STEALING THE
LANGUAGE

Alicia Suskin Ostriker

STEALING THE LANGUAGE

The Emergence of Women's Poetry in America

BEACON PRESS · BOSTON

Beacon Press
25 Beacon Street
Boston, Massachusetts 02108

Beacon Press books are published under the auspices
of the Unitarian Universalist Association
of Congregations in North America.

92 91 90 89 88 87 86   8 7 6 5 4 3 2 1

Library of Congress Cataloging in Publication Data
Ostriker, Alicia.
    Stealing the language.

    Bibliography: p.
    Includes index.
    1. American poetry—Women authors—History and
criticism.   2. American poetry—20th century—History
and criticism.   3. Women in literature.   4. Women and
literature—United States.   5. Feminism and literature—
United States.   6. Women—United States—Language.
I. Title.
PS147.08 1986   811'.009'9287   85-47949
ISBN 0-8070-6302-9

The following sections have been previously published:
    "Being Nobody Together" from chapter 2 was published in *Parnassus: Poetry in Review*.
    "In Mind: The Divided Self and Women's Poetry" from chapter 2 was published in *Midwest Quarterly*.
    "Body Language" from chapter 3 was published in *The State of the Language*, edited by Leonard Michaels and Christopher Ricks (University of California Press, 1980).
    "What Are Patterns For?: Anger and Polarization in Women's Poetry" from chapter 4 was published in *Feminist Studies*.
    "The Thieves of Language: Women's Poetry and Revisionist Mythmaking" from chapter 6 was published in *Signs*.

For my mother,
Beatrice Suskin Smith,
the first woman poet in my life

Contents

Acknowledgments

The writers and friends who made this work possible for me are many. First among poets in my life is William Blake, rule-breaker and revolutionary, who wrote that the road of excess leads to the palace of wisdom and that what is now proved was once only imagined. To study Blake is to acquire an appetite for the conceptually and emotionally difficult in poetry, and a thirst for the visionary. Reading women poets whose insights are often painful, threatening, and confusing has been a challenge comparable to reading Blake. Simone de Beauvoir's *The Second Sex* and Virginia Woolf's *A Room of One's Own* were watershed books. Essential perspectives on women's cultural position and women's writing have come from the pathbreaking work of Patricia Spacks, Ellen Moers, Elaine Showalter, Sandra Gilbert, and Susan Gubar. Louise Bernikow, Suzanne Juhasz, Emily Stipes Watts, Albert Gelpi, and Cheryl Walker have helped me understand the poetic grandmothers; Lynda Koolish has been a brilliant guide to contemporary feminist poetry and especially to the radical work of lesbian, black, and third-world poets. I am grateful to the keen intelligence and encouragement of Diana George, Susan Friedman, and Rachel Blau DuPlessis. Others who have prodded my thinking and writing include Kate Ellis, Diane Middlebrook, Barbara Gelpi, Patricia Dienstfrey, Leigh Bienen, Elizabeth Socolow, Cynthia Gooding, and Sheila Solomon. I am grateful to Joseph Boles for introducing me to H.D. and for being an exemplary feminist critic, and to Martha Smith for her bold reading of Emily Dickinson. I am indebted to J. P. Ostriker for his unswerving commitment to intellectual honesty and clarity in his own work and in mine and for his high standards in prose. Joanne Wyckoff, my editor at Beacon Press, has offered essential enthusiasm and advice. Paula Harris and Ruth Yeselson provided invaluable help in the final preparation of the manuscript. To Rutgers University and the Rockefeller Foundation I owe two years freed from teaching, without which this book would have been impossible. Finally I must thank the poets, for writing and continuing to write and for changing my life and my mind.

Grateful acknowledgment is made to the following for permission to reprint: For the lines from "euridice" from *I am not a Practising Angel* (Crossing Press, 1980), "Anybody could write this poem," from *Mountain Moving Day* (Crossing Press, 1973), and "Putting it all Down in Black and White," from *The Shameless Hussy* (Crossing Press, 1980) by Alta, copyright © by Alta, by permission of the author and publisher; from "She Considers Evading Him," "At first I was given centuries," and "Power Politics" from *Power Politics* by Margaret Atwood (Toronto: House of Anansi Press, 1971), and the lines from "This Is a Photograph of Me" and "The City Planners" from *Circle Game* by Margaret Atwood, copyright © 1966 Margaret Atwood, by permission of the author and of House of Anansi Press, Toronto; from "More and More" and "A Fortification" from *The Animals in that Country* by Margaret Atwood © Oxford University Press (Canadian Branch) 1968, by permission of the publisher; from "Circe/Mud Poems" and "Siren Song" from *You are Happy*, by Margaret Atwood, copyright © 1974 by Margaret Atwood, by permission of Harper & Row, Publishers, Inc.; from "A Cycle of Women" by Sharon Barba, from *Rising Tide: 20th Century Women Poets* (Washington Square Press, 1973), by permission of the author; from *Homage to Mistress Bradstreet* by John Berryman, copyright © 1956 by John Berryman, renewed © 1984 by Mrs. Kate Berryman, by permission of Farrar, Straus, & Giroux; from "Roosters," "Invitation to Miss Marianne Moore," "In the Waiting Room" and "The Moose" from *The Complete Poems* by Elizabeth Bishop, copyright © 1941, 1948, 1971, 1972, 1976 by Elizabeth Bishop, by permission of Farrar, Straus, & Giroux; from "I Saw Eternity" and "Alchemist" from *The Blue Estuaries* by Louise Bogan, copyright 1922, copyright © renewed 1949, 1968 by Louise Bogan, by permission of Farrar, Straus, & Giroux; the lines from "Maenad" and "Circe" from *Beginning with O* by Olga Broumas, by permission of Yale University Press; from "Fire" from *Casting Stones* by Helen Chasin, reprinted by permission of the author and Little, Brown; from "Miss Rosie" and "If I stand in my window" from *Good Times* by Lucille Clifton, copyright © 1972, Alfred A. Knopf, Inc., reprinted by permission of the publisher; from "she understands me" from *An Ordinary Woman* by Lucille Clifton, copyright © 1974 by Lucille Clifton, reprinted by permission of Curtis Brown, Ltd; from "Suicide Note" from *Maps and Windows* by Jane Cooper, copyright © 1973 by Jane Cooper, by permission of Macmillan Publishing Company; from "Trilogy" from *Trilogy* by H. D., copyright © 1973 by Norman Holmes Pearson, from "Helen In Egypt" from *Helen in Egypt* by H. D., copyright © 1961 by Norman Holmes Pearson, and from "Fragment Thirty-Six" from *Collected Poems: 1912–1944*, by H. D., copyright © 1983 by the estate of Hilda Doolittle, reprinted by permission of New Directions Publishing Corporation; from "The Argument" and "August Hallucination" from *Cleared for Landing* by Ann Darr, © Ann Darr, by permission of Dryad Press, 1978; from "Gaelic Legacy" from *St. Ann's Gut* by Ann Darr, by permission of William Morrow & Co., Inc.; from "Neural Folds" from *Self-portrait with Hand Microscope* by Lucille Day, (Berkeley Poets Workshop and Press, 1982), by permission of author and publisher; from "The Mirror Poems" from *Empress of the Death House* by Toi Derricotte (Lotus Press, 1978), by permission of the author; the lines from the poems from *The Poems of Emily Dickinson*, edited by Thomas H. Johnson, Cambridge, Mass.: The Belknap Press of Harvard University Press, Copyright 1951, © 1955, 1979, 1983 by the President and Fellows of Harvard College, reprinted by permission of the publishers and trustees of Amherst College; lines from the poems from *The Complete Poems of Emily Dickinson*, edited by Thomas H. Johnson, copyright 1929 by Martha Dickinson Bianchi, © 1957 by Mary L. Hampson, reprinted by permission of Little, Brown; from "Circling the Pond" from *Newspaper Stories* by Patricia Dienstfrey by permission of the author and Berkeley Poets Workshop and Press; from "The Party," "Jeanne Poems, #5," and "The Colors of Brick" from *Selected Poems* by Diane DiPrima (North Atlantic Books, 1975) by permission of the author; from "Undertow" from *Wells* by Rachel Blau DuPlessis, © Rachel Blau DuPlessis, 1980, by permission of the author; from "Beginning Journals" from *Us: Women* by Marjorie Fletcher (Alice James Books, 1973) by permission of the author; from "The Colonel" from *The Country Between Us* by Carolyn Forche, copyright © 1981 by Carolyn Forche, by permission of Harper & Row, Publishers, Inc.; from "Like a Woman in the Kitchen" from *Letters from the Floating World* by Siv Cedering Fox, by permission of the University of Pittsburgh Press, © 1984 by Siv Cedering; from "Both You Say" from *Mother is* by Siv Cedering Fox, by permission of Stein and Day Publishers; from "Flood" and "Coincidental," "The Story of Emma Slide," and "The Recognition" from *New Shoes* by Kathleen Fraser, copyright © 1978 by Kathleen Fraser, by permission of the author and Harper & Row, Publishers, Inc; from "Talking to Myself Talking to You" from *Each Next* by Kathleen Fraser, by permission of the author; from "On Refusing Your Invitation to Come to Dinner" from

Queen of Darkness, by Celia Gilbert, copyright © 1977 by Celia Gilbert, by permission of The Viking Press; from "The Intruder" from *In the 4th World* by Sandra Gilbert, © 1979 The University of Alabama Press, by permission of the publisher; from "Suicide" by Sandra Gilbert, from *Epoch*, issue 13 xi 85, by permission of the publisher; from "Woman with Tongue in Cheek" by Daniella Gioseffi from *Eggs in the Lake* (Boa Editions, Ltd., Rockport, NY), © 1979 by Daniella Gioseffi, by permission of the author; from "Woman Poem" from *Black Feeling Black Talk/Judgment* by Nikki Giovanni (William Morrow & Co., Inc., 1984) and the lines from "Poems for a Lady Whose Voice I Like" from *The Women and the Men* (William Morrow & Co., Inc., 1975), by permission of the publisher; from "Aphrodite" and "Grandmother" from *Descending Figure* by Louise Gluck, copyright 1980 by Louise Gluck, by permission of the author and Ecco Press, 1980; from "It's Cool Outside and Bright" by Madelon Springnettrer (Gohlke) from *The Normal Heart*, © 1981, by permission of New Rivers Press; from "Notes" from *Permanent Wave* by Miriam Goodman, © Miriam Goodman and Alice James Books, by permission of author and publisher; from "Love Came Along," "A Woman Is Talking to Death," and "She Who" from *The Work of a Common Woman* by Judy Grahn, copyright © Judy Grahn, by permission of author and The Crossing Press; from "A Woman Defending Herself," "I Like to Think of Harriet Tubman," and "Mother and Child" from *Like the Iris of an Eye* by Susan Griffin, copyright © 1976 by Susan Griffin, by permission of Harper & Row, Publishers, Inc.; from "Elegy" from *Presentation Piece* by Marilyn Hacker (Viking Press, 1974), copyright © 1974 by Marilyn Hacker, by permission of the author; from "Canto de Nada" by Jessica Hagedorn, from *Four Young Women* edited by Kenneth Rexroth (McGraw Hill, 1973), by permission of the author; from "Fix Me a Salami Sandwich, He Said," "When Mama Came Here as a Gold Panner," and "The Last Voyage of the Eudora Dawn" from *Manhattan as a Second Language* by Jana Harris, copyright © 1982 by Jana Harris, by permission of Harper & Row, Publishers, Inc.; from "Dear Friend, My Priest" from *A Packet Beating like a Heart* by Eloise Klein Healy (Books of a Feather Press, 1981), by permission of the author; from "I Used to Have Fur" from *Very Close and Very Slow* by Judith Henschmeyer; from "Bitter Pills for the Dark Ladies," "Aging," and "Ars Poetica" from *Fruits and Vegetables* by Erica Jong, copyright © 1968 by Erica Mann Jong, reprinted by permission of Holt, Rinehart and Winston, Publishers; from "Case in Point" from *Passion* by June Jordan, copyright (1980) by June Jordan, and from "Fragments from a Parable," "Who Look at Me," "Getting Down to Get Over," and "These Poems" from *Things that I Do in the Dark* by June

Jordan, copyright © 1967, 1968, 1969, 1970, 1971, 1972, 1973, 1974, 1975, 1977 by June Jordan, by permission of Beacon Press; from "Love Lust Poem" and "Freak Show and Finale" from *Word Alchemy* by Lenore Kandel (Grove Press, 1970), by permission of Grove Press, Inc.; from "Cages" from *From Room to Room* by Jane Kenyon (Alice James Books), copyright © 1978 by Jane Kenyon, reprinted by permission of the author; from "Pro Femina," copyright © 1963 by Carolyn Kizer from *Knock upon Silence*, by permission of the author and Doubleday & Company, Inc.; the lines from untitled poem from *Oh I Can't She Says* by Phyllis Koestenbaum (Christopher's Books, 1980) reprinted by permission of the author and publisher; from "Bed" from *In the Temperate Zone* by Judith Kroll (Charles Scribner's, 1973), by permission of the author; from "Sestina for our Revolution" from *More Palomino, Please, More Fuschia*, by Marilyn Krysyl (Cleveland State University Poetry Center, 1980), copyright © 1980 by Marilyn Krysyl, by permission of the author and publisher; from "After Love," "Running Away Together," "The Envelope," "Changing the Children," "Thinking of Death and Dog Food," "Body and Soul," and "Pea Patch" from *Our Ground Time Here Will Be Brief* by Maxine Kumin, copyright © 1969, 1971, 1973, 1976, 1977, 1978, 1979 by Maxine Kumin, by permission of Viking Penguin, Inc.; from "Holding Fast" from *Making the Park* by Marina La Palma (Kelsey Street Press, 1976), by permission of the author and publisher; from "Sunday Afternoon" from *Denise Levertov: Collected Earlier Poems 1940–60*, copyright © 1958 by Denise Levertov Goodman, from "In Mind," "Hypocrite Woman," and "Song for Ishtar" from *O Taste and See*, copyright © 1962, 1963 by Denise Levertov Goodman ("In Mind" was first published in *Poetry*), from "The Women" and "A Poem at Christmas" from *The Freeing of the Dust*, copyright, © 1975 by Denise Levertov Goodman, from "The Goddess" from *With Eyes at the Back of our Heads*, copyright, © 1959 by Denise Levertov, and from "The Fountain" from *Poems 1960–1967*, copyright, © 1961 by Denise Levertov Goodman, reprinted by permission of New Directions Publishing Corporation; from "The No More Apologizing, the No More Little Laughing Blues" from *Up State Madonna* by Lyn Lifshin (Crossing Press, 1975) by permission of author and publisher; from "Portrait," "Meet," and "The House of Yemanja" from *The Black Unicorn, Poems* by Audre Lorde, copyright, © 1978 by Audre Lorde, by permission of W. W. Norton & Company, Inc.; from "The Brown Menace," "Prologue," and "The Woman Thing" from *Chosen Poems, Old and New*, by Audre Lorde, copyright, © 1982, 1976, 1974, 1973, 1970, 1968 by Audre Lorde, by permission of W. W. Norton & Company, Inc.; from "Power" from *The Black Unicorn* by Audre Lorde,

© 1976 by Marge Piercy, by permission of the author and Alfred A. Knopf, Inc.; from *The Collected Poems* by Sylvia Plath, the lines from "Tulips," "In Plaster," "Lady Lazarus," copyright, © 1962 by Ted Hughes, from "Daddy," "Elm," and "Cut," copyright, © 1963 by Ted Hughes, and from "Metaphors," copyright, © 1960 by Ted Hughes, by permission of Harper & Row, Publishers, Inc.; from "Mushrooms" from *Colossus* by Sylvia Plath, copyright, © 1968 by Alfred A. Knopf, Inc., by permission of the publisher; from "Three Women" from *The Collected Poems* by Sylvia Plath, by permission of Olwyn Hughes; from "Late" and "Nursing Mother" from *Admit Impediment* by Marie Ponsot by permission of Alfred A. Knopf, copyright, © 1981; from "Snapshots of a Daughter-in-Law," "The Mirror in Which Two Are Seen as One," "The Planetarium," "Natural Resources," "Diving Into the Wreck," "Two Songs," "Leaflets," "The Blue Ghazals," "Necessities of Life," "The Knight," "The Burning of Paper Instead of Children," and "The Phenomenology of Anger," from *The Fact of a Doorframe, Poems, Selected and New, 1950–84* by Adrienne Rich, copyright, © 1984 by Adrienne Rich, copyright, © 1975, 1978, by W. W. Norton & Company, Inc., copyright, © 1981 by Adrienne Rich, by permission of the author and W. W. Norton & Company, Inc.; from "Jesus Was Crucified," copyright, © 1969 by Carolyn Rodgers from *How I Got Ovah*, by permission of Doubleday & Company, Inc.; from *The Collected Poems* by Muriel Rukeyser, "Myth," and "Despisals," copyright, 1973 © by Muriel Rukeyser, and from "Orpheus," copyright 1951 © and 1979 © by Muriel Rukeyser, reprinted by permission of International Creative Management, Inc.; from "My Sisters, O My Sisters" and "How to Believe the Legends I am Told" from *Selected Poems of May Sarton*, edited by Serena Sue Hilsinger and Lois Brynes, copyright, © 1978 by May Sarton, by permission of W. W. Norton & Company, Inc.; from "Housewife" from *All My Pretty Ones* by Anne Sexton, copyright © by Anne Sexton, from "Little Girl," "The Addict," "Wanting to Die," and "Those Times" from *Live or Die* by Anne Sexton, copyright © 1966 by Anne Sexton, from "Snow White," "Red Riding Hood," "Briar Rose," and "The Frog Prince" from *Transformations* by Anne Sexton, copyright, © 1971 by Anne Sexton, from "In Celebration," and "For My Lover . . . ," from *Love Poems* by Anne Sexton, copyright, © 1967, 1968, 1969 by Anne Sexton, from "Words for Dr. Y" and "Letters to Dr. Y" from *Words for Dr. Y* by Anne Sexton, copyright, © 1978 by Linda Grey Sexton and Loring Conant, Jr., executors of the Will of Anne Sexton, from "Jesus Awake," "Jesus Suckles," "Jesus Unborn," "The Author of the Jesus Letters," "Jesus Raises up the Harlot," and "Mother and Daughter" from *The Book of Folly* by Anne Sexton, copyright, © 1972 by Anne Sexton, from "Double Image," and "For John Who Begs Me" from *To Bedlam and Part Way Back* by Anne Sexton, copyright, © 1960 by Anne Sexton, and from "Rowing" from *The Awful Rowing Toward God* by Anne Sexton, copyright, © 1975 by Loring Conant, Jr., executor of the Estate of Anne Sexton, all excerpts reprinted by permission of Houghton Mifflin Company; from *For Colored Girls who Have Considered Suicide/When the Rainbow is Enuf* by Ntozake Shange, copyright, © 1975, 1976, 1977 by Ntozake Shange, by permission of Macmillan Publishing Company; from "wow . . . you're just like a man," "a conversation with all my selves," and "inquiry" from *Nappy Edges* by Ntozake Shange, copyright, © 1972, 1974, 1975, 1976, 1977, 1978 by Ntozake Shange, by permission of St. Martin's Press, Inc.; from "The Swimmer" by Elizabeth Ann Socolow from *Contemporary Writing From New Jersey* (William H. Wise & Co., 1980) by permission of the author; from "A Sonnet—Patriarchal Poetry" from *Bee Time and Other Pieces* by Gertrude Stein (Yale University Press) copyright, © 1953, by permission of the publisher; from "The Poster" by Lynn Luria Sukenick, by permission of the author; from "Evolution," © 1954, renewed © 1982 by May Swenson, "Bleeding," © 1970 by May Swenson, "Out of My Head," © 1963 by May Swenson, "Question," © 1954, renewed © 1982 by May Swenson, and "Bronco Busting Event #1" © 1976 by May Swenson from *Things Taking Place* (Little, Brown, 1978) by permission of the author; from "I Am Not Yours" from *Collected Poems* by Sara Teasdale, copyright 1915 by Macmillan Publishing Company, renewed 1943 by Mamie T. Wheless, by permission of Macmillan Publishing Company; from "Witch" by Jean Tepperman, by permission of the author; from "Death by Aesthetics," "Advice to a God," and "The Fear of Flying" from *Merciful Disguises* by Mona Van Duyn, copyright, © 1973 by Mona Van Duyn, and the lines from "Leda" and "Leda Reconsidered" from *To See to Take* by Mona Van Duyn, copyright, © 1970 by Mona Van Duyn, by permission of Atheneum Publishers, Inc.; from "No More Soft Talk," "Love Song for OK Ready," and "Caves" from *The Motorcycle Betrayal Poems* by Diane Wakoski (Simon & Schuster, 1971), from "In Gratitude to Beethoven" from *Inside the Blood Factory* (Doubleday, 1970), from "George Washington and the Loss of His Teeth," "George Washington and the Invention of Dynamite," "The Father of My Country," and "George Washington: the Whole Man" from *Trilogy* (Doubleday, 1974), by permission of the author; from "Beauty" from *The Magellanic Clouds* by Diane Wakoski, by permission of Black Sparrow Press; from "How to tell a story" from the book *The Man Who Shook Hands* by Diane Wakoski, copyright, © 1978 by Diane Wakoski, reprinted by permission of the author and Doubleday & Company, Inc.; from "Fast Speaking Woman" from *Fast Speaking Woman* by Anne Waldman (City Lights Books, Inc., 1975, 1978), by permission of the author; from "Sanctuary" from *Collected Poems* by Elinor Wylie (Alfred A. Knopf, 1966) by permission of the publisher; from "Sailing to Byzantium," (Copyright © 1928 by Macmillan Publishing Company, renewed 1956 by Bertha Georgie Yeats), "A Prayer for My Daughter" (Copyright 1924 by Macmillan Publishing Company, renewed 1952 by Bertha Georgie Yeats), and from "Adam's Curse" (New York: Macmillan, 1956) by William Butler Yeats from *Collected Poems*, by permission of Macmillan (New York) and Michael Yeats and Macmillan (London) Ltd.

Introduction

I am obnoxious to each carping tongue
Who says my hand a needle better fits.

Thus briskly wrote the pilgrim mother Anne Bradstreet in the "Prologue" to her book of poems, first published in 1650, adding, "If what I
do prove well it won't advance, / They'll say it's stolen, or else it was by
chance." Two stanzas later the first woman poet in America apologized:

Men have precedency and still excel . . .
Men can do best and women know it well.
Preeminence in each and all is yours;
Yet grant some small acknowledgment of ours.[1]

A fraction over three centuries later, Erica Jong observed in "Bitter Pills
for the Dark Ladies" (1968) just how small the acknowledgment could
be:

If they let you out   it's as Supermansaint
& the ultimate praise is always a question of nots:
     viz. not like a woman
     viz. "certainly not another poetess"

meanin'
     she got a cunt but she don't talk funny
     & he's a nigger but he don't smell funny
& the only good poetess is a dead.[2]

The "certainly not another poetess" remark was Robert Lowell's at the
advent of Sylvia Plath's *Ariel*, and Plath, who certainly did not want to
be another poetess, might well have been pleased by it. She was not the
first woman to be praised in this fashion, for it has always been custom-

ary when praising women writers to say that they do not write like most other women. The commendatory couplets written by Bradstreet's brother-in-law began, "If women, I with women may compare, / Your works are solid, others weak as air."[3] T. S. Eliot concluded an essay on Marianne Moore with "one final, and 'magnificent' compliment" on her work: "one never forgets that it is written by a woman; but . . . one never thinks of this particularly as anything but a positive virtue."[4] Theodore Roethke declared Louise Bogan an exception to the run of women poets, whose typical deficiencies included a set of "esthetic and moral shortcomings":

> the spinning out; the embroidering of trivial themes; a concern with the mere surfaces of life—that special province of the feminine talent in prose—hiding from the real agonies of the spirit; refusing to face up to what existence is; lyric or religious posturing; running between the boudoir and the altar; stamping a tiny foot against God or lapsing into a sententiousness that implies the author has re-invented integrity; carrying on excessively against Fate, about time; lamenting the lot of the woman; caterwauling; writing the same poem about fifty times, and so on."[5]

We may note that Roethke disparages in women poets characteristics which would be commended in men. As Sandra Gilbert and Susan Gubar observe, "shaking a Promethean male fist 'against God' is one perfectly reasonable male strategy, apparently, but stamping a 'tiny' feminine foot is quite another."[6]

All of us know, or think we know, what a poetess is, and, to paraphrase Marianne Moore, we too dislike her. But what has been the impact of this dislike—on the reputations of women already producing and on the ambitions of those who hope to produce good poetry?

Like many of the poets I discuss in this book, I received my literary education in the 1950s and early 1960s. My opinions on poetry were therefore formed predominantly by reading male poets and by the dicta of professors and critics who eloquently and reverently represented what Matthew Arnold called "the best that has been thought and said" in western culture. That their eloquence veiled gender bias, and that what they believed to be "universal" was only partial, did not occur to me. Subsequently I have come to believe that we cannot measure the work of women poets, past or present, without a thorough—and if possible demystified—awareness of the critical context in which they have composed and continue to compose their work. We need to recognize that our customary literary language is systematically gendered in ways that

influence what we approve and disapprove of, making it extremely difficult for us to acknowledge certain kinds of originality—of difference—
in women poets.

Like poetic argument, critical argument often conducts itself through
metaphor. We need first of all, therefore, to become aware that some of
our most compelling terms of critical discourse imply that serious poetry
is more or less identical with potent masculinity. Emerson toward the
close of his essay "The Poet" hears with his mind's ear "these throbs and
heart-beatings at the door of the assembly, to the end namely that
thought may be ejaculated as Logos, or Word." Elsewhere he cries,
"give me initiative, spermatic, prophesying, man-making words."[7] The
metaphor of the pen as the penis has a long literary history.[8] In our own
time we are impressed by the heroic notion of literary succession as a
"battle among strong equals, father and son as mighty opposites, Laius
and Oedipus at the crossroads."[9] Sometimes the metaphor may involve
size rather than force, as when we admire "greatness" or "stature" or
"high" achievement, or when a critic asks:

> Who are the major and crucial American poets, both in literary
> excellence and in the difference they make to their successors? Two
> American poets pre-eminently answer this description: Whitman
> and Pound. The other nineteenth century poets pass through
> Whitman's legs like Lilliputians."[10]

Has the critic been reading Bradstreet on the subject of "preeminence"
(itself a metaphor; "eminence" means elevation or protuberance)? Obviously we cannot fancy any poets passing between Emily Dickinson's
legs; consequently she is not a major and crucial American poet.

We seldom encounter, in praise of women poets, terms like *great,
powerful, forceful, masterly, violent, large,* or *true.* The language used
to express literary admiration in general presumes the masculinity of the
author, the work, and the act of creation—but not if the author is a
woman. Complimentary adjectives of choice then shift toward the di-
minutives: *graceful, subtle, elegant, delicate, cryptic,* and, above all,
modest; for the most continuous term of approbation for a woman poet
from the early nineteenth century to the day before yesterday has been
modesty. We are perhaps not surprised that an anthologist of American
female poets in 1849 says that "the most worthy are the most modest,"[11]
since we think of the Victorian period as a nadir in women's history. But
in our own emancipated time Roy Harvey Pearce approves of Marianne
Moore because her "insights are as modest" as the scale of the world she
examines.[12] Elizabeth Bishop "is modest and she is dignified."[13] Louise

Bogan is "elegant and remarkably self-effacing" and stands "for public reticence."[14] Adrienne Rich's first poems "are neatly and modestly dressed, speak quietly but do not mumble, respect their elders but are not cowed by them, and do not tell fibs," according to W. H. Auden.[15] Most curiously, in the preface to *Ariel* already quoted, Lowell also commends Plath for "her hand of metal with its modest, womanish touch."[16] Was any male poet, even a young one, ever praised for being modest? Is it possible to be both "modest" and "great"?

One role of the critic is to discover the individual talent which alters the shape of literature. Yet originality has never protected the woman poet from the condescension of critics, and the terms of depreciation remain remarkably fixed despite changes in literary fashions. To take the most obvious example in American literature, the few poems Emily Dickinson published in her lifetime were editorially emended, their odd prosody normalized, their quirky metaphors conventionalized. To her mentor and posthumous editor T. W. Higginson, Dickinson was "my half-cracked poetess," and the neurotic-spinster motif has remained a staple of Dickinson criticism; in 1971 her psychiatrist-biographer John Cody concluded that the frustration of Dickinson's romantic life was responsible for the emergence of her genius:

> If in spite of her wifely and motherly duties, she had still felt the need to express herself in verse, what would her subject matter have been? Would art have sprung from fulfillment, gratification, and completeness as abundantly as it did from longing, frustration, and deprivation?[17]

A writer who in 1971 could believe that "wifely and motherly duties" could constitute "fulfillment, gratification, and completeness" for a woman was not reading many women writers; but the belief that what is convenient for men is fulfilling to women dies hard. It is difficult to imagine a writer speaking in this vein of Shelley, Keats, or even D. H. Lawrence, for we do not reduce male creativity to the presence or absence of a love life. Another staple notion has been the idea that Dickinson wrote good poetry not as other poets do, by marrying genius to effort, but—in Anne Bradstreet's phrase—"by chance." To R. P. Blackmur,

> she was neither a professional poet nor an amateur; she was a private poet who wrote indefatigably as some women cook or knit. Her gift for words and the cultural predicament of her time drove her to poetry instead of antimacassars.[18]

This is to say: women do busywork, Dickinson was a woman, therefore her poetry is busywork. But it would be as reasonable to remark that Ezra Pound wrote the *Cantos* indefatigably as some men work on an assembly line, and that his gift for words and his cultural predicament drove him to poetry instead of bowling. Similarly, when John Crowe Ransom comments on the first edition of Dickinson's poems, which attempts to reproduce the poet's idiosyncratic grammar, punctuation, lineation—an edition made feasible by the literary public's familiarity with the far more idiosyncratic habits of E. E. Cummings, Eliot, and Pound—he finds her "a little home-keeping person" who never learned the concessions poets must make to printers, publishers, and the public. Of her nature poems he observes that "the woman poet as a type . . . makes flights into nature rather too easily and upon errands which do not have metaphysical importance enough to justify so radical a strategy." Male poets engage in quests; women poets run errands.[19] What we may call the "accident" theory of female creativity persists in, among others, David Porter, whose *Dickinson: The Modern Idiom* argues that Dickinson's evasions of "reality" inadvertently anticipate the radical gestures of postmodernism.[20]

Accusations of "privacy" and "escapism" have pursued other women poets besides Dickinson. From Douglas Bush's massive *Mythology and the Romantic Tradition in English Poetry* comes the pronouncement that "H. D. is a poet of escape" whose Greece "has no connection with the Greece of historic actuality," although this is not a complaint Bush registers about the Greece of Keats, Matthew Arnold, or Edgar Allan Poe.[21] From Hugh Kenner's *The Pound Era* we learn that H. D.'s Imagism was a pebble in the great Pound stream and that her first published poem "is 'about' her taut state of mind, a wried stasis like a sterile homecoming, and a homecoming not to a person but to a mute numinous ikon. That was to be, over and over, the story of her life. Ahead lay marriage, childbirth, desertion, bisexual miseries, and Freud's couch."[22] *The Pound Era* appeared years after the publication of H. D.'s major works, *Trilogy* and *Helen in Egypt*, yet Kenner implies that H. D. expired in neurosis after composing a few enigmatic lyrics. Similarly, there are the Freudian critics who discover that H. D.'s epic structures were substitutes for her missing penis,[23] and Dennis Donaghue, who scolds her for "resorting" to images of dream and myth.[24]

The discomfort provoked by original women is half-articulated by Yvor Winters writing on Dickinson. Commenting on "I like to see it lap the miles," Winters dislikes "the quality of silly playfulness which renders it abominable" and which he finds diffused throughout her writing so that "her best poems . . . can never be isolated certainly and defensibly from her defects; yet she is a poetic genius of the highest order, and this ambiguity in one's feeling about her is profoundly disturbing." [25] Winters' essay is entitled "The Limits of Criticism," and his confusion is evidently genuine, yet it does not lead him to guess that an ostensibly objective critical methodology may itself be defective, or that Dickinson's playfulness may not be merely offensive and accidental but subversive and strategic: a means of registering feminine powerlessness and of attempting to overcome it. [26]

While few critics are as perspicacious or as honest as Yvor Winters, it is not difficult to multiply examples of gender-linked criticism inexorably diminishing the accomplishment of women poets under the authoritative guise of aesthetic standards. Originality in a woman poet is censured by the commentator or is invisible to him because it does not resemble masculine originalities with which he is already familiar. The woman poet who writes problematically on religious, political, or social issues is irrelevant, sententious, or silly. The feminist poet is strident. The emotionally intense poet is neurotic. Above all, the poet who attempts to explore female experience is dismissed as self-absorbed, private, escapist, nonuniversal—although, as Carolyn Kizer puts it, women writers "are the custodians of the world's best-kept secret: / Merely the private lives of one-half of humanity." [27]

As several major studies of women's writing have demonstrated, the woman writer throughout most of our history has had to state her self-definitions in code, disguising passion as piety, rebellion as obedience. [28] "Tell all the truth but tell it slant" speaks for writers who in every century have been inhibited both by economic and legal dependence and by the awareness that *true writer* signifies assertion while *true woman* signifies submission. Insofar as poetry ranks above fiction in our hierarchies of genre, women poets have been discouraged from literary ambition even more than women novelists. Occasionally a critic expresses some slight hesitation over his capacity to judge a woman poet adequately, a hint of a sense that his mode of criticism may, in Winters' phrase, have limits beyond which it cannot successfully be applied. That an individual woman poet might achieve greatness not because she can be fitted into existing literary strictures but because she violates them—just as great male poets often violate them—is a disturbing notion. That a submerged tradition of women's poetry should exist, following certain rules of its own, is more disturbing. Most disturbing of all is the moment when the submerged tradition surfaces and when much of what we think we know about "women" and "poetry" is called into question.

2

My subject is the extraordinary tide of poetry by American women in our own time. An increasing proportion of this work is explicitly female in the sense that the writers have chosen to explore experiences central to their sex and to find forms and styles appropriate to their exploration. These writers are, I believe, challenging and transforming the history of poetry. They constitute a literary movement comparable to romanticism or modernism in our literary past. Often polemical and self-conscious at their centers, such movements involve multitudes of writers both major and minor. It is notoriously difficult to define precisely what Rimbaud called the "*quelque chose* DE NOUVEAU" which they bring about; and yet they change the way we think and feel forever.

I take 1960 as an approximate point of departure. Among the breakthrough and highly influential books published between 1960 and 1965 were Muriel Rukeyser's *The Speed of Darkness* (1960), Anne Sexton's *To Bedlam and Part Way Back* (1960) and *All My Pretty Ones* (1962), Adrienne Rich's *Snapshots of a Daughter-in-Law* (1963), and Sylvia Plath's *Ariel* (1965). Almost at the same moment appeared Denise Levertov's *With Eyes at the Back of our Heads* (1959), *The Jacob's Ladder* (1961), and *O Taste and See* (1963), Margaret Atwood's *Double Persephone* (1959), Mona Van Duyn's *Valentines to the Wide World* (1959), H.D.'s *Helen in Egypt* (1960), Gwendolyn Brooks' *The Bean Eaters* (1960) and *Selected Poems* (1963), Diane Wakoski's *Coins and Coffins* (1961), Maxine Kumin's *The Privilege* (1965), and Carolyn Kizer's *Knock upon Silence* (1965).

In the late 1960s and early 1970s, poetry by Black women, including Lucille Clifton, Audre Lorde, Nikki Giovanni, and June Jordan, began to proliferate, as did poetry by lesbian, third-world, and working-class women, and the political dimension of women's writing became increasingly visible.[29] Judy Grahn identified hers as the generation which "began wresting poetry from the exclusive clutches of the sons and daughters of the American upperclass and returning it to the basic groups from which it seeped and sprung"; June Jordan celebrated the "New World Poets"—Whitman's children—whose work demands "an end to feudalism, caste, privilege, and the violence of power."[30] Many of the poets in this book were active opponents of American involvement in Vietnam; the critique of war and violence is a central motif in women's poems. But the women's poetry movement has never been simply political. Apolitical poets such as May Swenson, Elizabeth Bishop, and May Sarton, for example, are of the highest relevance when we ask questions about the relation of woman and nature, woman and creativity, woman and myth.

My intention is not primarily to survey individual achievements. Books have been written on many of the poets I include in this study, but few critics have attempted to understand the powerful collective voice in which they participate. My intention is to gain perspective on an emerging image, to describe a woman's equivalent of what Whitman meant when he said he heard America singing in varied voices mysteriously united. The question I have asked myself is this: what happens when "we who are writing women and strange monsters," in May Sarton's phrase, begin to write with a freedom and boldness that no generation of women in literary history has ever known?

At the grassroots level it is clear that a women's movement exists in poetry as in society at large, antedating and to some extent inspiring contemporary feminism in its more political branches, while in turn being fueled by feminist thought and action and its creation of more conscious and courageous readers. Dozens of little magazines and small presses have sprung up which print only women's poetry. Universities across the country run series of women's poetry readings, as do, on a more modest level, bookstores and coffeehouses. Conferences of women's poetry occur and recur. Anthologies of women's poetry multiply. The audience on which these activities depend takes its poetry avidly and personally. One young woman poet I know, Helen Cooper, calls the work of other women "survival tools." Another poet, Eloise Healy, writes me from California:

> About women poets. I like them and read them because I think they're writing more exciting poetry than most men. Their poetry is about discovery and breaking new ground and it feels more like life to me . . . like work that comes to grips with what I feel is essential in all arts—what are we doing with our lives? Why do we do it? How do we see each other? How can we change what we have into what we want?

Among commercial and university presses, good women poets are widely published and recognized for their individual voices. Their books on the whole receive thoughtful reviews, written with clearer understanding and less condescension every year. Presently it is the exception rather than the rule to see a woman writer praised for being unlike other women. True, instead of "certainly not another poetess," the highest praise in some circles is "certainly not another feminist," but even this is changing. What has not changed is that most critics and professors of literature, including modern literature, deny that "women's poetry," as distinct from poetry by individual women, exists. Some women writers agree. Some will not permit their work to appear in women's anthologies.

The superficial plausibility of this position rests partly on the unacknowledged conviction of our culture that "woman poet" means "inferior poet" and partly on the undeniable fact that women writers are a diverse lot, adhering to no single set of beliefs, doctrines, styles, or subjects. Yet we do not hesitate to use the term "American poetry" (or "French poetry" or "Russian poetry") on the grounds that American (or French or Russian) poets are diverse. Should we call Whitman, Frost, and Stevens "poets" but not "American poets"? Did Pound's expatriation make him any less quintessentially American, or did Joyce's make him less Irish? From a global perspective, the more deeply an artist represents the ethos of a nation, the more likely that artist is to represent humanity. In the particular we discover the universal. Homer was perfectly Greek, Dante perfectly Italian, Shakespeare perfectly English, Goethe perfectly German. Our own national literature, significantly, remained mediocre as long as we clung to English models and an apologetic vision of ourselves as a cultural backwater. At the moment in the midnineteenth century when we began to write in the vigorous American idiom, our literature began to arrive at global status. Of women's poetry the same may be said. Insofar as it attempts timidly to adjust itself to literary standards which exclude the female, it dooms itself to insignificance. Where it speaks in its own array of voices, it enlarges literature.

The belief that true poetry is genderless—which is a disguised form of believing that true poetry is masculine—means that we have not learned to see women poets generically, to recognize the tradition they belong to, or to discuss either the limitations or the strengths of that tradition. It also means that individual women writers are read askew. Without a sense of the multiple and complex patterns of thought, feeling, verbal resonance, and even vocabulary shared by women writers, we cannot read any woman adequately. Time and again we will overlook some central shaping principle not only in a Rich or a Plath but in a Marianne Moore or an Elizabeth Bishop, in the same way as critics have misread Emily Dickinson. For writers necessarily articulate gendered experience just as they necessarily articulate the spirit of a nationality, an age, a language. In what follows I therefore make the assumption that "women's poetry" exists in much the same sense that "American poetry" exists. It has a history. It has a terrain. Many of its practitioners believe it has something like a language.

3

Chapter one is a survey of the past. Women's poetry in America, as else-where, from its inception has been ghettoized, confined as a special case within a pale of limitations. The individual woman writer has inevitably registered the effects of definitions of "woman" and "woman poet" not initially created by herself and accepted with complex and changing mixes of acquiescence, evasion, rebellion, and misery. In the Colonial period the fetters were relatively light, and the few women poets who wrote in this period seem comparatively unconstrained, in part because they were too few to be categorized. These women wrote on both public and private themes in a way which became impossible thereafter. In the nineteenth century, while the number of women writing multiplied tremendously, the cultural restrictions on them became crippling. A newly genteel middle class required inspirational images of angelic womanhood within the "separate sphere" of domestic life which was supposed to be exclusively feminine. Among women poets a painful tension developed in this period between aspiration and self-effacement: the most powerful theme in nineteenth-century female verse was renunciation, and its most interesting strategy was what I shall call duplicity. With the advent of modernism, some women began writing more openly of sexual passion, some became leading inventors of avant-garde form, some became social critics, and the general quality of women's poetry rose precipitously. Yet almost all this work continued to register the traces of feminine confinement and constraint; and, not coincidentally, the dominant criticism continued to disparage, neglect, and misread the woman poet.

Like every literary movement, contemporary women's poetry in part perpetuates and in part denounces and renounces its past. Women writing today tend to continue what Louise Bogan identified as the key contribution of their grandmothers to the life of American poetry: "the line of feeling." At the same time, much of their vitality derives from an explosive attempt to overcome the mental and moral confinement they identify with these grandmothers, and this effort has both thematic and formal consequences.

Thematically, a number of connected motifs in women's poetry today are especially noteworthy; they are examined in chapters two through six. Chapter two proposes that the central project of the women's poetry movement is a quest for autonomous self-definition and discusses a set of images for female identity which register the condition of marginality: nonexistence, invisibility, muteness, blurredness, deformity.

Each of these images may be understood as a variation on the theme of a divided self, rooted in the authorized dualities of the culture. When defining a personal identity, women tend to begin with their bodies and, moreover, to interpret external reality through the medium of the body. The idea that other authorities are untrustworthy but "the body cannot lie" is central here. Chapter three therefore examines an array of attitudes to the body, ranging from a sense of its vulnerability to a sense of its power, and concludes with a consideration of the way women write about nature, or the world's body, as continuous or equivalent with their own.

Chapter four examines the subject of anger and violence in women's poetry as it is connected with dualistic scripts of dominance and submission in private and public life. I argue here that violence against the self and against the other are equivalent expressions of rage at entrapment in gender-polarized relationships, and that satiric and retaliatory poems which dismantle the myth of the male as lover, hero, father, and God are designed to confirm polarization and hierarchy as intolerable.

Chapter five turns to the question of female desire, attempting to show how an "imperative of intimacy"—touch, mutuality, the ability to challenge self/other boundaries—shapes the way women write love poetry, poetry about family, about spiritual ancestresses and sisters, about political life, and about self-integration. The impulse here is to define an identity which is not merely personal but communal and which may be experienced as "plural" within and without. This impulse commonly extends itself toward the poem's audience, in poems created to function not as closed artifacts but as personal transactions between poets and readers.

The idea that women writers have been imprisoned in an "oppressor's language" which denies them access to authoritative expression is a common thread throughout this book, and I suggest the variety of strategies women use to subvert and overcome this denial. In chapter six I consider a major strategy—revisionist mythmaking—as a means of exploring and attempting to transform the self and the culture. Myths are the sanctuaries of language where our meanings for "male" and "female" are stored; to rewrite them from a female point of view is to discover new possibilities for meaning.

As I will try to show, this sequence of motifs constitutes an extended investigation of culturally repressed elements in female identity. I will also try to make clear how the subjects women choose to speak on, and their emotional and intellectual discoveries, generate particular formal and stylistic decisions, often designed to disrupt and alter our sense of literary norms. Formally, for example, many women poets today seem inclined toward a certain hardness of tone, which I call the "exoskeletal style," fluctuating somewhere between the acerbic and the abrasive. Obviously one intention of such a style is to avoid the fluttery poetess stigma. Another intention may be a humorous exaggeration of the woman-as-monster stereotype and a resolution to be hanged for a sheep instead of a lamb. Do you find me strident? Do I make you uncomfortable? Very well, then, let me make you very uncomfortable, would be the message here. Another, not humorous, effect is to capture the attention required to do what Conrad said all writers yearn for, "to make you *see*." Many women writers feel that they suffer from invisibility, inaudibility—including invisibility and inaudibility to themselves—which a hard-edge, crystalline, no-nonsense style is designed to overcome.

At the same time, this writing tends to be passionate rather than distant, and to defy conventional divisions between "the line of feeling" and the activity of the intellect, between life and art, and between writer and reader. A warning is therefore appropriate here for readers who were trained, as I was, not to mistake the "I" in a poem for a real person. The training has its uses, but also its limitations. For most of the poems in this book, academic distinctions between the self and what we in the classroom call the "persona" move to vanishing point. When a woman poet today says "I," she is likely to mean herself, as intensely as her imagination and her verbal skills permit, much as Wordsworth or Keats did, or Blake, or Milton, or John Donne of the Holy Sonnets, before Eliot's "extinction of personality" became the mandatory twentieth-century initiation ritual for young American poets, and before the death of the author became a popular critical fiction. When masks and disguises govern the poems, as is often the case for example in Sylvia Plath, Margaret Atwood, and Diane Wakoski, it is not to entertain us but because the mask has grown into the flesh. It is the fact that the question of identity is a real one, for which the thinking woman may have no satisfactory answer, that turns her resolutely inward. The same fact will make her poetry urgent and emotional, as feelings she has forbidden herself to acknowledge have permission to erupt into the poem—and she cannot know who she is until she lets them. Often these long-hidden, long-repressed feelings will be painful to both poet and reader. Because it is passionate, because it is often either keenly bitter or keenly idealistic, and because it attempts to involve the reader personally, such poetry tends to irritate readers trained in post–World War II literary values. Yet another source of irritation may be women's humor, which is often vulgar. Aristophanes and Rabelais were vulgar as well, with the comparable intention of deflating pomp and dignity and reminding us that our minds reside in bodies. The critical insistence that poetry should be universal often presupposes a far too narrow notion of what is universal, which women's current inventiveness may help overcome.

Each idea, each feeling, each poetic strategy I discuss appears in the work of many more writers than I am able to quote, and some of those I quote will be familiar names while some will not, precisely because I want to make the point that the ideas, the feelings, are not merely the property of individuals. Indeed, the experienced and exploratory reader of women's poetry will be able to supplement the poets and poems named here with many others.

4

Since I complain of critics whose judgments seem to me a disguise, conscious or otherwise, for bias, I should state as well as I can my own positions as a critic. First, as a feminist critic I have come to believe that there exists a body of poetry by women which illuminates the condition of women and therefore of humanity in an unprecedented way, and which is exciting enough as poetry, as art, not merely to be accepted into the literary mainstream but to influence the stream's course. I do not see this body of writing as one that somehow secedes or withdraws from literature. On the contrary, I think it augments and enlivens literature. Second, my methods are inductive. I attempt to read by the light that poems themselves emit, rather than by the fixed beam of one or another theory which might shine where a poem is not and leave in darkness the place where it is. The proper business of theory is to help us comprehend the principles that have generated actual works of art, in all their contradictory turbulence. Where critical dicta and works of art fail to coincide, it is the dicta that need to change. Third, my taste is eclectic. I admire closed and open forms, the pungency of colloquial idiom and the play of literary puns and allusions; evocative metaphor and clean abstraction; the disparate voices of lyric cry, satiric jibe, conversational inflection, prophetic incantation. The house of poetry has many mansions, and among the attractions of the women's poetry movement is its encouragement of diversity.

Personally, of course, I seek poems that speak to my personal condition. All critics do so, although some do not like to admit it. As a lover of art I seek poems that feed my hunger for significant form. As a poet I seek inspiration, models, and a sense of poetic community. I have written this book because I have encountered so many poems by women that are important to me as personal revelation, as artifact, and as examples of courage. Included in my array of women are heterosexual and lesbian poets, women of color and white women, middle-class poets who use language acceptable to the academic critic, working-class poets who write in street talk, and avant-garde poets who are testing the boundaries of language. Some of these poets identify themselves as feminists, some are highly political, some do not even like to identify themselves as women. For the most part I have chosen to concentrate on the terrain these writers explore in common rather than on the real and sometimes bitter divisions between them, while trying to indicate, for the interested reader, areas of significant difference and debate.

Above all, I have concerned myself with language and have tried to offer the reader phrases, lines, and passages which are compact and alive, witty, wild, wise, and vigorous, words which articulate, swiftly and memorably, large and complicated realities. Because this work takes the form of a survey, I have discussed in detail only a fraction of the poems I would have enjoyed discussing. I hope nevertheless that the shock of pleasure at seeing something beautifully said will occur again and again to my readers as it has to me, and that they will be drawn into further investigation of these poets and poems.

1 I'm Nobody:
Women's Poetry, 1650–1960

We think back through our mothers, if we are women.
—Virginia Woolf, A Room of One's Own [1]

Our mothers and grandmothers, some of them: moving to music
not yet written. And they waited.
—Alice Walker, "In Search of Our Mothers' Gardens" [2]

Every literary movement has its roots in a past which it at once perpetuates, repudiates, and transforms. For women, the past is doubled. We have a shared and canonized literary heritage written overwhelmingly by men, in which woman appears primarily as virgin or whore, angel or vixen, love-object, temptress, or muse. As Simone de Beauvoir definitively puts it, the female in a man's writing is always Other than the self, the stuff of dream and nightmare. [3] We also have a long line of uncanonized poetic ancestresses who have contrived to articulate, often in highly coded form, images of woman—and of reality—which are in crucial respects quite different from men's. It is their submerged tradition which I trace in this chapter.

To a certain extent the history of women's poetry in America is a tale of confinements. Throughout her existence the woman poet has needed to be proven virtuously female to legitimize her vocation as a poet. In the nineteenth century the genteel poetry and the genteel ideal of femininity, which stressed the heart and denied the head, was a perfect glass slipper; those who were not Cinderella had to shed blood to fit it, and these wounds are not healed yet. Even in the more liberated climate of the twentieth century, as we shall see, the divorce of mind from body and private from public remains a powerful constraint on women writers. And we shall also see that criticism of women poets in every period systematically and condescendingly obscures their achievements. Each of these confinements—the inhibition of ambition, acquiescence in definitions created by others, self-defeating division between heart and head, critical depreciation—is being challenged by contemporary woman poets.

But that is not the whole story. When we think back through our mothers we find weakness; we also find power. As writers from Virginia Woolf to Alice Walker make clear, women poets need strong mothers; and I use the Bloomian term not because I believe that the woman poet's achievement depends on killing and superseding her predecessor. Rather than Oedipus and Laius at the crossroads, the model among women writers, critics as well as poets, is Demeter and Kore: except that it is the daughter who descends to Hades, step by step, to retrieve and revive a mother who has been raped, or perhaps seduced, by a powerful male god. For as the mother returns to earth, the daughter expects to blossom.[4] We will find, then, in this chapter, poets who are memorable for their wit, grace, and technical skill; who do not merely submit to a dominant culture but also write to subvert that culture; and who, most significantly, represent the possibility of alternative vision.

2

Now say, have women worth? Or have they none?
Or had they some, but with our Queen is't gone?
　　—Anne Bradstreet, "In Honor of that High and Mighty
　　　Princess Queen Elizabeth of Happy Memory"[5]

A woman's reading, thinking, and writing were a potential danger to her community and herself in the Massachusetts Bay Colony to which the eighteen-year-old Anne Bradstreet sailed on the *Arbella* in 1630 with her father, Thomas Dudley, and her husband, Simon Bradstreet. At Boston as elsewhere in the Colonies, it was understood that freedom consisted of submission to higher authority. For a woman this meant that her relation to man was as man's to God: "He is her lord, and she is to be subject to him, yet in a way of liberty, not bondage; and a true wife counts her subjection her freedom."[6] Cautionary examples of deviant female behavior included Bradstreet's neighbor Anne Hutchinson, who was tried for heresy and banished from Massachusetts in 1637, her mentor John Cotton having testified against her and preached against women who spoke in church: "The woman is more subject to error than a man . . . and therefore might soon prove a seducer if she became a teacher."[7] A bright young woman named Ann Hopkins, wife of the governor of Hartford-upon-Connecticut, lost her reason and was brought to Boston in 1645 for medical help, according to the censorious John Winthrop,

> by occasion of her giving herself wholly to reading and writing, and had written many books . . . For if she had attended her household affairs, and such things as belong to women, and had not gone out of her way and calling to meddle in such things as are proper for men, whose minds are stronger, etc., she had kept her wits, and might have improved them usefully and honorably in the place God had set her.[8]

Thus when John Woodbridge published his sister-in-law Anne Bradstreet's poems in London in 1650 under the title *The Tenth Muse, Newly Sprung Up in America*, he garnished his preface not only with praise for the poet's "great variety of Wit and Learning, full of delight," but also with various assurances.[9] The reader is humorously advised that he will certainly like the book "unless men turn more peevish than women" and "envy the inferior sex." One book's excellence must not be construed as attacking men's general superiority. Woodbridge's commendatory couplets take the same note:

> Some books of women I have heard of late,
> Perused some, so witless, intricate,
> So void of sense, and truth, as if to err
> Were only wished (acting above their sphere) . . .
> What you have done, the sun shall witness bear,
> That for a woman's work 'tis very rare.   (p. 5)

That the poet has not neglected the duties of her sphere is essential to mention. Bradstreet is "esteemed," says Woodbridge,

> for her gracious demeanour, her eminent parts, her pious conversation, her courteous disposition, her exact diligence in her place, and discrete managing of her family occasions, and more than so, these poems are the fruit but of some few hours, curtailed from her sleep and other refreshments.   (p. 3)

Finally Woodbridge declares that Bradstreet herself did not desire publication and that he presents without her knowledge and against her wishes "what she resolved . . . should never see the sun." Perhaps so. Bradstreet's privileged position within a socially prominent family—

both her father and her husband were to become governors—accounts in large part for the acceptability of her writing.[10] It also accounts for her philosophical direction in this first book, which is secular, in the ambitious tradition of Renaissance humanism, rather than religious. At the same time, everything in Bradstreet's record indicates that she was indeed a loving and devoted wife and mother, competent housewife, and dutiful woman. And the poet's persona is insistently humble.

In the prologue to the *Quaternions*, Bradstreet laments her "foolish, broken, blemish'd Muse" for several stanzas. The poem was begun as a response to a poem of her father's on the four parts of the world, and her dedicatory poem to him apologizes for her "lowly pen" and assures him that her work cannot compete in merit with his. The long, unfinished work "The Four Monarchies" concludes with an apology. In "The Author to Her Book," composed for a second edition of *The Tenth Muse*, she amusingly retouches the original portrait of the modest housewife, viewing her book as an "ill-form'd offspring of my feeble brain" who has unwisely been exhibited in public:

> At thy return my blushing was not small,
> My rambling brat (in print) should mother call,
> I cast thee by as one unfit for light,
> Thy visage was so irksome in my sight;
> Yet being mine own, at length affection would
> Thy blemishes amend, if so I could:
> I washed thy face, but more defects I saw,
> And rubbing off a spot still made a flaw.
> I stretched thy joints to make thee even feet,
> Yet still thou run'st more hobbling than is meet;
> In better dress to trim thee was my mind,
> But nought save homespun cloth i' th'house I find.   (p. 221)

How are we to understand Bradstreet's self-effacement? A number of critics have speculated that this elaborate modesty is neither strictly sincere nor merely strategic, but tongue-in-cheek. We can read it as a *jeu d'esprit*, like the first sonnet of Sir Philip Sidney's *Astrophel and Stella*, artfully claiming artlessness. The poetry-maternity conceit, extended with such comic detail, gives the female poet a peculiar authority and incidentally introduces an original subject in English poetry, the realistic depiction of mother and child.[11] Significantly, nothing in this preface suggests that the poet has written on such unwomanly subjects as natural history, physiology, the history of civilization, and politics.

Notwithstanding its self-effacing introduction, the tone of Bradstreet's *Quaternions* is so confident and high-spirited that one suspects the poem was begun before the passage to America, when the author was still a clever young woman displaying her gifts to her father's learned and approving household. In the first *Quaternion* the four elements fire, air, earth, and water are personified as rivalrous sisters, each boasting of her "good" and her "rage," that is, of her usefulness to humanity and her destructive power. The debate begins quietly, grows contentious, and ends in a stalemate.

In the second *Quaternion* the elements' daughters, the four humors choler, blood, melancholy, and phlegm, take turns praising their advantages to Man's physical and moral constitution, insulting each other grossly. The debate ends when Phlegm, the weakest of the sisters, wins through kindness and makes all four join hands:

> Let Sanguine with her hot hand Choler hold,
> To take her moist my moisture will be bold:
> My cold, cold Melancholy's hand shall clasp;
> Her dry, dry Choler's other hand shall grasp . . .
> Nor be discern'd, here's water, earth, air, fire,
> But here's a compact body whole entire.   (p. 50)

The intention, of course, is to show "how diverse natures make one unity," and the seventeenth-century science is not Bradstreet's invention. But a number of points about this poem are surprising. First, neither God nor his hierarchical chain of being appears in it. The poem concerns Nature, personifying her femaleness in a lively way yet giving no hint that Nature is subordinate to Spirit. Moreover, if, as one critic has speculated, the poem is a portrait of contemporary theological turmoil,[12] it may equally well be a gently satiric commentary on the folly of political, religious, or domestic controversy in general. If so, it is rather interesting to see a young woman metaphorically proposing that men contending for superior status resemble girls squabbling in a kitchen and that they might learn to resolve "this rashness" like sisters, by forgetting the drive for superiority and realizing that "unless we agree, all falls into confusion." The idea that cosmic order may rest on cooperation rather than hierarchy and subordination does not animate other seventeenth-century philosophic poems either in England or America. It is not in du Bartas' well-known *Divine Weeks*, Bradstreet's source. Nor, in a period given to wit and grandiosity, do we elsewhere find such tolerant humor on such large subjects. But a gynocentric pulling down of cosmic vanities will become a recurrent theme in women's later poetry.

The third *Quaternion* adapts the idea of "a compact body whole entire" to the Ages of Man, and the device of personal monologue again gives freshness to a bookish theme. Childhood's self-portrait includes a detailed rendering of maternal care, complete with nursing and teething. Youth spiritedly describes his virtues (bravery, liveliness, affability) and vices (wildness, violence, foppishness). Middle Age is by turns the laborer, farmer, rich man, clergyman, political man, and man of learning, who admits that "envy gnaws if any do surmount, / I hate not to be held in high'st account" (p. 60). Old Age, finally, recounts the history and politics of Bradstreet's own times, mourning the decline of England after Elizabeth.

Bradstreet's two other political poems, "Dialogue Between Old England and New" and the celebration "In Honor of That High and Mighty Princess Queen Elizabeth," both lament conflict and praise civic harmony and prosperity. The poem commending Elizabeth cites her antifactional politics, her victory against Spain, her Irish policies, and her explorations—"Was ever people better ruled than hers? / Was ever land more happy, freed from stirs?"—and moves to its well-known peroration:

> Now say, have women worth? Or have they none?
> Or had they some, but with our Queen is't gone?
> Nay masculines, you have thus taxed us long,
> But she, though dead, will vindicate our wrong.
> Let such as say our sex is void of reason,
> Know 'tis a slander now but once was treason.   (pp. 197–98)

If the pilgrim mother had to wear the disguise—perhaps it was a reality—of modesty, her queenly heroine made an excellent compensation. This is the first in a long line of heroine poems by women.

Like her public poems, the personal pieces found among Bradstreet's papers after her death and posthumously published are in a plain, unornamented style, composed of prim and trim couplets and quatrains. Here too we find intimate touches, not only in the autobiographical pieces about the burning of her house and the poem "Before the Birth of One of Her Children," which expresses her fear of dying in childbirth. The devotional poems, which deal mostly with her will to submit to God's will, are personalized by their occasions—prayers for a son's safe return from a journey, thanks for deliverance from sickness, relinquishment to God of a dead grandchild—and by the specific physical self of a woman who anticipates the grave as "the bed Christ did perfume" and looks forward to a heaven where "No fainting fits shall me assail, / Nor grinding pains my body frail" (pp. 294–95). In the meditative poems where adversity or the remembrance of mortality teaches her to reject the things of this world in favor of the treasures of the next, Bradstreet nonetheless affectionately enumerates this world's attractions. The poems to her husband bespeak assurance of mutual love and friendship. When he is absent, she is punningly the "loving hind that (hartless) wants her deer" or a turtledove or mullet seeking its mate.

Most interesting among the domestic poems is one written when Bradstreet was forty-seven, "In Reference to Her Children, 23 June, 1659." She again comfortably describes herself as a natural creature: "I had eight birds hatched in one nest, / Four cocks there were, and hens the rest." As in "The Poet to her Book," Bradstreet identifies the roles of mother and poet—but without apology. Her wings have protected, her songs have instructed her young; she hopes that they in their nests will do likewise for theirs. They having flown, she having grown old,

> My age I will not once lament,
> But sing, my time so near is spent,
> And from the top bough take my flight
> Into a country beyond sight,
> Where old ones instantly grow young,
> And there with seraphims set song.   (pp. 232–34)

Meanwhile her eight children are to remember that it was their mother who "Taught what was good and what was ill, / What would save life and what would kill" before she would let them fly, and she will thus live among them after her death. The desire for immortality in heaven, combined with a continuing audience on earth, was a standard seventeenth-century trope. Her bird-mother-poet conceit, sustained with ease and grace through these valedictory ninety-five lines, tells us that Bradstreet had at last found an authoritative poetic persona—and in that least likely of places, her biological role.

Bradstreet's work contains elements which appear again and again in later women's writing. Female powerlessness and low cultural status mean that a meek poetic persona will be standard for Puritan and non-Puritan alike. Many women poets, including Emily Dickinson and the young Marianne Moore, will be published only thanks to the efforts of others. Gestures of bold assertion followed by retraction will form a recurrent pattern. Set against this, there will be female voices expressing pride in their ability to instruct or, later, to feel and experience life. Philosophically, a distaste for dualism, hierarchy, and vertical metaphors, and a preference for "a compact body whole entire" organized through balances rather than superior-inferior structures, will be a core female position. So will loving attachment to nature and the body[13] and a willingness to identify the self with animals.

In the depiction of relationships, unity through mutual balance almost universally signals happiness in women's poems, while dominance-submission relations (including those between God and the individual woman) are associated with suffering and death. This will be the case even when the poet ostensibly endorses such relationships, as Bradstreet does when submitting to the God who corrects her prosperity through pain. Humor will be for later women, as for Bradstreet, a mode by which one charmingly says the unsayable. Historic and mythic heroines will provide a means of self-exploration, self-projection, self-defense. And other women will dwell, of course, on the domestic scene. Yet no other, from Bradstreet's time to our own, will exhibit Bradstreet's wholeness, for no other will write with equal firmness and authority on matters as private as a mother's trouble with a baby's teething and as public as the history of the world.

Following Bradstreet, America was almost entirely barren of poetry in general and poetry by women in particular for about a century. Emily Watts in *The Poetry of American Women* has located no women's poetry preserved in the mid-Atlantic states before the mid-eighteenth century, or from the South before the nineteenth.[14] In New England, Jane Turrell (1708–1735) was, like Bradstreet, the daughter of a privileged family, and Phyllis Wheatley (1753?–1784) was America's first black poet. Turrell's husband omitted her "Pieces of Wit and Humour" in the posthumous edition of her poems because "her Heart was set upon graver and better subjects."[15] Wheatley, brought as a slave to this country at the age of five or six, was educated and encouraged to write by her master, John Wheatley, a Boston man, who also introduced her to London society. The primary object of Wheatley's friends, and her poetry, was to demonstrate "that Negroes, black as Cain, / May be refin'd, and join th'angelic train."[16] She therefore wrote neoclassic patriotic poems, elegies, compliments to various personages, and panegyrics on virtue, for the most part indistinguishable from other late-eighteenth-century verse. But her longest poem is an example of what was to become one of the most important escape hatches in women's poetry: the treatment of a mythological heroine. Wheatley's "Niobe in Distress for Her Children Slain by Apollo" is taken from Ovid, but the heavy degree of melodramatic woe in her rendition suggests that it may be a veiled portrait of her own powerlessness—or even, more radically, a lament on behalf of the mother from whom she herself had been torn.

By the late eighteenth century, American Puritanism had sufficiently subsided, and prosperity—meaning schooling and leisure for increasing numbers of daughters and wives—had sufficiently advanced, to produce several notable women poets, including Mercy Otis Warren (1728–1824), Ann Eliza Bleecker (1752–1783), and Susanna Rowson (1762–1824). These women wrote in a variety of styles, using public as well as domestic settings and images, and they illustrate as well as any other poets of the period the simultaneous fashions of neoclassic wit, post-Miltonic sublimity, and pre-Romantic sensibility characteristic of their age. All of them became interesting poets in part because revolution acted on social custom as a shifting of continental plates acts on the earth's surface, making rifts and mountains. Theirs was a time of political upheaval, when women who would otherwise have led protected lives were thrown, or threw themselves, into the public sphere, as the claims of patriotism and the notions of liberty and resistance to tyranny were able temporarily to override the claims of female modesty. Like Bradstreet's, their poetry of wit represents a degree of freedom and intelligence which was killed in the next century by the advancing doctrine of "separate spheres," the triumph of genteel poetry, and the ghettoization of women's writing.

Mercy Warren, one of the liveliest and most sociable ladies of the Revolutionary period, daughter of a prominent judge, wife of a future general, and lifelong friend of John and Abigail Adams, had for years been penning religious and domestic verse while raising her five sons. She wrote to John Adams in 1773, at the age of forty-five, asking whether it would be proper for a female to compose political satire in the patriotic cause. "Must not the female Character suffer," she fretted, "and will she not be suspected as deficient in the most amiable part thereof, if she indulges her pen to paint in the darkest shades even those whose Vice and Vanity have rendered [them] contemptible?" Adams reassured her that "the faithfull Historian delineates Characters truly, let the Censure fall where it will," and gallantly added that he knew of no geniuses ancient or modern who had attained "the tender, the pathetic the keen and severe, and at the same time the Soft, the Sweet, the amiable and the pure in greater perfection" than herself.[17] Warren proceeded to write political farces populated by wicked and cowardly Tories, and Drydenesque blank-verse tragedies teaching that the fall of nations results from corruption in high places and the failure of citizens to defend Liberty. Warren's romantic heroines in these plays are given to weeping and swooning, but their mothers are able to resist tyrants and lead men to battle in a national emergency. Her mock-heroic celebration of the Boston Tea Party, "The Squabble of the Sea Nymphs," is also organized by females something like herself:

> The fair Salacia, victory, victory sings,
> In spite of heroes, demi gods, or kings,
> She bids defiance to the servile train,
> The pimps and sychophants of George's reign.[18]

Ann Eliza Bleecker, a less aggressive spirit than Warren, destroyed everything she wrote before her marriage in 1769. Most of the rest, given to friends and visitors to her rural home in upstate New York, disappeared; the remains were published posthumously by her daughter, also a poet. Though Bleecker is the first of a long line of female poets said to compose extemporaneously for the amusement of friends rather than to satisfy personal ambition, her *vers de societé* is in fact fun, and in some of it her ambitiousness is only lightly disguised. She has a mock-heroic passage on a widow goose's search for a new husband, a wicked epigram on a narcissistic gentleman friend, and a mock-pastoral on the occasion of a New Year's morning after a drunken party, in which the poet compares herself to Orpheus:

> Impatient trees, to hear his strain,
>   Rent from the ground their roots—
> Such is my fate, as his was then
>   Surrounded here—by brutes.[19]

Another ostensibly lighthearted piece depicts a search for inspiration in which she is shuttled back and forth between the Muses and Apollo, who are too busy to be bothered with her, and finally finds the goddess of Wisdom, from whom "I cannot fear rejection." Bleecker's longer poems include a satire on country neighbors, descriptions of rural beauty, patriotic pieces, and a number of melancholy personal lyrics arising from her daughter's death after the family's flight from Burgoyne's marauding troops in 1777. In these poems—the first in America about personal tragedy—she defends her grief against those who urge resignation; and as much as she dares, she despairingly challenges God: "Father of the Creation wide, / Why hast thou not to man deny'd / The silken tye of love?" Later, in the classic submission pattern of women, she justifies God's ways to herself and thanks him for restraining her impulses to suicide. But Bleecker failed to recover from depression and lived only five years after her child's death.

Susanna Rowson, daughter of a British naval officer whose property was confiscated after the Revolution and then the wife of a feckless husband she satirized in the novel *Sarah, the Exemplary Wife*, of which the moral is "Do not marry a fool," was the first woman in America to earn her living by her pen. Rowson wrote *Charlotte Temple*, the new nation's first best-seller and the model for seduced-and-abandoned stories thereafter. She was also an actress, playwright, editor of a magazine, mistress of a school for girls, and poet, and her verse reflects the changing taste of her era. Her early poems include rousing and sometimes rowdy songs, like the drinking song from one of her plays, in which the sailors "toss off a glass to a favorite lass, / To America, Commerce and Freedom." Though this song, with several of her others, was "sung, during the first quarter of this century, all over the country," her biographer apologizes that "it is certainly too boisterous for the pen of a lady; but it must be remembered that the author was the daughter of a sailor" and promises that "her later poems, as her later life . . . are more serious, elevated, and devotional."[20] They are also, needless to say, more dull.

Since Rowson was a writer with a sturdy sense of her audience, we can assume her poetic opinions on the woman question were representative for her time. Her patriotic-romantic comedy *The Slaves in Algiers, or, a Struggle for Freedom* concerns a group of Americans held for ransom by pirates. The heroines range from saucy slave to self-sacrificing maiden to virtuous and indomitable mother, all of whom believe in liberty and also believe that "woman was never formed to be the abject slave of man . . . I feel that I was born free, and while I have life, I will struggle to remain so." The slave, significantly, has been tutored in independence by one who "came from that land, where virtue in either sex is the only mark of superiority—she was an American." Rowson's epilogue imagines an audience of ladies who slightly misinterpret her message, thinking

> She says that we should have supreme dominion,
> And in good truth we're all of her opinion,
> Women were born for universal sway,
> Men to adore, be silent, and obey,

whom she gently corrects:

> To bind the truant, that's inclined to roam,
> Good humour makes a paradise at home.
> To raise the fall'n—to pity and forgive,
> This is our noblest, best prerogative.
> By these, pursuing nature's gentle plan,
> We hold in silken chains—the lordly tyrant Man.[21]

The idea that the true American woman is both independent and useful domestically and socially appears in a number of Rowson's "miscellaneous poems." "Rights of Women" argues that American women should be grateful for the "right" to run their homes and help the sick and poor instead of living in idleness. "Women as They Are" is a hilarious send-up of feminine types: the dizzy beauty; the dull-witted housewife who can cook but do nothing else ("What is she fit for, but an upper servant"); the "accomplished belle" who sings, dances, and flirts in French and whose husband will find her a "fluttering insect" and want to kill her; the weeping novel reader; the screaming shrew. In the end the poet turns to the men who enjoy the satire and tells them if they want better wives than these they should learn to "treat us, scorning custom's rules, / As reasonable beings, not as fools."[22] In her "Dialogue—Mary and Lucretia," one of Rowson's many writings for her girl students, a good girl converts a giddy one to the values of study and sewing clothing for the poor. Throughout her work Rowson, like Bradstreet and Warren, writes with vigor, humor, and authority.

Except for Bradstreet, these are forgotten poets. And Bradstreet, who is usually represented in anthologies by her more submissive pieces, has been peculiarly served by admirers as well as critics. If, for example, we look to John Berryman's *Homage to Mistress Bradstreet* for the tribute of one poet to another, we will be misled.

Berryman's poem brilliantly depicts Bradstreet's sense of her own unprettiness, the physical and spiritual hardness of her life, and the moral staunchness of her response to that life, which may be why he wrote about her, as he wrote about Anne Frank: theirs was a staunchness he personally lacked and craved. The dazzling primary invention of the poem is Berryman's imagined projection of himself "across the centuries" as Bradstreet's lover, her would-be seducer, entering her consciousness as the temptation to sensuality which she ultimately rejects. At the work's center is a magnificent description of childbirth from a woman's point of view. But what of Bradstreet's poetry? The second stanza of *Homage* begins:

I doubt if Simon than this blast, that sea,
spares from his rigour for your poetry
more. We are on each other's hands
Who care. Both of our worlds unhanded us.[23]

Berryman implies that the husband to whom Bradstreet wrote a series of quite satisfied love poems appreciated her less than he, Berryman, would have and that she was neglected by her world—an odd notion

because she was very highly praised in her own time.[24] This opening
may be seen as good seducer's tactics, and *Homage* does not return to
the subject of Bradstreet's poetry until the interchange of stanza 12:

> Versing, I shroud among the dynasties;
> quaternion on quaternion, tireless I phrase
> anything past, dead, far,
> sacred, for a barbarous place.
> —To please your wintry father? All this bald
> abstract didactic rhyme I read appalled
> harassed for your fame
> mistress neither of fiery nor velvet verse.

No more is said until stanza 42, where the aging Bradstreet complains:

> The proportioned, spiritless poems accumulate.
> And they publish them
> away in brutish London, for a hollow crown.

And that is all. With such admirers, a poet needs no detractors. One
would scarcely rush to read Bradstreet after this introduction, and it is
difficult to avoid the conclusion that Berryman created, out of his own
yearning, a lover-anima-muse figure who would never be seen as a col-
league, collaborator, or equal.

Berryman is less peremptory than Moses Coit Tyler, in whose history
of Colonial literature Bradstreet is "lamentable rubbish,"[25] or Charles
Eliot Norton who, in editing her poems as an act of New England piety,
saw in them "no grace and charm of spontaneous lyrical utterance."[26]
Bradstreet's more charitable critics usually insist that her early work is
worthless because it is impersonal and attempts to "escape" her actual
existence, while her later poems "place her conclusively in literature"
because they are personal: "No more Ages of Man, no more Assyrian
monarchs; but poems in response to the simple events in a woman's
life."[27] If interested in her Puritanism, they miss her playfulness. The
critic who sees latent rebellion and possible theological satire in the
Quaternions discusses the protagonists of "Four Elements" and "Four
Humours" as if they were men, not women. Histories of American literature have yet to recognize that the Bradstreet opus constitutes something astonishingly original: a woman who as a philosophic poet takes
all knowledge as her province and interprets it from a distinctly female
point of view, who as a lyric and meditative poet offers a model of emotional and spiritual struggle concluding in success, and who finds in her
biological role a poetic authority unavailable to her brethren. What ob-

scures the achievements of Bradstreet and her late-eighteenth-century daughters from us, however, is the large white fog of the nineteenth century.

3

We need in woman the completion of our own natures; that her finer, clearer, and purer vision should pierce for us the mysteries that are hidden from our senses, strengthened, but dulled, in the rude shocks of the out-door world, from which she is screened, by her pursuits, to be the minister of God to us . . . We care little for any of the mathematicians, metaphysicians, or politicians, who, as shamelessly as Helen, quit their sphere. Intellect in women so directed we do not admire, and of affection such women are incapable. There is something divine in women, and she whose vocation it is to write, has some sort of inspiration, which relieves her from the processes and accidents of knowledge, to display only wisdom, in all the ranges of gentleness, and all the forms of grace.
     —Rufus Griswold, The Memorial: Written by Friends of the Late Mrs. Osgood [28]

Ah! woman still
Must veil the shrine
Where feeling feeds the fire divine.
     —Frances Osgood, "A Reply" [29]

The poetess as we know and despise her is the creation of post-Revolution America. She emerges during a period of rapid commercial and territorial expansion, when the most significant social movement was the growth of an urban middle class, priding itself on money and refinement, which required a population of idle daughters and wives to demonstrate that possession of wealth and to be in charge of that refinement. While reformers throughout the nineteenth century reprimanded the ornamental woman and urged her to be less narcissistic and more useful, skillful, self-respectful, and serious-minded, powerful social pressures dictated otherwise. It is in this period that literary culture, along with religion, lost its link with political power and became the property of middle-class ladies who were expected to dwell in the "separate sphere" of domestic tranquillity where, sheltered from the horrid shocks of commerce and the sordidness of politics, they would provide comfort, high-mindedness, and a satisfying evidence of their prosperity to the men whose business was business.

Respectable Colonial women at times were printers, blacksmiths, shopkeepers, and of course midwives. In the early nineteenth century the number of women working at trades and crafts decreased, and females were excluded from the newly licensed profession of medicine. Home industry, which had included spinning and weaving, food preserving, shoemaking, quilting, soapmaking, candlemaking, and the care of animals if the family was rural, declined as cities grew and factory manufacture advanced. Urban husbands worked outside their homes, not in them. With the shift away from productive labor for women came a shifting understanding of woman's relation to man. For the Puritans, the daughter of Eve was mentally and morally man's inferior, her subordination mandated by St. Paul. Yet she was God's equal child and, like a man, could earn praise through performance of duty.

In the enlightened eighteenth century, it was sometimes allowed that man's dominion, not necessarily just, was on the whole required for the smooth functioning of civilization. This is the position, for example, of *The Lady's New Year's Gift, or, Advice to a Daughter,* which went through fifteen American editions between 1688 and 1765. Its advice on "how to live with a Husband," though he be faithless, a drunkard, stupid (in which case "the Wife insensibly getteth a right of Governing in the Vacancy"), or a weakling (which is almost as good as his being dead, in which case the wife gets dominion over his property), is essentially a manual for saving appearances and taking the reins:

> You must be very dextrous, if when your Husband shall resolve to be an Ass, you do not take care he may be your Ass; but you must go skillfully about it . . . In short, the surest and most approved method will be to do like a wise Minister to an easy Prince; first give him the Orders you afterwards receive from him.[30]

This sort of candor disappears in the sentimental nineteenth century. Ann Douglas in *The Feminization of American Culture* cites Horace Bushnell, a liberal minister instructing his daughter in the new age with no mention of Eve's sin or the inferiority of the sex. On the contrary, she is by nature, and should be, "above all . . . unselfish." Her mission is "that she shall seem to have alighted here for the world's comfort and blessing . . . all the ways of selfishness are specially at variance with her beautiful errand."[31] In 1830 the *Ladies Magazine,* one of a burgeoning number of publications devoted to an exclusively female audience, eulogizes the True Woman: "See, she sits, she walks, she speaks, she looks—unutterable things! Inspiration springs up in her very paths—it follows her foot-steps. A halo of glory encircles her, and illumines her whole orbit. With her, man not only feels safe, but is actually renovated. For he approaches her with an awe, a reverence, and an affection which before he knew not he possessed." [32]

Douglas notes that in the absence of economically significant labor or political power, the True Woman was supposed to exercise "Influence," and especially she was supposed to exercise a purifying and restorative influence which the coarse irreligiousness of men was likely to require. One of the best beloved fictional plots in this period was the redemption of a brute male by a pure female. Another was the seduction and abandonment by a brute male of a pure female, who subsequently dies. Men were by nature more inclined to wickedness than women because their greater animal vigor and stronger intellects led them astray from the paths of simple faith. Women were by nature more religious, more submissive, more physically frail, and more sexually pure than men. While men were made for lives of action, women were made for the tender vocation of love. Into their hands fell the finer things in life, and from them the harsh realities were to be veiled.

As culture during the first half of the nineteenth century came to signify uplift, poetry ascended to a vaguely floating position above fiction and drama. The novelist or playwright might deal in matters scandalous and dangerous, if only to urge a pious moral. But satire as a major literary form was dead, in America as in England. Poetry now was "elevated"—the word is ubiquitous in nineteenth-century criticism—and the poet was, as Emily Dickinson's biographer George Whicher puts it, "a beautiful soul standing apart from the crass occupations of life." [33] The woman poet, even more than the male, needed to avoid taint. As editor Sarah Hale, herself a poet, explained in an early issue of the *Ladies Magazine*, "The path of poetry, like every other path in life, is to the tread of woman exceedingly circumscribed. She may not revel in the luxuriance of fancies, images and thoughts, or indulge in the license of choosing themes at will, like the lords of creation." [34]

Two mid-century anthologies represent the dominant taste of the period. Caroline May's *American Female Poets*, the less pretentious, explains in its preface that poetry "is the language of the affections" and that most of the poems in the volume spring from "home, with its quiet joys, its deep pure sympathies, and its secret sorrows." [35] Rufus Griswold, influential man of letters and compiler of the very successful *Female Poets of America*, is somewhat more complex. Arguing that the development of female genius is destined to redeem America from the charge of excess devotion to business and politics, he insists that women are capable not merely of feelings but of "mental superiority." [36] His commentaries on individual women poets often commend them for qualities of mind and intelligence. But Griswold also makes clear what the public required and what it could not tolerate, in female geniuses, however intelligent. "We turn," he wrote in a memorial to one poetess, "from the jar of senates, from politics, theologians, philosophies, and all forms of intellectual trial and conflict, to that portion of the literature which they have given us, coming like dews and flowers after glaciers and rocks, the hush of music after the tragedy, silence and rest after turmoil and action." However, as for "the ruder sort of women . . . casting aside their own eminence, for which they are too base, and seeking after ours, for which they are too weak, they are hermaphroditic disturbers of the peace of both."[37]

In a period when women poets as well as novelists were outselling men (and precipitating remarks like Hawthorne's about the "d———d mob of scribbling women"), the most predictable compliments of the woman poet tell us that she is personally modest, that she writes naturally and spontaneously from the heart, and that she cares nothing for fame. The biographer of Phoebe Cary, a bachelor woman poet known as a bright conversationalist, writes that "she maintained invariably a gentle reserve . . . her wit had no sting, her frankness and sincerity were those of a child, and she was always 'pure womanly.'" When compared to Sappho, "Phoebe accepted the comparison smilingly, in silence, but with a natural, modest pleasure."[38] Since a woman's poetry was to be natural rather than studied, Maria Osgood "sung simply in conformity to a law of her existence."[39] Ann Lynch's poems are "naturally and generally unpremeditated effusions."[40] Lydia Sigourney "sings impulsively from an atmosphere of affectionate, pious and elevated sentiment, rather than from the consciousness of subjective ability."[41] And since refinement in a woman meant personal self-effacement, Caroline May notes that when she asked her authoresses for biographical data, "Several of our correspondents declared their fancies to be their only facts; others that they had done nothing all their lives, and some—with a modesty most extreme—that they had not lived at all."[42]

In sum, what the genteel tradition demanded of the ladies was that they bare their hearts, gracefully and without making an unseemly spectacle of themselves. They were not to reveal that they had heads, let alone loins. They were not to demonstrate ambition. They were not to lecture on public issues or to speculate on philosophical or religious ones. A woman able to sing in this cage was respectable. A woman who tried to sing outside it was a whore—Griswold's shameless Helen—or a monster.

The most dramatic effect of this nineteenth-century view of women

and women poets was the precipitous decline of poems by women on
public subjects. Like Susanna Rowson, whose early work included
rowdy sailor songs, and whose later work is domestic and dutiful, a
number of women poets in the early part of the century made a sort of
backward journey from experience to innocence. Sarah Wentworth
Morton in 1790 published *Ouabi: An Indian Tale in Four Cantos*, fea-
turing noble and ignoble savages and a hero who flees the corruptions
of Europe for the Adamic wilds of Illinois, but her later poems are
personal lyrics. Eliza Townsend wrote a celebrated ode denouncing
Napoleon in 1909 before settling down to years of religious poetry.
Hannah Gould, whose father fought in the Revolution, wrote patriotic
ballads early and nature poetry later. Even the young Lydia Sigourney,
later to become the subject of Mark Twain's wonderful parody for her
incessant lugubrious elegies, published in 1822 a five-canto work on the
settlement of the American continent and "the duties of its present masters toward the aborigines." Throughout the first half of the century
women continued to write Indian romances, patriotic verse, and poems
on themes like abolition, missionary work, and the need of benevolence
for the unfortunate. Later come poems by women protesting the Mexi-
can War and the Spanish-American War, poems defending the "fallen
woman," and temperance ballads. Emotions women could not express
about their personal powerlessness were acceptable in the form of compassion and indignation over the sufferings of others. But poetry on social issues remains a comparatively minor strain in this period.

In the overwhelming mass of nineteenth-century female poetry, the
setting is either "the sacred retirement of home" or the inspirational
world of nature in which every brook laughs, every mountain is lofty,
every sunset cloud is angel-hued. Love and death are favorite themes,
but love excludes sexuality, and death scenes are vague on bodily details
beyond a fevered or pale cheek, preferring to concentrate on the sorrow
or despair of the mourners and the consolations of faith. If the object of
love is a man, his noble nature is exhorted, or he is idealized and absent, or his unresponsiveness is the occasion for the poet to express patient endurance. Much more often, the beloved is a child. The dead,
too, are commonly children. They may also be gallant soldiers, fellow
poets, beloved friends, or other inspirational adults. Sometimes it is the
example of their pure and noble lives which soothes the grieving poet;
sometimes it is the fact that they have gone to a higher place and are
now angels. Since the typical poem is contemplative and its real subject
is the state of the poet's ardent yet submissive soul, it usually contains
little action, much aspiration. Joy, grief, and duty figure prominently,
and there are scores of poems on Hope:

Hidden, and deep, and never dry,
   Or flowing, or at rest,
A living spring of hope doth lie
   In every human breast.

or

May Hope her anchor lend amid the storm,
And o'er the tempest rear her angel form;
May sweet Benevolence, whose words are peace
To the rude whirlwind softly whisper—cease![43]

Describing the literature of this period, Ann Douglas argues that "the feminization of culture" was a revenge of the powerless, whereby women and their allies—disestablished and effeminate fellow-traveling men of letters, primarily clergymen—established an antiintellectual, antihistorical, antiheroic, and morbidly sentimental bourgeois ethos dominated by a "debased religiosity" and filling the needs of consumerism.[44] That most women's writing during the early and mid-nineteenth century is sentimental is undeniable. It is also evident that the sentimentality is a result of authors' pretending not to know, not to feel, what they do know and feel. Inflated, exclamatory rhetoric is a device employed when a poet is supposed to seem natural and impulsive but is obliged to repress awareness of her body and her ego. Flights to sublimity arrive at banality when the actual world of men, women, and manners is restricted material. Soporific meters without prosodic experimentation arise when the intention is to please and soothe. Butter and sugar make a cloying diet, but if meat, fish, game, and salt are forbidden by the authorities, one will live on sweets.

At the same time, Douglas' dismissal as *ipso facto* trivial the "domestic and personal" worlds in which, alone, women could be "genuine authorities"[45] seems to reflect a familiar misogynist bias rather than a literary judgment. Louise Bogan's *Achievement in American Poetry* three decades ago suggested that nineteenth-century women were to be applauded for maintaining what she calls "the line of feeling" in American poetry, arguing that the "poetic intensity which wavers and fades out and often completely fails in poetry written by men, on the feminine side moves on unbroken."[46] Emily Stipes Watts points out that the pessimism of women poets and their failure to encounter the Divinity or identify with the Oversoul may be as valid a representation of the American experience as the Adamic optimism of their brethren.[47] However sentimentalized the treatment, it is worth acknowledging that death was a reality which women poets commonly confronted personally and which their male compeers usually ignored. Before hospitals and funeral establishments professionalized these matters, it was women, not men, who tended sickbeds and laid out the dead; it is small wonder if their poems are morbid.

Several recent critics have proposed that the conflict in a woman writer between the assertion required of her as writer and the submission required of her as woman may generate her most exciting writing.[48] Margaret Homans argues that the deviousness triggered in Emily Dickinson by a set of poetic conventions which exclude her is itself quintessentially poetic: Dickinson "finds in language's doubleness, paradoxically, a way around the hierarchizing dualism" that impedes other nineteenth-century women poets.[49] Cheryl Walker's study of nineteenth-century women's poetry finds that its most consistent and intense motif is vacillation regarding power, and that the contrary pulls of desire and renunciation are encoded in a multiplicity of ways. She cites the pattern of the "free bird" poem in which the poet sees some winged creature as an emblem of pride and courage and then proceeds to reject such a life as too lofty and lonely for her; the "sanctuary" poem in which retirement means not rest and refreshment, as it does in poems by men, but a desperate retreat from pain and danger; the death-wish poem in which sanctuary and tomb are one; and an almost universal identification of poetry and suffering, absent from mid-nineteenth-century men's poetry in America but pervasive in women's poetry, as if feminine ambition and punishment for that ambition were necessarily inseparable.

The lady poets insist that one must choose between love and fame since, as Emma Embury puts it in "Madame de Stael,"

Oh, Love is not for such as thee:
    The gentle and the mild,
The beautiful thus blest may be,
    But never Fame's proud child . . .

Only in lowly places sleep
    Life's flowers of sweet perfume,
And they who climb Fame's mountain-steep
    Must mourn their own high doom.[50]

Yet the permissible subject of love seems often in women's poems to be a disguised means of treating the theme of power, and love is often equated with suffering. Walker thus concludes that if "the nightingale's burden" of self-suppression "is antique to the degree that it approves accommodation, it is modern in the sense in which it betrays a divided mind."[51]

Even in the first half of the century we find a number of women poets whose surface piety, purity, and passivity plainly exist in tension with quite other feelings. Maria Brooks (1795–1845), who adopted the cosmopolitan pen name Maria del Occidente, was a warm-blooded manipulative lady who contrived to make both Robert Southey and Rufus Griswold (whose mistress she may at one time have been) her literary patrons, and to win a *succès d'estime* for a six-canto piece of erotic mythology entitled *Zophiël, or the Bride of Seven*. The plot of this poem involves a fallen angel smitten with love for a panting but pure Hebrew maiden, and its viewpoint is distinctly voyeuristic. We see the flimsily dressed heroine's limbs disposed in a number of fetching positions— awake, asleep, swooning, brought captive to an exotic court where all eyes find her beautiful "in every limb, joint, vein,"

Save that her lip, like some bud-bursting flower,
  Just scorned the bounds of symmetry, perchance,
But by its rashness gained an added power,
  Heightening perfection to luxuriance.

We see the angel materializing in her chamber wearing little more than wings, as his tender form

Modest emerged, as might a youth beseem;
  Save a slight scarf, his beauty bare, and white
As cygnet's bosom on some silver stream
  Or young Narcissus, when to woo the light
Of its first morn, that floweret open springs;
  And near the maid he comes with timid gaze,
And gently fans her.[52]

The angel kills a series of the heroine's prospective bridegrooms, one of whom dies of bliss in her arms, entangled with her hair as she tries to save his life. After a number of episodes influenced by both Milton and Byron, the heroine nearly succumbs to her evil lover and "the gushing torrent of attracted sense" but is rescued by the appearance of her divinely appointed true betrothed. It is a fascinating plot not only for its sexuality but for its violence; fantasies of male deaths in women's poems scarcely appear again until the mid-twentieth century. Anticipating T. S. Eliot, Brooks appended to her poem a set of bookish notes on exotic regions and comparative religion, which helped give the poem prestige. Griswold, in recommending *Zophiël*, says, "There is not perhaps in the English language a poem containing a greater variety of thought, description and incident" without "an impure or irreligious sentiment."[53] Caroline May, agreeing that it is a work of genius, rather chokingly remarks that "the story is one that cannot attract much interest, or elicit much sympathy, but the fine thoughts scattered through it amply reward those who read it through."[54] Among these thoughts is a complex piece on "wild Ambition," described as the destroyer of heaven, the "subtle fire" of Eve, and the tormentor of "the fiercely struggling soul," yet also the source of Song and the means whereby mankind defies death. Though set in the angel's mouth, this is one of the few nineteenth-century poems in which a woman's ambivalence about fame concludes triumphantly in its favor.

Another writer whose ardor strains the boundaries of gentility is Frances Osgood (1811–1850).[55] Like Brooks, Osgood writes love poetry that reads like flesh and blood, some of it evidently stemming from a soured marriage and a romance with Edgar Allan Poe. One of Osgood's favorite roles was the ingenue, and in some poems she sounds girlishly infatuated, or girlishly sophisticated in the manner that Edna St. Vincent Millay's "A Few Figs from Thistles" would later make famous:

> Have I caught you at last, gentle rover?
>   Do I see you at length at my feet?
> Will you own yourself, sighing, my lover?
>   This triumph is sudden as sweet!
>
> Long vainly I strove to allure him;
>   *That* tender endeavor is past;
> My task must be, *now*, to endure him!
>   Heighho! but I've caught him at last![56]

But other poems deal in closer detail with what Osgood calls "the fetter 'neath the flower" of love: its capacity to imprison women. In one the speaker begs her absent husband to save her from the temptation of adultery:

> Return with those cold eyes to me
>   And chill my soul once more
> Back to the loveless apathy
>   It learn'd so well before!

In another she confesses an eager desire to be anything her neglectful love desires:

> I'd be a gem, and drink light from the sun,
>   To glad thee with, if gems thy fancy won;

Were birds thy joy, I'd light with docile glee
Upon thy hand, and shut my wings for thee![57]

She would be, in this poem, "pliant as clouds" if he would only pay
attention to her. She would be, in fact, precisely the passive, identityless
thing that the doctrine of True Womanhood defined by the vocation of
love requires. One of Osgood's more astonishing poems almost rebels:
"Yes! Lower to the Level" scornfully bids an untrue lover to "join the
faithless revel" and destroy his own honor, predicting that one day,
haunted by the memory of "love's purer air," he will curse and hate his
degenerate life too late. The last stanza preserves the speaker's saint-
liness by declaring that even then she would gladly suffer for him if she
could. Still more complicated emotionally are two poems in which a
mother prays for the death of children. In the first, "Ashes of Roses," the
mother cannot bear her sick child's suffering, and the poem closes with
the wish to die and rejoin the child in heaven where she can "tend" it
again. In "A Mother's Prayer in Illness" she fears that her daughters will
never receive the love they deserve in "this rough world," whose "wild
discord" will bring them only pain, and prays "Ah, take them first, my
Father, and then me!"[58] All these poems maintain the proprieties of
pure feeling and woman's loving self-effacement. That the commitment
to love expected of a woman may destroy her identity, and that women
may feel conflicting emotions—including rage and guilt—about the
children as well as the men they love, was not something Osgood's age
was ready to acknowledge. But the veils in her case are thin.

4

A step like a pattering child's in entry & in glided a little plain
woman with two smooth bands of reddish hair . . . in a very plain
& exquisitely clean white pique & a blue net worsted shawl. She
came to me with two day lilies which she put in a sort of childlike
way into my hand & said "These are my introduction" in a soft
frightened breathless childlike voice—
—Thomas Wentworth Higginson[59]

Dare you see a soul *at the White Heat?*
—Emily Dickinson[60]

In writers such as Brooks and Osgood, the ambivalence pervasive
among nineteenth-century poetesses is peculiarly strong. In Emily

Dickinson, ambivalence ascends to an artistic principle which I shall here call duplicity and which places Dickinson among the great writers of the English language while enabling her to illuminate the precise dilemma of the woman writer.

As Walker and others have demonstrated, the parallels between Dickinson and other women poets of her day are multiple and central.[61] In adopting the persona of the shy recluse, delicately afraid of strangers, too sensitive for the marketplace, Dickinson did precisely what the ideal poetess was supposed to do. For the domestic setting, the exploration of intense personal feeling, and the creation of poetic capital out of deprivation, she had dozens of feminine examples. The theme of the forbidden lover, the renunciation of love as well as ambition, the sense of vulnerability to pain as well as ecstasy, the fascination with death, the presentation of the self as a child, the need for sanctuary, the idea of a compensating afterlife—all this was deeply within the feminine tradition by Dickinson's time.

Yet Dickinson emphatically rejects the cult of True Womanhood. "God keep me from what they call *households*," wrote the twenty-year-old Emily (*L*, p. 99), and she organized her family situation so that her sister Lavinia, not herself, did most of the household drudgery ordinarily required of spinsters. Nothing in her poetry idealizes the female life as one of virtuous service to others. Her love poetry is demandingly passionate rather than gently affectionate, and much of it was written to her sister-in-law, Susan Gilbert Dickinson. Describing nature she is usually not "inspiring" but exact; no decent poetess would have noted how the bird on her front walk "bit an Angleworm in Halves— / And ate the fellow—Raw" (*P*, 328).

Confronting authority—theological, social, literary—Dickinson both submits and defies. The patriarchal God of her Puritan forebears elicits from her not only awe but anger at his masculine distance and power. If at times she coyly plays his "little girl," he is nevertheless the biblical bully who

> On Moses seemed to fasten
> With tantalizing play
> As Boy should deal with lesser Boy—
> To prove Ability— (*P*, 597)

He is "mastiff," "Inquisitor," the sneering "Mighty Merchant" who refuses to sell his goods. He is "Burglar—Banker—Father!" pretending gentleness, he hurls the thunderbolt "That scalps—your naked Soul"

(*P*, 315). He is indifferent to suffering: "Of course—I prayed—And did God Care?" (*P*, 376).

Toward human authority, too, Dickinson's tone is subversive. "They shut me up in Prose" (*P*, 613), locking her in a closet as a child to keep her quiet, never guessing they might as soon shut a bird in a pound. Where other women poets sometimes criticized their sisters for insufficient moral seriousness, Dickinson mocked: "What soft—Cherubic Creatures / These Gentlewomen are" with their "dimity Convictions" (*P*, 401). Her poems on the institution of marriage are elliptically but profoundly ironic. Her poems on her own powers as a poet are covertly yet fiercely boastful and defiant. Notwithstanding the role of timid poetess she played for Higginson, her "business is Circumference," and though "I cannot dance upon my Toes— / no Man instructed me—" (*P*, 326), she is secretly as "full as Opera" minus the placards.

Yet subversion is not rebellion. The Dickinson who feels herself to be a loaded gun, Vesuvius at home, a bomb abroad, is also a daisy, a mouse, a wren, the helpless and terrified creature who significantly misquotes Genesis in declaring that "In all the circumference of Expression, those guileless words of Adam and Eve were never surpassed, 'I was afraid and hid myself'" (*L*, p. 946). She is "zero at the bone" when confronted with that most phallic of beings, the "narrow fellow in the grass" (*P*, 986). Masked, elusive, playful in language as in the evasive persona of her "supposed self" (*L*, p. 268), she uses self-division as a recurrent motif in her poems, from the confession—or boast—that "Mirth is the Mail of Anguish" (*P*, 165), to the dread of "Ourself behind ourself concealed" (*P*, 670), to the terrifying experience of feeling "a Cleaving in my Mind" (*P*, 937). Conversely, if Dickinson's relations with God parallel her relations with men, in which they are always strong and she is always weak, it is also probable that Dickinson's portrayal of male power is a description of the frightening power in her own poetry.[62]

In her most striking statement of the position she shared with many women poets who had less skill and courage than she, Emily Dickinson wrote that she was Nobody at approximately the same moment as Walt Whitman was claiming to be everybody. Let us then examine, to the point of seeing the quintessential duplicity in it, that signature poem:

I'm Nobody! Who are you?
Are you—Nobody—too?
Then there's a pair of us! Don't tell!
They'd banish us—you know!

How dreary—to be—Somebody!
How public—like a Frog—
To tell your name—the livelong June—
To an admiring Bog!   (P, 288)

"I'm Nobody!" is a particularly keen example of the many poems in which Dickinson plucks spiritual success from material defeat by making a virtue of deprivation. Its tone is the naughty childlike tone Dickinson often uses to express the condition of powerlessness, and there are two modulations of it. First, a timid conspiratorial whisper which sounds as if it is coming from behind the sofa issues a warning against candid utterance, seeming to express, though possibly with a giggle, a real fear. "They'd banish us" resembles "They'd punish us," but it reveals a need to remain included within "their" powerful circle, however inconspicuously. In the second stanza girlish boldness succeeds girlish timidity; the pact between "the pair of us" has been settled during the stanza break, and secrecy has been assured. Completing the first stanza's implied set of antitheses, Nobody mockingly dissects Somebody. The world of substantial existence is boring, publicity is vulgarity, and public utterance is ludicrously vain in both senses of the term: the vainglorious orator must puff himself egotistically for his audience, but his audience is stupid and his utterance therefore futile. The word "tell" appears in each stanza as a kind of invisible pivot, causing the idea of speech to dominate both. It is understood without telling that the world of Nobody is intimate, playful, innocent, while the world of Somebody is insensitive, pompous, corrupt.

That is one reading, but there is another. We as readers are invited to join Nobody. If we agree, we become Nobody's audience, enjoying her wit and our mutual superiority to Somebody. She is our leader. We admire her, modest as she is. If everyone agrees, Somebody will be left announcing his presence to empty air, a Frog minus his Bog, his centrality as well as his sense of virtue having been prettily usurped by the subversive Nobody. The issue, of course, is power, and even we who are charmed or abashed into joining Emily fictively behind the sofa may prefer to be Somebody when we get the chance. And might she not, perhaps, have preferred it herself? The better we enjoy Nobody's removing Somebody to an undangerous distance, the better we discern her resemblance to Shakespeare's proud Coriolanus, retorting, when sentenced by Rome to banishment, "I banish you!"

A poem like this is duplicitous in that it means both what it says and its opposite. I use the term *duplicitous* rather than *ironic* because in irony the unstated meaning cancels the stated one; here, contrary meanings coexist with equal force, because they have equal force within the poet. Dickinson genuinely despises publicity and power, prefers the private and powerless life—and the reverse is equally true. We may say the same about many of her poems in praise of deprivation: they reject what they commend, commend what they reject. Their delight, their strength, derives from their doubleness. Doubleness similarly governs, as Margaret Homans has shown, many of Dickinson's poems about the relation of language to nature, of masculinity to femininity, and of the self to the self.[63]

Poetic doubleness makes excellent aesthetic sense if we assume with Coleridge that all art consists in the harmonizing of opposites, and if we believe that the highest art is that which presses most matter and spirit into least space. The duplicity which arises when an idea must be simultaneously denied and affirmed—when, in other words, the poet is driven by something forbidden to express but impossible to repress—is a means of creating high artistic excitement, and Dickinson is far from being its exclusive practitioner. "The Ancient Mariner," which morally deplores the evil it poetically glamorizes, is riddled with duplicity. It was duplicity, this flashing of things forbidden, that T. S. Eliot sensed and disapproved of, and that Ernest Jones partially explained, in *Hamlet.* Blake's Milton, a poet who is of the devil's party without knowing it, is the most duplicitous poet in the language. As Donald Hall acutely remarks, "When a poet says that he is doing north, look and see if he is not actually doing south. Chances are that his bent is so entirely south that he must swear total allegiance to north in order to cover the globe."[64]

For women writers in the nineteenth century, duplicity was the one royal road to artistic triumph, whether in England or America. As a consequence, the greatest women writers are usually the most profoundly and excitingly duplicitous. *Pride and Prejudice,* for example, depicts a society based on class and custom, vanity and stupidity, asks us to respect it, and centers on the understanding that in order to catch a desirable man one must not chase him. Indeed, to embody a desirable integrity herself, a financially deprived heroine like Elizabeth Bennett must be quite unconscious that she wants a tremendously wealthy hero like Mr. Darcy, though the audience knows it well. Likewise, *The Mill on the Floss* cannot permit itself to say that a heroine as passionate and intelligent as her author deserves to survive or that the old-fashioned country life over which George Eliot expends so much nostalgia is essentially evil and its morality wicked. Yet where does this novel's intense power come from, if not the unspoken pressure of precisely these ideas within it? Christina Rossetti's "Goblin Market," that long-disregarded tissue of erotic Victorianism or Victorian eroticism, is brilliantly duplicitous as regards female sexuality in its oral dimensions. We feel the darts of what is not said, of what cannot be said because it is unthinkably dangerous, as poetic energy.[65] By contrast, a work like Elizabeth Barrett Browning's *Aurora Leigh* is artistically cruder, beginning as it does with extreme declarations of female artistic and intellectual independence and ending with the heroine's chastened embracing of an idealized romantic love. Idea B follows and more or less cancels idea A instead of being held in charged suspension with A throughout the whole work of art. Rather than a dance of duplicity, we may call this maneuver the retraction shuffle. *Aurora Leigh* is a large-scale version of the "free bird" poem, with its acceptance of the idea that, for a woman, the proper goal is not fame but love. But this returns us to the originating premise of Dickinson's signature: the implicit recognition that an autonomous female identity is supposed not to exist.

Richard Wilbur, in describing Dickinson's gift for "Sumptuous Destitution," suggests that "for her there were three major privations: she was deprived of an orthodox and steady religious faith; she was deprived of love; she was deprived of literary recognition."[66] Though close to the unpleasant truth, this formulation implies a passivity which Dickinson's career does not substantiate. As a young woman during the Great Awakening, Dickinson refused to surrender herself to Christ, though her schoolmates, friends, and every other member of her family submitted. When she fell in love, it was with the strictly unavailable "Master"—whatever his identity—and with Susan Gilbert Dickinson. Invited to publish, she resisted. Had she done otherwise, she might have become a pious gentlewoman, a submerged wife, and a popular poetess. She rejected all three roles because the getting of them would have meant the losing of self: God, Love, or Fame might be the Ocean that "would eat me up" (*P*, 520).

Higginson's judgments of her poems, and the editorial prettyings of the few printed in her lifetime, indicate that Dickinson would have been a fool to seek fame for her work as she was writing it. The first volume of her poems appeared in 1890, heavily edited, and the first accurate text was not published until 1955. Dickinson's artistry exceeds others' because, although she may have feared much, she did not fear her own mind. She never retreats from an insight, never withdraws or retracts, but bears it out to the edge of doom, in language and rhythms formed to reflect precisely the swiftness, compactness, and drama of that single subject, her mind. Consequently she illuminates more fully than any other the situation of the nineteenth-century woman poet in America; and consequently she was unpublishable. What the same mind would have accomplished had it lived in a world where it could seek God, Love, Fame, without the certainty that it would be destroyed if it tried, we have no way to guess. She is America's first radically experimental poet, and is the first woman poet whose poetic language and structures systematically register and resist the dominance of masculinity and rationality in culture—through play, through parody, through evasion and illogic, and through the device of duplicity which makes possible the secret transmission of opposed messages within a single poem. These are strategies, as we will see, which her immediate successors practice and which are still practiced by women poets today.

5

O beautiful Forever!
O grandiose Everlasting!
Now, now, now,
I break you into pieces,
I feed you to the ground.
        —Louise Bogan, "I Saw Eternity"[67]

For authorities whose hopes
are shaped by mercenaries?
Writers entrapped by
tea time fame and by
commuters' comforts? Not for these
the paper nautilus
constructs her thin glass shell.
        —Marianne Moore, "The Paper Nautilus"[68]

By the time Dickinson's poems were published in 1890, the literary and social climate had changed radically from the period in which they were begun.[69] In the expanding economy following the Civil War, many women were joining the work force, many were involved in humanitarian causes, many joined—and many more read about—an increasingly belligerent feminist movement. In America the success, however notorious, of Whitman, and the imported fashions of French symbolism and English Pre-Raphaelite poetry and letters made certain liberties and certain aesthetic positions newly conceivable. When in 1881 Ella Wheeler Wilcox achieved a scandalous fame with her *Poems of Passion*, a book full of scenes "where madness melts in bliss, / And in the convulsive rapture of a kiss," she was said to "out-Swinburne Swinburne and out-Whitman Whitman."[70] America was now debating the New Woman, ancestress of the flapper, and the doctrine of separate spheres was fading slightly along with Victorian requirements of cradle-to-grave feminine innocence. Women were beginning to enter higher education, and women's poems were now appearing along with men's in elite literary journals as well as the ladies' magazines.[71]

The arrival of modernism on the American literary scene precipitated two distinct styles in women's poetry. The first was an extension and refinement of the traditional lyric style which concentrated on intense personal feeling. The second, a more radical break from the immediate past, was formally innovative and intellectually assertive but avoided autobiography. Both schools assert the feminine self, both subvert masculine authority more boldly than women poets had dared do before—though the daring, as we shall see, has made little impact on masculine critical consciousness.

In Lizette Reese (1856–1935) and Louise Guiney (1861–1920), later in Adelaide Crapsey (1878–1914), Sara Teasdale (1884–1933), Elinor Wylie (1885–1928), Edna Millay (1892–1950), Genevieve Taggard (1894–1948), Louise Bogan (1897–1970), and others, a style emerged which was artistically self-conscious, highly crafted, and musical. Abstractions wane—or are retained for questioning and definition. Clarity and irony replace the ornate fogginess of the mid-century. Much of this poetry is, of course, about love, but love now includes passion and physical sensation. The world itself now is seen as irreducibly physical, and the self is no longer identified as undefined yearning spirit. It is body, as in Bogan's "Alchemist":

> I burned my life, that I might find
> A passion wholly of the mind,
> Thought divorced from eye and bone,
> Ecstasy come to breath alone.
> I broke my life, to seek relief
> From the flawed light of love and grief.
> With mounting beat the utter fire
> Burned existence and desire.
> It died low, ceased its sudden thresh.
> I had found unmysterious flesh—
> Not the mind's avid substance—still
> Passionate beyond the will.[72]

Cheryl Walker has observed that the advent of burning kisses in women's lives and poems brought less power and freedom than they may have expected. Though they repudiated their sentimental ancestresses, these women's poems from the turn of the century to the Bohemian 1920s and beyond still commonly imply an identification of love and suffering. The feminine self still means a capacity for intense feeling, and there is still a large component of renunciation, martyrdom, secret sorrow, and pain caused by immoderate emotion.[73]

Many lyrics of this period quintessentially represent motifs in nineteenth-century female poetry and anticipate ideas that later women will deal with even more explicitly. Adelaide Crapsey's once-famous "To the Dead in the Churchyard Underneath My Window," written as she was dying of consumption, epitomizes the pattern of feminine rebellion defeated by masculine authority—for the voice of her physician telling her to "lie still and rest" is one with the voice of Death—and anticipates the "doctor" and "hospital" poems Plath, Sexton, and many other women will write in the mid-twentieth century.[74] In Sara Teasdale's "I Am Not Yours," love is a desired oblivion and loss of self that makes one think backward to Osgood and forward to the end of Plath's "Ariel":

I am not yours, not lost in you,
    Not lost, although I long to be
Lost as a candle lit at noon,
    Lost as a snowflake in the sea.

You love me, and I find you still
    A spirit beautiful and bright,
Yet I am I, who long to be
    Lost as a light is lost in light.

Oh plunge me deep in love—put out
    My senses, leave me deaf and blind,
Swept by the tempest of your love,
    A taper in a rushing wind.[75]

Reese, Guiney, Teasdale, and Wylie all wrote poems entitled "Sanctuary," and the dark side of that theme in nineteenth-century women's poems finds its perfect representation in Wylie's ironic version, where the speaker is directing a bricklayer in the construction of her "marvellous wall":

Full as a crystal cup with drink
Is my cell with dreams, quiet and cool . . .
Stop, old man! You must leave a chink;
How can I breathe? *You can't, you fool!*[76]

All of these are implicitly poems about the dilemma of the woman in a masculine culture, and the poets who follow "the line of feeling" often write explicitly on this subject. One thinks of Crapsey's proto-feminist

"Susanna and the Elders" and "The Witch"; of Wylie's "Now Let No Charitable Hope"; of Millay's scornful rewriting of Homer in "An Ancient Gesture" and her scorn toward husband and lover in Sonnets XXXI and XLI; of Bogan's "Medusa," "Cassandra" and "Women"—to name a very few. The war of genders simmers close to the surface in much of this work, sometimes approaching the discovery that masculine culture with its insistence on hierarchical dualisms is intrinsically antagonistic to the feminine identity: when Bogan in "I Saw Eternity" declares that the great abstractions of high poetry will spoil the stomachs of birds and mice as they have spoiled her mind, she arrives close to the bitter vision of a poet like Margaret Atwood.

Yet many of these poems ring a note of celebration or defiance, and it would be a mistake to see these "feminine" poems as bounded by suffering and victimization. Indeed, the further one moves into the twentieth century, the more the dominant tone in women lyric poets is pride—as in Teasdale's late poems of joyful isolation and in much of Wylie, Bogan, and Millay. If Millay was the darling of her time, it was perhaps not for her poems of sorrow but because she sounded most keenly the new note of feminine arrogance, burning her candle at both ends, letting her Daphne cry "I am off;—to heel, Apollo!" and defying death:

> Wine from these grapes I shall be treading surely
> Morning and noon and night until I die.
> Stained with these grapes I shall lie down to die . . .
> Three women come to wash me clean
> Shall not erase this stain.[77]

These women composed the first substantial body of lyric poetry which is worth anything in the United States. Their work as a whole can bear comparison with Elizabethan and Jacobean song, Caroline lyric and Pre-Raphaelite verse. Yet their collective impact is not acknowledged as a movement, nor has it had an impact on critical theory.

There are several reasons for this neglect, all perhaps subsumed in the observation that men, not women, have written most of the literary manifestos in the twentieth century. Modest as her grandmothers when it came to self-promotion, the female lyric poet of the 1920s typically relied on others to create her reputation. She did not make common cause with women of the past, whose piety she was trying to reject, or with the cohorts who were her rivals for male regard.[78] Moreover, modernism took another direction, away from beauty as such, song as such. The great male moderns concern themselves with the decline of western values, the death of God, man's alienation from nature. If there is any single thing in common among Eliot, Pound, Frost, Stevens, and

Williams, it is that these giant figures labor under a sense of devastating loss, which is seen as historical and social, and their work is a wrestling to erect some other saving structure. The women, however, tend to write like pagans, as if the death of God (and His civilization, and His culture, and His myths) were no loss to them. Indeed, it may have been a relief. A corollary difference is that the women write personally, whereas the reigning doctrine of modernism became impersonality: Yeats' "all that is merely personal soon rots," or the "extinction of personality" called for by Eliot.

Above and beyond these causes, it is clear that the very femininity of these poets defeated them. Feminine experience—a feminine voice— for many critics sounds inevitably trivial or distressing. One might quote, from the age of New Criticism, perhaps dozens of examples of individual poems by women about which critics simply miss the point. John Crowe Ransom, in a 1938 essay on Edna St. Vincent Millay entitled "The Poet as Woman," comes as close as anyone to explaining why:

> She is an artist. She is also a woman. No poet ever registered herself more deliberately in that light. She therefore fascinates the male reviewer but at the same time horrifies him a little too. He will probably swing between attachment and antipathy, which may be the very attitudes provoked in him by generic woman in the flesh, as well as by the literary remains of Emily Dickinson, Elizabeth Barrett, Christina Rossetti, and doubtless, if we only had enough of her, Sappho herself . . . A woman lives for love, if we will but project that term to cover all her tender fixations upon natural objects of sense. Her devotion to them is more than gallant, it is fierce and importunate, and cannot but be exemplary to the hardened male observer.

The male, Ransom explains, has pursued a more intellectual "line of development":

> Man distinguishes himself from woman by intellect, but he should keep it feminized. He knows he should not abandon sensibility and tenderness, though perhaps he has generally done so . . . But the problem does not arise for a woman. Less pliant, safer as a biological organism, she remains fixed in her famous attitudes, and is indifferent to intellectuality. I mean, of course, comparatively indifferent; more so than a man.

Following this opening, Ransom's essay goes on to say that "the limitation of Miss Millay . . . is her lack of intellectual interest," more precisely defined as "deficiency in masculinity," but after a disparaging analysis of several individual poems and phases of Millay's work, he concludes that her "quite positive talent" is best at

> a vein of poetry which is spontaneous, straightforward in diction, and excitingly womanlike; a distinguished objective record of a natural woman's mind. The structures are transparently simple and the effects are immediate . . . Her best subjects are death . . . personal moods . . . and natural objects which call up her love or pity.[79]

The first part of this essay acknowledges male antipathy for female artists and almost confesses a bad conscience about it, a half-awareness that men may be deficient in emotion, before swiveling to conclude that, on the contrary, women are deficient in intellect. The second portion, if one altered "excitingly womanlike" to "truly" or "purely womanlike," could be Rufus Griswold.

If we agree that Ransom was speaking for the male reviewer, we can understand why another set of women, with the advent of modernism, strove to escape the ghetto of feminine poetry by the leaps and bounds of undisguised intelligence. Amy Lowell (1874–1924) and Gertrude Stein (1875–1946) are the shock troops here, followed by Mina Loy (1882–1966), H.D. (1886–1961), and Marianne Moore (1887–1972). In an age when it was widely believed "that women are the cause of modernism, whatever that is"—as one journalist put it[80]—these writers were at the provocative edge of the avant-garde. Lowell not only championed imagism and *vers libre* but wrote translations and pastiches of Japanese poetry. Stein invented a syntax of teasing and generous evasiveness, substituting a cheerful indeterminacy for representation, a continuous present for linear time, repetition for narrative, and diffuseness of focus for grammatical subordination.[81] Loy dissected free love in a clinical free verse icy with Latinisms. H.D.'s earliest poems were the model imagist lyrics, and her intensive use of Greek and Egyptian myth, and of hermetic as well as Christian symbolism, parallels what poets like Yeats, Pound, and Eliot were doing. Marianne Moore invented a new system of prosody and new forms of intertextual allusion, and was to William Carlos Williams "our saint . . . in whom we all instinctually felt our purpose come together . . . like a rafter holding up the superstructure of our uncompleted building."[82]

When these determinedly cerebral poets address the woman question, it is with a characteristic impersonality. Amy Lowell in "The Sisters" begins by remarking how queer women poets are and ends, after imagining meetings with Sappho, Emily Dickinson, and Elizabeth Barrett Browning, by rejecting all three as models for herself. In "A

Critical Fable," Lowell's rollicking fantasy debate with her conservative ancestor and predecessor James Russell Lowell, she defends Dickinson and attacks male bias against women poets as a desire "to love them and shear them of victory." But her own treatment of Sara Teasdale damns by faint praise—"Of course it is true that she's not intellectual"—and her breezy tone disguises the personal painfulness of her theme of male cultural dominance as well as her personal competitiveness with her sister poets.[83] Fifty years later, Carolyn Kizer's "Pro Femina" will adopt the same strategy.

Gertrude Stein in "Patriarchal Poetry"—a term she invented—offers the definitive parodic opus on the subject of the masculine and feminine voices within culture and creates the model for one of the final works I consider in this book, Susan Griffin's *Woman and Nature: The Roaring Inside Her.* On the one hand the poem repeats phrases like "Patriarchal Poetry their origin and their history," "Patriarchal poetry makes no mistake," and "Patriarchal poetry is the same as Patriotic Poetry." Against this authoritative pomp and bluster we hear the labial and sibilant whispers of phrases like "let her be," "let her try," "let her be shy," "let her to be what he said." Included in the poem is a "sonnet" summarizing, tongue firmly in cheek, the relation patriarchal poetry (and society) considers exemplary between man and wife:

To the wife of my bosom
All happiness from everything
And her husband.
May he be good and considerate
Gay and cheerful and restful.
And make her the best wife
In the world
The happiest and most content
With reason.
To the wife of my bosom
Whose transcendent virtues
Are those to be the most admired
Loved and adored and indeed
Her virtues are all inclusive
Her virtues her beauty and her beauties
Her charms her qualities her joyous nature
All of it makes her husband
A proud and happy man.[84]

Mina Loy, for whom Stein was a "Curie / of the laboratory / of vocabulary," became the first woman poet to examine female sexual experience with a combination of scandalous candor and formal rigor. Her

"Parturition"—an unpunctuated and grammatically fragmented exercise in the "spatial contours" of self and poem—begins

> I am the centre
> Of a circle of pain
> Exceeding its boundaries in every direction,

and moves toward a definition of female libido, a "lascivious revelation." Her "Love Songs," contemporary with J. Alfred Prufrock's, un-
sentimentally describe

> Pig Cupid   his rosy snout
> Rooting erotic garbage
> "Once upon a time"
> Pulls a weed   white and star-topped
> Among wild oats   sewn in mucous membrane

and conclude with a sardonic salute to "Love — — — the preeminent
litterateur," which dismisses not simply an individual lover but an entire
tradition of poetry as mere male posturing.[85]
     Even more than Lowell, Stein, and Loy, H.D. challenges male au-
thority in literature and culture. Among her early lyric poems, "Helen"
implies that men and nations hate the woman-as-erotic-object they
claim to love, until they can embalm her as art. In "Demeter" the
Greek mother-goddess rejects the torpid image men have made of
her and announces "enough of tale, myth, mystery, precedent," as
Adrienne Rich will fifty years later set aside "the book of myths / in
which / our names do not appear." H.D.'s "Callypso Speaks" and "Eurydice" angrily attack not only Odysseus and Orpheus but the venerable
literary tradition of the egocentric male as hero, lover, poet. As recent
feminist criticism demonstrates, H.D.'s late visionary work beginning
with the war poems of Trilogy (1944–46) is governed by the determination to dismantle orthodox patriarchal structures and to pursue a buried
female truth.[86] Trilogy, composed, like Four Quartets, as a response to
the disintegration of self and civilization in World War II, imagines a
heterodox Christianity antipodal to Eliot's, gradually centering itself in
the vision of a "Lady" who has "none of her usual attributes":

> she carries a book but it is not
> the tome of the ancient wisdom,
>
> the pages, I imagine, are the blank pages
> of the unwritten volume of the new.[87]

By the close of *Trilogy* the poet has written something like a new Gnostic Gospel, fusing the persons of the virgin-mother and the Magdalene and delicately proposing an ultimately matriarchal base for all of western culture.

Among the most provocative figures in *Trilogy* is a set of variations on the armored, hidden, enclosed self of Dickinson. The anguish of World War II and her experience of the blitz turn the poet into a shellfish whose jaws "snap shut / / at invasion of the limitless" (p. 9), but from this enclosure she finds it possible to "beget" the pearl-of-great-price which is art. Later, the words of the poet are described not as Logos but as "anagrams, cryptograms, / little boxes, conditioned / / to hatch butterflies" (p. 53). Still later, the image for enclosure is a crucible in which words fuse and are transformed (p. 71). And when the Lady appears to H.D., "she is Psyche . . . out of the cocoon" (p. 103). The image, in sum, is a triumphal one of the poet's imagination as protection, disguise, and creative womb.

Marianne Moore's early long poem "Marriage" hides—under its elliptical surface—a rather absolute critique of patriarchy and its central institution.[88] "Men have power / and sometimes one is made to feel it," she remarks coolly. Adam "experiences a solemn joy / in seeing that he becomes an idol"; and Eve observes that "Men are monopolists / Of 'stars, garters, buttons / and other shining baubles'—unfit to be the guardians / of another person's happiness." The stars and garters are of course emblems of imperial power, and the shining baubles men possess presumably include their women. Associations of masculine authority, complacency, and violence appear also in Moore's poems "To Statecraft Embalmed," "Pedantic Literalist," "Critics and Connoisseurs," "The Labours of Hercules," "To Military Progress," and "To a Steam Roller"—all under a beguiling veil of charmingly deployed erudition and wordplay. At times the veil thins almost to transparency. "Sojourn in the Whale," nominally about England's oppression— "swallowing"—of Ireland, is also about men and women. Thus the poet addresses Ireland:

you have lived and lived on every kind of shortage . . .
          and have heard men say:
"There is a feminine temperament in direct contrast to ours,

which makes her do these things. Circumscribed by a
    heritage of blindness and native
    incompetence, she will be wise and will be forced to give in.
Compelled by experience, she will turn back;

water seeks its own level":
   and you have smiled. "Water in motion is far
   from level." You have seen it, when obstacles happened to bar
the path, rise automatically. (p. 90)

Yet Moore herself remains level, appearing merely amused by this little allegory.

Like Dickinson's shyness, Moore's was real, and it disguised an equally real arrogance. Moore's proliferating bestiary of creatures in protective armor and camouflage are not only personal self-portraits in code, as many critics have observed. They imply over and over the necessary timidities and disguises of a brilliant woman in a world where literary authority is male. William Carlos Williams' memoir of Moore recalls how "she would laugh with a gesture of withdrawal after making some able assertion as if you yourself had made it and she were agreeing with you."[89] Her *Paris Review* interview is a self-presentation of the poet as self-deprecating literary virgin pulled reluctantly to the altar of publication.[90] Moore's snail, whose "contractility is a virtue / as modesty is a virtue," is herself as artist, with a "principle that is hid." The shelled creature in "The Paper Nautilus" is explicitly feminine, a mother, and a creatrix—the roles of creation and procreation are for her one, as they are for H.D. in *Trilogy*—whose natural enemies are the powerful and comfortable "authorities" and "writers" of a society founded, in both the economic and the military sense, on the mercenary. The shell built by the nautilus in which her eggs will be "hid but not crushed" is a portrait of the artist as duplicitous woman. What Donald Hall notes of Moore's style might also be said of Dickinson, and for the same reasons:

> It is typical of Miss Moore's poetry that the meaning is equivocal
> . . . She gives and takes away in the same motion so that often,
> just as one believes he understands, the words start to fold back
> on themselves and an exactly opposite meaning begins to seem
> plausible.[91]

What Moore's "undermining modesty" undermines is the same structures of power, in the worlds of political and intellectual life, that feminist poets and critics have recently attacked less modestly.

The work of Lowell and Stein, Loy, Moore and H.D., and their successors amounts to a challenge. Now say, have women wit, or have they not? It is very clear that these women have. They are analytical, cosmopolitan, erudite, brilliant, and they address the world of society and nature, history and literature, in a way which the lyric poets, absorbed in their feelings, appear not to do. At the same time they remain masked women. While making sure, to paraphrase Frost, that nobody could call them poetesses, they keep "human sexual relationships at a measured and chiseled distance," as Adrienne Rich writes of Moore and Elizabeth Bishop.[92] "If it is unpermissible, in fact fatal / to be personal," as Moore says in the late poem "To a Giraffe," the cost of admission to critical esteem was, for women, elimination of the personal self as a fit subject for poems—though the personal self fuels many a masterpiece by male poets. William Gass has speculated that Stein's stylistic virtuosity constituted "a desire to gain by artifice a safety from the world" and from the issue of her own sexuality.[93] Carolyn Burke regards Mina Loy's "evasive self-presentation as typical of the women modernists."[94] Again, where Eliot, Pound, Frost, Stevens, and Williams openly wrestle and grapple, defying the materialism and chaos of their times, the women modernists veil their critique of culture behind a dazzle of stylistics, a film of distance—Lowell's jocularity, Stein's wordplay, Loy's jagged form, H.D.'s Greece, Moore's enameled objects and embroidered quotations. Moore in an early poem says that "the passion for setting people right is itself an afflictive disease. / Distaste which takes no credit to itself is best." Randall Jarrell complains of Moore:

> In her poems morality usually is simplified into self-abnegation . . . Some of the poems have the manners of ladies who learned a little before birth not to mention money, who neither point nor touch, and who scrupulously abstain from the mixed, live vulgarity of life . . . We are uncomfortable—or else too comfortable—in a world in which feeling, affection, charity, are so entirely divorced from sexuality and power, the bonds of the flesh.[95]

Yet would a sexual and powerful Marianne Moore have met with the respect accorded the chaste and ladylike, self-effacing spinster in the tricorne? There is no reason to think so. Amy Lowell's skill at self-promotion was defeated, of course, by the larger skill of her enemy Ezra Pound amid jests of "Amygism" and jocular allusions to the poet's obesity and cigar smoking. Stein remained a figure of the coteries. Mina Loy, championed early by Pound and Eliot, scandalously famous in her time, fell silent and was forgotten. H.D., known as "the perfect imagiste" long after she had outgrown that diminutive label, continued to be represented in anthologies by her earliest and least disturbing poems, while her late work was dismissed as escapist by the few critics who noticed it.[96] The aura of lesbianism about Lowell and Stein, of bisexuality about H.D., and of sexual cynicism about Loy, almost certainly inhibited their critical acceptability within the academy. As to Moore, the connection between the personal and sexual self-effacement which was one source of the respect she received in elite poetic and critical circles, and the limitations which readers have complained of in her work, can scarcely be doubted. To advocates and critics alike she has been the preeminent poet of the filigreed and polished surface, who is "unassuming" and "unpretentious" and whose "humility is vast." That her anger and her ambition were equally vast has not been noticed. She has been all too thoroughly accepted, represented in anthologies by her most maidenly and least threatening work, and her subversiveness has been virtually invisible.

What becomes of women's poetry after the explosion of early modernism? Elizabeth Bishop, Moore's successor as the eminently acceptable woman poet among academic critics, is a warmer and more sensuous writer than Moore and writes of passion and politics more directly than any of the early women modernists. Yet Bishop too is esteemed for reticence, and it is usually the "colored" people in her poems—the poor, the servants—who are identified with strong emotion. In an early poem still considered to be among her finest, we may see a capsule representation of the invisible constraints inhibiting poets who would be ladies, as Bishop comes close to assailing a world of violence and territoriality—and then retreats. The first two-thirds of "Roosters," which appeared in *North and South*, her first book, in 1946, is a strong and brilliant parody of male brutality and male aesthetics:

The crown of red
set on your little head
is charged with all your fighting blood,

yes, that excrescence
makes a most virile presence,
plus all that vulgar beauty of iridescence.[97]

But Bishop's cruelly graphic portrayal of a mass cockfight—evidently emblematic of World War II—is followed by a meditation on the spiritual sin of St. Peter. The cock, suddenly transformed to a sculpture outside the Lateran, now stands for "inescapable hope, the pivot," and at the poem's close comes a tranquil description of sunrise. Imagery of the physical violence of cocks is thus succeeded not only by Christian moralizing on forgiveness but by a static use of the icon—brute life replaced by sacred (and forgiving) art—and by what is, after all, the cliché of the dawn. "Roosters" is finally a withdrawal of a familiar sort, its two parts rather crudely tacked together, ultimately detaching itself from what Pound called "an old bitch gone in the teeth, a botched civilization."

If the muting of the female throughout our literature requires a poetry able to assert the female self, while the terrors of our century require a poetry able to murder and re-create all that we know of civilization, neither the women poets who wrote personally from the heart, nor those who wrote impersonally from the mind, were yet unconfined enough to undertake such a task. To their successors remained the effort of attempting to synthesize the divisions they represented—and a first step would be the recognition that this needed to be done.

There is also a third style in twentieth-century women's poetry less well known than the styles of the lyricist and the modernist innovator. Louise Bernikow in her pathbreaking anthology *The World Split Open* points out that our folk tradition includes anonymous nineteenth-century ballads by working women in the textile mills of the North and South which lead directly to the union songs of Aunt Molly Jackson, Sarah Gunning, and Ella May Wiggins, and that the 1920s was a period of women blues singers such as Ma Rainey and Bessie Smith who composed words like

> I woke up this morning
> My head was sore as a board . . .
> My man beat me last night
> With five feet of chopped up cord

and

> There's nineteen men living in my neighborhood
> Eighteen of them are fools and the one ain't no doggone good.[98]

Ann Stanford in *The Women Poets in America* observes that many late-nineteenth-century women poets, including Julia Ward Howe and Emma Lazarus, wrote on humanitarian issues, and that later women have followed them. In the twentieth century a steady stream of political poetry by white women—Lola Ridge, Genevieve Taggard, the later Edna St. Vincent Millay, Marya Zaturenska, Babette Deutsch, Muriel Rukeyser—and black women—Angelina Grimké, Georgia Douglas Johnson, Anne Spencer, Margaret Walker, Gwendolyn Brooks—appeared before 1945. Some of this work is melancholy in tone, some angry, some hopeful:

> Let us believe in the flesh, the hope made flesh . . .
> Though death has overrun our desperate walls
> And panic has us in a corner, cold,
> Do hope, do cling; by the great atom, by the cell . . .
> Flesh, that pale prophet that survives all fates,
> Will, if it matters, make a more human race,

writes the Quaker pacifist Hildegarde Flanner.[99] In *For My People*, Margaret Walker creates the folk heroine Kissie Lee, who transforms herself from victim to woman warrior who "died with her boots on switching blades / On Talladega Mountain in the likker raids," alongside better-known black heroes such as John Henry.[100] "Not Sappho, Sacco," was the cry of Muriel Rukeyser as a young protest poet.[101] In the left-wing literary atmosphere of the thirties and early forties, the poetry of social conscience was taken seriously by, for example, important anthologists like Louis Untermeyer. But this fashion faded. The prevailing literary climate of America's postwar years was socially and politically conservative, nostalgic, stylistically formalist. Its dominant tone was ironic disillusion with self and society. With the dominion of the New Critics, as one chronicler of the literary 1950s observes, "modernism, like an aging evangelical religion, had rigidified into an orthodoxy."[102] Like other orthodoxies, this one was unfriendly to women. What Beat poetry and more recently Black poetry, Native American poetry, and women's poetry since 1960 demonstrates is that poetry springing from the will to change was hibernating but not dead.

6

> Well,
> she's long about her coming, who must be
> more merciless to herself than history.
> —Adrienne Rich, "Snapshots of a Daughter-in-Law."[103]

The poet Jane Cooper, in a classic essay on the damaging literary atmosphere internalized by women in the 1940s and 1950s, recounts being told by a fellow classmate in the Iowa Writers' Workshop that "to be a woman poet was 'a contradiction in terms.'" At Princeton she learned that "men's praise of women's poetry didn't seem to go much beyond Marianne Moore and Elizabeth Bishop" and that "women have trouble managing traditional meters with authority and verve and also can't handle long lines." John Berryman was an instructor at Princeton when Cooper arrived, and in his first conversation with her he asked her to write a poem about roosters; Elizabeth Bishop had written a poem about roosters. Cooper had been writing love poems and a series of poems about World War II. She experienced personal difficulties and "wondered whether I had been 'castrating.'" In the early 1950s, for a variety of reasons, she stopped writing poetry for several years.[104]

In her essay "When We Dead Awaken," Adrienne Rich also describes growing up in the 1940s and 1950s as a poet under the tutelage of male literary masters from whom she learned "that poetry should be 'universal,' which meant, of course, unfemale." Throughout her early poems, Rich explains, "formalism was part of the strategy—like asbestos gloves, it allowed me to handle material I couldn't pick up barehanded." She was following, in other words, the intellectual line in women's poetry, which required distancing of personal feeling and cautiousness regarding public issues. Her first two books were well received, the incendiary potential of poems like "Aunt Jennifer's Tigers" and "An Unsaid Word" well hidden from poet as well as reader. Yet by the time the second volume was published, she considered herself a failure and had begun to suffer a protracted crisis in which she felt unable to make coherent sense of her life as a woman, wife, and mother, her life as a poet, her beliefs about violence and social change. She "was looking desperately for clues, because if there were no clues then I thought I might be insane." Toward the end of this crisis, Rich wrote her first poem "about experiencing myself as a woman." Although she had not yet "found the courage . . . to use the pronoun 'I'—the woman in the poem is always 'she'—"Snapshots of a Daughter-in-Law" was the poet's breakthrough.[105]

Written over a period of two years, and retaining the form of fragments and jottings, "Snapshots" is a radical critique of woman's place as a beautiful object in a man's world. A quote from Horace praising a "sweetly laughing, sweetly speaking" girl is ironically juxtaposed with the image of a woman shaving her legs. A phrase from a Shakespeare song is followed by a bitter attack on drunken gallantries. One section "concerns a woman who is going mad; she is haunted by voices telling her to resist and rebel, voices which she can hear but not obey." Another reminds us that Mary Wollstonecraft, the first feminist writer in England, "was labelled harpy, shrew and whore." Another contains the realization that "the thinking woman" who has absorbed great literature and philosophy thereby becomes her own worst intellectual enemy. But by the end of "Snapshots" the poet is prophesying the advent of a new being, in whom the muted demands of the mothers and grandmothers burst into life:

> Her mind full to the wind, I see her plunge
> breasted and glancing through the currents,
> taking the light upon her
> at least as beautiful as any boy
> or helicopter,
>   poised, still coming,

her fine blades making the air wince
but her cargo
no promise then:
delivered
palpable
ours.

These were the years, in America, of McCarthy hysteria and Eisen-
hower quietism, of the cold war, of the civil rights movement, of the
Bay of Pigs, the beginning of the war in Vietnam, the beginning of
the antiwar movement. In the late 1950s and early 1960s every woman's
magazine in the country preached the joy of wifehood and the creativity
of domesticity for women, much as a century before every woman's
magazine had preached the sacredness of woman's separate sphere and
the beauty of female selflessness. A smaller proportion of college students and professional people were women in 1959 than in 1929.

Contemporaneous with Cooper and Rich, other poets believed they
were going mad. Others were coming to the conviction that they were
invisible, inaudible. Others were deciding that they would write about
their most intimate experiences as women even if it killed them. A few
were beginning to see connections between history and private life.
A few were starting to recognize, with a horrified clarity never before
achieved by women writers, that western culture was riddled root and
branch with a violence and a misogyny that were intimately connected.
Some were deciding, although it had never before been possible to be
both fully woman and fully poet, that they would turn, and stand, and
fight.

2 Divided Selves:
The Quest for Identity

not not not
myself
is it myself?
    —Rachel Blau DuPlessis, "Undertow"[1]

And I have no face, I have wanted to efface myself.
    —Sylvia Plath, "Tulips"[2]

At the core of the women's poetry movement is the quest for autonomous self-definition. Shaping that quest is a heritage, external and internal, which opposes female autonomy. "If we don't name ourselves we are nothing," says Audre Lorde. "If the world defines you it will define you to your disadvantage."[3] Yet women have always been defined, and have permitted themselves to be defined, by the "world" of masculine culture, so that to name ourselves seems absurd. Adrienne Rich describes the difficulty in a complex and reverberating metaphor derived from Matthew Arnold's image of the alienated self in late Victorian society: "Wandering between two worlds, one dead, / The other powerless to be born."[4] In Rich's version we move from the abstract to the fleshly and from impossibility to imperative. A woman seeking her identity is like a woman attempting to give birth to herself:

your mother dead and you unborn
your two hands grasping your head
drawing it down against the blade of life
your nerves the nerves of a midwife
learning her trade[5]

How then do women poets today go about naming themselves? Before answering this question we must first examine an array of images which register women's sense of identity as marginality, inferiority, inadequacy; poems in which the self is seen as nonexistent, invisible, mute, dissolving, or deformed. Each of these images may be understood as a variation on a key theme; to be a creative woman in a gender-polarized culture is to be a divided self. As we shall see, both the structure of the split self in women's poems, and the characteristically acerbic voice used by many women poets to articulate their dilemma, compose a reflection and critique of cultural dualism.

In a sense, contemporary women's poetry commences with the dread of nonexistence. If a single woman poet exists to whom women poets today trace themselves, that poet must be the Emily Dickinson who identified herself as Nobody. In our time as in hers, there is a common perception that a woman, a woman poet, has—is supposed to have— no self.

Superficially this would seem to be a generically human rather than a generically female problem. John Donne, a poet approximately as devious and knotted as Emily Dickinson, calls himself "a quintessence of nothingness" in "The Nocturnall on St. Lucie's Day." Wallace Stevens' man with a mind of winter, who is "nothing himself, beholds / Nothing that is not there, and the nothing that is." A conviction of personal nonexistence is surely among the permanent motifs in human life and art. Dickinson's nonexistence, however, is firmly social. She is not Nothing compared to Something, but Nobody compared to Somebody. It is not God or Nature but other people who exclude her—or, as she claims, from whose felicity she absents herself.

When Nobody inhabits the poetry of contemporary American women, her plight continues to be social rather than theological or metaphysical. For the twentieth-century poet continues to live in a society which first of all discourages the possibility of an autonomous female identity by defining womanliness primarily in terms of love— selfless connubial love, ecstatic romantic love, nurturing maternal love. Thus Karen Horney in the 1930s claimed that "the overvaluation of love" caused women cripplingly to see their primary goal as "extorting from fate a man . . . by giving proof of one's own weakness, dependence and helplessness." Much of Simone de Beauvoir's *The Second Sex* is a massive elaboration of Byron's observation that "Men's love is of men's life a thing apart; / 'Tis woman's whole existence" and an insistence that the vocation of love keeps women weak, passive, and humanly crippled. A long string of subsequent feminist manifestos has of course objected to the absorption of women's lives by the sponge of romance.[6]

Among poets, the perception that romantic love tends to submerge rather than fulfill a woman's identity begins to appear as far back as Maria Osgood and Emily Dickinson. Still, to be without an admirer, as every young woman learns, is to be Nobody, and the imagery of nonentity is widespread in contemporary women's love poems. "As for me," writes Anne Sexton in "For My Lover, Returning to His Wife," "I am a watercolor. / I wash off." At the end of a love affair, having played her whole hand only to find, "as I turned over card after card, nothing in sequence," the poet and ex-pilot Ann Darr writes, "I look / in the mirror, see nothing." The West Coast feminist poet Judy Grahn summarizes many a parallel story of romantic loss in a sardonic poem that begins "Love came along and saved me . . . didn't I have / company in my nothing?" and ends:

> & then one day Love left to go save someone else.
> Love ran off with all my self-esteem my sense of being
> wonderful and all my nothing.
> Now I am in the hole.[7]

Where the situation is not explicitly romantic, a woman poet's nonentity commonly derives from related aspects of feminine socialization, such as the obligation to be modest, to be kind, to be caring. "Women's need to appear modest, certainly my own need, is almost as powerful as the need to be nice," writes Jane Cooper in her portrait of the artist as self-effacing woman poet,[8] and Cooper's "Suicide Note," faintly echoing Dickinson's opposition of child and adult, silence and speech, moves a step further:

> It's not that I'm out of touch—
> a child stranded on a shoal
> looking back without feeling
> at the grownups still playing on the beach.

> It's just that everyone else's
> needs seem so urgent!
> Already I've ceased to exist
> at my end of this conversation—

The urgency of the needs of others can also explain Patricia Dienstfrey's mysterious disappearance in "Circling the Pond," when, in a blurring

and dreamlike mirror a child stands "waiting for an answer." How, asks
the poet, can she answer, or even speak?

> Half my tongue is ivory.
> Half is shadow. Half
> of each plate
> I fill is empty.
> A leg seems to be missing,
> teeth and fingers.

> In my dreams I am completely
> missing.
> I pass through groups
> like a breeze
> at skin temperature.
> Children follow me,
> stumble and tilt.
> They're mine, of course—
> my own little ones.

Though the speaker is perplexed by her own absence, it is clear to the
reader that being a missing person has something to do with having "my
own little ones," that is, with motherhood. According to many women
poets, the mothering of others is death to the self. A cloud's "slow
effacement at the wind's hand" is one of Sylvia Plath's images for motherhood, while in "Tulips," attempting through illness to escape the claims
of husband and children who are "little smiling hooks," Plath mutters,
"I am nobody; I have nothing to do with explosions. / I have given my
name and my day-clothes up to the nurses."[9]

Behind the absences implied by the feminine role in romance and
nurture, telling us that a woman cannot exist in herself but only through
her lovers and her children, yawn yet greater vacuities. "I'm just a
rim / around some damp chilly air," observes Diane Wakoski in "Caves."
Cooper resigns herself to childlessness: "suppose you are an empty box?"
Or, as Sandra McPherson remarks, "The female genital, like the blank
page anticipating the poem, / is an absence, a not me, which I occupy."[10]

Images of women who define themselves as blank by virtue—or
rather by defect—of their gender, though striking in a post-Freud era,
reflect a far older tradition, in which women are ideally featureless, requiring men to form them. The critic Susan Gubar, fascinated with the
connections between female creativity and images of female purity and
nonentity, traces this tradition back to the blank marble awaiting life
under Pygmalion's touch, and forward to such instances as Othello's

question, "Was this fair paper, this most goodly book, Made to write 'Whore' upon?" and the image of the innocent Pansy in *Portrait of a Lady* as a "sheet of blank paper" compared with the experienced Madame Merle who reveals "unmistakeable blots." [11] We have become familiar with the mythic and literary convention of man as creator and woman as his creation, and we should probably do well to remember that norms of female sexual purity, which amount to another sort of requirement of blankness, featurelessness, nonexistence, are not a thing of the distant past. The posture of modesty, conspicuous in Emily Dickinson or Marianne Moore, retains a significant place in feminine self-definitions today. The contemporary woman who declares herself to be Nobody, nowhere, empty and blank, registers the continuing power of a culture which defines her as, at her best, genitally defective, sexually pure, and personally self-effacing. Nobody is, in effect, a perfectly good woman.

She is not, however, a perfectly satisfied one, as we see when we consider those figures designed most forcefully to articulate her condition: invisibility and muteness.

2

Let the woman learn in silence, with all subjection. But I suffer not a woman to teach, nor to usurp authority over the man, but to be in silence. For Adam was first formed, then Eve.
—1 Tim. 2:11–13

never tell a mirror you are black
it will see you as a rainbow
never tell a mirror you are white
it will make you disappear
—Toi Derricotte, "The Mirror Poems" [12]

she's been dead so long
closed in silence so long
she doesn't know the sound
of her own voice.
—Ntozake Shange, *For Colored Girls* [13]

If a woman who dares to assert herself invites punishment, invisibility and muteness are predictable responses, painful and perhaps also tactical. As we recall, Dickinson's Nobody is invisible, inaudible, and deucedly clever. Margaret Atwood's "This Is a Photograph of Me," which opens her *Collected Poems*, is likewise a poem about invisibility, childishness, and strategy and is among our most neatly ironic poems in its implied catalog of feminine stereotypes. The banality of the title, first of all, is strategic. The poem splits into two halves. The opening half explains that although the photograph looks smeared, "you" can make out a landscape with a small frame house on a slope and a lake and some hills in the background. The poem's second half is enclosed in a parenthesis, a visual device denoting modesty and self-suppression:

(The photograph was taken
the day after I drowned.

I am in the lake, in the center
of the picture, just under the surface.

It is difficult to say where
precisely, or to say
how large or small I am:
the effect of water
on light is a distortion

but if you look long enough,
eventually
you will be able to see me.)

This is typical Atwood in its flat tone with the twin undertones of acerbity and yearning, and in its complicated manipulation of social and literary convention. The idea of self as photograph might be an amusing commentary on the ubiquity of technology in our lives; self as illegible photograph makes the amusement more sinister. The poet's apparent intention to invite/frustrate "you" is a variant of feminine sexual teasing. There is an ironizing of Whitman's "look for me under your bootsoles" and his identification of self with continent; there is a reminder that the reader's rational inclination to fix objects and their importance ("how large or small") "precisely" is necessarily deflected by "distortion." Most conspicuously, Atwood engages in semicomic play with a cluster of stereotypic images and ideas associated with femininity. Woman is archaic mystery. She is "in the center of the picture." She is to be identified with natural landscape, domesticity, and water. She is a romantically submerged lady of the lake. Or she is like Wordsworth's Lucy, "Rolled round in earth's diurnal course / With rocks and stones and trees," a pre-text for a poet's elegiac text. *Cherchez la femme,* says the poem, but given Atwood's framing artifice and her stress on the idea of misperception, we may legitimately take the last lines ironically, as if they were saying, "You will be able to persuade yourself you see me; but you will be mistaken."

Yet the ironic reading of this poem to which we postmoderns instinctively turn is a half reading, just as the innocent Dickinson without her subversive self is a fractional Dickinson. Atwood's posthumous voice, like Dickinson's in poems such as "I died for Beauty," may be a means of asserting a real identity not to be confused with blurred and distorted surface images—or with what can die. We may read the poem not merely as a tease but as an earnest game, an adult version of the game of the child who hides and hopes to be found. If we set the rational and judgmental aggressiveness of "to say" against the patient receptiveness of "to see," the final lines emerge from irony into earnestness, like a photograph emerging from its negative, and carry the whole poem along with them. The poet insists on our knowing that she is difficult to discover, submerged—and possibly hostile—yet discoverable. Thus Atwood's invisibility looks in two directions. It resists discovery, it yearns for discovery.

Other poets also use the figure of invisibility as a feminine attribute. *Invisible Woman* is the title of a volume of poems by Joyce Carol Oates, whose postscript explains that "a woman often feels 'invisible' in a public sense precisely because her physical being . . . figures so prominently in her identity." In Suzanne Berger's "Vita," "We are all trapped in an accident / that makes us invisible" is the wistful message of her mother's aging eyes in a family photo. Marge Piercy's caustic "in the men's room(s)" chronicles the familiar disappointment of the young woman intellectual who hopes to be one of the boys who "were talking of integrity and existential ennui / while the women ran out for six-packs and had abortions." She thinks she is different, but to be is to be perceived, and eventually she learns "how their eyes perceived me":

When I brought my aerial maps of Sartre or Marx,
they said, she is trying to attract our attention,
she is offering up her breasts and thighs.
I walked on eggs, their tremulous equal,
they saw a fish peddlar hawking in the street.

Questions of perception, politics, and male-female roles converge in another well-known feminist parable, Robin Morgan's "The Invisible Woman," a mini-version of the classic Ralph Ellison novel. Morgan's invisible woman

sees others quite clearly,
including the doctor who patiently tells her
she isn't invisible,
and pities the doctor, who must be mad
to stand there in the asylum corridor
talking and gesturing
to nothing at all.

The invisible woman has great compassion.
So, after a while, she pulls on her body
like a rumpled glove, and switches on her voice
to comfort the elated doctor with words.
Better to suffer this prominence
Than for the poor young doctor to learn
he himself is insane.
Only the strong can know that.[14]

Like Dickinson's playful twirling of power relations, this is both funny
and not so funny. While the doctor's self-delusion is amusing, the condition of a woman who believes herself to be "nothing at all" is not
amusing. Moreover, though the doctor's concern for the madwoman is
professional and simpleminded while hers for him is personal and
subtle (as well as condescending), we are not dealing with a familiar
reversal of the "much madness is divinest sense . . . much sense the
starkest madness" sort. The poem presumes but does not rest on the familiarity of such formulations. Society, it proposes, may be a large mental institution whose authorities may themselves be insane. It scarcely
follows that the "invisible woman" is sane. Playing as she does a typically nurturing-condescending feminine role toward her ostensible pro-
tector and guide, is she his moral superior? Or is she merely repro-
ducing, as Phyllis Chesler's *Women and Madness* might suggest, the
patterns which made her crazy in the first place?[15] The multiple analogy
emerges: to be a compassionate female is to be a good nigger is to be
invisible is to be insane. Moral value is not social value. Ellison's hero,
too, sees others quite clearly. But knowledge is not power and cannot
bring Ellison's invisible black man out of his underground shelter, any
more than it can extract Morgan's madonna from her madhouse.
   An even harsher figure for a sense of inadequate existence than invisibility, at least to poets, is muteness. Our sense of modernism in Anglo-
American poetry commences with J. Alfred Prufrock, alienated from his
body, pinned insectlike to the wall by the stabbing stares of the socially
adapted, intimidated by the ghosts of heroes he can never emulate, hu-
miliated by the all-too-desirable and inaccessible opposite sex, exclaim-

ing, "It is impossible to say just what I mean!" His inability to speak is Prufrock's essential characteristic. Voiceless himself, Prufrock has heard mermaids singing to each other but does not think they will sing to him. When human voices wake him, he drowns.

Women will recognize certain features of Prufrock's predicament as coinciding with their own, in particular the linked dilemmas of feeling oneself a mere object in the eyes of the other sex and being unable to participate in its mode of discourse—which all the while one half-envies, half-despises. Other aspects of Prufrock's problem, such as his sense of disjunction between significant heroes of the past and his insignificant self, are less relevant. The general problem of rich literary, philosophical, and social traditions that have been lost in a culturally depleted present era is a central issue in modernism—but not, as a rule, for modern women. On the contrary, as we have seen, the female modernists Lowell, Stein, Loy, H.D. and Moore were already casting a skeptical eye on the claims of masculine tradition. That women are culturally muted not only in the present but in the scannable past, as far back into recorded history as we can trace, has become a commonplace of feminist criticism and cultural history, and is reflected in the absence of nostalgia from contemporary women's poetry.[16]

Among women poets, the inability to speak signals, however, just as it does in Prufrock, a state of passivity, marginality, self-hate. As in Prufrock, and as in women's invisibility poems, there is usually a sexual script. The poet is perhaps erotically dependent. "When I am voiceless / be my lips," Suzanne Berger begs a lover in a poem called "The Mending." Or if Ann Darr loses a lover, she knows why: "Of course, the horoscope said / keep silent . . . Talking too much, I told you too much." Louise Glück, a poet fascinated with border states between existence and nonexistence, in "Portrait" imagines herself a child drawing a figure that is only an outline, "white all through," until a lover draws the heart, and in "Grandmother" Glück becomes a child watching Grandmother wait for Grandfather to come home. "That is what marriage is," thinks the child, and when Grandfather tenderly kisses Grandmother, Glück comments, "it might as well have been / his hand over her mouth." In a poem of unreturned love, Adrienne Rich describes "my swirling wants. Your frozen lips. / The grammar turned and attacked me." To love a man is to be dependent on him. To be dependent is to be silenced. Prufrock believes he must speak, assuming a completeness and assurance he does not have, to obtain feminine approval. Women, by contrast, feel that to gain male approval they must remain silent. An initially entertaining indictment of feminine dependence is Celia Gilbert's "Little Devil," where the devil a woman can't exorcise is named "Leave-The-Bills-To-Me . . . Don't-Move-I'll-Do-It." Coming to love him, she regresses to an infancy where "He is the dearest one, he is the voice, he is control." The same poet, refusing a dinner invitation, explains that she is "forgetting the language" necessary in such situations, when

> the men around the table laugh,
> argue, agree,
> then pause politely
> while we speak . . .
> when we've finished,
> politely,
> they turn to the real conversation,
> the unspoken expectation of applause.

A collection of poems on these themes—muted women in love, muted women at the dinner table—would fill a volume. We do not speak, the poems insist, because men do not listen; they laugh at us, they wish us to be the listeners. They are powerful and we need their approval.

On a larger scale, of course, female silence is a political and historical as well as a psychosocial phenomenon. Many of Marge Piercy's more raucously feminist poems concern themselves with "unlearning to not speak" as an act which is necessary not only for individual healing but to gain access to political power. A dominant theme in Adrienne Rich is the poet's wrestling with "the oppressor's language" of a patriarchal civilization that permits and perpetuates not only the wars of the sexes but all wars, not only sexual hierarchy but all hierarchy, all forms of dominance and thus all human damage. What Rich calls "a book of myths / in which / our names do not appear" may be all of recorded history and literature, from which the actualities of female experience have been erased. In "Heroines," Rich addresses the women who enjoyed sufficient class privilege in the nineteenth century to become active figures in abolitionism and women's rights, remembering for them "when you open your mouth in public / human excrement / is flung at you." Susan Griffin's *Woman and Nature: The Roaring Inside Her* elaborately examines the theological and metaphysical rationales for women's muteness.[17] A formidable body of feminist literary theory has argued that female experience is systematically excluded from all forms of public discourse.[18] As we shall see toward the close of this book, the most visionary writing by women poets is also what Rich has called "re-vision," aiming "not to pass on a tradition but to break its hold over us."[19] For Rich and for the many writers who have been influenced by her, the inherited language is what history was for Stephen Dedalus: a nightmare from which they are trying to escape.

Finally there is the bitter truth that the power to speak may rest not only on economic, political, and legal power but on ordinary physical strength. In "Case in Point" the black poet June Jordan addresses a non-feminist older woman who claims "there is no silence peculiar / to the female." Jordan couches her reply in deliberately meticulous diction referring repeatedly and ironically to acts of speech:

I have decided I have something to say
about female silence: so to speak
these are my 2 ¢ on the subject.

What she has to say is a description of a "recent situation" which happened to be a rape:

Today is 2 weeks after the fact
of that man straddling
his knees either side of my chest
his hairy arm and powerful left hand
forcing my arms and my hands over my head
flat to the pillow while he rammed
what he described as his quote big dick
unquote into my mouth
and shouted out: "D'ya want to swallow
my big dick: well, do ya?"

He was being rhetorical.
My silence was peculiar
to the female.

Madelon Gohlke's "It's Cool Outside and Bright" describes a parallel conjunction of rape and silence:

Bruises are flooding to my skin
on my arms, my legs, my neck.
He thinks I'm hysterical, but I can't scream.
I can hardly even talk.
"Please take me home, please, please."
I'm a virgin. I have never known pain.
But I'm not. Look, I'll unbutton my blouse.[20]

Whatever the historic and social causes of silence in Prufrock and his lonely crowd of alienated modernist brethren, they do not include the powerlessness of the female who must buy love with silence, the female excluded from public discourse, the female subject to physical violation.

3

More and more frequently the edges
of me dissolve.
    —Margaret Atwood, "More and More"[21]

A woman in the shape of a monster
a monster in the shape of a woman
the skies are full of them
    —Adrienne Rich, "Planetarium"[22]

The tendency of feminine identity to dissolve into its relationships
may be reimprinted in every generation not merely by the fiat of patriarchy but by the mother-daughter bond. According to the influential
speculations of Nancy Chodorow in *The Reproduction of Mothering*,
mothers treat sons as differentiated beings but daughters as extensions of
themselves; daughters persist in their preoedipal attachment to their
mothers. One consequence is that females tend to experience themselves not as autonomous selves but as enmeshed in, and defined by,
their relations with others. "The daughter herself then comes not to recognize, or to have difficulty recognizing, herself as a separate person.
She experiences herself, rather, as a continuation or extension of . . .
her mother in particular, and later of the world in general."[23]

The idea that women develop a blurred identity through identification with mother figures is beautifully illustrated in two celebrated
poems by poets who are in almost every way diametrically opposed to
each other, Elizabeth Bishop and Anne Sexton. Bishop, among the
most personally reticent of modern poets, is a successor to Marianne
Moore in the sharpness of her observer's eye, the affectionateness of a
sensibility that searches out oddness and obscurity to celebrate, and the
perfection of her artistry. That we learn, reading Bishop's poems, much
about her environments whether exotic or domestic and little about herself, locates her within the long tradition of feminine self-effacement
and disguise. By the 1970s, however, some of Bishop's poems were ven-
turing to the tidal edge of self-exploration.

"In the Waiting Room" is the opening piece of *Geography III*, Bishop's
last published volume. The poem begins with herself as a child of almost seven who sits reading the *National Geographic* on a winter eve-
ning in a crowded dentist's waiting room while waiting for an aunt. The
magazine contains photographs of a volcano's "inside . . . full of ashes"
and in eruption; white explorers; and some primitive women whose
"breasts were horrifying." Suddenly, "from inside"—the second time
this word appears in the poem, and we assume it means inside the den-

tist's office—the child hears a cry of pain. She identifies the voice at first as her foolish aunt's and then with surprise as her own, coming from her own mouth. When she tries to remind herself who she is, disorientation increases. "I felt: you are an *I*, / you are an *Elizabeth*, / you are one of *them*," and the unanswerable question surfaces: "*Why* should you be one, too?"

> I knew that nothing stranger
> had ever happened, that nothing
> stranger could ever happen.
> Why should I be my aunt,
> or me, or anyone?
> What similarities—
> boots, hands, the family voice
> I felt in my throat, or even
> The *National Geographic*
> and those awful hanging breasts—
> held us all together
> or made us all just one?
> How—I didn't know any
> word for it—how "unlikely" . . .
> How had I come to be here,
> like them, and overhear
> a cry of pain that could have
> got loud and worse but hadn't?

The child feels she, they, are falling off the world into empty space; then that the waiting room is sliding under a succession of great waves; and then, abruptly, she is back to normal and all is firmly located. She is "in" the room, the "War" is "on," it is a winter night "outside," the place is Worcester, Mass., the date February 5, 1918.

"In the Waiting Room" is a plainly written poem, simple in diction, syntax, and narrative direction, governed by Bishop's usual tone of trustworthy casualness, the better to emphasize its disorienting vision of dissolved boundaries, as room becomes globe, globe threatens to become void, self and others become interchangeable. The wall between "outside" and "inside" collapses in the poem's center, when "inside" can refer to a volcano, a closed room, one's own throat, all able to erupt irrationally. The superlatively strange thing that has happened is the emergence of a sense of how provisional the existence of our individual selves is. Like Wordsworth's "fallings from us, vanishings," or the young Whitman's doubts of reality in "There was a child went forth," Bishop's realization that nothing stranger could happen is a realization on behalf of all. "In the Waiting Room" is widely admired as one of Bishop's finest poems. We need therefore to recognize that it is a woman's poem in a way that Whitman's and Wordsworth's are not. First, it takes place not outdoors but in a room—that archetypal trope for the feminine self. Then, it is no accident that the child's experience is triggered by a succession of female images—aunt, volcano, naked woman—or that it is experienced as powerfully, and perhaps permanently, disorienting. Does it make sense to perceive oneself normally as an individual? Or is the truth the "awful" truth that we are "just one" and that our individual selves are fictions? The poet does not presume to answer, although it is significant that she juxtaposes her vision to a reality in which the Great War is going on, since wars are fought by those who do not perceive themselves to be "just one" with their fellow men. Among the many ways we can take the title of this remarkable poem is to feel that the poet has waited a lifetime to write it and in some sense has never left the room it describes.

At an opposite pole from Bishop's deceptive balance and leisure is the nervous speed of Anne Sexton's famous "Housewife," a poem that crackles and is over almost before it starts, like a shorted fuse. Far from the proprieties of Bishop's career, Sexton is a poet who achieved instant popularity by writing with unprecedented intimacy about herself, festooning her poems with the dirty linen of female breakdown, madness, guilt, and sexuality. Note, however, how many details this cameo of a blurred self shares with Bishop's: the enclosed space that stands for oneself but is less stable than one expects; the physicality; the hint of primitive female monstrousness; the identification of one female with another.

"Housewife" is a wry critique of marriage as well as a definition of conventional womanhood, and it starts out with a pun. The joke becomes scatological in three lines, satiric in six, expands to myth and collapses to practicality in four more, and stops with a jolt.

Some women marry houses.
It's another kind of skin; it has a heart,
a mouth, a liver and bowel movements.
The walls are permanent and pink.
See how she sits on her knees all day,
faithfully washing herself down.
Men enter by force, drawn back like Jonah
into their fleshy mothers.
A woman *is* her mother.
That's the main thing.

Housewives are normal, yet the normal housewife is anything but what she appears to be. Having intentionally or otherwise married a house with which she will be more intimate than with any husband, the wife finds it a second body. As the poem tells us in its first hairpin turn, it must be her own body. We know how narcissistic women are; therefore the drudgery of housework is merely more narcissism. Husbands who enter women sexually, or come home at night, or concede their own natural mortality, do so reluctantly. To those who are trained to identify themselves as independent beings, the devouring wife-house-body is like Jonah's voracious whale. But men and their independence, or alienation, are a digression in this poem, the real point of which is woman's fixed identification with house, body, mother, her domestic and biological genesis and destiny. From "some women" to "she" to "men" to the singular "a woman," the poem's language tightens its vise. The final line may logically mean either that the identity of women and their mothers is the central fact about women or that it is the central fact about the world. Like the close of Keats' "Ode on a Grecian Urn" or the opening of Williams' "Red Wheel Barrow," this is a generalization of unlimited jurisdiction.

The depiction of mother identification as a burden or curse recurs throughout Sexton's early work and surfaces in many other poets. In Plath's shocking "Medusa," the mother is a clinging jellyfish, a placenta attached by the umbilicus of the poet's guilty anger toward her, an "eely tentacle" she wants to exorcise. June Jordan's "Fragments from a Parable" finds her "aggressively resisting" a powerful mother and wondering if she is or is not "an impermeable membrane." Louise Glück's "For My Mother," yearning backward as so many of her poems do toward the serenity of preexistence, insists, "It was better when we were / together in one body." Motherly attachment in these poems means infantilism and shapelessness for both mother and daughter, absorbed in each other, neither one capable of independent self-definition.[24]

The fear that femaleness means formlessness takes another form, not necessarily connected with the idea of excess attachment, although the guilts and resentments associated with attachment must be a hidden motif here, just as sexual purity is a hidden motif when women lament their blankness. This last and most violent figure for an identity that fails to achieve wholeness is the figure of the monster-woman, an image with a long genealogy. As numerous women writers, most recently Sandra Gilbert and Susan Gubar in *The Madwoman in the Attic*, have observed, the image of woman as monster recurs throughout western myth and literature from the Sphinx and Lilith onward. Greek mythology gives us Medusa with her snaky hair. Grendel's dam lurks evilly at the bottom of her pool in *Beowulf*, our one remaining Anglo-Saxon epic. Renaissance poetry includes the rich inventions in *The Faerie Queene* of Spenser's Errour, a woman above the waist but a "lothsome, filthie, foul" serpent beneath, and his Duessa, a witch whose nether parts are vilely misshapen. Milton's Sin copulates with her father Satan and breeds hellhounds who endlessly reenter and reemerge, barking and howling, from her womb. Pope and Swift fill Augustan satire with mythically disgusting females. In all such cases, and of course in the general history of misogyny, it is assumed that female sexuality is inherently vile and dangerous.[25]

Disobedient, clever, or intellectual women have often been damned as deformed by men's pens. Higginson described Dickinson's metrical "gait" as "spasmodic" and "uncontrolled" (does this amount to one criticism or two?). Mary Wollstonecraft was a "hyena in petticoats" to Horace Walpole. In our own century similar strictures are not lacking. A short list might include Pound's portrait of an intellectual hostess, with its veiled suggestion that she is a stagnant depository of sexual detritus— "Your mind and you are our Sargasso Sea"—or Hemingway on Gertrude Stein, or the castrating neurasthenic wife in *The Waste Land*, with her electrical hair. During the last few decades John Berryman's ostensibly loving portrait of Anne Bradstreet depicts her verse as boring and her person as unbeautiful and makes much of her deforming dropsy; Allen Ginsberg re-creates a mad and monstrous mother as his muse in "Kaddish"; Robert Bly in a passionate antiwar poem successfully resurrects "The Teeth Mother Naked at Last." That such poetry may express implicit dread of something dangerously female within the male self, as well as dread of actual (or fantasy) women, augments rather than diminishes its misogynist force.

To be a woman and a creator rather than simply a procreator is to be "uncontrolled" and so to doom oneself—if a thinking woman internalizes some of the most powerful images in our culture—to monstrosity. Much of *The Madwoman in the Attic* traces the image, in nineteenth-century women's writing, of the monster the author fears she is or secretly craves to be as against the angel she wishes to be or to appear. Among contemporary women poets, fascination with deformity seems also to capture a sense—guilty or gloating, defensive or aggressive—of unacceptable personal power: nature untamed, gone haywire, unregulated and therefore horrible. *Monster* is the title of Robin Morgan's first book, and an important theme for many other poets. There is, however, the striking difference that the misshapenness which in earlier women's writing is projected onto a doppelganger and punished or killed is now disconcerting but unsubdued.

Cynthia Macdonald, a dazzlingly witty poet who has become a mistress of monsters, reminds us in "Celebrating the Freak":

The freak is   the other
The freak wears   on the outside what we conceal

But Macdonald's freaks are more than bizarre; they multiply and amplify themselves. Her imagination generates spectacular pregnancies like that of "All Mouth," who yearned for greater completion and gave birth to "All Ear," whose "frustration mounted" and used "its own stirrup," lashing itself with language until it produced the punning "All Eye"; or Aphrodite's impregnation from a poisoned tomato given her by Hermes, resulting in the birth of Hermaphrodite, with "The mushroom velvet of its penis and testes, / The anemone satin of its vulva"; or the dwarf that grows into a giant, eats people who say it is too long, and uses them as fertilizer because it believes in growing things. Her catalogs of deformities are announcements of perverse value, as in "How to Order a Freak":

Neatly. Precisely. Survey its hump.
Chart its topography. Fathom its veined secrets. See
Following pages for our complete spine of hunchbacks.

Usually too big rather than too small, Macdonald's creatures are often grossly hilarious and not infrequently violent. Other poets drawn to deformity include Atwood, whose "Speeches for Dr. Frankenstein" is a history of metamorphosis escaped from the creator's control. In Atwood's "Songs of the Transformed," furious vitality and hatred of humanity are the primary attributes of a once-human bestiary. "She Considers Evading Him," a poem in a series on modern love, has the speaker ironically warn her lover that she may metamorphose to various forms out of male mythologies, becoming a Daphne-like virgin or a distended earth mother:

I could grow bark and
become a shrub

or switch back in time
to the woman image left
in cave rubble, the drowned
stomach bulbed with fertility,
face a tiny bead, a
lump, queen of the termites.

The West Coast Beat poet Diane Di Prima in her book-length *Loba* and the experimental playwright-poet Rochelle Owens in the "Wild Woman" of her *Joe 82 Creation Poems* have reinvented images of primitive female violence. If such poems imply that female fecundity breeds deformity when it takes verbal instead of biological form, Adrienne Rich insists that culture, not nature, determines the process. Rich's "Incipience" depicts two women who have the bodies of birds of prey, but only in the dreams of a man sleeping in the next room. The misshapen constellations in "Planetarium" are "doing penance for impetuousness." But Rich, too, probing for the undiscovered identity, finds a violent potential:

> If I am flesh sunning on rock
> if I am brain burning in fluorescent light
>
> if I am dream like a wire with fire
> throbbing along it
>
> if I am death to man
> I have to know it [26]

This disturbing suggestion may be read in two ways. The poet may be "death to man" in actuality, or she may be "death to man" in his image of her. (Indeed, perhaps she is "death to man" because of the potential energy implied by her combination of body, intelligence, and imagination, if the image of a whole and powerful woman is the ultimate threat to men's self-esteem.) Either way, she needs to know. But how can she know? As we have seen, external authority either gives us lessons in sweetly singing, sweetly speaking for someone else's benefit, or it assures us that we are visible when we know we are not, or it mutes us, or it insinuates that we are monsters. Yet if we are not what our fathers and mothers taught us a good girl was, not what our teachers expected, not what our lovers desire and suppose, nor what literature tells us, what are we then? The effort of self-definition yields, at least in the first instance, an array of images reflecting female marginality. The next point we need to discover is how all these images represent not a whole (and dismayingly inadequate) self but a portion of something larger.

4

> I know not what to do,
> my mind is reft:

is song's gift best?
is love's gift loveliest? . . .
as two white wrestlers
standing for a match,
ready to turn and clutch
yet never shake muscle nor nerve nor tendon;
so my mind waits
to grapple with my mind,
yet I lie quiet,
I would seem at rest.
       —H.D., "Fragment Thirty-Six"[27]

I'd allowed myself to be cut in two. Woman sawn apart
in a wooden crate, wearing a bathing suit, smiling, a trick
done with mirrors, I read it in a comic book; only with me
there had been an accident and I came apart.
       —Margaret Atwood, *Surfacing*[28]

The conviction that "love" and "song" are opposed choices for a woman—that she is forbidden to be both lover/beloved and artist—dates from the mid-nineteenth century and retains considerable force within our culture and within women's minds. It is one way of saying that "woman poet" is a contradiction in terms. As H.D. represents the problem, self-division is exacerbated by a feminine need to "seem at rest." The terms of the division, love versus song, represent the authorized dualities of the culture as regards women, and a ladylike "I" lets the dualities freeze in place. In Atwood's version we see not only entrapment but complicity. Her surrender to self-division is an acquiescence in images that seem vulgar and harmless illusions but become all too real. With these passages on the split self we arrive at a landscape that has been illustrated by poet after poet, poem after poem, in works of such evident impact that to read them is plainly to hit a psychic bedrock.[29]

Consider, as examples of escalating extremity in the representation of a divided identity, works by the three well-known poets Denise Levertov, Diane Wakoski, and Sylvia Plath. In most respects these writers are conspicuously different from each other. Levertov, an Englishwoman who emigrated to the United States in 1948, has been associated with the Black Mountain School and with the influence of William Carlos Williams. Her writing is lyric, idealistic, inclined toward a mysticism kept grounded in this world by her love of "the authentic" of daily experience. Diane Wakoski is a Californian strongly influenced by Surrealism, whose favorite landscapes are the desert, the moon, and the highway of the motorcyclist, and whose favorite men and animals are skillfully predatory wilderness creatures. Wakoski writes in an aggressive style, at once prose-flat in its rhythms and hyper-vivid in its stark images, and has invented for herself a mythicized autobiography in which the crucial features are the desertion by her father, the weakness of her mother, the suicide of an incestuous brother, and a destiny of being rejected by men she loves due to her lack of beauty. Plath, an archetypal example of meteoric poetic self-destructiveness, developed in the course of a few years from an academic formalism not unlike the early work of Rich to a brilliantly polished original style. *Ariel*, published in 1965 after the poet's suicide at the age of thirty, gave many readers their first taste of unapologetic anger in a woman's poems. Posthumous publications, including Plath's autobiographical novel *The Bell Jar*, her letters to her mother, and her journals, have filled in the portrait of a young woman racked by contradictory desires for success as a woman— through prettiness, popularity, joyous daughterhood, wifehood, and motherhood—and success as a writer; a writer, unfortunately, uniquely skilled at representing precisely those dark immoderate passions forbidden to the happy woman: hatred of her parents, repressed fury at all mankind, desire and dread of personal freedom, obsessive fascination with pain, violence, death.

Levertov in the poem "In Mind" discovers two incompatible selves: one a woman

> of innocence, unadorned but
> fair-featured, and smelling of
> apples or grass. She wears
> a utopian smock . . .
> And there's a
> turbulent moon-ridden girl
> or old woman, or both,
> dressed in opals and rags, feathers
> and torn taffeta.

The first "is kind" but lacks imagination. The second "knows strange songs" but is not kind. A self approved by others, modest, decorous, and humanistically valuable (this self has written, we may suppose, Levertov's poems of social and political idealism), stands against a darker, more mysterious, and dangerous self. Both are natural—it is not a question of one being real, one hypocritical—although the latter might better be called preternatural. Levertov, perhaps the sweetest and most life-celebratory of poets writing today, nevertheless writes of a "coldness to life," an inner-directedness which seems "unwomanly" because it is insufficiently nurturing of others. Or she writes of cherishing a "madness . . . blue poison, green pain in the mind's veins," though she has always been the sanest of her friends, the one they came to for comfort.

This split between a tame and a wild self is central in Levertov as far back as the early "The Earthwoman and the Waterwoman." Her "Sunday Afternoon" describes how a coffee merchant's daughters, after taking First Communion and eating "the banquet of mangoes and bridal cake,"

> lay down
> for a long siesta, and their white dresses
> lay beside them in quietness . . .
> But as the afternoon
> burned to a close they rose . . .
> among the halfbuilt villas
> alive, alive, kicking a basketball, wearing
> other new dresses, of bloodred velvet.

It is delightful here to see domestic passivity alternating with recreational vigor, a meal including prophetic wedding cake followed by a basketball game, innocent white leading without conflict to erotic red. The reason for the lack of conflict, of course, is that these females are prepubescent. Grown women enjoy less flexibility. Levertov's Rose White and Rose Red in "An Embroidery (I)" are separate beings, as are the two figures of "The Woman," a later and more astringent poem, where "the one in homespun / you hunger for / when you are lonesome" alternates with "the one in crazy feathers" who "wearies you." The poet remarks that she wearies herself, that the homespun one is weary too, and concludes:

> Alas,
> they are not two but one,
> pierce the flesh of one, the other
> halfway across the world, will shriek,
> her blood will run. Can you endure
> life with two brides, bridegroom?[30]

We may attribute the violence in "The Woman," as well as its quiet hinting at generic male insensitivity, atypical for Levertov, to the fact that it was written during the Vietnam War. Rage at war tends to make misanthropes of the mildest women.

Young women of unrevolutionary temperament often warm to Levertov's work because it expresses both clearly and gently a dilemma they find in themselves. More flamboyantly, Diane Wakoski in "Beauty" parades a self something like Levertov's moon-ridden girl, asking:

> and if I cut off my long hair,
> if I stopped speaking,
> if I stopped dreaming for other people about parts of the car,
> stopped handing them tall creamy flowered silks,
> and loosing the magnificent hawks to fly in their direction . . .
> if I stopped crying for the salvation of the tea ceremony,
> stopped rushing in excitedly with a spiky bird-of-paradise,
> and never let them see how accurate my pistol-shooting is,
> who would I be? [31]

The dilemma in Wakoski is also a common one. On the one hand is the poet's pride, vitality, and flashing imaginative energy unconfined by gender stereotypes (note her typically spectacular repertoire including parts of the car and pistol-shooting adjacent to flowered silks and the tea ceremony). This vitality is crossed by a self-destructive dependence on others for its confirmation. "Where is the real me I want them all to love," she asks self-mockingly, as she swings from one father-lover figure to another—George Washington whom she excoriates at one end of her pendulum, Beethoven to whom she clings at the other, the King of Spain who would be Eros to her Psyche, and the easy riders whom she invites to make her life difficult in between.

The two most thoroughly elaborated personae in the myths Wakoski has elaborated about herself are the poet, master of her craft, "the eye of the world," a proud, controlling, even predatory force, whom she often describes in male pronouns, and the woman deserted in childhood by her father, desperately in need of love and doomed to be rejected by all her lovers. [32] The first of these personae is fiercely strong, hard as a rock, poetically abundant—a poet's abundance consists of her range of images, and Wakoski's is wide and wild as any surrealist's, possibly wider and wilder than any other American poet's. The other is pathetically needy, barren as a moonscape, wilted as the pink dress she cannot wear because it reminds her of a lover's betrayal. Wakoski's work vividly illustrates the All or Nothing syndrome in female romantic fantasies. Her two selves are appropriately also an All and a Nothing, a Strong and a Weak. When the poet speaks of their relationship she claims that the poet comes into being as a compensation for the lonely self, using, for example, the "dreamlike image in order to present a painful reality that if described in everyday terms would seem mundane and unworthy." Typical Wakoski interviews assert:

My poetry is about beauty and how it rescues us, if only through our fantasy lives, from what is mundane and dull.

The act of writing is an act of completion. If you get what you want, you don't write about it. You write about what you don't get.[33]

In Wakoski's view the weak, personal, "real" self generates the strong poetic "fantasy" self. But on the other hand, a strong poetic self may beget a weak personal self, in a twentieth-century version of the nineteenth-century conviction that ambition is unfeminine and that true femininity reveals itself through one's capacity for romantic suffering. We seem close to a Dickinsonian duplicity here. If strength, independence, aggressiveness are masculine qualities in our culture, the woman who has such qualities in abundance can expect to see herself as abnormal, unfeminine—and perhaps this is intolerable. Consequently the strong woman who needs to deny/punish herself for her strength might contrive to design an unhappy love life for herself; might believe that this destiny is due to powers beyond her control, like a father's desertion or a plain face; might anchor her power to her weakness. That she should succeed in both art and love might well seem to her, and to us, unthinkable.

As a number of commentators have observed, the most brilliant single split-self poem of our time is Sylvia Plath's "In Plaster," composed while the poet was hospitalized with appendicitis.[34] "In Plaster" describes a relationship between a self and a plaster cast, unfolding in three stages which are made to seem psychologically inevitable. First, the poem's two personae are presented. The "absolutely white person" is "certainly the superior one." "She doesn't need food, she is one of the real saints." She is "so cold." When the speaker hits her, "she [holds] still, like a true pacifist." The speaker, on the contrary, is "the old yellow one . . . ugly and hairy." Far from the blank purity of the plaster saint, she writhes with negative passions directed against the uncomplaining double.

During the poem's second stage the speaker announces that the relationship is developing advantageously. She decides that the other one wants love and that the situation can be exploited:

Without me, she wouldn't exist, so of course she was grateful.
I gave her a soul, I bloomed out of her as a rose
Blooms out of a vase of not very valuable porcelain,
And it was I who attracted everybody's attention.

Now Plath's hatred and fear modulate to condescension, as the plaster self appears to enjoy servitude. "You could tell almost at once she had a slave mentality." But as the speaker comes to admire and need the other's care, "our relationship grew more intense" and also unstable, and the poem moves into its final phase. The speaker decides that her saint is growing irritable and that the care is deteriorating. The saint, she concludes, resents wasting her life on a half-corpse and secretly hopes the speaker will die. Dependence and passivity now reverse, as the formerly confident speaker discovers

> I wasn't in any position to get rid of her.
> She'd supported me for so long I was quite limp—
> I had even forgotten how to walk or sit.

At the poem's conclusion, the speaker is craftily conciliatory. Though the relationship is "like living with my own coffin," she plots revenge:

> One day I shall manage without her,
> And she'll perish with emptiness then, and begin to miss me.

Conceivably the ending means that the speaker plans to return to wholeness and health. Another possibility, supported by the poem's opening exclamation—"I shall never get out of this!"—as well as by the physical decline of the speaker in the course of the poem and by the resemblance of her final declaration to a suicide threat, is that she will get her revenge by dying, an appropriate denouement since the opposite of a saint is a sinner and we know what the wages of sin are. "In Plaster" is a tour de force of extreme solipsism. Nothing and nobody exists inside the poem but "I" and "she," and the poem illustrates the tight connection between passivity, dependence, solipsism, and self-loathing.

"In Plaster" is dated 18 March 1961. In the spring and summer of 1961 Plath was writing in *The Bell Jar* about her breakdown and suicide attempt in the summer of her eighteenth year. *The Bell Jar* suggests two connected readings for "In Plaster." It is peopled with characters who are versions of the plaster saint, successful and confident role players on whom the heroine, Esther, depends and whom she dislikes. But the resentment is a private secret, never publicly expressed. Esther's good-student, prize-winning personality is all compliance, designed to please and not offend her mother, her boyfriend's mother, her college teachers, the fluffy lady writer who has given her one scholarship, the staff of the fashion magazine which has given her another, not to mention other girls, her boyfriend, and other men—anyone, in short, whom she perceives as having power. Her public personality is, in other words, the very image of a plaster saint itself, and so is implicitly both necessary and despicable, despicable because necessary. "My head ached. Why did I attract these weird old women? . . . they all wanted to adopt me in some way, and, for the price of their care and influence, have me resemble them." But Esther herself attempts to imitate almost everyone influential whom she encounters. While skiing recklessly downhill on the way to breaking her leg in two places, she sees her life as "year after year of doubleness and smiles and compromise."[35] Hence, in part, the suicide attempt of *The Bell Jar*, and hence also the "ugly and hairy" self-image of "In Plaster" and its implied momentum toward self-destruction.

As with Wakoski but even more extremely, Plath's divided selves lock into place. There is a public self designed to please others, which is so perfect that it drives all antisocial "ugly" impulses back into secrecy, where they seethe and increase. Or there is an "ugly" self so distressing that an unbreakable self of "whiteness and beauty" must be invented to mask it. Either way, division is self-perpetuating. The Sylvia Plath who played perfect daughter, schoolgirl, eager young woman of letters and hard-working wife, and wrote the painfully cheerful *Letters Home*, created and was created by the Sylvia Plath who hated obedient role playing and wrote the angry and self-punishing *The Bell Jar* and *Ariel*.

Wild self and tame self in Levertov, strong rational poet and weak emotional woman in Wakoski, perfect external and ugly internal selves in Plath—never far from the surface in all this work is the sense that self-division is culturally prescribed, wholeness culturally forbidden, to the woman and the woman poet. The cleavage in the brain is inherited from Dickinson and other ancestresses. It appears conspicuously in Atwood, Sexton, Rich, and many lesser-known poets.[36] Invisibility and muteness, dissolving and distorted selves are images of it. And as a recurrent image in R. D. Laing's representation of the schizophrenic personality suggests, a disguised form of the double self pervades women's poetry even when no split is explicitly mentioned.

For Laing, schizophrenia "is a special strategy that a person invents in order to live in an unlivable situation,"[37] typically a situation of family tyranny disguised as love. Schizoid personalities suffer what he calls ontological insecurity, and what our women poets call nonexistence, invisibility, and muteness. Unable to feel their existence confirmed by others, they cannot affirm it for themselves; their "identity and autonomy are always in question" privately. Such an individual, says Laing, may create a false self organized to comply with the expectations of others, while the true self remains a detached, hyperconscious, critical observer. This sort of temporary dissociation is normal as an escape re-action in threatening or disagreeable situations. To the schizophrenic, however, reality is permanently threatening and unpleasant, so that all activity seems void contrivance or performance—and dissociation be-comes not only chronic but progressive. The false self, says Laing, "is compulsively compliant to the will of others," (p. 102) its excessive goodness being reinforced by the secret self's dread of being unmasked. The false self may not only obey but impersonate or caricature the hated, controlling person, while the true self in its increasingly doomed search for security, baffled by fear of the "helplessness and bewilderment which would be the inevitable start to being oneself," may degenerate into fantasies of transparency, loss of the body, lethal magic powers. Consciousness becomes charged with hostility, fear, envy; ever more elaborate games "of pretense and equivocation" are played with others, while the inner self may subject itself to experiences of pain and terror in the elusive pursuit of convincing itself it is alive. To the outer world the psychotic "appears to be extremely narcissistic and exhibitionistic. In fact he hates himself and is terrified to reveal himself to others." [38]

It is ironic that an analysis designed to describe a psychotic person-ality resembles so closely a normal woman's dilemma. One key concept in Laing's analysis needs reformulating, however, if it is to be adequate to the poems I have been discussing and to the many poems by women that resemble them—if not, indeed, to the clinical schizophrenic. The idea of "false self" and "true self" is a theorist's imposition—the terms do not occur in Laing's patients' recorded fantasies—a residue, perhaps, of Aristotelian logic. To suppose that the mind, or the self, cannot truly encompass both X and Y is like supposing that a tree cannot truly en-compass both roots and leaves. The split selves in women's poems are both true, both false—or rather their truth or falsity is not the issue. The issue is division: that the halves do not combine to a whole, as if a tree had roots and leaves but no trunk. The issue is that the left foot is cut off from the right, the right from the left, and that the division re-flects and is reinforced by our culture's limited images of feminine personality. [39]

Among Laing's most provocative images, derived from Wilhelm Reich's metaphor of character armor as the layer of an individual per-sonality designed to protect the vulnerable interior, is the image of "pet-rification." [40] The schizoid, Laing observes, may fear being turned to stone or into a robot or automaton; or he may believe he can turn others to stone. He is in fact doing what he fears: mounting a rigid outer per-sonality for himself while defensively depersonalizing others.

Of such a pattern, "In Plaster" is a particularly striking example, but images of self as stone, or armor, or metal, are extremely common in women's poems, whether or not they include explicit statements of self-division. Often the precise point is that the self was once soft but has become self-protectively hard. Often there is more than a hint that the self is imitating, exaggerating, or caricaturing the hardness of an enemy who once controlled it and made it suffer. Thus the poem can be at once an embodiment of self-protection and an act of hostility. A poem by Judith Hemschemeyer begins

> I used to have fur
> and dimensions
> and handles
>
> I got drunk at parties
> and let people in
>
> Now I know better

Presently she is an almost completed "sphere / made of plates / of vanadium poems . . . your hands / glance off me now . . . your words are filed / and worked on / and bolted into place." The change from organic to inorganic, irregularly shaped to smoothly spherical, spontaneous to calculating, is also explicitly a change from life to art, or at any rate artifact. The poet's new ability to resist and even exploit the hands and words of the invading "you" is punitive as well as defensive.

Similarly punitive is Louise Glück's "Aphrodite," a succinctly angry poem about failed marriage, which appropriates the Odysseus-Penelope story and exploits the Greek habit of personifying rocky headlands as goddesses. To adventuring men, the story of life should terminate joyously in a harbor, where they expect after life's wanderings to find no drudge but a welcoming goddess. However, Glück takes her metaphor from the obvious anatomical locus for a woman's sense of the distinction between permeable and impermeable:

> In time, the young wife
> naturally hardens . . .
> On a hill, the armless figure
> welcomes the delinquent boat,
> her thighs cemented shut, barring
> the fault in the rock.

We have moved far from Dickinson's "Mirth is the Mail of Anguish," from Marianne Moore's humorous acceptance of a need for self-protection in her many poems on armored animals, and from the protective/creative images of shells and cocoons in Marianne Moore and H.D. The figure of armor in contemporary women's poems almost invariably signifies sterility, and it is never mirthful. Margaret Atwood's "A Fortification," our most chillingly painful armored-self poem, perhaps suggests why mirth is no longer an option in a world of high technology. Atwood raids science fiction for images of a rational self-protection which links consciousness itself to aggression. Daily to awaken and open her eyes, says Atwood, is to trigger an automatic closing of hydraulic doors. Consciousness, a control panel, "whispers softly as a diamond/ cutting glass." To get up is to "extend the feet / into my body which is a metal spacesuit":

> I have armed myself, yes I am safe: safe:
> the grass can't hurt me.
> My senses swivel like guns in their fixed sockets:
> I am barriered from leaves and blood.

Fear of the natural, the dreamlife, and the unguarded subconscious requires that one transform oneself into artifact, even to the extent of making organs of sensation, which in nature are organs of receptivity, into weapons. To fear what is natural is to become absurd, and it is to become symbolically male instead of symbolically female. "A Fortification" divides, like "This Is a Photograph of Me," into two halves, with the above stanza as pivot. The conclusion describes a tantalizing glimpse of another self, "the one that has real skin, real hair," at the moment of its diurnal disappearance "down the line of cells / back to the lost forest of being vulnerable."[41]

All such poems, aligning themselves around stated or implied dualities, at least one of which is the duality between vulnerable nature and invulnerable art, intersect illuminatingly with one of the most famous poems of the modern era, Yeats' "Sailing to Byzantium." Yeats in this poem rejects the sensual music of nature's cycle in which, as an old man, he can no longer participate except by dying. To the "dying generations" of fish, flesh, and fowl, he prefers "Monuments of unageing intellect," and to the scarecrow rags of the body he prefers the soul. Leaving the country of life he sails to the holy city of art, where he longs to be gathered "Into the artifice of eternity" and to assume the form of a precious object:

> Once out of nature I shall never take
> My bodily form from any natural thing,

But such a form as Grecian goldsmiths make
Of hammered gold and gold enamelling.[42]

How beautiful this is, indeed how feminine, compared with the stony
and metal voices of our women. To compare is apparently to apprehend
a melancholy gap between the strongest yearnings of men and of women.
For one thing it is not dying that the women object to and want to defend themselves against, but being hurt, wronged, violated. Second,
when they see themselves as artifacts it is not beauty and preciousness
that they envision. A plaster cast and a space suit are more functional,
less pleasing, than a singing golden bird in a fantasy emperor's court.
Finally, unlike Yeats, the women do not really want to be secure, hard,
dispassionate objects. They hate it. The flat inflections of their voices
say they hate it. They are angry, despising in themselves the necessity, or
what they take to be the necessity, of their petrification. Of this split between a self that desires and one that dreads human contact, we see little
in contemporary men's poetry. Neither do we see the "elaborate game of
pretence and equivocation" so firmly embedded in the poetic strategies
of writers like Atwood, Plath, Wakoski, Glück: this game that no longer
repeats the flirtatious duplicities of Dickinson yet cannot escape from
fragmentation. The nearest things to it, John Ashbery's elusive coyness,
Mark Strand's evanescences, are quite without the desperation of the
female. That the women's poetry movement today stresses power rather
than beauty we have known for some time. A primary source of that
power is women's struggle with and against a divided self, experienced at
once as inescapable—"I shall never get out of this"—and unbearable.

5

I shall speak about women's writing: about what it will do. Woman
must write her self: must write about women and bring women to
writing, from which they have been driven away as violently as
from their bodies—for the same reasons, by the same law, with
the same fatal goal. Woman must put herself into the text—as
into the world and into history—by her own movement . . . And
why don't you write? Write! Writing is for you, you are for you;
your body is yours, take it.
—Hélène Cixous, "The Laugh of the Medusa"[43]

I am a wind-swayed bridge, a crossroads inhabited by whirlwinds
. . . You say my name is ambivalence? Think of me as Shiva, a

many-armed and legged body with one foot on brown soil, one on white, one in straight society, one in the gay world, the man's world, the women's, one limb in the literary world, another in the working class, the socialist, and the occult worlds. A sort of spider woman hanging by one thin strand of web.

Who, me confused? Ambivalent? Not so. Only your labels split me.

—Gloria Anzaldúa, "La Prieta"[44]

If an empty identity and a divided self are what women see in themselves, that is not what they desire. Assertions of nonexistence, invisibility, and muteness on the one hand, stony or metallic rigidity, formlessness, and deformity on the other, are signals of crisis, signs of a fragmented being unable to unify itself, unable to tolerate some part of itself that is necessary for its wholeness, yet unwilling to remain scattered.

Two sorts of poetic results emerge from the quest for identity in women's poetry, one relating to style, one to content, both contributing to what we must finally recognize as a gynocentric poetics. Attentive readers will have noticed that many of the passages quoted in this chapter seem stylistically hard, cold, rigid, and rational rather than soft, warm, pliable, and sensitive. Individual variations of this tone, which effectively makes a poem's surface an exoskeleton dividing poet from reader, are extremely common among women poets since 1960. Among poets for whom a primary theme is physical or emotional vulnerability, it is virtually universal. Absent from their voices are the musicality of lyric and the familiar speech rhythms of conversational poetry, although the voice edges toward incantation in a poet like Plath, and poets like Atwood and Macdonald often devise sour pastiches of conversational phrases and locutions of public address. Parody and mockery seem the flesh and blood of the exoskeletal style, fear and rage govern its nerves, and we are meant to feel that we could throw a hammer at these poetic surfaces and not break them.

The artist's stance in many of these poems seems to identify aggressive-defensiveness with the art of writing, and this stance is clearly ungracious, ungentle, unladylike. From the point of view of poetic reputation, so much the better. The woman poet who adopts an impermeable tone is in less danger of being dismissed as sentimental or overemotional by critics; "certainly not another poetess" was Lowell's posthumous tribute to Plath for the steely implacability of *Ariel*. To approach the strategy of this style from another angle, we need look no further than Laing's observation that an ontologically uneasy person may adopt, to the point of caricature, the personality of his oppressor. Control, impersonality, and dispassionateness are supposedly normative masculine virtues in any case, and are favored by the contemporary literary climate. The cooler the voice, the warmer the reception, is a good rule of thumb. An intelligent woman poet may have every reason in the world to construct, as her fortress, a perversely exaggerated version of an acceptable style.

An intelligent reader, on the other hand, need not be fooled. The exaggerated style invites us to understand that it means both what it seems and the opposite, like the broken grail in Frost's "Directive," hidden "so the wrong ones can't find it." It appears that the intention is to draw us closer while repelling us, to demand everything of us while promising nothing, as in Wakoski's announcement:

> My rock is the mountain.
> Love me
> if you can.
> I will not make it easy for you
> any more.[45]

Or, as Atwood says while making herself invisible,

> eventually
> you will be able to see me.[46]

We have no equivalent of Dickinson's charm, no ingratiating seductions of the reader, in contemporary women's poetry. Yet to look hard at the hard style in women's poetry is to see its duplicity, as scintillating in our time as Dickinson's was in hers. To look at it hard enough is to see it melt away like a magic mirror, letting us step through. In fact, the equivocal treatment of the reader as lover-antagonist—a formal invention elegantly designed to illuminate the dilemma of inadequate self-hood—is, as I hope to show, one aspect of a larger reorientation of the relation between artist and audience in women's poetry.

Turning from style to substance, it is immediately apparent that women who seek themselves will include the material of their daily lives and feelings in their poems. The roles of daughter, wife, mother, the routines of domesticity, the classroom, the job market—these become subjects to redeem from soap opera, situation comedy, and Harlequin romance. For women of color, working-class women, lesbian women, it becomes possible to release imprisoned strata of experience into the daylight of language.[47] The legitimization as literary of what has been excluded from literature is one result of all literary movements and is the one respect in which art is, like science, an accretive enterprise. No subject was fit for poetry in writing's dawn but gods and heroes. In the

Renaissance, no character below the rank of gentleman could enter a literary work save as a clown. Nineteenth-century poetry legitimized children, the poor, and the insane; so the moment has come for what one anthology calls "ordinary women." [48]

When the republic of letters annexes a new province, it is immediately revealed to be different, and more complex, than we thought while it was a blank spot, like Conrad's Congo, on the cultural map. We did not know love was so complicated, before Petrarch's sonnets and Dante's *Vita Nuova*, or that little boys were so sensitive, before Rousseau and Dickens. The blankness of woman has made her the perfect field for creative male fantasy; Gauguin's *Soyez Mystérieuses* is, as the West Coast poet Kathleen Fraser has observed, a motto engraved above the backside of a nude female lying "perfectly / voluptuous / in mud." [49] When this female turns over, Fraser imagines that she will want "to re-write" herself and her environment. As Adrienne Rich reminds us in her powerful quest poem "Diving into the Wreck," "the words are purposes. The words are maps." [50] We need to trace the complications encountered when women poets begin to draw their own maps of the female body, the female passions, the female mind and spirit, demystifying these mysteries.

3 Body Language:
The Release of Anatomy

The American artist has sometimes avoided [her femininity], by
getting her mental hysterectomy early. She will often not speak for
female experience even when the men do. She will be the angel-
artist, with celestially muted lower parts. Sometimes, in any of
the arts, where women's work remains beautifully mandarin or
minor, it may be not because of their womanhood but from their
lack of it.
  —Hortense Calisher, "No Important Woman Writer" [1]

We sat across the table.
he said, cut off your hands.
they are always poking at things.
they might touch me.
I said yes.

Food grew cold on the table.
he said, burn your body.
it is not clean and smells like sex.
it rubs my mind sore.
I said yes.

I love you, I said.
that's very nice, he said
I like to be loved,
that makes me happy.
Have you cut off your hands yet?
      —Marge Piercy, "The Friend" [2]

Oh, darling, let your body in,
let it tie you in,

in comfort . . . .
What I want to say, Linda,
is that there is nothing in your body that lies.
　　　—Anne Sexton, "Little Girl, My String Bean, My Lovely
　　　　Woman"[3]

One of the ways we recognize a poetess—which is to say a woman poet locked into sentimentality by her inhibitions—is that she steers clear of anatomical references. As womanly inhibition declines, we grow aware of its sources in dualistic ideology, gender polarization, and the dread of female sexuality. One of the ways we recognize that a woman writer has taken some kind of liberating jump is that her muted parts begin to explain themselves.

During the last two decades, American women poets have been writing about their bodies with decreasing embarrassment and increasing enthusiasm. They write about the sensations of making love. They write about eating and sitting on the toilet. They write about their faces and hands, their arms, their breasts, their wombs, their menstrual periods. Necks and throats, knees and teeth. They write about giving birth, giving suck, growing old. Poems about abortion, poems about breast surgery, poems about rape, have become part of women's poetic repertoire. In sum, whether or not they deal directly with the self, or with sexuality as such, contemporary women poets employ anatomical imagery both more frequently and far more intimately than male poets.[4] Their female audiences enjoy this. Male readers, and indeed conservative critics of any stripe, tend to be made uncomfortable by women's body imagery, to feel that it is inartistic, and to take it as evidence of the writer's shallowness, narcissism, and unseemly aggressiveness. More than one writer has observed the consequences of female candor. As Ntozake Shange remarks, when women writers "start alla this foolishness bout their bodies & blood & kids & what's really goin on at home," their men friends usually flee the scene "in fear of becoming unclean."[5] For the issue is not in fact an aesthetic one but reaches deeply into the question of what our bodies mean to us.

It is of course difficult for any of us to evade the mental yardstick which seems to have been let down from heaven like Jacob's ladder, governing thousands of years of religion, philosophy, and literature, according to which the mortal and corruptible flesh imprisons the immortal and incorruptible soul, the body is base and the mind is exalted. We have no known "high" culture without hierarchical thinking and no hierarchical thinking that fails to categorize the body as "low." If anatomy is destiny, we all want to escape it. From Plato to St. Paul, and from St. Paul to Freud, civilization means vertical mobility: one transcends the body to achieve anything of spiritual or public worth. As to woman: woman in both our sacred and secular mythologies *is* the flesh, when men write about her, whether to express revulsion at her physicality and sexuality or "to flatter beauty's ignorant ear," as Yeats says, and thereby gain control of it. She has been discouraged from writing about the flesh herself, just as she has been forbidden to assume control over her sexual and reproductive life. Socially or intellectually, a free woman is a dangerous woman.

Within the last few decades, however, a woman desirous of freedom, Simone de Beauvoir, has made the most massive and elaborate philosophical case that artistic creativity and female biology are natural foes. More recently, a group of feminist theorists has insisted to the contrary that female creativity is and should be intrinsically carnal, basing itself in women's unique maternal relations and sexual sensations. Both these positions need to be considered as part of the context of contemporary women's poetry.

The idea that the female body is a creative woman's chief liability has never been so fully argued and documented as in *The Second Sex*, which, since its first publication in France in 1949 and in the United States in 1953, has been the great-godmother of all feminist texts.[6] For de Beauvoir, who believes that the goal of civilization is release from our bondage to nature, the prison of the flesh is no metaphor. Male biology, because its strength and independence encourage masculine acts of control, acts relatively to man's advantage. Female biology, because it is organized to serve the species (the ends of procreation) rather than the individual, is a handicap.

> From birth, the species has taken possession of woman and tends to tighten its grasp . . . at puberty the species reasserts its claim . . . this whole occurrence has the aspect of a *crisis*. Not without resistance does the body of woman permit the species to take over; and this struggle is weakening and dangerous . . . Many of the ovarian secretions function for the benefit of the egg, promoting its maturation and adapting the uterus to its requirements . . . the woman is adapted to the needs of the egg rather than to her own requirements. (pp. 29–31)

On the menstrual cycle:

> From puberty to menopause woman is the theatre of a play that unfolds within her and in which she is not personally concerned . . . the menstrual cycle is a burden, and a useless one from the point of view of the individual. (p. 31)

On pregnancy, chilbirth and lactation, and finally the menopause:

> Woman experiences a more profound alienation when fertiliza-
> tion has occurred . . . gestation is a fatiguing task of no individual
> benefit to the woman . . . Childbirth itself is painful and danger-
> ous . . . Nursing is also a tiring service . . . In the end woman
> escapes the iron grasp of the species by way of still another serious
> crisis; the phenomena of the menopause . . . Woman is now de-
> livered from the servitude imposed by her female nature . . . her
> vitality is unimpaired . . . she is no longer the prey of overwhelm-
> ing forces; . . . she and her body are one . . . Often, indeed, this
> release from female physiology is expressed in a health, a balance,
> a vigor that they lacked before.   (pp. 33–35)

Historically, de Beauvoir explains female subordination as a necessary outcome of advancing technology and civilization, commencing
with the transition from nomadic to agricultural economies in which
women, tied to domestic life and the bearing and rearing of children,
could only minimally participate. Identified with the Nature which
men have sought to conquer, woman has remained trapped, forced by
her body to serve as the eternal Other, an emblem perhaps of sacred
mysteries, but a physical, social, and political inferior. Biologically a
victim of the species, she becomes by extension a victim of culture.

The Second Sex contends that woman's physiological inferiorities "do
not condemn her to remain in this subordinate role forever," since civilization has advanced to a degree which makes biology a relatively
minor factor in human life. Liberty and equality, the elimination of
woman's diminishing role as Other, will benefit society as well as women
themselves:

> Women are "clinging," they are a dead weight, and they suffer for
> it; the point is that their situation is like that of a parasite sucking
> out the living strength of another organism. Let them be provided
> with living strength of their own, let them have the means to at-
> tack the world and wrest from it their own subsistence, and their
> dependence will be abolished—that of man also. There is no
> doubt that both men and women will profit greatly from the new
> situation   (p. 805)

De Beauvoir's rejection of female subordination is forceful and com-
bative. But below the ring of her battle cry sounds a steady drone, difficult to distinguish from the voice of patriarchy itself, with its metaphors
of attacking, wrestling, and profit. Existentialist ethics in this respect
marries Platonic mind-body dualism with modern—indeed capitalist—

individualism. The Jacob's ladder without the religious machinery leaves behind a psychic yardstick which is still vertical, still judgmental; it indicates that in order for a woman to achieve full humanity, she must reject or minimize whatever is imposed on her by the physical body. The inferior life of "immanence" dictated by feminine anatomy must become the superior life of "transcendence" willed and dictated by the striving individual ego. The woman past menopause becomes the one model of the free and healthy female being.

While *The Second Sex* decrees that we must disentangle the laws of nature from the laws of men, de Beauvoir does not ask how much a European or American woman's experience of physical frailty and alienation from the body may be culturally produced. She does not suggest that certain attributes she identifies with female biology, such as devotion of self to species, or cooperation with nature rather than conquest of it, might be adapted by men to the advantage of society, or might give actual satisfaction to the self. Nor, though their political fruits have been questioned as mixed blessings in this century, does the author at any point challenge the traditionally male values of "independence," the "ego," the "individual," the activities of striving, attack, and conquest.

From her privileging of "transcendence" over "immanence," it follows that de Beauvoir cannot take women artists seriously. She allows that they aptly describe "their own inner life, their experience, their own universes . . . they present their experience, still warm, through savory adjectives and carnal figures of speech" (p. 790), and they are good at recording facts. But for her these strengths are weaknesses, dooming a woman to intellectual mediocrity. She agrees with Stendahl that "all the geniuses who are born *women* are lost to the public good."

While contemporary feminist critics have found these positions highly debatable, de Beauvoir's ideas nevertheless powerfully articulate the dominant assumptions of a phallocentric culture and literature. Consequently, radical French feminists of the school of *l'Écriture féminine* have contended that to "inscribe the body" for a woman writer does not simply promote female self-expression but constitutes a subversion of patriarchy and patriarchal discourse, substituting female libido for male, sexual pleasure or *jouissance* for logic and convention.

For the Marxist linguist Julia Kristeva, founder of the avant-garde journal *Tel quel*, women's linguistic essence is "negative, at odds with what already exists . . . something that cannot be represented, something that is not said," and preoedipal, representing the blissful fusion with the mother that all social organization attempts to overcome and deny; woman's role as writer is then to "reject everything finite, definite, structured, loaded with meaning, in the existing state of society."[7]

Hélène Cixous' manifesto "The Laugh of the Medusa" identifies women's writing with an illimitable, explosive physicality and sexuality: "Almost everything is yet to be written by women about femininity; about their sexuality, that is, its infinite and mobile complexity . . . More body, hence more writing . . . Her libido is cosmic, just as her unconscious is worldwide."[8] The post-Lacanian psychoanalyst Luce Irigaray similarly claims that the unique disruptiveness of women's writing derives from the diffuseness of her sexuality:

> *woman has sex organs just about everywhere.* She experiences pleasure almost everywhere . . . That is undoubtedly the reason she is called temperamental, incomprehensible, perturbed, capricious—not to mention her language in which "she" goes off in all directions and in which "he" is unable to discern the coherence of any meaning.[9]

The novelist Chantal Chawaf, among others, advocates an antilogocentric woman's language:

> In order to reconnect the book with the body and with pleasure, we must disintellectualize writing . . . . And this language, as it develops, will not degenerate and dry up, will not go back to the fleshless academicism, the stereotypical and senile discourses that we reject.[10]

Among American writers, Mary Daly, Susan Griffin, and Adrienne Rich have championed the transformative power of a writing grounded in the body: "In order to live a fully human life," argues Rich in *Of Woman Born: Motherhood as Experience and Institution*, "we require not only control of our bodies . . . we must touch the unity and resonance of our physicality, the corporeal ground of our intelligence."[11]

Such writers have been challenged by other feminists as reiterating an unacceptable biologism and as reinforcing a dualism in language and society which has always been used to justify the marginalization of women. The demand that the woman writer must embrace a disintellectualized, preoedipal carnality may be as prescriptive as the demand that she remain disembodied.[12] It is with this debate in mind, however, that we must examine what happens when contemporary American women poets "inscribe the body."

In the work this chapter considers, an important form of subversion has already taken place. The familiar vertical standard has disappeared; body is not assumed to be morally or metaphysically inferior to some higher principle. On the contrary, it is taken first of all as a reliable reality—"the body cannot lie"—and by extension as the medium whereby realities beyond the body are interpreted, their codes read. Rather than a uniform dwelling on *jouissance* or a concerted use of the body as a rhetorical instrument for the overthrow of phallocentric discourse, however, we must recognize in this work a wide range of representative attitudes or stances regarding bodily experiences, associated with a range of poetic strategies. In the following sections I look at poems which reject the body on account of its vulnerability, poems which respond ambivalently to the body on account of its conventional status as "beautiful," and poems which affirm the body as a source of power. Throughout, it will be important to note the reinterpretations of other matters which follow from reinterpreting the body. Finally I will look at a category of poetry which has been central to our tradition for centuries, nature poetry, and consider the impact of women's sense of the body on their readings of nature.

2

All Greece hates
the still eyes in the white face,
the lustre as of olives
where she stands,
and the white hands . . . .

could love indeed the maid,
only if she were laid,
white ash amid funereal cypresses.
    —H.D., "Helen" [13]

And the body, what about the body?
Sometimes it is my favorite child . . . .
And sometimes my body disgusts me.
Filling and emptying it disgusts me.
    —Jane Kenyon, "Cages" [14]

Did this happen to your mother? . . .
Did your sister throw up a lot?
    —Alice Walker, "Did This Happen to Your Mother" [15]

Male poets who despise the flesh traditionally do so for two associated reasons. The flesh is both corrupt and corruptible; that is, it is both inherently sinful and inherently subject to change and death. The former grievance is expressed morally, the latter lyrically—and with the understanding that in the youth and prime of life, the flesh is a source of pleasure.

A large number of women poets since the 1960s appear to view the body as a source essentially of pain, not pleasure. We may view these poets as continuing the traditional association of feminine sensibility with suffering which we saw taking hold in the nineteenth century and as illustrating de Beauvoir's categorization of the female body as weak and vulnerable. What they do not do, however, is posit any higher, purer, transcendent principle as relief or consolation. As has already been suggested in poems associating female muteness with acts of rape, and as we will see more elaborately in the next chapter, rape and physical violence are for many women paradigmatic of women's position in male society. There exists a subgenre of poems in which a woman's flesh and blood are manipulated by a condescending doctor figure. The damaged bodies of war victims, the hungry bodies of famine victims are acutely important images in the work of Adrienne Rich, Muriel Rukeyser, Denise Levertov, Carolyn Forché, Sharon Olds, and many other poets. Margaret Atwood's chief figures for alienation are bodily fragmentation and an endangered landscape. Among Ai's men and women, victims of contemporary poverty and of history's nightmares, physical violence is a norm. The female body in Louise Glück is phantomlike, passive. Bodies in Joyce Carol Oates are almost always in stasis, frozen, trapped, figures for terror. The black poets Audre Lorde, June Jordan, and Ntozake Shange write powerfully and angrily of white violence against black and of male violence against females.

Women also seem drawn to portray psychic hurt in somatic terms. Lynn Sukenick's "The Poster" describes a lover's contempt:

> He tells me I am boring.
> He hollows out a space inside my chest
> as a whittler would do it,
> carefully, coolly,
> whistling a tune
> everyone knows and likes.

May Swenson's "Bleeding" describes the contempt more extremely, but the metaphoric structure is the same: a passive and penetrable self, an aggressive and phallic instrument of attack:

> Stop bleeding   said the knife.
> I would if I   could said the cut.

Stop bleeding   you make me messy with this blood.
I'm sorry said   the cut.

The cut apologizes, in a voice that we will by now recognize as famil-
iarly feminine, for being hurt. The knife replies that it "can't stand
bleeding" and wants to be shiny; and it sinks in deeper. While she avoids
assigning genders to the cut and the knife, Swenson brilliantly epitomizes the connection between physical and emotional vulnerability in
women as it plays itself out in a context of obsessive violence and loath-
ing for the body and for emotion. Visually, the slash that runs down the
page of "Bleeding" represents both feminine anatomy and the psychic
split that divides victim from victimizer.

The normal processes of a woman's body may also feel like imprison-
ment, as in Lisel Mueller's "Life of a Queen," which summarizes the
biological cycle of a queen bee. "They build a pendulous chamber / for
her, and stuff her with sweets" is how it starts, and "A crew disas-
sembles / her royal cell" is how it ends. The opening of Anne Sexton's
"Snow White" comparably perceives the female body as passive object,
a medium of exchange in modern commercial society as in Levi-
Strauss' primitive tropics:

No matter what life you lead
the virgin is a lovely number:
cheeks as fragile as cigarette paper,
arms and legs made of Limoges,
lips like Vin Du Rhône,
rolling her china-blue doll eyes
open and shut.
Open to say,
Good Day Mama,
and shut for the thrust
of the unicorn.[16]

To understand the connection between physical vulnerability and
ironic self-rejection in women poets, it is useful to consider Sylvia Plath,
who appears most thoroughly to have internalized the larger culture's
principles of flesh-rejection and aspiration toward transcendence.[17]
Plath's work is filled with body images both internal and external: skin,
blood, skulls, feet, mouths and tongues, wounds, bone, lungs, heart
and veins, legs and arms. She writes of both male and female bodies.
She also projects human anatomy into the natural world. The moon is
"a face in its own right, / White as a knuckle and terribly upset"
(p. 173). Goldfish ponds being drained "collapse like lungs" (p. 130).

An elm speaks like a woman pregnant or cancer-ridden—one cannot
tell the difference:

> I am terrified by this dark thing
> That sleeps in me;
> All day I feel its soft, feathery turnings, its malignity.   (p. 193)

Tulips, when the poet is hospitalized, have "sudden tongues" and "eat
my oxygen." They breathe

> Lightly, through their white swaddlings, like an awful baby.
> Their redness talks to my wound, it corresponds. . . .
> They are opening like the mouth of some great African
>   cat.   (pp. 161–62)

In "Totem," the projection of biology outward is global and primitive:
"the world is blood-hot and personal" (p. 264).

Throughout most of Plath's writing, what is organic is approximately
coterminous with what suffers. Her poetry offers fragments of beings,
not whole persons. A critic observes:

> The living flesh is felt as . . . a prey to axes, doctors' needles,
> butchers' and surgeons' knives, poison, snakes and tentacles, acids,
> vampires, leeches, bats and bees, jails and brutal boots. Small
> animals are butchered and eaten, man's flesh can undergo the
> final indignity of being cut to pieces and used as an object . . .
> Subjects and metaphors include a cut, a contusion, the tragedy of
> thalidomide, fever, an accident, a wound, paralysis, a burial, ani-
> mal and human sacrifice, the burning of heretics, lands devas-
> tated by wars, extermination camps: her poetry is a "garden of tor-
> tures" in which mutilation and annihilation take nightmarishly
> protean forms.[18]

A number of Plath's persistent motifs can be decoded with de Beauvoir's help as referring to the feminine body specifically. Plath's imagery
of strangulation implies in extreme form the woman fatally imprisoned
and stifled by her own body. An infant is "stealer of cells, stealer of
beauty" in "The Fearful." Children are hooks sticking in one's skin, and
placenta and umbilical cord threaten the poet in "Medusa." Most painfully, her imagery of laceration suggests woman's essential anatomical
condition, shameful to endure, difficult to confess—as in "Cut," where
the poet runs through a set of brilliant metaphors for the thumb she has
just sliced with a kitchen knife "instead of an onion." All the metaphors
are masculine and military: "Little pilgrim . . . Redcoats . . . Homun-
culus . . . Kamikaze man," until the finale:

How you jump—
Trepanned veteran,
Dirty girl,
Thumb stump.   (pp. 235–36)

What, after all, is more humiliating in our culture than being a bleeding, dirty girl? As in Swenson's "Bleeding," the coded allusion to menstruation points to a primary locus of woman hatred in the culture and hence of woman hatred within the female self.

At the same time, the landscape of war and mutilation in a poem like "Getting There," the references to Jews and Nazis in "Daddy" and "Lady Lazarus," the "Hiroshima ash" of "Fever 103," and even the sour commercial comedy of "The Applicant," in which a wife is sold like a household appliance and only the mutilated man can be normal enough to marry, reinforce Plath's vision of worldly existence as at worst holocaust, at best tawdry sideshow. The drama of social and political life plays out, on a nightmarishly large scale, the victimization of the body.

Plath imagines the possibility of detachment from body and world in two ways. The first of these is the distancing of experience through poetic manipulation; the second is death. In some of the late poems, these solutions coalesce.

The modern masters had taught the superiority of art to the absurdity of life, and Plath in the 1950s was a good student.[19] Her early verse employs tight formal structures, bookish diction, an armory of allusions to sanctioned works of art and literature, and a consistently ironic impersonality of tone, which has everything to do with controlling experience, little to do with dwelling in it. The looser, less traditional forms of her late work intensify rather than relax our sense of the poet's control. She manipulates rhyme and off-rhyme, regular and irregular meter, with the casualness of a juggler tossing knives, and her mature mastery of colloquial idiom illustrates her contempt for the vulgar and cruel social relations which generate such idiom. She becomes a mocker of the vernacular, using language against itself. We note the slowed-down scorn of the final phrase in "Lady Lazarus":

The peanut-crunching crowd
shoves in to see
Them unwrap me hand and foot—
The big strip tease,   (p. 245)

and the ironic use of the popular term "adores" in "Daddy":

Every woman adores a Fascist,
The boot in the face.   (p. 223)

According to A. A. Alvarez, Plath called "Daddy" a piece of "light verse" a few days after she wrote it, and in her BBC note on it she remarked coolly, as if it were nothing personal,

> Here is a poem spoken by a girl with an Electra complex. Her father died while she thought he was God. Her case is complicated by the fact that her father was also a Nazi and her mother very possibly part Jewish . . . she has to act out the awful little allegory once over before she is free of it.   (p. 293)

The poem itself says "I"; the poet cannot do so. Like Eliot condescending to say, "I gotta use words when I talk to you," the artist of *Ariel* is "too pure for you or anyone."

As Plath's artistic control increased, so did her vision of possible release, into a state of purification and perfection equivalent to the perfection of art. The implicit equation is clear as early as "Two Views of a Cadaver Room," which places a real-life scene with corpses next to the "panorama of smoke and slaughter" in a Brueghel painting. In "The Disquieting Muses," Plath rejects her mother's cheery songs and stories for the three bald and faceless figures she accepts as artistic guides. And in *Ariel*, the poet "unpeels" herself from her body in poem after poem, lets her body "flake" away, annihilates the "trash" of flesh which disgusts her because it would make her kin to the ogling peanut-crunching crowd. She transforms herself from gross matter to "a pure acetylene virgin" rising toward heaven or to dew evaporating in the sunrise—but transcendence always means death. When self-inflicted, it spells triumph. And if she fears and scorns death's perfection as well as life's imperfection ("Perfection is terrible, it cannot have children" [p. 262]; "This is what it is to be complete. It is horrible" [p. 198]), self-annihilation is nevertheless the ultimately artistic, ultimately ironic response to humiliation.

Had Plath lived, she might have discovered another exit from the locked compartment; possibly through motherhood, about which she wrote her only poems of unambiguous sensual pleasure. As it is, she imagined one further form of transcendence. The veiled and jadelike woman in "Purdah," who says of her bridegroom "I am his," proceeds to envision herself the tigress who will kill him. The daughter in "Daddy" who lives passively and fearfully "like a foot," adores "the boot in the face," and lets her "pretty red heart" be bitten in two, finally accomplishes her ritual murder of the father she loves and hates. "Lady Lazarus" reduces Lucifer, God, the killer of Jews, and the poet's doctor to a single brutal exploitative figure. Given the poem's title, this figure is also the one who in the Gospels raises Lazarus, speaks of laying up treasures in heaven, and is himself resurrected after death. To that "enemy," that male authority, the poet replies:

> I am your opus,
> I am your valuable,
> The pure gold baby . . .
>
> Ash, ash—
> You poke and stir.
> Flesh, bone, there is nothing there—
>
> A cake of soap,
> A wedding ring,
> A gold filling.
>
> Herr God, Herr Lucifer,
> Beware
> Beware.
>
> Out of the ash
> I rise with my red hair
> And I eat men like air.   (p. 246–47)

In the Plath scheme, then, if transcendence is a solution to the problem of the body, it merely means joining the killers instead of the killed. It is not this vision which de Beauvoir anticipates when she asks women to "attack the world." But when the physical self is made an object, trash, subject to harm and worthy of destruction, its most ardent impossible dream may be to destroy its maker.

Plath is, as Alvarez early recognized, a poet whose "particular gift is to clarify and intensify the received world." [20] We may view her work aesthetically as a radical extension of the mode of disenchanted alienation in the Eliot-Auden-Lowell line. We may view it morally as a capitulation to weakness, a self-indulgence. Perhaps it is both. In any case, the identification of woman and body, body and vulnerability, vulnerability and irony—which in effect responds to the implacable indifference or cruelty of the world by internalizing it—is a common phenomenon in women's poetry of the last twenty years. As we will see in the following chapter, this pattern is part of a larger pattern involving female anger at a world of oppressive polarization and hierarchy in which all relationships seem to be relationships of dominance and submission.

3

> Our masks, always in peril
> —Carolyn Kizer, "Pro Femina"[21]

As W. B. Yeats has the "beautiful mild woman" who was Maud Gonne's sister observe in "Adam's Curse,"

> To be born woman is to know—
> Although they do not speak of it at school—
> That we must labour to be beautiful.[22]

In reply, one may imagine a chorus of not-so-mild women poets remarking: you said it. The labors of beauty have not been traditionally spoken of in male poetry, outside of misogynist attacks on the foulness of the painted woman, like Swift's "Celia." But they are now, commonly to hilarious effect, in women's poetry. Honor Moore's poem "My Mother's Moustache" gives a wry and detailed account of adolescence with and without depilatories. Karen Swenson tells of a bosom which never attains movie star amplitude and hopes (with oral metaphors in the Spenser-to-Keats tradition) to find a man who will settle for dumplings at the feast of life. Kathleen Fraser writes "Poem in Which My Legs Are Accepted." The opening poem of Diane Wakoski's *Motorcycle Betrayal Poems* complains about "this ridiculous face / of lemon rinds/ and vinegar cruets." Grumbling with the voice of multitudes in "Woman Poem," Nikki Giovanni summarizes:

> it's a sex object if you're pretty
> and no love
> or love and no sex if you're fat
> get back fat black woman be a mother
> grandmother strong thing . . .

Beauty, when a woman stops to think about it, means bondage. In "A Work of Artifice," Marge Piercy compares the feminine fate with that of a bonsai tree, artificially miniature:

> It is your nature
> to be small and cosy,
> domestic and weak;
> how lucky, little tree . . .
> With living creatures
> one must begin very early
> to dwarf their growth:

the bound feet,
the crippled brain,
the hair in curlers,
the hands you
love to touch.

The adaptation of advertising language in the final lines grimly indicates both commercial-economic and emotional reasons for woman's
bondage. Her face is someone else's fortune. But what can she do? She
needs to be loved. In a tone only slightly less bitter than Piercy's,
Carolyn Kizer in "Pro Femina" talks "about women of letters, for I'm in
the racket," and addresses the unique dilemma of the lady with brains
and ambition:

Our masks, always in peril of smearing or cracking,
In need of continuous check in the mirror or silverware,
Keep us in thrall to ourselves, concerned with our surfaces.

Men, says Kizer, do not have this problem. Even male fashions are
"hard-fibered . . . designed to achieve self-forgetfulness":

So, sister, forget yourself a few times and see where it gets you:
Up the creek, alone with your talent, sans everything else.
You can wait for the menopause, and catch up on your
    reading. . . .
Meanwhile, have you used your mind today?
What pomegranate raised you from the dead,
Springing, full-grown, from your own head, Athena?

While quizzical poems on the topic of beauty versus truth as applied
to cosmetics will admittedly weigh lightly in most literary scales, they
typically embody two interesting stylistic decisions. First, these poems
refuse rather than cultivate formal distance. No persona, no gloss of verbal refinement, intervenes between the poet and her sense of personal
inadequacy or between herself and her audience. As readers we are
asked to participate in the predicament of someone who wants to be
beautiful while challenging, implicitly or explicitly, the standards or
value of beauty for a woman, and who does not pretend to transcend
the situation. It would be inappropriate to make the poem itself too
beautiful.

Second, the poems are comic. Comedy prevents the poet from laps-
ing into naive self-exposure, and a comic stance enables writer and
reader to agree that the predicament is, after all, innately ridiculous.

Not a life or death matter, is it? Clowning shows that we have perspective. Or perhaps we laugh to erase the frown lines in the mirror? The rollicking meter and jaunty-to-blustery tone of "Pro Femina," unlike Kizer's more usual lyric style, serve the same function as a woman's preening: they make a disguise for a naked emotion, as paint for a woman's naked face.

Possibly the funniest, certainly the most outrageous, poem of this subgenre is Erica Jong's tour de force "Aging," subtitled "balm for a 27th birthday." Jong at the outset presents herself as

> Hooked for two years now on wrinkled creams   creams for
> crowsfeet   ugly lines (if only there were one!)
> any perfumed grease   which promises youth   beauty
> not truth   but all I need on earth
>
> I've been studying   how women age
>   how
>
> it starts around the eyes   so you can tell
> a woman of 22 from one of 28 merely by
> a faint scribbling near the lids   a subtle crinkle

She imagines through several stanzas the advancing track of the wrinkles, as "ruin proceeds downwards" and the face begins to resemble "the tragic mask." Her tone grows increasingly nervous. But the poem is undergoing a transformation of its own, from self-mocking panic to self-loving acceptance. Though "the neck will give you away," and the chin in spite of facelifts "will never quite love your bones as it once did,"

> the belly may be kept firm through numerous pregnancies
> by means of sit-ups   jogging   dancing   (think of
>   Russian ballerinas)
>   & the cunt
> as far as I know is ageless   possibly immortal   becoming
>   simply
> more open   more quick to understand   more dry-eyed
>   than at 22
>
>   which
>
>   after all   is what you were dying for   (as you ravaged
>   islands of turtles   beehives   oysterbeds   the udders
>   of cows)

desperate to censor changes which you simply might have
    let play
over you   lying back   listening   opening yourself
      letting the years make love the only way   (poor
    blunderers)
                           they know [23]

When a woman is naturally narcissistic, she might as well go the whole hog. Beauty is, Jong reminds us, as beauty does. During the first half of the poem Jong provides us with incidental lexical amusements such as a play on "lines" and "plotting" in a woman's face or her writing, both of which show "promise" of "deepening." The wicked four-letter term "cunt" at the poem's crux has been cunningly prepared for by suggestions that decline in one aspect may bring ascendance in another. If the term shocks, we may be obliged to ask ourselves what we thought feminine attractiveness was all about. The remainder of the poem gracefully offers the pun on "what you were dying for" and concludes with a deft inversion of a centuries-old poetic convention. Time, the enemy of love in lyric poetry since the Greek *Anthologia*, has become a sequence of lovers—blundering, presumably young and inexperienced lovers at that—to whom a woman, ripe with herself, can condescend.

Jong writes less successfully when she attempts to make narcissism look sublime rather than ridiculous, and poems of self-examination in this surface sense seem generally to need a Dickensian mail of mirth. Humor can effectively spotlight problems which are naggingly real if trivial; the comic-autobiographical mode has become a major option in women's writing.

4

It is that dream world Anais speaks of
that dark watery place
where everything is female
where you open the door of the house
and she waits upstairs
the way you knew she would
and her hair floats over the world . . .
Until she rises as though from the sea
not on the half-shell this time
nothing to laugh at
and not as delicate as he imagined her:

a woman big-hipped, beautiful, and fierce.
—Sharon Barba, "A Cycle of Women"[24]

When women write to praise the body rather than to attack or joke about it, their most significant technique is revisionist metaphor. Water, moon, earth, and living things, the natural as opposed to the artificial, provide the common sources of imagery for women poets engaged in commending the physical self, just as they always have for men describing women; but the images are turned to new directions. Rather than supporting traditional interpretations of woman as desired and dreaded Other, they resist these meanings and imply alternatives. Here is where American women poets come closest to the prescriptions of l'Écriture féminine, whether or not their poems are explicitly ideological.

Three metaphors will serve as examples of women's alternative vision: flower, water, and earth. The identification of woman with flower is at least as old as the Roman de la Rose. Elizabethan poets agreed that "Beauty is but a flower / Which wrinkles will devour." Keats urged the melancholy lover to glut his sorrow on a rose, a wealth of globed peonies, or his mistress's peerless eyes, all of which dwell with beauty that must die. Poets have seen both woman and flower from without, whether in erotic poetry, poetry of witty seduction, or poetry of reflection on the transience and mutability of life. But when Diane Wakoski compares an armful of roses first with skin and then with internal organs, the focus changes:

The full roses with all their petals like the wrinkles of laughter
on your face as you bend to kiss someone
are bursting on the bush,
spotting my arm, as I carry a bundle of them
to my friends;
they seem to have come out of my skin
on this hot fragrant night,
and I imagine the inside of my body
glowing, phosphorescent, with strange flower faces
looking out from the duodenum
or the soft liver,
white as my belly, the eyes always disbelieving
the ugly processes that make a living body.

In their particularized detail—color, texture—as well as dramatic quality, these flowers resemble Plath's poppies and tulips. We experience not "beauty" but an overwhelming vividness, energy, and terror in the sense of self as living, therefore mortal, organism. The rapid and radical alterations of focus in Wakoski's lines blur spatial distinctions between night and roses, face, arm, and the inside of the body, until everything seems equally bursting, hot, fragrant, and in flux. The extreme vitality of flowers and body approaches the obscene, as in Plath it approaches the predatory. Though wrinkled, there is nothing frail or weak in the blossoms of either woman poet. That the identification of flowers with feminine sexuality can be unnerving when it ceases to be a dead metaphor and is resurrected as a genuine sensual observation is the point in a Marina La Palma poem:

> In a shop there are dark red
> and purple flowers growing from a pot.
> My fingers hesitate, then press against their
> folds—which yield only a little
> and give no sign that they've been touched.
> "Like intestines" the woman says.
> To me they are inside
> vagina convoluted folds.
> I hesitate before I say it
> thinking it might shock her
> obvious and careful point of view.[25]

A second image is water. When Adrienne Rich writes her major quest poem "Diving into the Wreck," or when Sharon Barba in "A Cycle of Women" imagines entering "that dark watery place," both poets accept a woman-water identification held in common with Shakespeare's Cleopatra, identified with the fertile and capricious Nile, or with Milton's Eve, whose first act in *Paradise Lost* is to kneel and behold her own image in water, where Adam at the moment of his creation sprang upright and looked at the sky. We recall the sea-mother in Whitman's "Out of the Cradle" and the mermaids of Prufrock's plunge into memory, into fantasy, into that brief moment of womblike ease before he wakes and chokes on mortal air. Throughout our literature, descent into water signifies danger or death, consistently associated with the feminine. If Conrad recommends "in the destructive element immerse," he does not mean to minimize its alien quality.

Women poets who make the same plunge also evoke the dangerous and the mysterious, but they tend at the same time to evoke a sense of trust. As the image of the flower shifts in women's poems to represent force instead of frailty, the image of water comes to mean security instead of dread. It is alien, and yet it is home, where one will not be hurt. Rich notes that relaxation rather than force is required to maneuver underwater, and she is confident of finding treasure as well as devastation.

At the deepest point in "Diving into the Wreck" she becomes her deepest self, the androgyne: "I am she . . . I am he." Sharon Barba anticipates, in "The Cycle of Women," that a new Venus will be born from the watery place of the female unconscious and the line of mothers, who will be stronger and less delicate than Botticelli's Venus. Elizabeth Anne Socolow, in a memoir of her own mother, recalls just such an erotic woman—a "tremendous swimmer" who lost wedding band after wedding band in the ocean as if returning to goddesslike purity:

> In the surf, her fingers pleated by immersion,
> she lost rings,
> forgotten dimestore earrings,
> rhinestone brooches clasping shut
> the bosom of her bathingsuit
> because he objected to sharing her deep cleavage
> with strangers on the beach.
>
> Out of the water climbing,
> sturdy thighs over the white shore foam,
> her suit drooped,
> brooches taken by the ocean.
> She studied as she climbed,
> her fingers.

For Marge Piercy in "Unclench Yourself," water is again erotic and female, and the act of copulation is a river of "brown waters" into which a fearful lover must "come all the way" as she promises him he will not drown but will see visions of living things too tender for air.[26] As we will see in chapter five, water for women poets becomes a key image in the representation of erotic gratification, evoking both bodily and emotional intimacies and standing for the dissolving of boundaries not only between self and lover but between lovers and nature.

A third and most compendious image for woman's body is earth. Adored as mother, revered as virgin in the mythologies of countless cultures, Earth is of course always other than the celebrant. "I sing the earth, firmly founded mother of all, venerable grandmother, supporting on her soil all that lives," begins a Homeric hymn. But as de Beauvoir observes, from the moment that man perceives the soil as subject to his tools and his technology, the status of earth declines. She becomes the principle of passive material life divided from the mental or spiritual; and she is always subject to conquest. Annette Kolodny's wittily titled *The Lay of the Land* traces the recurrent metaphor of land-as-woman in American life and letters from ecstatic evocations of the New World's maidenhead in documents of sixteenth-century explorers to the nightmare image of monster-with-child in Norman Mailer, showing how the power of men's fantasies depends consistently on a vision of nature and woman, as alive, fecund, and essentially mindless.[27]

Women who identify their own bodies with earth, however, tend not merely to celebrate the concept of fecundity but to link earth's powers with a critical and subversive intelligence, or with the creative imagination itself. Yosana Akiko in "Mountain Moving Day" makes the mountain a symbol both of women's bodies and of their awakening consciousness. Meridel LeSueur declares, "What strikes you, my sisters, strikes us all. The global earth / is resonant, communicative." Judith McCombs, whose volume *Against Nature: Wilderness Poems* is a critique both of the will to conquer and the will to sentimentalize nature, suggests in "Loving a Mountain" what sensible attitudes might be toward women's, and the earth's, physical, emotional and intellectual existence. While McCombs avoids the feminine pronoun, the parallels between mountain and housewife/mother are unmistakable and amusing:

Learn where the mountain
is tired, where it's unwilling to hold any more,
underfoot or over your head. Learn
the days when the ledges are happy & the great folds smile,
basking like pigs in the light. Stop being jealous
of the dust & the fauna: they got here first
& besides have adapted
better than you will: of course the mountain prefers
them. Learn when it wants you
to get off its back: stop staring, stop grabbing,
stop thinking of it.

The idea of a consciousness indivisible from the earthy body appears as well in Anne Sexton's notorious "In Celebration of My Uterus," a poem which finds unity where the culture propagates division: between a woman's sexuality and her spirituality, her creativity and her procreativity, herself and other women, her private and her public self. It begins with a medical misdiagnosis which is a striking trope for the culture's misdiagnosis of women. Sexton's opening is euphoric, buoyant, hyperbolic:

They wanted to cut you out
but they will not . . .
They said you were sick unto dying
but they were wrong.

You are singing like a school girl.
You are not torn.

The poem's central portion compares the uterus with "soil of the fields
. . . roots," and the poet announces, in an engaging combination of
insouciant self-confidence and generosity:

Each cell has a life.
There is enough here to please a nation.
It is enough that the populace own these goods.
Any person, any commonwealth would say of it,
"It is good this year that we may plant again,
and think forward to a harvest."

Then comes another shift, as the poet announces that

Many women are singing together of this:
one is in a shoe factory cursing the machine,
one is at the aquarium tending a seal,
one is dull at the wheel of her Ford,
one is at the toll gate collecting,
one is tying the cord of a calf in Arizona,
one is straddling a cello in Russia,
one is shifting pots on the stove in Egypt,
one is painting her bedroom walls moon color,
one is dying but remembering a breakfast,
one is stretching on her mat in Thailand,
one is wiping the ass of her child,
one is staring out the window of a train
in the middle of Wyoming and one is
anywhere and some are everywhere and all
seem to be singing, although some can not
sing a note. [28]

Sexton's willingness to be flamboyant, to be exhibitionistic, even to be
silly, in a poem of this sort, engages our sympathies. Euphoria is called
for, is appropriate, when one is found not to have cancer. At the same
time, we are being asked to accept some novel notions. The abundance
and fertility of the poet's imagination in inventing her group of women
of all types, from all regions of the globe, must be understood as parallel
to, or an extension of, her uterine health. And the primal selves of
women (presumably also with healthy wombs) "everywhere," notwithstanding appearances, combine to express her joy.
    A chorale of far-flung women cannot be observed from without, pre-

cisely as the continued vitality and fertility of the womb have evaded external discernment. As matter, so spirit. Both, according to this poem, lie within, in the realm of the immanent rather than the transcendent. The function of spirit is to celebrate matter, not to subdue or escape it, and women become mutually connected beings by the participation of spirit in the principle of flesh they commonly share. Sexton has used a conventional fertility-and-harvest symbolism to lure us into a set of perceptions radically opposed to those of the vertical standard.[29]

But Sexton's affirmation occurs in a world defined as exclusively feminine. For a woman, perhaps the most decisively difficult act is to think of herself as powerful, or as more powerful than a man, and capable of influencing the outward world without sacrificing femaleness. Paradoxically, the biological condition which is conventionally seen as most imprisoning woman may also be seen as empowering her, as in Robin Morgan's "The Network of the Imaginary Mother."[30]

Morgan's work has undergone a metamorphosis. In her first volume, *Monster*, published in 1972, the poet is angry but nonetheless a victim: she "ought to be born one-breasted or male / or mindless." In the title piece, a feminist revolution is "labor agony" for her, she is ready to "kick and kill" men into freedom, and wishes her feminine tears were bullets. She accepts the appellation her small son, looking at her genitals, has given her, and concludes, "I am a monster. / And I am proud." Her 1977 volume, *Lady of the Beasts*, is less defensive, more exploratory. In "The Network of the Imaginary Mother," she describes a conversion from flesh-loathing to flesh-affirmation while nursing her dying mother, and defines her biological capacities in terms of goddess-figures including Kali, Demeter, Isis, African and pre-Columbian madonnas, representing a triumphant will to love and nurture. Her husband in this poem is Osiris, a "consort." Her son extends from herself, and the mother-son dyad is set in opposition to the history of patriarchal violence. A key passage describes the act of nursing as simultaneously personal and political. In this lucid and reverberating instance of the woman artist as thief-getting-her-own-back, it is not the God-man of the gospels but a nursing woman who says to her own son, and by extension all children, envisioning a world unthreatened by violence and famine:

Take. Eat. This is my body,
this real milk, thin, sweet, bluish,
which I give for the life of the world . . .
an honest nourishment
alone able to sustain you.

Biological fact and spiritual significance here become indistinguishable.
If Morgan's vision of power, like Plath's of revenge, is fantasy, it is nevertheless shared by many women writers, as we will see in chapter five.
The idea of a maternal politics implies a coherent and consistent world-
view which would eliminate the burden of conflict between humanity
and nature, between individual and species, between woman's body and
social change.

5

for the word *tree* I have been shown a tree
and for the word *rock* I have been shown a rock,
for stream, for cloud, for star
this place has provided firm implication and answering
   but where he is the image for *longing*:
      —A. R. Ammons, *Sphere: The Form of a Motion* [31]

      the longing
      that i know
is in the Stone also
      —May Swenson, "Evolution" [32]

We know ourselves to be made from this earth. We know this
earth is made from our bodies. For we see ourselves. And we are
nature. We are nature seeing nature. We are nature with a concept of nature.
      —Susan Griffin, *Woman and Nature* [33]

Contemporary women poets who name their bodies through nature
and natural processes tend, we have seen, to propose transformed
meanings for these images and hence for themselves. This leads to a
larger question. Can we find in women's poetry a revisionist view of the
world's body, of nature?

The critic Estella Lauter has argued that women poets today are collectively generating a new myth of the relationship between consciousness and the natural order, which involves neither subservience nor
special status for the human. Nature in this myth may be variously personified as mother, sibling, alternate self, but is always that in which we
are embedded rather than that from which we are divided. The significant point to Griffin's "we are nature with a concept of nature," in
Lauter's view, is that it neither abandons the idea of consciousness nor

assumes that consciousness precipitates a loss of naturalness.[34] Judith McCombs similarly suggests that a "myth of woman allied with nature" is emerging in many women writers for whom nature is neither virginal, nor seductive, nor maternally bounteous, yet is equivalent to, at a level with, the female self.[35]

Given such hypotheses, it is significant that a poet as meticulous in his naturalism as A. R. Ammons retains traces of the vertical standard which locates mind above matter and leaves him stranded—half self-pitying, half self-congratulatory—in a world to which he does not finally belong. In the dedicatory poem of Ammons' long philosophical *Sphere*, addressed to Harold Bloom, the poet stands at a "summit" only to find that "having been brought this far by nature I have been / brought out of nature / and nothing here shows me the image of myself"; for he discovers, surveying rocks, trees and outer space, that "nothing answered my word *longing.*" Nature, he concludes, has shut him out, and his defining activity as a poet is the creation of "an image for *longing*" made imperative by this exclusion. By contrast, Susan Griffin imagines penetrating an earth that feels, suffers, and endures like herself:

> As I go into her, she pierces my heart. As I penetrate further, she unveils me. When I have reached her center, I am weeping openly. I have known her all my life, yet she reveals stories to me, and these stories are revelations and I am transformed . . . She is as delicate as I am; I know her sentience; I feel her pain and my own pain comes into me, and my own pain grows large and I grasp this pain with my hands, and I open my mouth to this pain, I taste, I know, and I know why she goes on, under great weight, with this great thirst, in drought, in starvation, with intelligence in every act does she survive disaster.[36]

Again by contrast, May Swenson in "Evolution" takes for granted both connection and distinction between human and other forms of existence, declaring with nursery rhyme charm—as if nothing could be more obvious—that as "the stone / would like to be / Alive like me," and the tree would like to be mobile, and the lion to be articulate, so she yearns for the stone's endurance, the tree's annual rebirths, the lion's lawlessness.

Swenson, one of the chief nature poets writing in America today, is playfully matter-of-fact when dealing with man's wish to transcend nature, remarking, "Earth will not let go our foot" (p. 91), or teasingly deflating the stance of the alienated intellectual:

```
        If I could get
   out  of my
  head  and
  into  the
 world.
        What am I saying?
   Out  of my
 head?
        Isn't my
 head
   in   the
 world?          ("Out of my Head," p. 215)
```

She is similarly impudent when encountering the mind-body problem. "Body my house / my horse my hound / what will I do / when you are fallen," she asks ("Question," p. 292). In "Ending," she tries to picture her soul exiting her body—through her big toe—and imagines the soul's transparence as "his little jelly / belly." Swenson's humorous comfort with her own body extends to the body of the world. She can describe a physicist's model of an expanding and contracting universe as a large lung periodically inhaling and exhaling ("Models of the Universe," p. 155). Her poems can believably and without sentiment imagine what it is like being a cat, a lion, a bee, a caterpillar-turned-butterfly, a bull in a bullring, a chick being born, a bronco in a rodeo who

```
        bursts into five-way
  motion: bucks, pitches, swivels, humps, and twists,
  an all-over-body-sneeze, ("Bronco Busting Event #1," p. 10)
```

or a mother ape being suckled while briskly delousing her infant, in a poem significantly and generically entitled "Motherhood" (pp. 132–33). Whatever she describes, Swenson's extraordinary tactility, her feel for texture and structure, her perfect renderings of motion, bespeak a mind lovingly engaged by the physical.

Like Swenson, Maxine Kumin assumes without question our rootedness in nature. Kumin has for twenty years explored the pastoral tragi-comedy of what she calls "the continuum," describing the daily acts of a family and farm life nested among animal and plant lives. For Kumin there is no hierarchy: humans, animals, and plants uncannily resemble each other, are often metaphorically interchangeable, enjoy the same energies, and suffer the same downfalls. "Feeding Time" means the poet feeds horses, dog, birds, cat, and finally herself and her husband,

"My soup, your bread . . . slicings and soppings" in twin blue bowls, while "Time that blows on the kettle's rim / waits to carry us off." [37] Love defies more than one kind of boundary: in "The Incest Dream" a sorrowing hangman brings her beloved dying brother's severed penis, "pressed as faithfully / as a wild flower," for the poet to keep "and lie back down in my lucky shame" (p. 27). When the brother has died, "Retrospect in the Kitchen" (p. 29) tells of the forty pounds of plums she takes from his tree and carries three thousand miles to preserve: "Love's royal color / the burst purple fruit bob up."

The making of preserves is a recurrent image in Kumin's poems and is a metaphor for what she wants to do with those she loves as both poet and woman. Creatures surround her, she sees and touches them, she foresees their doom. At times she is their doom's guilty agent, as when lambs must be slaughtered or woodchucks shot. At times she contemplates the uses of horseflesh and human flesh, her mare and herself:

Amanda, you'll be going
to Alpo or to Gaines
when you run out of luck;
the flesh flensed from your bones
your mammoth rib cage rowing
away to the renderer's
a dry canoe on a truck

while I foresee my corpse
slid feet first into fire
light as the baker's loaf
to make of me at least
a pint of potash spoor.
I'm something to sweeten the crops
when the clock hand stops.   ("Thinking of Death and Dog
    Food," p. 139)

With the same sensuous precision, she applauds life's persistence, as young plants in the pea patch

        saying dance with me,
    saying do me, dangle their intricate
    nuggety scrota,   ("Pea Patch," p. 11)

or plowed fields "release a sweet rancidness / warm as sperm," ("Relearning the Language of April," p. 12). The tender bawdiness of such metaphors is typical for Kumin, enabling her to be celebratory without sentimentality. Kumin has spoken of her poems of kinship and parenting as "tribal poems," [38] and if one feels in her nature poems as well a practical, nonmystical, humorous, and resolute relationship to a world perceived as animate and mortal, this too is "tribal."

A final example may suggest how women poets are delicately but firmly reversing the assumption of man's division from nature. One of Robert Frost's most characteristic poems, "The Most of It," describes the futile efforts of his protagonist to provoke from the wilderness a "counter-love, original response." [39] All the answer he receives for his cries is the apparition of a great buck who swims the lake, "And stumbled through the rocks with horny tread, / And forced the underbrush—and that was all." We may read "The Most of It" as emblematic of nature's indifference to man or, more ironically, as illustrating man's incapacity to love what is authentically natural. Either way, communication is impossible.

To the pessimism of this parable, Elizabeth Bishop lays an allaying hand in "The Moose," one of her last and finest poems. [40] Almost every element in "The Moose" seems to respond to something in "The Most of It." For Frost's *isolé* who "thought he kept the universe alone," we have a quotidian busful of folk traveling through Canadian back country at nightfall. For his (possibly self-deluded) cries of lonely love, we have the soothing murmurs of the elderly couple Bishop half-hears, half-invents at the back of the bus recounting old tales of lives and deaths. Finally, for the violent appearance and disappearance of the buck, Bishop gives us a moose who emerges from "the impenetrable wood," stops the bus, and sniffs at it. Symbolically impressive in size ("Towering"), its aura combines spiritual loftiness and domestic familiarity—it is "high as a church, / homely as a house / (or, safe as houses)." As the passengers gaze, one recognizes—"Look! It's a she!"—and the recognition leads to Bishop's quiet climax:

> Taking her time,
> she looks the bus over,
> grand, otherworldly.
> Why, why do we feel
> (we all feel) this sweet
> sensation of joy?

The magic of this epiphany has everything to do with synthesis, nothing to do with alienation. The femaleness of nature has manifested itself in a creature that responds and is responded to. Both passengers and moose "look," and the bus driver after the event echoes, "Look at that, would you," as if completing the triplet utterance of fairy tale or ritual. The community of passengers is crystallized into unity by the encounter, and the poet is mysteriously able to speak for them all. "The Moose" is, as always with Bishop, low-key, casual, undidactic. But we are, as readers, tacitly asked a question. Why do we feel this joy? The answer can only be that we have recognized, in nature, ourselves.

6

Don't you get tired of wanting
to live forever?
Don't you get tired of saying Onward?
　　—Margaret Atwood, "Circe/Mud Poems"[41]

but lust too is a jewel
a sweet flower and what
pure happiness to know
all our high-toned questions
breed in a lively animal.
　　—Adrienne Rich, "Two Songs"[42]

Poets have perennially occupied themselves with discovering analogies between the macrocosm of the world and the microcosm of the self. For many women poets at present, the microcosm means, emphatically, a physical self from which it is neither possible nor desirable to divide mental or emotional existence. A particular endeavor of twentieth-century thought has involved a questioning of distinctions between private and public life in order to understand how each influences and reflects the other. Here too, women poets seem inclined to insist that we begin with the body to understand the body politic. None of these poets seems disposed to celebrate a world of "transcendent" public action at the cost of minimizing the given physical self. Neither do they advocate the body at the expense of intelligence.

For some, the dominant experience of life in the flesh is suffering. We can scarcely deny the public validity of such an apprehension in the light of history. For other writers, the relation between private and public means a conflict between what used to be called appearance and reality. To cosmetize or not to cosmetize? This is a battle fought on the fields of the skin as well as on more dignified terrain. For still others, the body is felt as a strength, a kind of connective tissue uniting human beings at a level beneath the particularities of individual ego or circumstance, a set of capacities both socially and personally valuable. Finally, in their treatment of nature as continuous rather than discontinuous with the human self, we find perhaps the largest outcome of women's inclination to identify the self first of all with the body, and the body with reality.

Compared with the variety and richness of work by women in this area, that of most male poets at present appears constrained and un-original. The exceptions—poets such as Ginsberg, Bly, and Kinnell, for whom identity is inescapably anatomical—make the general polariza-tion clear. If we may say that women have contrived to make a conti-nental landscape out of the secret gardens to which they have been forcefully confined, we may say by the same token that men have en-dured a certain self-imposed exile. Distance remains a virtue in the male poetic establishment, almost like a corollary of the training which defines the masculine body exclusively as tool or weapon, forbids it to acknowledge weakness or pain, and deprives it accordingly of much po-tential sensitivity to pleasure—a sensuous man is an "effeminate" man—apart from the pleasures associated with combat or conquest. Control—of mind over matter, of orderly word over disorderly emo-tion—remains a literary desideratum. The discourse of male bonding may derive from big and little game hunting and the tennis court, or from allusions to the responses of women in bed. These are the safe, sane, blushproof topics.

Yet we are just beginning, in fields outside of literature such as ge-netics, biochemistry, biosociology, neurophysiology, and neurophysics, to decipher the code of our natural selves. We have scarcely arrived at the threshhold of examining the relations between body, mind, and be-havior. What we will learn will be complex and unpredictable, and will require poets for its interpretation. As we enter this new project of hu-man self-examination it will be valuable to remember, as Adrienne Rich points out, that our inquiring intellects cannot be detached from our sexuality. And as Margaret Atwood's earth goddess reminds the hero who is about to sail away, we cannot transcend mortality by wanting to.

Men also look in mirrors, experience troublesome and delicious sen-sations, contribute to the generation of species, and ride throughout their lifetimes the tide of emotions influenced by glandular secretions. They too get ill, grow old and withered, and are, in sum, precisely as rooted in nature as women. Will they in due time acknowledge this condition? Will women begin comparing the bodies of men to flowers? Confronting old age, Yeats divided himself into two beings: an old man craving fiery purification from the flesh and an old woman—Crazy

Jane—raucously declaring her satisfaction with it. We must assume that the discoveries women poets are making about bodily experience, and the verbal strategies employed to name their discoveries, will enter common usage and become readily available to men as well as women. Crazy Jane stands at the foot of the tower, inviting the man to come down.

4 *Herr God, Herr Lucifer: Anger, Violence, and Polarization*

I am asham'd that women are so simple,
To offer war where they should kneel for peace,
Or seek for rule, supremacy and sway,
When they are bound to serve, love and obey.
    —Shakespeare, *The Taming of the Shrew* [1]

They fucked me over because I was wrong . . .
which is exactly like South Africa
penetrating into Namibia . . .
and if
after Namibia and if after Angola and if after Zimbabwe
and if after all of my kinsmen and women resist even to
self-immolation of the villages
we lose nevertheless what will the big boys say will they
claim my consent
    —June Jordan, "Poem About My Rights" [2]

If Mary's eyes were Mary's mouth
she would not stammer b b but
but say straight
I hate.
    —Phyllis Koestenbaum, "oh I can't she says" [3]

Is anger literary? Is it gendered? Among the passions dignified by literature, anger commands a secure place. "Sing, Goddess, the anger of Peleus' son Achilles" is Homer's opening directive to the Muse in *The*

Iliad. Wrathful deities provide the motivating energy for much of Greek legend, epic, and tragic drama, and without this passion we would have no quarrel between Achilles and Menelaus, no slaughter of the suitors at the end of *The Odyssey*, no Prometheus or Oedipus. A conception of aggrieved divinity continues to validate the power of rage in postclassical literature. "Touch me with noble anger," Lear begs the gods. "And let not women's weapons, water drops, / Stain my man's cheeks"; and we mysteriously believe that the old king's wrath, as if it reflected some infusion of a divine attribute, is indeed noble, heroic, heightening.

The poet-prophets Milton and Blake draw deeply on funds of Old Testament ire. The visionary Dante sets his political foes in Hell, by the grace of the Love that moves the sun and the other stars. Jonathan Swift, resting where savage indignation no longer lacerates his heart, reminds us that anger is the driving force of satire. Among the great modern poets, disgust, fury, and rage animate Lawrence, Pound, and Jeffers to dramatic effect. Williams, offended at puritanism and pedantry, burns down an entire library in *Paterson.* The Russian poet Mandelstam exclaims, "Literary anger! Without you, how could I have eaten the earth's salt?"[4]

A proudly angry or indignant man who writes a fierce poem, a violent polemic, a bitter manifesto, may thereby influence literary history. An indignant woman, on the other hand, is privately a nuisance, publicly a joke, at least since the Middle Ages.[5] *Shrew, virago, harridan, termagent, fishwife, battle-ax,* and *scold* are terms for which the language possesses no male equivalent. Even our contemporary term *bitch* lacks a proper mate, for a bitch is a woman with a cruel tongue, and the verb form signifies "to complain," but a bastard can be a bastard without a word spoken. Thanks to the asymmetry of male and female roles in life and art, Shakespeare's Kate in *The Taming of the Shrew,* whose sharp wit makes her so theatrically attractive, must be tormented and tamed by her husband into connubial submissiveness. Nietzsche's remark, "Woman learns how to hate in the degree that she forgets how to charm," expresses the continuing social consensus, as does, a bit later, Yeats' "A Prayer for My Daughter." Hoping his infant girl will become the generous mistress of a ceremonious household rather than a troublemaking political activist like Maud Gonne, Yeats prays, "An intellectual hatred is the worst, / So let her think opinions are accursed."[6] At best, if she has the good luck to be beautiful, the angry woman becomes an aesthetic-erotic object:

> Or if thy mistress some rich anger shows,
>> Imprison her soft hand, and let her rave,
>> And feed deep, deep, upon her peerless eyes.[7]

Keats loves it, as the saying goes, when she's mad. But the literary expression of female indignation, personal or collective, by women writers is unacceptable. "Hence she was labelled harpy, shrew and whore," recalls Adrienne Rich of Mary Wollstonecraft. When Elizabeth Barrett Browning published the abolitionist poem "A Curse for a Nation" in *Poems Before Congress*, the reviewer for *Blackwood's* thought she had been "seized with a fit of insanity" and hoped she would remember in the future that "to bless and not to curse is woman's function."[8] Caroline Kizer opens "Pro Femina" by summarizing the dilemma of witty Kate's post-Freudian counterpart:

From Sappho to myself, consider the fate of women.
How unwomanly to discuss it! Like a noose or an albatross
     necktie,
The clinical sobriquet hangs us: cod-piece coveters.[9]

To consider and discuss are masculine activities; to question women's fate is to question nature, for nature and destiny are one; a woman who places herself in a category with Sappho is immodest; the obvious diagnosis is penis envy. "Albatross necktie" picturesquely suggests the guilt women suffer, as at a primal crime, when they fail to accept their fate. As the critic Jane Marcus comprehensively observes, "the terrible swift sword is for fathers and kings, not daughters and subjects."[10] For the articulation of female anger, like female body language, is culturally taboo, and a woman who breaks this taboo does so at her own peril.

To remember the history of the shrew is to begin to understand the suave tone of Virginia Woolf in *A Room of One's Own* (1928), ironically wondering why there are no great women poets while imagining one or another potentially great woman poet over the centuries, "crazed with the torture that her gift had put her to." The most eloquent argument against anger in women's writing appears, duplicitously enough, in a work which seems designed to induce it. Woolf has several linked objectives in *A Room of One's Own*. One is to dissect the economic, social, and intellectual system of patriarchy under which women have been barred from writing. A second is to define the conditions of economic and social independence under which creativity can occur. A third is to define art itself, in its highest form.

Woolf argues neither that rage defeminizes a woman nor that it subjects her to hostile criticism, but only that it produces inferior art. Of Shakespeare, her model of the perfect artist, she declares, "All desire to protest, to preach, to proclaim an injury, to pay off a score, to make the world the witness of some hardship or grievance, was fired out of him and consumed. Therefore his poetry flows from him free and unimpeded." Jane Austen, Woolf's epitome of the successful woman artist, likewise wrote "without hate, without bitterness, without fear, without protest, without preaching." In contrast, of the seventeenth-century poet Lady Winchelsea, Woolf feels it "a thousand pities that the woman . . . whose mind was turned to nature and reflection, should have been forced to anger and bitterness." Commenting on Duchess Margaret of Newcastle, who wrote that "women live like Bats or Owls, labour like Beasts, and die like Worms," Woolf regrets that Margaret's "passion for poetry" was "disfigured and deformed" by rage. Comparing Austen and Charlotte Brontë to the latter's disfavor, her primary charge is that Brontë's work is "deformed and twisted" by indignation. Toward the close of the essay, Woolf summarizes her contention that art and protest are intrinsically incompatible:

> It is fatal for a woman to lay the least stress on any grievance; to plead even with justice any cause; in any way to speak consciously as a woman . . . for anything written with that conscious bias is doomed to death. It ceases to be fertilized.[11]

The tuned ear may hear faintly echoing, in Woolf's metaphors of artistic deformity, the conviction that the unsubmissive woman is unnatural, a physical monstrosity. The idea that even a touch of indignation dooms a work to death on aesthetic grounds suggests—is it unwittingly?—the more literal punishments of women which *A Room of One's Own* has already chronicled. We remember the endless line of penalizing fathers and patronizing professors to whom creative women have had to bow; we remember Woolf's hypothetical Judith Shakespeare, her brother's equal, dead at the crossroads of the Elephant and Castle. Woolf's sense of great art as sublimation, elevated above the experiences whence it arises, cleansed of the stains of personal feeling, expressed a modernist creed which she shares, for example, with Eliot and Joyce—and which has an unmistakable aura of sexual taboo clinging to it.

A few passages near the conclusion of *A Room of One's Own* directly subvert the author's position:

> So long as you write what you wish to write, that is all that matters; and whether it matters for ages or only for hours, nobody can say. But to sacrifice a hair of the head of your vision, a shade of its colour, in deference to some Headmaster with a silver pot in his hand or to some professor with a measuring rod up his sleeve, is the most abject treachery, and the sacrifice of wealth and chastity

which used to be said to be the greatest of human disasters, a mere flea-bite in comparison.[12]

For what if a woman's vision is angry? What if the hair on the head of her vision stands up hissing like Medusa's? It is difficult to imagine that, in Woolf's phrasing, "if we have the habit of freedom and the courage to write exactly as we think," women will want to tiptoe around the expression of anger. Yet can one be simultaneously angry and a great artist? The question seems baffling—so artful is Woolf, so persuasive even now is modernist aestheticism—until we cease thinking about Shakespeare for a moment and think about Dante.

Woolf's own strategy, of course, is quintessentially duplicitous. On the one hand she defines the sufferings of female intellect under patriarchy, employing novelistic and rhetorical skills that might make a stone weep with rage; on the other hand her tone remains light, arch, merely mocking, condemning the passion she provokes. It is as if the *Communist Manifesto* were written in a charmingly ironic style and expressly reminded the working classes at all costs to avoid revolution. It is agitating and exasperating that Woolf should appear so cool, and it is the most perfect signal of a simmering under the censor's lid.

Between Woolf's time and our own, a revolution has occurred. For many readers, and for many writers, the overwhelming sensation to be gotten from contemporary women's poetry is the smell of camouflage burning, the crackle of spite, free at last, the whirl and rush of flamelike rage that has so often swept the soul, and as often been damped down, so that we never thought there could be words for it. A moment arrives when the volcano erupts, the simmering blood boils over, the fire breaks out. Like the imperative of "writing the body," the imperative of this moment has become almost an axiom in feminist poetry and criticism. "It is always what is under pressure in us," remarks Adrienne Rich in an essay on Dickinson called "Vesuvius at Home," "especially under pressure of concealment—that explodes in poetry." "I still couldn't believe—I still can't—how angry I could become," writes Robin Morgan, describing "something like a five-thousand-year buried anger." "Strong women," writes Audre Lorde, "know the taste / of their own hatred." Susan Griffin's "A Woman Defending Herself" chants a litany: "You are a woman who is angry. / You are a woman who is tired. / You are a woman clear in her rage. / And they are afraid of you."[13] The release of what we could call suppressed passion, were the passion not so thoroughly informed by astute analysis, becomes one of the most recognizable signs of the new poetry.

The critic Jane Marcus, exploring the history of repression, disguise, and articulation of anger in women's writing, argues that "self-preservation is the source of anger" and is necessary for the artist. Marcus' conclusion expresses a common feminist faith: "When the fires of our rage have burnt out, think how clear the air will be for our daughters. They will write in joy and freedom only after we have written in anger."[14] But the story of female rage as a literary phenomenon is more subtle than the expressive-purgative process implied by the quotes above. We can in fact distinguish within it three patterns of an increasing order of complexity: the victimization scenario and the attack on male domination; the response of violence; and the critique of polarization as such.

To begin, it is clear that the women's poetry movement coincides with an outpouring of what we can call victimization writing. Men in victimization poems embody a cultural script in which masculine power, intrinsically violent and tyrannical, dominates the concentric worlds of personal life and society, supported by myths of superior male rationality and, ultimately, male divinity. Women in victimization poems submit, angrily complying in their own powerlessness, as if three centuries had scarcely altered the confession of Shakespeare's Kate that a woman's man is "Thy lord, thy life, thy keeper, / Thy head, thy sovereign." Typically, victimization writing is clear, powerful, and accessible, deploying familiar gendered scenarios—relying, for the most part, on our ability to recognize the gendered gestures and rhetoric built into our culture.

Second, as a partial consequence of women's discovery of female victimization, we have an immense explosion of violence in women's poetry today, an articulation of a need which may indeed have been buried for three thousand years. Much of this writing is highly inventive in its deployment of gender-saturated metaphor and profoundly subversive both in its exploration of prohibited emotion and in its attack on our culture's systemic phallocentricity, that potent combination of might and right ascribed to the deity and his sons. The release of fantasy in these poems is a striking example of the volcanic return of the repressed. What has been less often recognized is that the violence in women's poems is directed as often against the self as against what Adrienne Rich calls the oppressor, and that here too we have the bringing into literary consciousness of elements long present and long denied in our psychic and cultural netherworlds.

Finally, as I will try to show in the last portion of this chapter, the most exploratory and experimental of women's anger poems, far from offering literary catharsis or suggesting that dominance-submission structures can be magically dissolved by a righteous retaliation, rather intensify our sense of an ineluctable polarization in which the author is herself entrapped and entraps her readers. Formally, conceptually and emotionally, such poems are difficult to read; but they are among the most impressive documents the women's poetry movement has produced.

2

By God! if wommen hadde written stories
As clerkes han withinne hir oratories,
They wolde han writen of men more wikednesse
Than al the mark of Adam may redresse.
        —Chaucer, "The Wife of Bath's Prologue" [15]

well i laughed the apologizing
oh i don't want no trouble laugh
over the years pretending to cook
pretending to like babying
my husband
        —Lyn Lifshin, "The No More Apologizing the No More
        Little Laughing Blues" [16]

every man I have loved
was like an army.
        —Marge Piercy "All Clear" [17]

Like charity, women's anger begins at home. During the early years of the women's movement in particular, feminist publications over-flowed with mad-housewife poems, off-our-back poems, poems of the oppressive husband, lover, father, poems describing rape, battery, ex-ploitation. The most interesting of these personal victimization poems tend to uncover the principles which animate persons and to suggest that dominance-submission patterns cut across social boundaries, as-signing comparably powerless roles to women of every social class and subculture. Thus, for example, Cynthia Macdonald takes a post-Ibsen view of bourgeois marriage in "A Family of Dolls' House Dolls," where a child describes a doll family in which the father is very smart but does not say anything nice to the mother even when she is wearing her ear-rings. The father is so smart he always looks things up when he can't answer them, even during dinner "when the maid is just passing him the platter." Similarly, in Marge Piercy's "Right Thinking Man," an au-tocrat of the breakfast table drops some choice ironies on the wife who after twenty years fails to understand "the perfection of egg protein/ neither runny nor turned to rubber" and turns to his professorial work:

> Advancing into his study he dabbles a forefinger
> in the fine dust on his desk and calls his wife
> who must go twitching to reprimand
> the black woman age forty-eight who cleans the apartment.
> Outside a Puerto Rican in a uniform
> is standing in the street to guard his door
> from the riffraff who make riots on television,
> in which the university that pays him owns much stock.

Masculine self-love and feminine self-suppression hipster-style are the themes in Diane Di Prima's cameo prose-poem "The Quarrel," in which the poet resents doing dishes while her lover works on his drawings, but feels it would be "uncool" to complain. "Hey, hon," he cheerfully informs her in the punch line, "It says here Picasso produces fourteen hours a day." Another snapshot of Bohemian domesticity is Jana Harris' "Fix Me a Salami Sandwich, He Said," which opens with the modern lover's complaint, "I don't wanna fix it myself / if you love me / you'll fix me a sandwich," and carries him through a set of grievances and remonstrances including "let's have coffee together for once,/ he said, / . . . . I don't like these raw vegetables / I don't like this smelly cheese / it smells like cunt, / he said, / it smells like I have pussy / all over my fingers."

In one of a series of victimization poems Harris has composed using tape-recorded interviews with working-class West Coast women, we learn how a gold miner's wife was beaten by the men she cooked and laundered for and "said she was spread so thin / she felt like glass." In another of Harris' poems, when a salmon fisher doesn't want to be told to come home sober, we get a poor woman's version of *The Mill on the Floss*:

> Women, he said
> his wood-grip gun
> smackin me across the face,
> I oughta kill you if I can't
> beat some sense into your head . . .
> And then, she said,
> it was just like bein
> a little girl back home
> playin Gin Rummy with my brother:
> When I'd win he'd come

at me with a hammer
and when I screamed
Ma'd slap my face, sayin,
you must have provoked him, Eudora.

Systematic abuse of women in Ntozake Shange's poetic drama *For Colored Girls Who Have Considered Suicide When the Rainbow Is Enuf* runs a gamut from sexual harassment ("come over here bitch cant ya see this is $5") to the insults men add to injury: "O baby, ya know i waz high, i'm sorry," "shut up, bitch, i told you i waz sorry." The play's scalding climax is the story told by Crystal of her lover Beau, who has come home crazy from combat in Southeast Asia. He beats her, cheats on her, knifes her, and in a final scene drops their two children out a window.[18]

The themes of male sexuality, brutality, and possessiveness also coincide in women's rape poems,[19] including Shange's anguished "With No Immediate Cause," Audre Lorde's "Need," and June Jordan's "The Rationale, or, She Drove Me Crazy," a linguistic tour de force in which we cannot tell the difference between an unattended woman getting raped and a Porsche on the street getting stolen. Adrienne Rich's "Rape" and Piercy's "Rape Poem" delineate the double abuse of a rape victim in a society which tacitly blames the victim:

There is no difference between being raped
and being bit on the ankle by a rattlesnake
except that people ask if your skirt was short
and why you were out alone anyhow.

Sexuality and violence often lie behind women's accusations of the father. Plath's "Daddy" is a domestic Nazi and an attractive devil; so is her husband. Rich in "After Dark" explores her rage at a father whose intellectual authoritarianism was a stuck record, repeating "I know you better than you know yourself." Her later "Sibling Mysteries" assails the father "that took, that took, whose taking seemed a law," who appropriated the mother's body desired by the daughter. Sonia Sanchez attacks a womanizing father who needs "so many black / perfumed bodies weeping" underneath him. Lynn Sukenick remembers a father's coldness to a mother and his excessive warmth to her. Judith Kroll's "daddy whose name / is death," after condemning the poet for flirting and tempting, comes to tuck her "in / & in / & in."[20]

The typical domestic victimization poem is dramatic or narrative. Like an effective fiction, it seizes the revealing gesture, the incriminating scrap of dialogue, to create a sense of documented authenticity.

Often it is obtrusively antiliterary. The black street talk in writers like Shange and Jordan, the working-class language in writers like Harris, diagram the skull beneath the skin of civilization. At the same time, the best of these poems function as a critique of language, revealing the connections between acts of domination and the rhetoric of domination, of which we are usually unconscious.

When the poet moves from personal to political life, where truth is commonly more atrocious than fiction and where figurative language may be suspect, devices associated with factual documentation are particularly useful. To a media-oriented reader, a pastiche of newspaper and newsmagazine prose styles can provide a rope of credibility which fastens the poet's metaphor—often appearing only at the poem's close— to earth. For example, Audre Lorde's "Power," a meditation on violence, turns on the shooting of a black child by a white policeman who

> stood over the boy with his cop shoes in childish blood
> and a voice said "Die you little motherfucker" and
> there are tapes to prove that. At his trial
> this policeman said in his own defense
> "I didn't notice the size or nothing else
> only the color." and
> there are tapes to prove that, too.

We, the audience, need to be told about those tapes, those proofs, in order to believe what we might otherwise prefer to doubt. This in turn prepares us to understand a more subtle manifestation of racial and sexual victimization which can only be expressed figuratively. The policeman, the poem goes on to say, was acquitted by eleven white men

> and one black woman who said
> "They convinced me" meaning
> they had dragged her 4′10″ black woman's frame
> over the hot coals of four centuries of white male approval
> until she let go the first real power she ever had
> and lined her own womb with cement
> to make a graveyard for our children.

Susan Griffin's "Breviary" describes, from the point of view of a photo-journalist, a massacre in which a girl is raped and killed and her mother stabbed. The poem juxtaposes this incident with surrealistic images of a sacrificed virgin, implying that the individual incident plays out a generic pattern of ritual violence against passive women which antedates and includes Christianity. Here again journalistic technique provides the credibility, while fantasy provides the interpretation of which journalism is incapable. Robin Morgan's "The Network of the Imaginary Mother" evokes visions of cross-cultural goddess figures punctuated with documented annals of witch burnings in England and Europe between the fifteenth and the mid-eighteenth centuries. Another poem, "Documentary," quotes an Ethiopian tribeswoman interviewed in a film describing her girlhood clitoridectomy, the rattling leg irons she wears "for decoration and for bondage," the scarification of her body after a tribal battle, and the custom that babies beat dogs, men beat girls and women:

> "His whip is always in his hand, and when you run
> he only sits. Where could you go? . . .
> Do women have erections or go cattle raiding
> or hunting?" she laughs. "Do women have erections or kill?
>   No,"
> she rattles, "women work. Women kill lice."

Part of the strategy of public poems which rely on journalism, photography, television, and so on, is that they remind us of how in ordinary life we trust what we have been taught to consider objective authority. But the poet's personal witness can also serve as authority, if the writing is journalistically flat and emotionless enough. Carolyn Forché's prose-poem "The Colonel," perhaps the most overwhelming single piece in her powerful volume *The Country Between Us*, begins plainly. "What you have heard is true. I was in his house." It recounts in short sentences the occasion of a dinner in a general's home in El Salvador, ending when the host, who has been served silently by his wife, leaves the table and returns with a grocery bag which he overturns on the table. It has been filled with human ears.

> They were
> like dried peach halves. There is no other way to say this. He took
> one of them in his hands, shook it in our faces, dropped it into a
> water glass. It came alive there. I am tired of fooling around he
> said. As for the rights of anyone, tell your people they can go fuck
> themselves. He swept the ears to the floor with his arm and held
> the last of his wine in the air. Something for your poetry, no? he
> said.[21]

As a number of these poems already indicate, women poets' indignation at male power is deepened by its rationale of rationality—by the assumption that masculinity represents the superiority of mind and reason, logical objectivity and civilization over mere female emotionality, subjectivity, and corporeality. Many victimization poems are therefore preoccupied with the demystifying of rationalism. Not surprisingly, female bitterness intensifies when it focuses on relationships which are ostensibly loving and on the figure drawn over and over by women in pain and rage, the logocentric lover-antagonist. We recall Plath's archetypally authoritarian male figure in "Lady Lazarus," the composite doctor—Nazi—sideshow manager whom she calls "Herr God, Herr Lucifer." In the eyes of this figure the poet is, she knows, an object to be manipulated, a freak, "your opus . . . your valuable." In Mona Van Duyn's complex and witty "Death by Aesthetics," the same unpleasant being appears as a physician-lover, probably also psychoanalyst, a glacial Doctor Feelgood:

> His fluoroscope hugs her. Soft the intemperate girl,
> disordered. Willing she lies while he unfolds
> her disease, but a stem of glass protects his fingertips
> from her heat, nor will he catch her cold . . .
>
> He hands her a paper. "Goodbye. Live quietly,
> make some new friends. I've seen these stubborn cases
> cured with time. My bill will arrive. Dear lady,
> it's been a most enjoyable diagnosis."

Enemy of the flesh and its sensations, avatar of control, the male is professional and ordered, the female is suppliant and dis-ordered. He is composed and at ease, she is dis-eased. In vain the poet begs for a more intimate connection, a more mutual encounter:

> Meet me, feel the way my body feels,
> and in my bounty of dews, fluxes and seasons,
> orificies, in my wastes and smells,
> see self.

He has already gone, saying, "Don't touch me," and his prescription reads "Separateness." Similar characters appear in Judy Hemschemeyer's "The Carpenters," Jana Harris' "What d'ya Get When You Cross a Gynecologist with a Xerox Machine" and many other doctor poems, all of which represent women as objects being probed by experts whose profession is to care for and heal, and who personally fear and despise, women's bodies.[22]

Contempt and violence, actual or latent, are of course linked. As we know at least from the time of de Sade, and as popular pornography

continues to confirm, masculine rationality nourishes itself on the hatred of female flesh and female emotion, which are perceived as vulnerable to harm and therefore deserving of it. The experimental poet and
playwright Rochelle Owens, in the ironically titled "The Power of Love:
He Wants Shih (Everything)," has composed a sadistic fantasy for a
practitioner of martial arts. The hero explains that a woman's love for
him is his weapon. As her feeling increases, his disappears and is replaced by a gratifying sense of mastery:

> It's heaven's will, shua hsi!
> In my mind I smear the mucus
> from my nose on her breasts . . .
> & drop ants into her two mouths . . .
> I fill up all her orifices—
> I'm very generous . . .
> & she calls me the divinity
> of mountains & streams &
> I think of how it would be
> to piss on her!

More generically, as we have already seen, May Swenson's "Bleeding"
takes the form of a dialogue between a cut and a knife, the former apologetic, the latter angry about being made "messy with this blood."
Though the poet assigns no explicit gender to these speakers—the masochistic cut in fact sounds very much like Shakespeare's Shylock—we
know the bleeding cut feels feminine, we know the knife which wants to
be hard and shiny feels masculine, and we know that our culture, like
both these characters, equates "bleeding" with "feeling" and despises
both. Similarly grim, we remember, is the dialogue in Marge Piercy's
"The Friend," in which a man across the table tells a woman to cut off
her hands because they poke and might touch him, to burn her body
because it is "not clean and smells like sex." She agrees and says she
loves him. He says he likes to be loved and asks if she has cut off her
hands yet. Scarcely less violent, and following similar quasi-ritual lines
which indicate through formal means that the victimization scenario is
habitual and predictable, are poems like Kathleen Fraser's "The Baker's
Daughter," Pat Dienstfrey's "A Solid Plot," Du Plessis' "Breasts," Jill
Hoffman's "The Emperor of Lies," and Celia Gilbert's "Life and Death
of Hero Stick." [23]

If man distinguishes himself by rationality, according to the victim-
ized woman, the rationalist man diminishes all he touches, including
himself, especially when rationalism crystallizes into ideology. Abstrac-

tion dehumanizes, and absolute abstraction dehumanizes absolutely. Of a *soi-disant* revolutionary leader, Piercy remarks:

> The will to be totally rational
> is the will to be made out of glass and steel:
> and to use others as if they were glass and steel.

Similarly dwelling on the crimes committed in Reason's name, Denise Levertov ironically observes that when "smart [i.e., antipersonnel] bombs replace / dumb bombs," the good future technologists who never threw spitballs in class can now aim "directly at the dumb perfection of living targets." Judith Leet's "Missile Launch Officer" describes a tour of duty in a sanitized underground chamber, prepared "for a task that was historical and awesome," in a language equally sanitized. Anne Sexton dreams nightly of a soldier who wants to shake hands. "It would be rude to say no," although he leaves her hand green with the intestines of massacre victims. The soldier explains it's his job as he lowers her into the pit with the other women and babies, "pointing his red penis right at me and saying, / *Don't take this personally.*" [24]

Like bulbs sending out spring shoots around an equestrian statue, clusters of gendered images group themselves around the figure of the male antagonist in women's poetry. Because rationality and control are metaphorically cold in our culture, images of deadly chill are prominent. "I wake to a mausoleum: you are here," says Plath in "The Rival." A woman who has had a miscarriage blames "the cold angels, the abstractions" in Plath's "Three Women." "Who froze the ground under his feet?" asks Erica Jong. A nocturnal intruder in a Sandra Gilbert poem has "a shard of ice / falling into each eye." Lynn Sukenick extends the observation: "Each time he looks at me with his frosty eyes / an animal dies in the local forest / and someone puts on a uniform."

Linked to imagery of abstraction and coldness are images of men as inorganic and mechanical. They wear armor, at once self-protective and self-imprisoning, which glides easily into weaponry. Rich wonders in "The Knight" whether a man can ever be freed of the bright metal which crushes him and leaves his eye "a lump of bitter jelly." "His codpiece gleams like a knife," observes Jong. Man's world in Atwood is "the rational whine of a power mower / cutting a straight swath in the discouraged grass." Piercy's left-wing organizer, dedicated to revolution, "turns himself into a paper clip . . . a vacuum cleaner . . . a machine gun." "If we opened that armor like a can," she asks, "would we find a robot? . . . the ghost of an inflated bond issue?"

Sylvia Plath's father is a stone statue, or the Roman Forum itself, in

"The Colossus." He is a shoe, a boot, and a black swastika in "Daddy."
Her Virgin Mary in "The Magi," recognizing the wise men as enemies,
sees their wisdom and purity as flatness and blankness and is repelled
and frightened by "the ethereal blanks of their face-ovals." The woman
who has miscarried in Plath's "Three Women" believes she has caught,
from the complacent men in the office where she is a secretary, "That
flat, flat, flatness from which ideas, destructions, / Bulldozers, guillo-
tines . . . proceed, / Endlessly proceed." Infertile beings, able to become "important men" only by forming "governments, parliaments, societies," jealous of women's and nature's rotundity, they remind her of
another all-male society:

> I see the Father conversing with the Son.
> Such flatness cannot but be holy.
> "Let us make a heaven," they say.
> Let us flatten and launder the grossness from these souls.

To the withholding man in "A Birthday Present," Plath cries, "O adding
machine . . . must you stamp each piece in purple, / Must you kill
what you can?"

As in this last metaphor, a parallel cluster of images associates man
with money and with the dismal science of economics. Male wealth, it
appears, is no emotional bargain for a woman, notwithstanding the
popularity of the marrying-up plot in female fictions. "Mr. Love," an
early Wakoski antihero, dresses in a blue business suit and fedora, black
patent leather shoes, and carries a glass cane filled with sharks and
whales. He says "I beg your pardon" twice when she tries to address
him, and so she discerns that he is a banker. Perhaps, thinks the reader,
he is Dickinson's God, that sanctioned thief of love whom might made
right. Piercy's revolutionary lover, who hoards love "as if tenderness
saved drew interest," is a capitalist as dangerous as those he battles.
Kathleen Fraser's lover in "Ships" admires her smooth exterior and decides to "order a dozen in different colors," while Van Duyn's "Advice to
a God" reminds Zeus of Danae, whom in the myth he seduced in the
form of a shower of gold—or, in the poet's terms:

> Whose every register your sexual coin
> Crammed full, whose ignorant bush mistook for sunshine
> The cold, brazen battering of your rain.[25]

Chill and remote, abstract and powerful—finally, as all roads in the
Roman Empire lead to Rome, all images of logocentric male dominance in a patriarchal society lead back to God. "Are not religion and

politics the same thing?" asked William Blake, with the idea of over-throwing both. If to Marxists and Freudians religion is the narcotic illusion upon which social stability depends, so from the woman's point of view as well the winning ace up any man's cheating sleeve is his assumed proximity to divinity, insisted on in all our religious traditions. Adam is God's image; Eve, a mere rib and sinful seductress, must in the post-Edenic world submit to her husband. St. Paul and Catholicism agree: as Christ is man's head, so man is woman's, for man was not created for woman, but she for him. Milton and Protestantism likewise agree: "He for God only, she for God in him."

The critic Emily Stipes Watts has observed that in contrast to American men poets, women poets seem peculiarly distant from God.[26] Where male Puritan writers experience numerous visions of God's living presence, Anne Bradstreet explains in her spiritual autobiography that her faith endured through lifelong doubt, without "any miracles to confirm me."[27] Bradstreet's devotional works are almost uniformly poems of submission to a God who corrects her prosperity by pain: sickness, the burning of a house, the death of a grandchild. Where Emerson, Thoreau, and Whitman engage in transcendental transactions with a God relieved of encumbering doctrine, Emily Dickinson retains an Old Testament Father who is mysterious, punitive, and irrevocably remote from herself. He is equally remote, though less dangerous, in the poems of her more pious nineteenth-century sisters, for whom faith promises predictable happiness in the afterlife in exchange for humble suffering here below, but who shrink from imagining either Judge or Redeemer as actual beings.

The contemporary woman poet labors less under this difficulty. What she sees when she looks at the ultimate patriarch is what she sees when she looks at the fathers, rulers, and husbands who are his mortal representatives: a fatal adversary, by whom she is enthralled. As Daniella Gioseffi says in "Woman with Tongue in Cheek,"

> He was Dr. Kildare and Emmett Kelly and Christ,
> he was Leonardo da Vinci and Albert Einstein and Louis
>   Pasteur,
> he was Napoleon and Clark Gable . . .

That is to say he thought he was; perhaps she thought so; perhaps she does still, regardless of knowing better. Women need, as we know, to look up to their men, in order to feel truly feminine. From a lightly mocking poem like Gioseffi's, it is a short step to Piercy's Right Thinking Man, the family tyrant whose egoism is supported by the intellectual

and theological history of the western world: "Plato sits on his right hand
and Aristotle on his left . . . ask any god. / He says they all think like
him." The misogynist professor in Judith Kroll's "Who to Look Out
For" insists that the clear and pure mind of God is polluted by
"Woman—a bagful of gimmicks." In another short step we reach Eloise
Healy's "Dear Friend, My Priest," a critique of the narrow deity necessarily adored by those for whom spirit and flesh must never mingle:

> Your god wears a mosaic suit
> of hard mirrors and his clothes are too small.
> They pinch him like metaphysics . . .
> He has never perspired, has no handkerchief.
> He is barely aware you worship him,
> fretting as he does about his own existence.

The jibe at modern theology hints that God the Father was made in the
image of man's frail *amour-propre*, and from here it is easy to arrive at
Sandra Gilbert's Uncle Death in "The Dream of the Deathpill," who
apologetically offers her a "deathpill . . . like the Eucharist," or Piercy's
Tarot Emperor in "Laying Down the Tower," who "exiled the Female
into blacks and women and colonies . . . invented agribusiness . . .
pissed mercury in the rivers and shat slag on the plains" and is finally
revealed as "the God of the Puritans playing war games on computers,"
or Marie Ponsot's Lord Slaughter, to whom humanity throughout history offers its boy children.[28] All such poems anticipate Mary Daly's
claim that "patriarchy is itself the prevailing religion of the entire
planet, and its essential message is necrophilia."[29] The true religion of
mankind, say these poems, is death worship. Masculine power, sterile
in itself, survives by ruthless suppression of whatever is organic and sensitive, within and outside itself. It creates a God in its own authoritarian
likeness to whom woman submits in her own despite, trapped by her
own gentleness, by her own avoidance of power.

This last point is of painful significance, for the poetry of victimization may direct one's horror almost equally against the hypocrite male's
inaccessibility to emotion and the female's compliance in her victimization. Men, in poems about masculine domination, are always authority
figures associated with technology, abstract and analytical thinking instead of feeling, a will to exercise control, and a gluttonous demand for
admiration. But the women are commonly helpless petitioners. All
they need is love, they make no demands, they will do anything and
permit anything to be done to them, they are all too ready to obey. They
as well as their antagonists believe that to feel is to bleed, and they

would rather bleed than cease to feel. Nor is it an accident that the scenes of female humiliation are often intimately physical. The body, to women, is what is real, but the presumably male idea of the uncleanness of the flesh, and of women's flesh in particular, which we inherit with the rest of our Judeo-Christian dreamlife baggage, is one idea that perhaps few women themselves evade. Self-disgust is a strong drink and to the passive woman an intoxicant: "Every woman adores a Fascist,/ The boot in the face."

Of the many contemporary poems describing the woe associated with love and marriage, among the strongest and saddest is Mona Van Duyn's "The Fear of Flying."[30] Van Duyn has a Browningesque gift for concentrating a short-story's worth of character and plot into a brief poem, and a mature grasp of the facts of marriage. The wife, about to leave on a trip, feels irrational panic. The poem tries to say why. It is not, she thinks, a fear of actual death. Nor has she any delusions about her husband. He is—and here the poem turns acid—a philanderer who plays by turns the cool sophisticated roué, the green youth ("with hair redyed"), the reassuring father figure, the hot sensualist. She recalls being deceived by his warm appearance: "then, if I leaned against you, I'd feel the sleet / Of your look, go numb at your blast / Of contempt." Why, despite her disillusioned scorn, does she dread leaving him? Ruefully she guesses at last, and the poem concludes with her discovery:

> It would seem that I still love you,
> and, like a schoolgirl deep in her first despair,
> I hate to go above you.

Readers of Van Duyn's vintage will recognize the quotation. In a once-popular poem of John Greenleaf Whittier, a boy remembers his first sweetheart and her bashful confidence after she has lost a spelling bee to him, "I hate to go above you . . . Because, you see, I love you." Van Duyn's punning conclusion, identifying physical flight with the concept of moral and intellectual superiority, finely exemplifies the culture's vertical standard of value and the well-trained woman's reluctance to transcend her allotted position.

3

> The air was pure anger . . .
> Breathing was worse than my Screaming Dream where

I try telling *it hurts* and they're glad for me
so grief boils in the bloodstream like rage.

After the smoke put the air out
it rested, hanging over a while: weather
from World War Two or what's coming

then the burnt light began sifting, the day
falling back down, grains of it, black
feathery stuff, skin, the next day
was dirt in the mouth, then all the time
a taste of scar tissue, a feel to the eyes of weeping
as if someone had tried to kill   kill or die.
          —Helen Chasin, "Fire" [31]

You have seen my father whip me.
You have seen me stroke my father's whip.
          —Anne Sexton, "The Death Baby" [32]

To the tacit or actual violence women experience themselves as en-during, many poets are responding with violent language, generating an extraordinary eruption of vengeance fantasies, often ingeniously em-ploying the gestures and signs of sexuality, twisting and inverting the plot of victimization. A man dies, a woman kills him, and the weapon is phallic. Or, since hell hath no fury like a woman scorned, the female is fiery. We become aggressively and punitively sexual, thereby embody-ing what is most dreaded and repressed in conventional feminine imag-ery. And at the same moment, we rewrite the male text.

The earliest and most famous of female vengeance poems in our time, Plath's imagined ritual slaying of the father she loves and hates in "Daddy," uses a quintessentially phallic instrument: "a stake in your fat black heart." As woman, child, and figurative Jew, she makes, we may say, her point. The veiled woman who is her husband's passive posses-sion in Plath's "Purdah" anticipates unloosing "The shriek in the bath,/ The cloak of holes," and the oblique allusion to Clytemnestra's stabbing of Agamemnon obliges the reader actively to imagine western litera-ture's most ancient scene of phallic woman and feminized male. To re-visit that scene is also, not coincidentally, to revisit the climax of T. S. Eliot's "Sweeney Among the Nightingales," where Agamemnon's cry and his "stiff dishonored shroud" are emblematic of the corruptness of sexuality in general and the murderousness of sensual women in particular.

In a central section of one of Adrienne Rich's most important poems,

"The Phenomenology of Anger," the poet dreams of becoming an acetylene torch to burn away the lie of her "true enemy." A composite figure
at once intimate and historical, the poet's enemy is both the killer of
babies in wartime and the unresponding lover. The poet's failed effort at
intimacy reinscribes, from the woman's point of view, the famous
neurotic-wife scene in *The Waste Land*, and strongly implies that he
who feels himself a victim of the wasteland is, if we look more deeply,
one of its creators. Imagery of suppressed potential fire, at once erotic
and destructive, runs through this poem. It is a governing image as well
in the "burning bush" of Marge Piercy's chantlike "A Just Anger" and
the demonic flaming woman in her "The Window of the Woman Burning." Audre Lorde's "The Women of Dan Dance," where female fires
warm what is alive, destroying only "what is already dead," parallels the
image of women's collective love as a "hose" turned on a city or a world
to destroy "poisons, parasites, rats, viruses," in Rich's "Hunger," dedicated to Lorde, which declares that no revolution yet has committed
itself to feeding the world's children.

In her more down-to-earth manner, Diane Wakoski dedicates *The
Motorcycle Betrayal Poems* "to all those men who betrayed me at one
time or another, in hopes they will fall off their motorcycles and break
their necks." In one of the poems of that volume, she imagines shooting
an indifferent lover in the back with a Thompson Contender and watching him topple over once for every man—from her father to the president—who has neglected her. In "They Eat Out," Atwood punctures,
with a fork, a self-important gentleman friend. A particularly ingenious
twist of the phallic knife occurs in Cynthia MacDonald's "Objets d'Art."
Having been told by a stranger in a railway station that she was "a real
ball-cutter," she goes into the business, finds that freezing is the best
method of preservation—and is interested, of course, only in volunteers:

It is an art like hypnosis
Which cannot be imposed on the unwilling victim.

As in Plath's "Purdah," the knives themselves remain tactfully unmentioned by the poem, and there is the added touch of true femininity in
the speaker who is devoted to making preserves. That the castrated man
wishes to be castrated is perhaps related to the popular notion that the
rape victim deserved to be raped. The notion that the fellow was asking
for it also governs Macdonald's "Reply to the Request from the Remaining Poet for Suicide Suggestions." A bridge, a gun, and a walk in front
of a car having been ruled out as unoriginal, MacDonald's persona suggests that her poet friend assemble his various children, stepchildren,

and wives for a group portrait with explosive flashbulb, thus assuring his
immortality at the moment of his extinction. He is to be sure to pose
holding one of his volumes with title visible. She has just sent him, air
freight, the Hasselblatt portrait camera and other required equipment.[33]
Explosion, like fire, seems to excite the female imagination.[34]

At times women's revenge fantasies are explicitly erotic. "Open him
as if for surgery," says Jong of an icy man. "Let the red knife love slide
in." In Margery Fletcher's "Fantasy, the dominant position," a woman
weaves and teases until "her husband is useless rags." Helen Adam's remarkable and hypnotic ballad "I Love My Love" sings of a beautiful
woman who is killed by her husband but destroys him from the grave by
wreathing him in her hissing, writhing, indestructibly growing Medusa-
like hair.[35] That some of these poems claim to express true love for the
men they unman enables them the more chillingly to reflect our identification of love with conquest.

At other times women's table-turning is more cerebral, less somatic,
addressing the logocentricity rather than the phallocentricity in male
dominance. Muriel Rukeyser's "Myth" recounts an unrecorded conversation between Oedipus and the Sphinx. The link between joking and
revenge, pivoting on a question of language, is central. Old and blind,
Oedipus wants to know where he went wrong and the Sphinx tells him
he answered her famous question incorrectly.

> "When I asked, What walks on four legs in the morning,
> two at noon, and three in the evening, you answered,
> Man. You didn't say anything about woman."
> "When you say Man," said Oedipus, "you include
> women too. Everyone knows that." She said,
> "That's what you think."

Judith Leet's heroine in "Overlooking the Pile of Bodies at One's Feet" is
a perfectly rational person who sincerely regrets that so many men die
for love of her. Slapstick role reversal governs Erica Jong's "Back to Africa," lifted from Frazer's *Golden Bough*, where a tribal custom encourages discontented women to be mystics while their husbands do the
housework and complain that they need a maid and never intended to
marry God. Marilyn Krysl's "To the Banker: Sestina Against Money"
imagines a tribe of hippie women kidnapping the banker, and her "Sestina for Bright Cloud" playfully plows under a fellow worker on the
commune who says plowing isn't women's work.[36]

Whether comedic or earnest, directly violent or merely malicious,
the revenge fantasy in women's poetry seems at first glance undupli-

citous. It tells a truth and tells it straight. The truth is that, as Auden says, "Those to whom evil is done / Do evil in return" or dream of doing it. Like the sterile flatness that Plath's character fears she has caught from the men around her, violence is contagious. Women's audiences, it should be remarked, are often most enthusiastic when the poetry threatens the most violence. No reader encountering these poems will be in further danger of mistaking women for the gentle sex.

That the burden of hatred these poems bear may itself be regarded as a poisonous waste product of patriarchy is a point made in at least two poems. Lorde's "Power," having recounted the story of the policeman acquitted of the black child's shooting, warns that her unexpressed rage is like an unconnected wire. One day that wire will set some "teenaged plug" into the nearest socket, to rape and burn some old white woman. The innocent will continue to suffer, and racial hatred will be a self-fulfilling prophecy. Levertov's "A Poem at Christmas, 1972" responds similarly to American bombing of North Vietnam. "Now I have lain awake imagining murder," the poem begins, describing the poet smashing windows until she reaches the secretary of state, whom she stabs. Disguised as a waitress, she hurls napalm at the president and some "small bombs designed / to explode at the pressure of a small child's weight" at his cohorts. She plays the scene over and over with fresh details—"*O, to kill / the killers!* . . . to this extremity," the poem ends, "the infection of their evil / thrusts us."[37]

Another extremity is suicide, the defiant gesture which modern psychologists have called murder in the 180th degree. To the powerless, self-destruction may seem the ultimately liberating act. "By suicide," says Artaud, "I free myself." If we trust Freud's early intuition, suicidal impulses spring from thwarted aggression—"no neurotic harbors thoughts of suicide which he has not turned back upon himself from murderous impulses against others"—or, according to a later formulation, from an "excessively strong super-ego raging against the ego."[38] In literature, the motifs of liberation, blocked hostility, and self-hatred converge in the classic literary case of Hamlet. Hamlet's unacted anger at his uncle turns inward; he is morally ashamed of his inaction and so doubly self-hating; and he is politically powerless.

For women who feel themselves encaged in dominance-compliance scenarios, the connection between the desire to die and the desire to kill is evidently very strong. Both derive from a conviction of powerlessness. Both, like madness, would bring the obliteration of consciousness. The interchangeability between anger against the other and anger against the self, and the link with a feared/desired insanity, is tellingly apparent in an entry in Alice James' diary:

reading in the library with waves of violent inclination suddenly invading my muscles taking some one of their myriad forms such as throwing myself out the window, or knocking off the head of the benignant pater as he sat with his silver locks, writing at his table, it used to seem to me that the only difference between me and the insane was that I had not only all the horrors and suffering of insanity but the duties of doctor, nurse and straitjacket imposed on me too.[39]

"Madness. Suicide. Murder. / Is there no way out but these?" asks Rich in "The Phenomenology of Anger." The victim hates the oppressor, hates the self for being unable to escape his influence, and hates consciousness for making her aware of her entrapment. If "The freedom of the wholly mad / to smear & play with her madness," or the freedom of death, seems preferable to Rich at the outset of this poem, she articulates a common crisis. Robin Morgan in the title poem of *Monster* dreams "of being killed or killing." Helen Chasin, at the exhausted conclusion of "Fire," having pursued an extended fire-anger analogy through painful personal and ominous global dimensions, reflects on the disaster "as if someone had tried to kill   kill or die." A set of lost-love poems by Ann Darr begins in self-blame, "I need a hair shirt and two / well-seamed apologies," and concludes, "I should have / cornered the market in ridiculous laughs. / I should have cut you to shreds."

If self-punishment is bottled hostility, it may also be an anteroom to that great judgment chamber in which one permits oneself to punish others. Consider the lady in a Marjory Fletcher poem:

She has headaches everyday at four.
She imagines a brain tumor and doctor's date-of-death.
She imagines . . . release and energy to name all names.

Plath's "Daddy" and "Lady Lazarus" both follow this pattern, of symbolic death and avenging resurrection, as if the poet must agree that her flesh is trash, worthy of annihilation, in order to rise from the grave to devour her foes, or as if the poet were giving her destructive impulses a mandate to shoot, provided only that they shoot her first, or, finally, as if it is another self, the inner self, posthumous and pure, released from the husk of the gross outer self, that does her violent bidding. Yet another probing version of the connection appears in Olga Broumas' "Maenad," where overt rage is a screen for covert self-hatred. "Hell has no fury like the fury of women. Scorned . . ." is the refrain of "Maenad," and Broumas, herself of Greek origin, reminds us that the original maenads—our culture's image of the irrationally angry woman—were not

rejected sweethearts but good Greek family women, trapped in patriarchal families where they were necessarily scorned by their sons, their
daughters, their own mothers, so that they despised themselves. Broumas' maenads "deny" the image of womanhood

> even to god
> as she laughs at them, scornfully
> through her cloven maw. Hell has no rage like this
> women's rage.[40]

Hamlet proposes freeing himself with a bare bodkin during one soliloquy, and during another considers taking arms against his sea of
troubles, that is, against himself. His hypothetical weapons are appropriate to the masculinity he does not quite possess. Ophelia, in the madness preceding her suicide, flirts and sings bawdy songs as she has
not had an opportunity to do while sane, but makes her own quietus
through the passive means of drowning. We ladies wear our rue with a
difference. As women's vengeance fantasies invert familiar sexual scenarios, so our suicide and self-punishment fantasies intensify these
same scenarios.

In *Women and Madness* psychologist Phyllis Chesler argues that the
submissiveness culturally imposed on girls and women is a chief cause
of mental illness among females and that conventional therapies exacer-
bate their illnesses by further imposing passive feminine behavior. This
hypothesis coincides with women poets' passive-erotic self-punishment
and suicide fantasies.[41] Robin Morgan's "The Improvisers" is a nightmare in which the poet flees a succession of sadists, from cruel mus-
cular lover to frustrated priest, only to reach a red-draped bed where the
original muscleman, whip coiled at thigh, awaits her masochistic
orders. Marilyn Hacker's elegy for Janis Joplin overhears the voice of the
singer's addiction:

> skag said:
> you are more famous than anyone
> out of West Texas, your hair is a
> monument, your voice preserved
> in honey, I love you, lie down.

Anne Sexton's "The Addict" explains that pill taking is a rehearsal for
death, using a male image for the pills—"I plant bombs inside / of myself"—and a vulnerably sexy image for herself—"I'm a little buttercup
in my yellow nightie." Sexton's "Wanting to Die" also sees suicide as "a
drug so sweet" and boasts as a woman might boast of a seduction:

Twice I have so simply declared myself,
have possessed the enemy, eaten the enemy,
have taken on his craft, his magic.

Still more explicitly, one of Sexton's "Letters to Dr. Y" identifies a sui-cidal impulse with the excitement attached to "the trapeze artist / who flies without a net," itself a quasi-sexual image, and finally confides,

to die whole,
riddled with nothing
but desire for it,
is like breakfast
after love.

Since death is conventionally a masculine figure in our culture, the feminine suicide conventionally perceives him as seducer. A less recog-nized but highly significant form of feminine self-punishing imagery is that which fastens on the self as diminutive, a child, an infant, or even an embryo. This shrinking imagery may serve several simultaneous pur-poses. It suggests a flinching gesture intended to avert attack or pain. It confirms woman's smallness, weakness and limited social scope. It re-turns her to a preoedipal state prior to the rigidity of gender differentia-tion. Above all it implies powerlessness and innocence—a sense that she is powerless and possibly a dread of being otherwise.

Thus Levertov's "Hypocrite Women," which accuses women of self-destructive compliance with male demands, ends with the exasperated comment "our dreams, / with what frivolity we have pared them / like toenails, clipped them like ends of / split hair." Self-destructiveness and the requirements of feminine attractiveness coincide here, as they do in Piercy's critique of women's self-deprecating laughter, "That diffident laugh that punctuates, / that giggle that apologizes . . . That little laugh sticking / in the throat like a chicken bone." Sandra Gilbert's "Suicide 2" pleads, "let me be small, let me be trivial, / let the soil / di-gest me." An almost identical image, only substituting amniotic water for placental soil, defines Kathleen Fraser's babyish Emma Slide, who "was so small . . . she was / all in a pool / in an overflowing of help me."

Several of Sexton's finest poems which evoke the hospitalization after her first breakdown and suicide attempt, including "You, Dr. Martin," "Music Swims Back to Me," "Ringing the Bells," "Lullaby," and "Cripples and Other Stories," involve regression to childhood. Later, "Making a Living" says that the poet's death is like being in the whale's belly. Finally, the hallucinatory "The Death Baby" defines the death she anticipates as a frozen infant, a doll, and a stone baby whom she will rock, and be rocked by, in her final moments.

Likewise regressive are Plath's suicide fantasies, which rearrange, over and over, key male, female, and infant images, as the poet imagines returning to a protected enclosure and the peace and security of the unborn. In "Suicide Off Egg Rock"—a suggestive place name—the speaker squirms under a masculine sun with a corrosive ray and wants to crawl into a female "pit of shadow." "The Hanging Man" suffers "bald white days in a shadeless socket," another image of a masculine and punishing sun. Nursery rhyme rhythms and language govern the clinging infantilism of "Daddy," where an early suicide attempt is an attempt to get "back to you," and its frustration means an enforced rebirth: ". . . they pulled me out of the sack / And they stuck me together with glue." "A Birthday Present," with its mysterious veils, its painless knife, and its pure baby's cry, invents a suicide that blends defloration and childbirth. The phantasmagoric wartime setting of "Getting There," with its phallic train and, again, the emergence of a pure baby, has a similar effect. The close of "Ariel" fuses elements of the child's cry, the male arrow, and the female dew evaporating. Together these images hurtle toward an extinguishing sun that is at once fiery exposure and womblike enclosure. And in "Lady Lazarus" the memories of attempted suicide are figuratively fetal:

> I rocked shut
> As a seashell.
> They had to call and call
> And pick the worms off me like sticky pearls . . .
>
> It's easy enough to do it in a cell.
> It's easy enough to do it and stay put.[42]

It is easy, we may assume, for Plath and for other women writers who are half or more than half in love with easeful death to follow the path of least symbolic resistance. Small, passive, harmless, protected, the unborn fetus is in her way ideally feminine. To die is to correct the error of having been born, and to do it on paper, leaving behind the phantom imprint of a small, curled thing, like a composite cause and cure of a feminine sea of troubles, is evidently a consummation devoutly to be wished. It is also a means of signaling, to the peanut-crunching crowd Plath feels her audience to be, "here is my true shape, this is the form you have made me assume, take a careful look at the performance you are paying for."

The critic A. A. Alvarez, who in *The Savage God* attempts to understand the meaning of suicide in the lives and work of modern artists, has proposed that self-destruction as a theme and as an actuality among artists reflects an increasingly inward response to a shared sense of intolerable public disaster which "is like, for a believer, the final, unbudgeable illumination that God is not good." The crucial fact of our times, argues Alvarez, is the spectre of meaningless unnatural death on a mass scale:

> Just as the decay of religious authority in the nineteenth century made life seem absurd by depriving it of any ultimate coherence, so the growth of modern technology has made death itself absurd by reducing it to a random happening totally unconnected with the inner rhythms and logic of the lives destroyed.[43]

The artist, who must attempt to grasp atrocity mentally, assimilate it personally, and find an individual language and a form for its meaningless horror, risks being absorbed by destruction, surrendering to it, becoming a self-destroyer. Thus we have not only Plath and Sexton, our female sacrifices, but the self-savaging Hart Crane, Dylan Thomas, Brendan Behan, Artaud, Delmore Schwartz, Pavese, Celan, Randall Jarrell, Hemingway, Berryman, Mayakovski, Modigliani, Gorki, Pollack, Rothko, all of whom, whatever their private histories, are victims of our shared history.

Were the critic to name the twentieth-century writers for whom violence against others—not self-destruction but the grand pageant of slaughter itself—is a primary theme, the list would be endless. That women writers now write violently against themselves and others signifies in part simply that we have deghettoized ourselves. We are doing what everyone in our sorry time is doing. Yet the absurdity and atrocity Alvarez notes retain a special meaning for women. If God the Father seems "not good" in a postholocaust world, he has always been the creative woman's adversary, whom the fact of holocaust merely makes it easier to assail. As to the lethal force of modern technology, woman is not its primary creator or deployer. Since women have been excluded from the labors of rationality, neither the three centuries of applied science which have generated our instruments of mass destruction, nor the political ideologies which have justified their use, have been women's work. Compared with man, for whom heroism retains a vestigial glamour apparently difficult to discard, and for whom mental as well as physical conquests are confirmations of masculinity, woman stands rather purely in the position of technology's victim. It is women's discovery that their assigned private and public roles are disastrously consistent, equally defined by passivity and submissiveness, neither affording an escape from the other, that ignites the intense fury of their writing.

4

The fire bites, the fire bites. Bites
to the little death. Bites

till she comes to nothing. Bites
on her own sweet tongue. She goes on. Biting.
    —Olga Broumas, "Circe"[44]

The concept of victimization alone cannot account for the hypnotic, seductive, almost glamorous, almost magic energy that shimmers about women's best violence poems, whether vengefully phallic, self-punishingly unltrafeminine, or, most angrily and helplessly, both. To approach the poetics as well as the politics of these poems, we must turn again to the principle of duplicity.

The duplicitous poem overtly transmits one message, covertly a contrary one. Dickinson likes being a marginal Nobody, would not for the world be an egotistical Somebody, the poem says; but by writing the poem she tries to usurp Somebody's role and, if we enjoy the poem, succeeds. At all costs we should show no trace of anger in our writing, says Woolf, while making certain to induce anger in her readers. While renouncing this earlier, coy sort of duplicity which pretends to accept passivity, the feminine violence poem advances into another doubleness that demands decoding. If "I want to kill" also means "I want to die," and "I want to die" means "I want to kill," poetic excitement arises from the charged presence of the unspoken message. The reader will experience the thrill, not necessarily conscious, of decoding a forbidden thing. Further, those poems which bring to consciousness the painful unity of the wish to kill/die, poems which make us believe that consciousness has altogether surrendered itself to that obliterating desire, may bear within themselves a secret contrary desire which we do not yet know how to read.

I here consider three extended poem sequences whose amplitude lets us examine what shorter poems obscure—the essentially duplicitous nature of female rage in poetry. Margaret Atwood's *Power Politics*, Diane Wakoski's *The George Washington Poems*, and Anne Sexton's "The Jesus

Papers" are major works, conceptually radical and formally experimental, each centering on the motif of female victimization within patriarchy. Depicting the patriarchal male as lover, hero, father, and God, the poems use a broad array of anger-generated devices to demystify, attack, and ridicule him and the cultural script he embodies. To the woman reader, the dismantling of masculine authority is gratifying. Yet in all three cases, rage and retaliation are made to seem ultimately inadequate to the woman poet's larger needs; retaliatory strategies confirm rather than transform the cruel patterns by which we live. To use Lucy Stone's memorable phrase, these poems deepen our disappointment.

Margaret Atwood's *Power Politics* (1971) is a quintessential dissection of the modern love affair as power struggle, in a world shadowed by intimate as well as international violence.[45] The book contains forty-five poems, in three sections, each introduced by an epigram. A shockingly perfect example of the victimization poem, using a figure that instantly crystallizes from romantic cliché to domesticity to horror, is the first epigram:

You fit into me
like a hook into an eye

a fish hook
an open eye   (p. 140)

Atwood's second poem, ominously called "he reappears," suggests like the opening of *Finnegans Wake* that an apparent beginning marks a recurrence in a cyclic pattern. The lover rises from a snowbank, three-headed and devious, with glowing red eyes; the innocent speaker tries to make friends with him. A mimesis of the horror movie or horror comic is sketched here, and the next poem explicitly identifies the course of true love with the banality of popular entertainment: "You take my hand and / I'm suddenly in a bad movie," this time a romantic costume drama. She stays to the end while others leave because "I paid my money, I / want to see what happens" (p. 142). What does happen is vulgar, defiling, and nightmarish, the lover clinging to her like celluloid.

Until this point, Atwood's materials and attitudes seem familiar. The speaker is an innocent if complicit female victim, associated with organic and domestic imagery. The "you" is a threatening male lover, associated with what is cold and inorganic. Sex is violence, love is a banal addiction involving the surrender of self to sentimental stereotype.

This classic male dominance–female victimization pattern runs like an Ariadne's thread through *Power Politics*. In the single poem where Atwood describes herself as feeling sensual pleasure, perhaps as having an orgasm, the experience is one of sudden brutal annihilation of body and mind, from which she only gradually recovers. Her most sympathetic description of lovemaking describes the lover as a hurt animal wildly trying to tear itself from a trap. Elsewhere he is a warrior, a statue. She bitterly hails him as "my beautiful wooden leader" in one poem about masculine heroism, and in another depicts him as standing with boot on prow "to hold the wooden body / under, soul in control."

But at least as commonly, we are running the maze dizzyingly backward. The female "I" is strong and manipulative. The male "you" is weak and pathetic. His substance, she says, is subhuman, boneless protoplasm infesting her garden. When he asks for old-fashioned idyllic love, she informs him brusquely that their modernized heads are attached to their bodies by rubber tubes and snaps, "This is the way it is, get used to it" (p. 148). Parodying T. S. Eliot, "After the agony in the guest / bedroom," she describes the drunken lover as a buffoonlike Jesus whom she proceeds, as a contemptuous Madonna, to crucify (p. 146). When they quarrel in a restaurant, she stabs him in the heart with her magic fork, causing a Superman balloon with flashing eyes and pop-music soundtrack to rise from his head. Again, she is a clinician of love in her rubber gloves and lab coat; he flees like a political prisoner. When he extends his hand she takes his fingerprints. "Please die I said / so I can write about it" (p. 149). When he is pursued by demons across a baking landscape, she offers traditional feminine comfort, spinning a soothing fantasy of rivers, trees, rain, only to conclude, "Now you have one enemy / instead of many" (p. 169).

Individually, these cruel poems can be read as responses to experiences of hurt so familiar they hardly need to be rehearsed, a gratifying release of female punitiveness, a vengeful eye for an eye. Atwood's early reviewers almost uniformly regard the book, with delight or distaste, as an antimale manifesto.[46] Yet Atwood has remarked that Amy Lowell's famous "Christ! What are patterns for?" made a strong impression on her as a girl and has explained that the book's subject is "certain mythologies, especially those involving victor/victim patterns, with their endless variations of pose, accusation, complicity and subversion of the human."[47] A reversed pattern remains a pattern. Jonathan Swift tells us that satire is a mirror in which the reader sees every face but his own; he might have added that the same is usually the case for the writer. As a satirist, Atwood is unusual in that she is equally contemptuous of the lover and of the self.

Female control in Atwood's work parallels male control in male writing. The author is the authority. The difference is that Atwood's style encourages no suspension of disbelief, no illusion of illusionlessness; these are, she makes clear, her poems, her nightmares, her definitions of "I" and "you," and her "distortions of you." The implication is that all power, not excluding the power of the writer to interpret a relationship, is intrinsically alienating and destructive. As Judith McCombs observes, the game of author/object played—and displayed—in *Power Politics* is as vicious as the game of victor/victim.[48] Or, worse, authorial control is itself a delusion. When the poet sees the lover as a science fiction monster, destroying cities and dripping blood, leaving her mutilated and barely escaping, she asks first, "How can I stop you" and then "Why did I create you" (p. 167). The lovers are hostile nations mapping each other's weaknesses, not because their hostility has a rational basis but because they cannot stop (p. 161). Throughout *Power Politics* scenes of danger, disaster, and destruction are played and replayed, escapes become entrapments, tender gestures transform themselves to attacks, and it seems impossible to distinguish between truth and lies, real and unreal motives, even life and death, in the poet's world of mirrors, water, maps, photographs, and games. Among the collection's strongest poems is "At first I was given centuries," where the lovers enact the roles of hunter-warrior and warrior's bride which Atwood first encountered in Amy Lowell's "Patterns":

At first I was given centuries
to wait in caves, in leather
tents, knowing you would never come back

Then it speeded up: only
several years between
the day you jangled off
into the mountains, and the day (it was
spring again) I rose from the embroidery
frame at the messenger's entrance.   (p. 154)

On one occasion the warrior "fails" to be killed according to plan and the bride must put up with him for life. The black comedy accelerates, with costume changes. When we reach the modern era, the best evenings are those when the explosion immediately follows the radio announcement. On other nights,

you jump up from
your chair without even touching your dinner

and I can scarcely kiss you goodbye
before you run out into the street and they shoot   (pp. 155)

At once horrible and trivial, like the deaths of television cartoon animals, the noble death of the lover has left the realm of romance and
entered the realm of farce. Atwood's final poem in *Power Politics* comes
after the couple has decided, like every good modern pair, to split up.
Called "He is last seen," it represents a final twist to the romantic cliché,
for now the lover is rising from underground, walking toward her carrying her death in the form of a paperweight.

Structurally, Atwood's sequence resembles a slide show. Vivid images
appear in succession. With the exception of the opening and closing
encounter-poems with their paradoxically interchangable titles, they
could be rearranged without altering the sense of the whole. One can
almost hear the whirr and click of the projector between slides. The sensation of stasis, or rather of furious running in place, is augmented by
the individual poems. Though saturated in violence, sprinkled with
terms denoting narrative progress, and full of the poet's insistent resolu-
tions to change the self or the situation, nothing happens in these poems.
They defy chronology and deny time. They present history itself as a set
of absurdly elastic repetitions. They "end without resolution," as one
critic says of Atwood's poems in general; "we arrive at our destination
and we confront an intensified version of our original predicament."[49]

The predicament is the lack of an exit. Atwood's title urges us first to
perceive intimate relationships as power struggles between individuals,
and second to understand that individual will and motive in love relationships is a delusion. "I" and "you" are playing parts blocked out for
them, which they can no more alter than they could alter the course of
a roller coaster by turning its steering wheel. The controlling realities of
their lives are historical and geopolitical. They merely enact in miniature what is acted on a large scale among the hostile nations. Terror of
one another precipitates obsessive self-defense; there is no mercy from
the powerful for the powerless; earnest idealism is a self-deception;
heroism is a conditioned reflex, a posturing, an unconscious wish for
annihilation.

Man as hero is more thoroughly if no more kindly examined in Diane Wakoski's *The George Washington Poems*, twenty-three deadpan surrealist farces woven like Maypole ribbons around the stiff figure of the
father of our country.[50] As Wakoski explains in a preface, the poems "address some man in my life as well as his alter ego, George Washington";
both figures represent "'the man's world,' with its militaristic origins and

the glorification of fact over feeling" (p. xiv). Like Atwood, Wakoski enjoys surprise. Here is the opening of the first poem in the series, entitled "George Washington and the Loss of His Teeth":

> The ultimate
> in the un-Romantic:
> false teeth
>
>> This room became a room where your heaviness
>> and my heaviness came together,
>> an overlay of flower petals once new and fresh
>> pasted together queerly, as for some lady's hat,
>> and finally false and stiff, love fearing
>> to lose itself, locks and keys become inevitable.
> The truth is that George cut down his father's cherry tree,
> his ax making chips of wood so sweet with sap they could be
> sucked, and he stripped the bark like old bandages
> from the tree for kindling.
> In this tree he defied his dead father,
> the man who could not give him an education and left him to
> suffer the ranting of Adams and others,
> those fat sap-cheeked men who said George did not know
>   enough
> to be president.   (p. 113)

Several kinds of female outrageousness coalesce here. The most obvious is the deflation of Washington's dignity in the opening three lines, but there is also the immediate digression from the historical subject to the poet's private life, the saucy "truth" compounded of history, biography, apocryphal anecdote, and the poet's lively imagination—which gives us an imaginary tree with real sweet chips cut from it—and the first-naming of "George," modeled perhaps on how we talk about popular politicians or media celebrities.

The poem's narrative continues: after chopping the tree down, George naps and dreams that his dead father attacks him "with a large penis swung over his / shoulder." He retaliates by spitting a torrent of cherry pits at his father, but his teeth come out with the pits. Later he has false teeth made from the cherry wood, but since the tree was his father's, "His lips closed painfully over the stiff set."

A moment's dip below Wakoski's whimsical surface reveals considerable allegorical logic. The political rebellion sanctified by history has its private oedipal motives, and the end product is a son who defeats his father only to become a rigid and comfortless duplicate of him. The "false" teeth and the "false" love of the poem's opening are alike in that both represent a decline from nature to artifact, and both are associated with weapons. "We all come to such battles with our own flesh," Wakoski comments, accusing her lover of spitting out "rocky white quartz sperm" that has ossified in her womb and of getting his own false teeth from "This room . . . built from the lumber of my thigh" that is "heavy with hate" (p. 113–14). Like George Washington, we infer, the lover too will become the ultimate in the un-Romantic, which, as Wakoski explains, is "classical."

This opening poem is the first and last time we see George Washington as a son, a person of passionate impulse. Subsequent poems depict him as an unemotional patriarch, propped up in the various masculine poses of governor, slaveowner and landowner, soldier, the face on coins and bills, the public figure waving at the crowd, a surrogate for the poet's absconding father, and the subject of a biography the poet quotes in the final piece, called, delightfully, GEORGE WASHINGTON, MAN AND MONUMENT. The Washington of popular lore also appears. The poet sleeps with her lover at an inn where Washington slept. She waits all night under the George Washington Bridge for George to keep a scholarly rendezvous with her, which of course he fails to do. He—or perhaps it is her lover—crosses the Delaware in a boat of razor blades. As Father of her Country, he is involved in a not-too-subtle anatomical pun.[51] The poet's pose, meanwhile, is that of earnest hero worshipper, explainer, and amorous pursuer through a series of caricatured American landscapes.

Some of the fun Wakoski has with her ostensible idol is direct and personal. He is a "tight-lipped man" unable to love or to make anything grow on his plantation. In "Patriotic Poem" the poet explains that she pines secretly for the more glamorous Alexander Hamilton but is loyal to George because he is "first president / and I need those firsts," notwithstanding his "absolute inability / to feel anything personal, or communicate it" (pp. 133–34). In "George Washington and the Invention of Dynamite," she commiserates with him for not beating Nobel to the punch:

We all
know the story of the famous discovery,
the inventor's guilt
and humanitarian needs.

George, she notices, is "different since this / crazy invention / and I wish I could restore you to your / original polite calm" (p. 131). In one of several particularly anachronistic poems poor George, naked with an erection, is being tittered at by two ladies in bikinis at Martha's Vineyard. Another finds him glancing at his Bulova saying he has always been afraid of anachronisms, at the very moment Baudelaire drives up in a Ford.

The systematic derangement of chronology reinforces Wakoski's tacit undermining of objective history. The seriousness of history and the dignity of male leadership and power within it are deflated not by direct and solemn critique, but by the poet's spirit of play, and by her aggressive foregrounding of her own fascinations and obsessions. Interpolating Washington into dramas of disconnection and failure suggesting the flip side of the American Dream, she manipulates him much as political leaders manipulate populations. The hero of national fame is at the personal level false and stiff, a wooden puppet containing so little emotional sap that Wakoski, with her sweeping loves and hates, her moments of arrogant haughtiness and abject humility, her terror and pain on the one hand, and her penchant for wicked nonsense on the other, easily upstages him. Upstaging is the poet's form of victory, of course, not simply over this particular man but over the mental and institutional structures mandated by masculinity. As political commentary, *The George Washington Poems* is both a fool's holiday and a declaration of independence, reminding us that authority resides where we the people bestow it, disappears where we withdraw it.

At the same time, to understand *The George Washington Poems* as predominantly satiric is to ignore their forceful emotionality. The long central poem "The Father of My Country" reconstructs the child Wakoski's desperate love and need of the absent, indifferent father who has created her identity:

Father living in my wide cheekbones and short feet,
Father in my Polish tantrums and my American speech . . .
Father who makes me dream in the dead of night of the falling
    cherry
blossoms, Father who makes me know all men will leave me
if I love them (pp. 141)

When at the poem's conclusion the poet enlists George Washington as father figure, it is with the remembered incredulous ecstasy of the six-year-old playing outside when her father made an unannounced appearance. "Father," she cries three times, "have you really come home?" (p. 143).

Identified at times with the indifferent lover as well as the indifferent father, Washington may also, the sequence hints, be an interior portion of herself. "We all come to such battles" marks one parallel between him and herself. He and she write each other "inspiring letters" (p. 125) and he is her friend and confidant. She and he both have jewels (his are magic pearls he finds in his shoe) that fail to help in their romances. Her blood "perhaps was shipped from Mt. Vernon / which was once a blood factory," and "the white house of my corpuscles / asks for new blood" (p. 133–134). When Wakoski praises Washington's executive capacity—

> George, you could not love or make anything
> around you grow,
> but you built and pushed and forced
> and largely by will
> shaped and defended things—real, substantial.   (p. 159)

she might be complimenting her own style as a poet. She is tempted to imitate him—"I should trim my hair straight . . . I should cut out all curves," (p. 163), though she rejects the temptation. In the sequence's last poem, ironically entitled "George Washington: The Whole Man," the poet announces her disappointment with Washington as a great man, but also depicts him as shifting through time, caressing her body and brain, "squeezing the thalamus, / fingering the spongy protrusions that make me dream" (p. 165), until he seems not only to touch but to dissolve into her identity. At least one interview confirms this subtext:

> I guess I think of my world as so female or feminine, or so much
> in the spirit of the anima, that the things that populated it ought to
> be masculine and of animus . . . bursting through the mirror of
> self and reflecting back . . . these characters that are both com-
> pletely outside the self and reflections of the self. The self you can
> never be in real life.[52]

Whether as hero-father-lover or as animus, George Washington stands in an equivocal relation to Wakoski's "I." His world is public, hers private. He is emotionally arid, she is emotionally juicy. She despises and mocks him and the historical-political existence in which, alone, he lives and moves and has his being. Yet she also takes him, and not only in jest, to be her creator, a necessary part of herself, a thing she wants and needs and can never possess—and there's the rub. As writers both Jungian and non-Jungian have found, what is experienced as the mas-culine principle within a female is more often a foe than a friend.[53] Given Wakoski's sense of the relations between herself and men, she can win all her battles and still lose her war, for the feminine self needs the animus but cannot believe it reciprocally needs her. Whether outside or within the self, the male remains Wakoski's antagonist.

A further dimension appears, and the stakes are higher, when the antagonist is unveiled as that male who stands behind every lover, father and hero: God himself. Anne Sexton's "The Jesus Papers," published in her 1972 collection *The Book of Folly*, is a mordantly comic dismantling of Christian myth from a female point of view, anticipating by several years the feminist critique of patriarchal religion triggered by Mary Daly's *Beyond God the Father* and at the same time demonstrating the crucial distinction between critique and transformation.[54] The woman poet here can analytically penetrate but cannot transcend—cannot imagine transcending—a patriarchal theology which swallows her alive. As in *Power Politics* and *The George Washington Poems*, an intellectually devastating subversion is equaled and canceled by an emotionally devastating submission.

"The Jesus Papers" begins with the most familiar and appealing image in Christian iconography, the Madonna and Child. "Jesus Suckles" places us within the consciousness of an infant who is at first engaged in a joyous and playful celebration of his connection with the mother whose "great white apples" make him "glad." This consciousness, exuberantly fertile in its metaphors, resembles Sexton's own consciousness in poems like "In Celebration of My Uterus," and for a similar reason. Sensuous bliss and abundance generate a blissfully abundant imagination:

> I'm a jelly-baby and you're my wife.
> You're a rock and I the fringy algae.
> You're a lily and I'm the bee that gets inside. . . .
> I'm a kid in a rowboat and you're the sea,
> the salt, you're every fish of importance.

But the erotic extravaganza is followed by a correction:

> No. No.
> All lies.
> I am small
> and you hold me.
> You give me milk
> and we are the same
> and I am glad.

Then another correction, still briefer:

> No. No.
> All lies.

I am a truck. I run everything.
I own you.   (pp. 337–38)

"Jesus Suckles" recalls Sexton's earlier autobiographical poem "Those Times," where she recounts childhood humiliations inflicted by her mother and says she did not know "that my life, in the end, / would run over my mother's like a truck" (p. 121). Unlike Sexton, however, "Jesus" is unapologetic. Thus we can see the infant as the poet's animus, a masculine self characterized by a guilt-free egoistic aggressiveness forbidden to the feminine Sexton, while at the same time he is precisely what Christian thought defines him as: a god who is also a boy child. To be a boy child, or to be a god, is to use the word "no." It is to deny, to divide. First metaphor, and then the blissful female connection that generates metaphor, must be sacrificed. To be a boy or a god means to seize power and possession, to reject nature, to embrace artifact, to transcend the erotic. Gospel accounts place this cruel moment—"Woman, what have I to do with thee"—in the god-man's adolescence. Psychoanalytic theory places it at the close of a boy's oedipal crisis, when he identifies with the father and turns away from the mother. Sexton locates it in his infancy, as a forethought of things to come. "Jesus Suckles" records the differentiation of Jesus from Mary, and also from the poet. When attached to the female, his imagination lives; when detached, it dies. Jesus does not speak in the first person again until his crucifixion.

Succeeding poems illustrate the consequences of a dualism whereby God becomes superior to Nature, Logos to Eros, the reality principle to the pleasure principle, and boys to their mothers. Figures for Eros and Logos segregate themselves. The natural world remains voluptuous and orgiastic, a ripe mélange of sex and food, where "Outdoors the kitties hung from their mother's tits / like sausages in a smokehouse," while Jesus stubbornly fasts and is celibate. "His sex," explains the narrator, "was sewn onto Him like a medal" (p. 338). When asleep he still desires Mary, but using his penis as a chisel he carves a *Pietà* and rehearses dying so that he can fuse with her at his death, when cross and woman are united "like a centerpiece" (p. 339).[55]

Sexton's version of sexual sublimation—the subduing of libidinal energy and redirecting of it for socially valued ends—deviates from the gospel according to Freud. Her Jesus is motivated not by a forbidding father but by an inner will to power which is incompatible with sensuous love. In Sexton's equation, to repress love is to seek death. Sexual sublimation is therefore the equivalent of the death wish and results ironically in the most routine sort of domestic artifact, "a centerpiece," presumably on a wholesome bourgeois table. "Jesus Raises Up the Harlot," perhaps the most shocking poem in the sequence, gives us the gospel according to de Sade. To save the harlot from sin, the savior "lances" her breasts, "those two boils of whoredom," with his thumbs, until the milk runs out. Afterward—and the poet's juxtaposition of biblical and contemporary diction is typical—

> The harlot followed Jesus around like a puppy
> for He had raised her up.
> Now she forsook her fornications
> and became His pet. (p. 340)

The relation of Son to Father is one of junior to senior charlatan in "Jesus Cooks," where the miracle of the loaves and fishes involves opening sardine cans "on the sly." In "Jesus Dies," the disagreeable aspects of the poet's role as self-publicizing agonized performer come into play. The crucifixion is represented as a sort of ultimate poetry reading, where Jesus' confession of his need for God is a half-infantile, half-competitive "man-to-man thing," and his attitude toward his audience is a mix of identification and contempt for its sensation-seeking.[56]

Until this point, "The Jesus Papers" has been roughly if selectively chronological. Instead of a resurrection, however, the next poem reverts to the Virgin Mary at the moment of the Annunciation. A reprise of sensuous imagery surrounding the Virgin is interrupted by a strange being who "lifts her chin firmly / and gazes at her with executioner's eyes." Consequently,

> Nine clocks spring open
> and smash themselves against the sun.
> The calendars of the world
> burn if you touch them.
> All this will be remembered.
> Now we will have a Christ. (p. 344)

Sexton's epilogue, "The Author of the Jesus Papers Speaks," confirms the defeat of sensuous femaleness by manipulative masculine control. It is a brief dream poem beginning with a rich female drama between the poet and a cow-mother who gives blood instead of milk. God interrupts and asks to be reassured that people like Christmas, and the poet goes to the well and pulls up a baby. God then gives her a gingerbread lady to put in her oven, explaining:

> When the cow gives blood
> and the Christ is born
> we must all eat sacrifices.
> We must all eat beautiful women.

This conclusion reiterates the paternal demand for submission beneath the idiom of affection, and Sexton's psychological, theological, and rhetorical implications are all painful. Seemingly wishing for sympathy and communication, engaging in a gesture of apparent gift-giving, God's "we must . . . we must" pretends to share with the poet a sense of fated necessity. But if "we" eat beautiful women, one of us thrives, one of us dies. To eat beautiful women is like the infant's suckling writ large and omnipotent, and the reader may wonder whether the notorious devouring mother is not a psychic screen for just such an unacceptable masculine wish, in the same way as we speculate that the concept of female penis envy was invented to screen male womb envy or breast envy.[57]

Theologically, the substitution of a gingerbread lady for the eucharist reminds us that the central ritual of Christianity, and of the Passover feast from which it takes its symbolism, derives from earlier religions in which the object of worship was the fertile and nourishing mother. Far, however, from implying that we should return to goddess worship, the gingerbread offering means that we, and especially we women, must kill and suppress the goddess anew. Rhetorically, God's authority extends to the language of the poem, as he successfully reduces a set of powerful female symbols to domesticity and powerlessness. What was a dream-cow in the poet's own framework becomes a cookie in God's framework. The poet's tacit compliance with God's will is consistent with female passivity throughout "The Jesus Papers." One's sense is that, though the poet has put up a brave analytical front, she is after all just another beautiful woman whom "we" can sacrifice and who is all too ready to sacrifice herself. However relentless her critique of male authority, she sees no way out of it. She has had many words, but God, who is Logos, has the last word.[58]

What light do these three ambitious sequences cast on the theme of anger in women's poetry? Most obviously, of course, they represent anger as a psychic necessity, both emotionally and intellectually. To be conscious, as a woman, is to be conscious of hurt and to demand reparation. If the best revenge is writing well, the demystifying power of these poems is a primal triumph. Yet to represent these works as simply advocating a purifying female rage would be to misrepresent their view of gender antagonism, of the poet's role, and of the relation between poem and audience.

First, all three sequences present the war of the sexes as a power struggle insusceptible of resolution, into which participants of both sexes are inescapably locked. Gender polarity means hostility, never more so than when it is disguised as love. This is the case whether we see the masculine figure in the poems as a genuine Other, a "real man," or as the poet's animus, her enemy within. It remains the case even when the roles of spirit and flesh, calculating mind and spontaneous feeling, authority and obedience, strength and weakness, reverse their usual gender attributions. When Atwood plays God, she remains as unable to rewrite a sadomasochistic script as when she plays victim. Wakoski's capacity for judgment and mockery does not reduce her hunger for love, nor does it cause the father-lover to satisfy her romantic longings. When Sexton dismantles the gentle Jesus of sentimental stereotype and reveals a sex-rejecting misogynist zealot, she increases rather than decreases our fear that there's no hiding place for women in religion.

Second, the authority of the poet in each of these sequences is employed as a weapon and is consequently self-defeating. The poet analyzes, categorizes, scrutinizes, superimposes female maps on male territory, uses comedy and parody to reduce the foe to ridicule. As poet, she tries to win rather than submit: a corrosive demystification is her mode of conquest. She becomes, in other words, precisely the phallic woman predicted by phallocentrism itself. What she does not do is synthesize opposites or imagine contexts larger than the ancient text of dualism. Like the smart fool in the tar baby story, the more she struggles against the rigid hierarchical scheme of patriarchy, the more she is trapped by it.

Third, these works are heavily surrealistic—absurd, bizarre, farcical, luridly nightmarish. In part they thereby demonstrate, and induce in the reader, an acute degree of psychic pain. The experience of reading *Power Politics*, *The George Washington Poems*, and "The Jesus Papers" is like walking barefoot on broken glass. But the surrealist mode subverts one's ability to accept suffering as ultimately necessary or ennobling. In contrast to tragic and lyric modes which persuade us that their visionary worlds are deeply true and must be accepted, surrealism persuades us that its world is arbitrary and questionable. The confusion between "truth" and "lies" insisted on in each of these sequences reinforces this subversive effect, as do key structural devices designed at every formal turn to disorient the reader: absence of connectives, jump cuts, shifting viewpoints; randomness of sequence and failure of closure in *Power Politics* and *The George Washington Poems*; progressive (but potholed) sequence followed by regression in "The Jesus Papers"; the collapse of past and present, the flaunted anachronisms. The polarized worlds these artists depict and the polarized personalities they inhabit—are they not, finally, ridiculous?

If we compare these sequences with familiar masculine works exploring dissatisfaction and alienation in a modernist context but without the seductive irrational sheen of surrealism—*Life Studies*, for example, or *The Dream Songs*—Lowell and Berryman appear relatively reconciled to their own and the world's bruised destinies. No better can be had, they seem to imply. As Adrienne Rich observes in "When We Dead Awaken," "to the eye of a feminist, the work of Western male poets now writing reveals a deep, fatalistic pessimism as to the possibilities of change, whether societal or personal." [59] By contrast, the violence, the bitterness, the self-mockery, the sense of absurd entrapment, along with the smoldering nonresignation of Atwood, Wakoski, and Sexton, suggest that the secret desire encoded in women's anger poems is a desire to imagine precisely what cannot be imagined within the poems themselves. The stronger the poems, the more emphatically dualistic they are—and the more they convey to a reader that the pattern of dualism is intolerable. When the tightly laced heroine in the formal garden of Amy Lowell's poem learns that her lover has died, significantly, "in a pattern called a war," she ends her poem with the exclamation "Christ! what are patterns for?" The poetry of women's anger continues to pursue that question in our time. "This is the way it is, get used to it" means what it says. It also means the opposite. [60]

5 The Imperative of Intimacy: Female Erotics, Female Poetics

The fateful question of the human species seems to me to be whether and to what extent the cultural process developed in it will succeed in mastering the derangements of communal life caused by the human instinct of aggression and self-destruction. In this connection, perhaps the phase through which we are at this moment passing deserves special interest. Men have brought their powers of subduing the forces of nature to such a pitch that by using them they could now very easily exterminate one another to the last man. They know this—hence arises a great part of their current unrest, their dejection, their mood of apprehension. And now it may be expected that the other of the two "heavenly forces," eternal Eros, will put forth his strength so as to maintain himself alongside of his equally immortal adversary.
    —Sigmund Freud, *Civilization and Its Discontents*[1]

i felt the joy of being a body,
of being inside a body, of
another body being inside my
body; the unbearable joy
        —Alta, "Putting It All Down in Black & White"[2]

we have lost all sense
of woman man each being
both you say
        —Siv Cedering Fox, "Both You Say"[3]

        Afterwards, the compromise.
        Bodies resume their boundaries . . .

Nothing is changed, except
there was a moment when
the wolf, the mongering wolf
who stands outside the self
lay lightly down, and slept.
—Maxine Kumin, "After Love"[4]

If the release of anger is a major element in women's poetry, so too is the release of a contrary passion which in part explains the vehemence of women's rage. "What do women want?" was a question ancient before Freud asked it. A provisional answer, were we to trust women's revenge poetry, would be that they want man's phallus, or what the phallus represents—the power to conquer and punish. Another answer, if we judge by the poetry of feminine desperation, is what the sibyl said to the boys in Petronius' *Satyricon*, which T. S. Eliot quotes as the epigraph to *The Waste Land*: "I want to die." The violent desires arising from the contemplation of powerlessness are suggestively interchangeable, and those women who express them most dramatically and thrillingly make clear at the same time that the wish to kill/die confirms a dualized world and a dualized sexuality.

We have now to look at a quite different form of female desire and to delineate an alternative portrait of female pleasure. For it is not only woman's aggressive impulses which have been thwarted and made taboo in her past life and literature. Her eroticism has suffered equally. Where female aggression has been twisted into manipulativeness, female ardor has been chained to submissiveness. To love, for a woman, has meant to yield, to "give herself." As we have known since Karen Horney and Simone de Beauvoir, the addiction to love relationships in which the woman is powerless and suppliant—what Rachel Blau Du Plessis calls "romantic thraldom"—is woman's peculiar curse.[5] Can it ever be otherwise? Can we imagine love not as the prop of the dependent woman but from the angle of an empowered one? Can we, as Carol Gilligan and other recent theorists of female development claim, "separate the description of care and connection" which characterizes feminine personalities "from the vocabulary of inequality and oppression"?[6]

From the poetry women are writing today, at least one general point emerges. The systematic gender-based polarities built into our culture are intolerable to many writers not only because they are perceived as oppressive to women and others, but because of intense yearnings for relationships defined by mutuality and interpenetration rather than by the culturally privileged grid of dominance and subordination, and because of powerfully rooted convictions that dualistic and hierarchical views of reality are falsifications. Mutuality, continuity, connection, identification, touch: this motif constitutes the imperative of intimacy

166 STEALING THE LANGUAGE

in women's writing, and in this motif we find the elements of a gynocentric erotics, metaphysics, poetics, constituting a radical challenge to
some of our most cherished cultural and psychic assumptions.

At the opening of *Civilization and Its Discontents* Freud quotes a
letter from Romain Rolland describing a "sensation of 'eternity,' a feeling as of something limitless, unbounded, something 'oceanic,'" which
he identifies as the core of religion. Freud does three things with this.
First he insists that he cannot "discover this oceanic feeling in myself"
and therefore concludes that it is an illusion. Second he traces this
"feeling of indissoluble connection, of belonging inseparately to the external world as a whole," to the feelings of the infant at the breast whose
"ego includes everything." "Normally," says Freud, "there is nothing we
are more certain of than the feeling of our self, our own ego. It seems to
us an independent unitary thing, sharply outlined against everything
else," except, he significantly adds, when love "threatens to obliterate
the boundaries between ego and object."

Having assumed that what "we" are certain of is nondelusory, Freud
goes on to point out that the independent ego forms itself as a result of
deprivation of the mother and concerns itself ever after with the will to
control others who may be sources of pleasure or pain. Thus the sense
of intimate connectedness is associated by Freud with "infantile helplessness," "limitless narcissism," and illusion, while the reality principle
brings us the autonomous ego, the "primary mutual hostility of human
beings," and the aggressiveness underlying all relationships. As to religion, Freud derives it of course not from the psychic residue of mother
love and the sense of "indissoluble connection" but from separation and
fear:

> The derivation of the need for religion from the child's feeling of
> helplessness and the longing it evokes for a father seem to me in-
> controvertible, especially since this feeling is kept alive per-
> petually by the fear of what the superior power of fate will bring.[7]

Over against this Freudian formulation we may consider the developing consensus of women writers who propose alternative female
structures in the areas of psychology, morality, religion, and literature,
based on connection rather than separation and modeled on the powerful continuity of the mother-daughter bond.[8] As Nancy Chodorow and
other psychologists have lately demonstrated, relationship is a central
term in female identity in contrast to the independence and autonomy
associated with maleness, and women's relationships tend to involve a
fluid sense of ego boundaries and body boundaries, at least partially as a
consequence of the intensity and persistence of mother-daughter bond-

ing. We have already seen how damaging a lack of autonomy may be. Yet feminist theorists, such as Carol Gilligan on the subject of ethics and Sara Ruddick in her speculations on "maternal thinking," have extrapolated from Chodorow in such a fashion as to suggest that female identity perceives itself as reciprocally both constituted by and constituting others, and have argued that a female pattern of fluid boundaries might be considered normal rather than aberrant and might be a source of social value.

Feminist literary critics have also found Chodorow's ideas generative.[9] Judith Kegan Gardiner, discussing the connection between female identity formation and female writing, suggests that because female identity is "less fixed, unitary and more flexible than male individuality," we can expect women writers to elude canonical genre distinctions; their writing "may blur the public and the private" and may be intensely personal and provoke personal identification on the part of the reader (she quotes Margaret Drabble generalizing her own response to Doris Lessing: "Most of us read books with this question in our mind: what does this say about my life?"). We can expect the subject of the mother-daughter relation to be central in women's writing and to reflect the ambivalence of the daughter who must both identify with and reject the mother. Finally, "woman writers often draw characters in whom traditionally male and female attributes of personality form a real and infrangible union."

Elizabeth Abel uses Chodorow to discuss the dynamics of female friendship in women's novels, showing how self-definition is accomplished through female bonding; she also outlines "a preoedipal psychoanalytic model for the creative process in all writers" opposed to Harold Bloom's oedipal theory. Mary Jacobus proposes that while "access to a male-dominated culture may equally be felt to bring with it alienation, repression, division, a silencing of the 'feminine,' a loss of women's inheritance," nevertheless "contemporary feminist criticism is more likely to stress pleasure than suffering—the freeing of repressed female desire; *jouissance* . . . as against the burden of womanhood," and she redefines "difference" to ally feminism and the avant-garde and challenge androcentric terms of discourse. Extending and exemplifying such convictions, Rachel Du Plessis defines a female aesthetic in the pathbreaking essay "For the Etruscans." Proposing the female "text as a form of intimacy . . . conversations with the reader or the self" characterized by "porousness and nonhierarchic stances" in both content and structure, Du Plessis boldly declares that the core position of the artist as woman is a "both/and vision" which "is the end of the either/or, dichotomized universe."

While it would clearly be mistaken to suppose that women's writing necessarily represents these or any other universal principles, it is evident that an assertive desire for intimacy looms very large in women's poetry today and that its implications for what we mean by art are significant. Several points must be emphasized about the poems I will cite in this chapter. First, these are poems which challenge the concept of the fixed self-other boundary. We find that satisfying pairings in women's poems join equivalent rather than polarized beings; that pleasure requires the elimination of hierarchy; that joy is the sensation of dissolved boundaries and the conviction that the walls between self and other have at least temporarily tumbled. This is the case in love poetry whether the work is heterosexual or lesbian. It is also the case in poetry not conventionally considered erotic—the poetry of maternity, of ancestresses and sisters, of muses and self-exploration. A corollary is that mind-body, public-private, sacred-profane distinctions are all likely to lapse in these poems. Second, the poems tend to stress female power as against feminine passivity, and the possibility or actuality of pleasure as against the older tide of suffering and victimization. This needs to be remembered because much feminist criticism rests on the assumption that female authors necessarily write from a position of powerlessness. Third, while these poems on intimate topics are necessarily personal, relying on what feminist critics have come to call the authority of experience as against traditional forms of authority, they are nonetheless transpersonal and principled. The individual case is felt to be general, the "I" to be a "we." Indeed, part of the point of this poetry lies with its discovery that "I" and "we" cannot be separated.

Stylistically, the imperative of intimacy tends to pull writers toward informal and "incorrect" uses of language. Among other sorts of "fracture of order" designed to combat the oppressor's language, earthiness, bawdry, and comedy abound, and most conspicuously so when the artist means to tell of the sacred and spiritual, for she is at pains to dissociate spirituality from theology and to reembed it firmly in the body. Unconventionally fluid and open forms are common in this work. Syntactic ambiguities are often extremely important. From time to time there surfaces a tone difficult to describe in our ordinary critical discourse: a species of irony, it seems, but vulgar and cheerful in contrast to the resigned and cruel ironies modernism teaches us to scent out as a primary signal of the cultivated author. This peculiar tone may be one of the chief contributions women are making to our literary and personal repertoires. Finally, and from the viewpoint of literary history most significantly, the breakdown of boundaries which is a central act in women's poetry commonly extends itself in these poems toward the reader, challenging and transforming the nature of the poem-audience transaction. *We Become New* is the title of an anthology of women's poetry, and appears to refer to the writers. We may also become new as readers.

2

I want to take off my clothes
and lie on cool sheets with you and show you
my fever
I want you to look   at me   and say
you're burning up.
      —Kathleen Fraser, "The Recognition" [10]

If I stand in my window
naked in my own house . . .
and if the man come to stop me . . .
let him watch my black body
push against my own glass
let him discover self
let him run naked through the streets
crying
praying in tongues
      —Lucille Clifton, "If I stand in my window" [11]

life without caution
the only worth living
love for a man
love for a woman
love for the facts
protectless

that self-defense be not
the arm's first motion
      —Adrienne Rich, "Leaflets" [12]

Who is burning up in Kathleen Fraser's poem? The poet, with her fever. What she wants is that the lover see it and say it. What she also wants and contrives to obtain in the poem, thanks to the convenience of omitted quotation marks, is an equivalence and ambivalence between the lover's body and her own. It is as if we could, by looking at another's fever, catch it; as if "you're burning up" might flash back and forth between two people like strobe lights. A similar fantasy animates, we remember, Mona Van Duyn's "intemperate girl," who wants her doctor-analyst-lover to "feel the way my body feels . . . spit up your text and taste my living texture," and in her dews, orifices, wastes, and smells "see self." [13] Whose self? To be intemperate is to be uncontrolled and tropical. Like Fraser, Van Duyn's girl must look flushed and fevered, and it is in this heightened erotic state that "self" may come to signify two persons simultaneously. Or, casually but marvelously, Lucille Clifton declares that the antagonistic white man seeing her naked body in the window will "discover self." But whose self does she mean? Or, rather, she does not say he will or he may. Like a priestess or a lady preacher, she uses the optative and says, "let him."

A white man who catches the contagious sacredness of a black woman's body and prays in tongues like a pentecostal Christian swept by the Spirit, is a miracle. A miracle in the optative. From seeing to bodily sharing to miraculous voicing is the desired sequence. The yearning to unlearn the learned instinctiveness of the insular gesture we associate with modern urban life recurs in the optative in Rich's "Leaflets," while the compressed grammatical ambivalence of "the only worth living" and the invented word "protectless" combine to create a sense of vulnerability made active. Thanks again to the lapse of grammar and punctuation, "protectless" can equally modify the facts, a woman, a man, and the impulsively loving self, creating the imagined case that is not yet the case. For it to become so, as the schooled reader will recognize, we must alter not only the ethos of societies which make caution and self-protection a necessity for the prudent individual—we who do not and never have lived like the lilies of the field. We must also apparently cast off one of the oldest dicta we as western intellectuals can remember, for our lofty conviction that the unexamined life is not worth living is perhaps part and parcel of an inability to love either each other or reality. What the passage suggests, omitting pronouns as it does, is that unstudied love is what I, you, he, she, they, anyone wants.

Need, want, look, touch, and *joy* are key terms in the poetics of intimacy. June Jordan's early exploration of the intersection between sexism and racism puts it in upper case: "WHO LOOK AT ME / WHO SEE," as does Diane Di Prima's "The Party:" "I NEED TO BE LOOKED AT / be seen / & not twice a week / I'm not a Brancusi bird." Another of Kathleen Fraser's poems, "What You Need," concludes, "You are brave. But you need to be touched." Nikki Giovanni complains, "I want to touch you & be touched . . . But you think I'm grabbing and I think you're shirking," and elsewhere asserts that touch is "the true revolution." Anne Sexton, who grew up among "people who seldom touched— / though touch is all," not only insists upon the absolute human value of openness, trust, and vulnerability throughout her work, but asserts that human intimacy accomplishes, if only briefly, what religion promises.

Touch for Sexton is "the kingdom / and the kingdom come," or "Zing! a resurrection." At the advent of any lovemaking, "Logos appears milking a star." Elsewhere in Sexton, even more boldly, the conventional concept of God as love translates to "When they fuck they are God . . . When they break away they are God . . . In the morning they butter their toast. / They don't say much. / They are still God." Sharing the same faith, Marge Piercy begins "Meditation in my Favorite Position" with the greeting "Peace, we have arrived . . . know you and be known, / please you and be pleased." This is St. Paul's rhapsody on love, but inverted: instead of seeing through a glass darkly on earth and expecting "to know, even as I am known" only when released from the flesh, we find that flesh alone makes knowledge possible. For these and other women, where Eros exits, Thanatos enters. If the heart is caught in a trap, explains Diane Wakoski,

> you can't gnaw it off and run away:
> to cut out the heart
> is to—
> this is obvious—
> cut out life.

Were it obvious to the poem's interlocutor, of course, Wakoski would not need to protest. Yet the poet Jean Valentine voices a thoroughly shared sense of female morality as well as a commentary on the long tradition of women's fearful sanctuary poems, when in the poem "Sanctuary" she criticizes the self as a prison-sanctuary which prevents us from entering another's mind to know "what it is like for you there." Asking herself what she most dreads, she answers, "Not listening. Now. Not watching. Safe inside my own skin. / To die, not having listened."[14]

In women's love poetry, the imperative of intimacy means goodbye to the hero, goodbye to the strong silent type. "It was never the crude pestle, the blind / ramrod we were after," says Adrienne Rich. "Merely a fellow-creature / with natural resources equal to our own." "I like my men / talky and / tender," explains Carol Bergé, and in poem after poem describing gratified desire, those husbands and lovers are praised who are most gentle and warm, releasing rather than repressing their own feminine qualities.[15] Scenes of role reversal and interchangeability are common in women's erotic poetry. An enlighteningly bawdy instance is "Like a Woman in the Kitchen" by Siv Cedering [Fox], where an amorous husband is not only feminized but maternalized. The husband talks while making love, Fox says, as if he were

> at home with the pots and pans
> and stirring . . .

it is the kind of talk
that knows that someone's listening:
    "Spread your legs.
    I have thought about your cunt
    all day. I like to feel it
    changing."

The poet obeys, she says, like a girl home from school being told to "dry
those glasses, taste some frosting, / lick the spoon," and is then herself
lifted and tasted as if she were a broth rich with "parsnips, turnips,
rutabaga," while she eats the marrow sucked from his bone. The tone is
matter-of-fact. Later, she declares, "we have lost all sense / of woman
man each being / both you say." To erase that difference is no doubt desired by many. A poem of John Donne boasts that he and a lady were
miraculously able to "forget the hee and shee." [16] However, Donne's occasion was not carnal, for it was the lady's virtue that he loved, compared with which her body was merely old clothes. To the male writer,
erasure of sexual difference depends on erasure of sexuality. Among
women, on the contrary, gender divisions attach to social roles and can
disappear in bodily encounters. Sex paradoxically brings the opportunity to shed or share gender. The husband in the Cedering poem is
masculine in that he gives instructions, feminine in that he cooks and
talks like a woman. The wife gets to play girl, cooking pot, and cook-
taster herself; and, it should be remarked, it is she who is doing the
boasting, conventionally a man's prerogative. The image of the male
mother reminds us that the mother is the primal erotic object for both
sexes.

Not surprisingly, women poets seem best satisfied with themselves
when they quit passivity and take some form of initiative, like Nikki
Giovanni in "The Seduction," forthrightly undressing her man while
he lectures her about revolutionary strategy, or Elizabeth Sargent, who
picks up and takes home a sailor, enjoys his battle tales, and is enter-
tained when asked if she is a virgin: "No, I'm a poet, I said. Fuck me
again." [17]

At times sexual role reversal tacitly inscribes itself when an ostensibly
neutral image of male-female sexuality evokes an extended history of
female associations. Thus Marge Piercy's "Unclench Yourself" envisions self and lover submerged in a brown stream, a clearly female image. When a lover compares Piercy with a rose, she corrects him, saying
that the rose represents their mutual embrace, but to the reader it remains a projection of the poet's sexuality. Similarly, Denise Levertov's
"The Ache of Marriage" sets husbands and wives like Noah's creatures
"in its belly," seeking salvation "two by two in the ark of / the ache of it."

The couple like the animals is nonpolarized, while the enclosing symbol of their pairing remains emphatically maternal.[18]

Such resonantly female symbols in women's erotic poems plainly signal the centrality rather than the marginality of female sexuality to women writers. As a general rule, however, women in love urge similitude in love. Pairs are often called "we," their genders minimized, their likenesses maximized, and ingenious arrays of nongendered metaphors help erase "the hee and shee" without erasing the physicality. Nikki Giovanni is as glad as mortar on a brick expecting another brick when her lover walks through the door. Ntozake Shange tells her lover that the mental space his love creates for her is "where the nile flows into the ganges . . . where the mississippi meets the amazon." A couple in an Eloise Healy poem is like wristbones, and a quarrel is a nail between them causing numbness they can feel for hours. In another Healy poem a couple is like a pile of old clothes, their colors fading together. When neglected in love, Healy compares herself to an old gray dog shoving its muzzle at the loved one's hand, hoping to shed all over the loved one's coat. As a Los Angelean, Healy appropriately describes love as merging onto a freeway at high speed, knowing that the other driver is adjusting to meet her and "wants it to go smooth."

For Adrienne Rich, lovers arriving at orgasm are like astronauts from separate nations reaching the moon, and their postcoital conversation is like moon-words: "Spasibo. Thanks. Okay." For athletic Maxine Kumin the same event when successful is like "the kind of hand-in-glove / expertise team workouts can evoke." For Lenore Kandel's hip exhibitionism, it is two trapeze artists, the first one yelling in upper case "CATCH ME" for a while, and finally "YOU CAUGHT ME! I LOVE YOU! Now it's *your* turn!" Meanwhile, back in the kitchen, Alice Mattison distinguishes herself and her husband from those whose "kisses are collisions" by a well-turned oral pun, "for us there's an overlapping." Domestically, women tend to envision love as something natural, normal, and shared, as in Lisel Mueller's "Love Like Salt" or Lucille Clifton's "Salt."[19]

Individually and collectively, such images demystify their subject. It is difficult to imagine any of these writers, or their attentive readers, tolerating with ease the role playing of unequals which remains the society's standard expectation in sexual relationships. The discovery of eros in the ordinary is important to women writers because, as Anne Snitow has pointed out,

> Men's idea of sex as transcendence, sex as transformation, has often been linked to the kind of mystification that conceals fear of women and the desire to repress their sexuality. The move toward using sex as a metaphor for something beyond the flesh has usu-

ally culminated in the glorious moment when the male writer
leaves his catalyst, the woman, behind.[20]

Possibly too we are seeing a recoil from the medieval identification of
love with death which has so profoundly influenced our culture, as cultural historians like De Rougemont and Bataille demonstrate[21] and
which caused Karen Horney to ask, in "The Dread of Woman":

> Are love and death more closely bound up with one another for
> the male than for the female . . . Does the man feel, side by side
> with his desire to conquer, a secret longing for extinction in the
> act of reunion . . . ?[22]

On the other hand, demystification should not be mistaken for a denial
of joy. In fact, women describe sexual ecstasy intensively, commonly
employing the idea of interpenetration between two lovers, the dissolving of boundaries between individual selves, and, at especially sensuous
moments, the elimination of distinctions between human and non-
human existence. "I am not sure where I leave off, where you begin,"
says Lenore Kandel. "Is there a difference, here in these soft permeable
membranes?"

"Permeable membranes" is a phrase used by more than one poet.
Ann Darr, Susan Griffin, and Margaret Atwood all use the figure of osmosis as the emblem of desire. Lucille Day, a neurochemist and biolo-
gist who describes an eroticized natural world, looks under the electron
microscope at the nerve cells bulbously developing in frog embryos:

> flowing inward, they move
> toward each other
>
> and when they finally meet,
> melding together, cell by cell,
> there is no explanation:
> they know who they are.
> I can almost hear them
> yammering in strange tongues.

This places us back alongside Lucille Clifton's man who speaks in
tongues, hearing the half-joking conceit of human (or cellular) elective
affinity as generating a sacred ur-language. The comic and the mystic
meet, and this breaking down of boundaries, this fluidity whereby microcosm and macrocosm exchange places and we reenter the natural
world from which we have been exiled, lies at the core of women's eroticism. Strikingly often, the key metaphors themselves involve water. In

Kumin's "We Are," the lovingly developed metaphor for a pair of lovers is that of a pond, complete with frogs whose legs open like very small children's, skimmed by water bugs, surrounded by blackberry bushes: "We teem, we overgrow." In another Kumin love poem,

> The water closing
> over us and the
> going down is all.
> Gills are given . . .
> Now we are new round
> mouths and no spines
> letting the water cover.
> It happens over
> and over, me in
> your body and you
> in mine.

In a poem by the bisexual Alta, a couple, neither conquering nor being conquered, makes love in a bedroom, and the result is

> the hot joy spilling
> puddles on the bed, the rug,
> the back yard, the earth
> happy with us, needing our joy.

"Anybody could write this poem. All you have to say is Yes," insists Alta in her title. It is a very different yes from Molly Bloom's, which never loses the distinction of the hee and shee. For Alta, "hot joy" dissolves the differentiation of genders, of self and other, of human and natural, of poet and reader, even of subject-object, as the poet's bed, rug, back yard, and earth transform themselves in mid-passage from passive receptacles to volitional consciousnesses; this poet tells us what Nora did not tell James Joyce.

A similar image of watery communion governs the evocation of lesbian love in Susan Griffin's "The Woman Who Swims in Her Tears," and submersion in a dream pond brings Adrienne Rich to a longed-for encounter with a woman lover and likeness in "Origins and History of Consciousness." Again, a woman lover is both child and mother in the Audre Lorde poem "Meet"; they are "women exchanging blood," and in another poem, "you create me against your thighs . . . my body / writes into your flesh / the poem / you make of me." Still again, in Daniella Gioseffi's quasi-surrealistic, quasi-pornographic "Paradise Is Not a Place," the pair of heterosexual lovers sail the seas on their mattress and ultimately fuse into a giant Mount Androgynous, which becomes a permanent tourist attraction in the mid-Pacific.[23] One would think of Donne's "Canonization," except that for Gioseffi as for women love poets typically, whether they are heterosexual or lesbian, sexuality does not signify transcendence of carnality or mortality, nor does it involve trials, tests, and obstacles. Where male sexuality, in keeping with its valorizing of conquest (of which courtly love is merely the inverse gesture), exploits metaphors of danger, risk, and death, female sexuality exploits metaphors of safety and security. Its most joyous act is a mutual letting go. Its images are of relaxation and immanence rather than strenuousness. The motion of love is down, not up: down toward the earth and water, down into the flesh, easily.

What then becomes of female eroticism beyond the bedroom door? To release sexual libido is to subvert social and political order, as we learn in male western literature from Euripides' *Bacchae* to Blake's *Marriage of Heaven and Hell*, from Rabelais to de Sade, and from Freud and Reich to Orwell's *1984*, where the triumph of Big Brother depends on the poisoning of sex. "The personal is the political" is a key feminist slogan, and the connection between erotic need and the need to be "disloyal to civilization" is central in feminist poetry.[24]

As gratified desire emerges from beings who are equivalent rather than polarized, sexual union becomes a figure in women's poems for every reunification needed by a divided humanity. Relationships between friends and lovers become paradigmatic for the conduct of political life. What resists the self-surrender of love and the commitment to human tenderness in the microcosm of personal relations is also what resists it in Vietnam, Africa, Harlem, and these poets want to break that resistance, tear off the armor. The intersections between practical politics and practical loving form a constant theme throughout Piercy's work. Again, according to Rich in "The Blue Ghazals," "The moment when a feeling enters a body / is political. This touch is political," because every human interaction must represent either connection or the will to dominance which is a refusal of connection. The old visions of escape—Matthew Arnold's "Ah, love, let us be true to one another" as a refuge from the death of God and the darkling plain of history—are impossible because public and private existence are indivisible. Thus the chilly lover in Rich's "Phenomenology of Anger" is simultaneously a defoliator of forests in Vietnam. By the same token, when in "Twenty-one Love Poems" Rich explores the effort of two women to live, love, and work together, she confronts the difficulties of choosing such a life in a city and a world hostile to love and to women. The ugliness and brutality of the city, the daily news of political atrocity and torture abroad, and the awareness of history and culture as chronicles of op-

pression, all drain the lover's power to love, so that "two women together is a work / nothing in civilization has made simple." [25]

One of the most powerful statements about the linked social and personal dimensions of women's love is Judy Grahn's underground classic
"A Woman Is Talking to Death," a long work which connects female
eroticism with the need to combat racism, misogyny, and class oppression. [26] The following passage is from a mock interrogation:

What about kissing? Have you kissed any women?

I have kissed many women.

When was the first woman you kissed with serious feeling?

The first woman ever I kissed was Josie, who I had loved at such
a distance for months. Josie was not only beautiful, she was
tough and handsome too. Josie had black hair and white teeth
and strong brown muscles. Then she dropped out of school
unexplained. When she came back she came back for one day
only, to finish the term, and there was a child in her. She was all
shame, pain, and defiance. Her eyes were as dark as the water
under the bridge and no one would talk to her, they laughed and
threw things at her. In the afternoon I walked across the front of
the class and looked deep into Josie's eyes and I picked up her
chin with my hand, because I loved her, because nothing like
her trouble would ever happen to me, because I hated it that she
was pregnant and unhappy, and an outcast. We were thirteen.

You didn't kiss her?

How does it feel to be thirteen and having a baby?

You didn't actually kiss her?

Between the interrogator's lascivious interest in lesbian kissing and the
poet's commitment to lesbian loving lies the shadow of what sexuality
means in our culture. When the questioner asks if she has held hands
with a woman, Grahn's affirmative includes "women who had been run
over, beaten up, deserted, starved, women who had been bitten by rats,"
as well as women who were dancing, climbing mountains, or "liked me
better than anyone." Asked if she has committed indecent acts with
women, she lists her acts of omission: failure to save suicidal women, to
love a love-hungry prostitute, to sleep with and comfort the lonely, to
fight for "our planet, our city, our meat and potatoes." In a later section

of the poem Grahn is knocked down in a diner by a Spanish-speaking youth who calls her "queer." Counterman and police prove indifferent. Weeks later it occurs to her that this might be Josie's son. In a still later section, she and her "pervert" friends encounter a fifty-five-year-old Chinese woman who has been raped by a cab driver and left bleeding in the snow. They kiss and try to reassure her, knowing it is not enough. Grahn burns with desire to rule the city with this woman. But she lets her go in the ambulance with the bored policemen, guiltily unable to enact her defiance and "get the real loving done."

The close of "A Woman Is Talking to Death" is Grahn's vow not to work for death or serve him but to spend her life so lovingly that she will leave nothing of herself for him but some fertilizer: "your pot is so empty / death, ho death / you shall be poor." This is a vow made implicitly by many other women poets, for whom self-examination means assuming an almost mystic responsibility for the lives of others. [27]

It would be a mistake to say that these female figures of fluid boundaries are merely literary tropes, objective correlatives of the subjective sensation of female pleasure. Though they certainly serve that function, they remind us also that our normal conception of self as rigidly bounded entity is a fiction, a mental habit true neither to our biochemical lives nor to the actualities of human interaction whereby in fact we are all interdependent "permeable membranes" continually penetrating and being penetrated by a world of others. The female erotic vision, then, amounts to a subversion of the identification of self with ego as bounded form committed to preserving its boundaries, and begins to propose an alternative scheme of larger units wherein the self is plural, a spinning array of multiple selves. For not only does the erotic female "I" perceive itself as equivalent to and interchanging with a loved one in moments of sexual encounter, and not only does it extend the sphere of the erotic to nature on the one hand and to political life on the other. It can also, as we shall see, perceive itself as composed of its parents, extended in its children, vitalized by the powers of spiritual ancestresses, determined to identify with and redeem the defeated, and engaged in a communal drama denoted by the omnipresent "we" of shared desire.

3

As men go to war—ignorant, foolhardy, vainglorious,
brave—so women to motherhood.
　　　—Celia Gilbert, "Voices" [28]

Mother
I write home
I am alone and
give me my
body back
     —Susan Griffin, "Mother and Child"[29]

The poet is a daughter. The poet may be a mother. Daughters write of parents and grandparents, mothers write of children, and, as Judith Kegan Gardiner suggests, the theme of the mother-child relationship has proven extraordinarily intense in contemporary women's poetry. More than the bond with any lover, the bond with a parent or with a child is absolute and noncontingent. For better or worse, as the saying goes. "A woman *is* her mother," Anne Sexton remarks. "I built you within me, a sealed world," Sharon Olds says to her daughter.[30] The permanence promised in marriage vows encapsulates the culture's attempt to make a nonbiological link the equal of a biological one. A bride and groom forsake their parents and cleave to one another, becoming one flesh. That is our metaphor, that is our wish. But a woman and her mother, or a woman and her child, already are one flesh whether she wishes it or not. The mother and the child occupy her and tug on her. As they commend and blame her, so she does herself. Their power over her seems infinite—until it lapses, frays, wanes, or until she breaks it. The fact is that she never can become a poet—never can become an autonomous being—unless that bond is broken. The bond with the mother. And the bond with the child, if she has a child. And then when it is broken, she wants to recover it. Without it, she is not whole.

A second reason for the intensity of the parent-child poem is that we here explore a primal erotic relationship, that emotion-laden intimacy antedating all others, on which perhaps all others are modeled. "The first knowledge any woman has of warmth, nourishment, tenderness, security, sensuality, mutuality, comes from her mother," Adrienne Rich points out in *Of Woman Born: Motherhood as Experience and Institution;*[31] it is on that intimacy that our lives once depended, and our child's life depends on it if we have a child. A third reason for intensity is cultural and literary: we are struggling against amnesia and denial. Good motherhood, in our culture, is selfless, cheerful, and deodorized. It does not include resentment, anger, violence, alienation, disappointment, grief, fear, exhaustion—or erotic pleasure. It is ahistorical and apolitical. It excludes the possibility of abortion. As to the child: sons grow independent, but not daughters. Our culture does not give us images of the daughter desperate for the mother's love, or desperate to escape it, or contemptuous of the mother, nor do we have an archetype of the Prodigal Daughter, who escapes and returns—not to a fatted calf but to her mother's body. As Rich has amply demonstrated in *Of Woman Born*, what we have is a flat and sanitized version of the mother-child relation, which is institutionally useful and experientially inauthentic. It is a version which dozens of women poets are working to overthrow. [32]

Because the mother as an autonomous subject has been excluded from literature, the first point to be made here suggesting the extraordinary significance of motherhood in women's poems is that there is no discontinuity between "motherhood" and "abortion" poems. Gwendolyn Brooks' widely anthologized "The Mother" is actually an abortion poem whose speaker articulates complex feelings of yearning, loss, guilt, and love toward the children she "got but did not get." Lucille Clifton's "The Lost Baby Poem" swears to an aborted child that she will be a mountain of strength to its future brothers and sisters. Summer Brenner and Diane Di Prima, among others, have written impassioned addresses to their aborted children. [33] On the other hand, the most euphoric mother-child poems usually imply that maternal euphoria is a form of cultural defiance. This may take the shape of Di Prima's deliberate hyperbole over a toddler, "when Jeannie wakes light starts . . . clotheslines untangle . . . when Jeannie sings / Bach listens," or Marilyn Krysl's wildly exuberant depiction of her daughter and herself in "Sestina Extolling the Pleasures of Creation," as they color a Dürer drawing of a rhinoceros and defeat the forces of depression and the difficulties of the sestina at once. Alta reminds herself that nursing a child was "not stained glass windows," the culturally mandated and cold artifice. Other poets describe nursing as a sensual or even quasi-adulterous encounter. Lucille Clifton's proud "Admonitions" allies herself with her sons against the law, with her daughters against predatory white men. [34] As poems of abortion are not inconsistent with powerful maternal feelings, so powerful maternal feelings are not inconsistent with subversion of social stereotype.

Because intensity depends on tension, our most exciting and disturbing mother-child poems tend to group themselves around the periods of infancy and adolescence, when the simultaneous union and division between parent and child generates maximum ambivalence. For the condition of motherhood is then most plainly perceived as both an enlargement and a loss of identity. [35] "Perfection is terrible, it cannot have children," remarks Sylvia Plath of the narcissistic and barren-by-definition "Munich Mannequins." Madeline Bass, advising a new mother, echoes "No more perfection. No circle," promising only that the future daughter will embody an affectionate separateness which the poet calls "a gracious mystery; we are all its daughters."

Kathleen Fraser's "Poem Wondering if I'm Pregnant" anticipates both gain ("is it you, penny face? is it you?") and loss ("thief I can't see . . . uncontrollable"), consistent parameters in maternal poetry. That a child is the uncontrollable other, absorbing and exhausting its mother, is a given in women's poems, often generating bizarre imagery. Infants fasten on and eat their mothers in poems by Cynthia Macdonald and Joan Larkin. In a Joyce Carol Oates poem, a monstrous baby grows "enormous, filling the room, the space." To Susan Griffin her daughter is the "innocent jailer." Plath's sense of pleasure at parturition is a torn one. The newborn of "Morning Song," which Plath designated as the opening poem in *Ariel*, gives the poet meaning, like a statue in an otherwise empty museum. Simultaneously the baby destroys the poet's previous essence—she is a cloud distilling a reflection which effaces her. And yet again she is solidly comic, "cow-heavy and floral in my Victorian nightgown," as she stumbles toward the infant's cry and the final lyric perception, "the clear vowels rise like balloons." Elsewhere, Plath's children can be either "you, ruby" and "the baby in the barn" ("Nick and the Candlestick") or "little smiling hooks" ("Tulips"). Miriam Goodman inverts Plath's effaced cloud metaphor for motherhood, claiming, "My spirit was smoke until it took a shape / for the sake of serving." Alice Mattison, who writes extensively of motherhood in the vein of the comic-grotesque, sees her fecundity surreally: in "Husband" she is a house in which babies emerge from jelly in every room, a tube bubbling babies forth at either end, who crawl up her thighs, cascade over her hips, "prodding me inside and out with new feet." Mattison compactly delineates the mutually frightening edge between love and violence in the most ordinary mother-infant encounter, as well as the triumph of its ordinarily safe resolution, in "The Crazy Baby." The baby keeps waking too soon for his feeding in the first stanza, keeps sleeping overtime in the second, and finally:

We have no issues, he and I, but life,
death; not stabbing him with the pin,
I change his diaper; not being eaten,
I let him suck.
I tell him, "Oh you dodo, you
crazy baby."

"Crazy" is of course what new mothers often fear they will become. Thus if the maternal love-talk on which an infant's emotional and ver-

bal growth will depend is a kind of ur-poetry, a half-nonsensical play
with syllables, it is also a hair's breadth from disaster: mother's craziness
safely averted once again and transformed to nurturant play. A similar
insight regarding maternal possessiveness is recorded in Anne Sexton's
modernized version of "Hansel and Gretel," which implies that the normal mother's nuzzlings of a child who is good enough to eat are controlled versions of a larger appetite: "My fritter, my bubbler, my chicken
biddy . . . / it is but one turn in the road / and I would be a cannibal!"
Sharon Olds, among our most eloquent celebrants of the erotic mother-
child relation, describes young mothers as themselves alert animals and
tranced infants, lost in the bliss of tending, the anguish of separation:

> Crossing the sill again, she inhales that
> peace like ether. Leaving again she
> enters the dream of murder, mutilation, her
> old self bleeding in pieces on the butcher paper
>   . . . she is
> struggling down the corridor, her own mother
> holding onto her ankles and bearing down.[36]

That the intimacy between mother and child is a two-way dependence, and its loss a grief, is the burden of many poems concerning the
child's adolescence; and often the poignant point made is that the rejection of mother by child is precisely the band knotting maternal generations. In a typical multigenerational poem, Ann Darr extracts a stiletto
from her ribs, returns it to her daughter, and explains that this is the
same blade she inherited from her mother, and she from hers. On
the other hand, Lucille Clifton boasts to her mother, "I have taken the
bones you hardened / and built daughters," and Maxine Kumin's "The
Envelope" daringly inverts the image of pregnancy to assert that mothers defy division and mortality by entering their daughters' bodies at the
hour of their death:

> Like those old pear-shaped Russian dolls that open
> at the middle to reveal another and another, down
> to the pea-sized irreducible minim,
> may we carry our mothers forth in our bellies.

As she bears her mother's "nervy" ghost under her navel, so her daughters will become envelopes for her and carry her onward, like a "chain
letter good for the next twenty-five / thousand days of their lives."[37]
    As in "The Envelope," Kumin's enduring theme is biological attach-
ment with its convergence of division and continuity. She is our fore-

most chronicler of kinship, for to Kumin, family extends well beyond the Freudian romantic triangle—"Sperm," for example, tragicomically traces the lives of seventeen look-alike cousins—and our shared biology stretches well beyond the human. The title poem of *Our Ground Time Here Will Be Brief*, an extended conceit on lifetimes and airports, envisions generations of the great-grandchildren's souls strewn like parsnip or celery seeds over the cloud pack. In the title poem of *The Retrieval System* people die but animals "retrieve" them. Two elderly departed aunts become ponies begging for apples; the dog has Father's brown eyes; a boy once loved, buried at sea in World War II, reappears in a yearling's gallop. To split wood is to release the soul of the beech and recall the soul of the lost friend, Anne Sexton, in "Splitting Wood at Six Above." [38]

Children, especially daughters, keep cropping up in Kumin's work, and her poems about growing and grown children consistently balance between the need to possess and the need to release, and between the pathos of Thanatos and the comedy of Eros. Parental fury ("Changing the Children") has the black-magic power to transform the adolescents into berating crow, accusatory porcupine, and "spider / forced to spin from her midseam / the saliva of false repentance," but eventually they come back, "much like ourselves . . . not a virgin among them." The adored children in "Family Reunion" are both "adult, professional, aloof," and "the almost-parents of your parents now." When she visits a daughter she loves "with secret frenzy" ("Leaving My Daughter's House"), Kumin admits she cannot penetrate the daughter's life or play other than a walk-on part, and compares herself with the second-rate horses in the stable next door who no matter how hard they try will never run at Ascot. Yet even division is a form of intimacy: at poem's end, mother and daughter have become paired horses,

> balancing on the bit that links us and keeps us
> from weeping o God! into each other's arms. [39]

That the mother desires an impossible closeness and accepts a separation which she tries to reinscribe as reunion is a central thread through Anne Sexton's family poetry as well as Maxine Kumin's, though the part played by time and natural cycles in Kumin is in Sexton played by the poet's mother, the determining figure whose "Double Image" she is and whom she hates and loves:

> On the first of September
> she looked at me

and said I gave her cancer.
They carved her sweet hills out
and still I couldn't answer.

Anger and pity dominate Sexton's poems to her mother—anger that she
was "the unwanted, the mistake / that Mother used to keep Father /
from his divorce," and pity because "I did not know that my life, in the
end, / would run over my mother's like a truck" ("Those Times . . .").
She wants, in the early elegy "The Division of Parts," both to "curse"
her mother and bring her "flapping back, old love . . . god-in-her-
moon . . . my Lady of my first words," and she writes with undimin-
ished identification and alienation of her need and deprivation in the
posthumous collection 45 Mercy Street. Toward her daughters, in
poems like "The Double Image," "A Little Uncomplicated Hymn,"
"The Fortress," and "Pain for a Daughter," Sexton at first asserts her passionate desire to love adequately, coupled with guilt over her failures.
Later there is urgent joy over a daughter's impending puberty—"Oh
darling, let your body in," she cries in "Little Girl, My Stringbean, My
Lovely Woman"—mixed with pride that she has been her daughter's
first lover no matter who enters afterward. Delight mixes with the
awareness that the daughter's advance is the mother's decline ("Mother
and Daughter").

> Linda, you are leaving
> your old body now.
> You've picked my pocket clean
> and you've racked up all my
> poker chips and left me empty . . .
>
> Question you about this
> and you will see my death
> drooling at these grey lips
> while you, my burglar, will eat
> fruit and pass the time of day.

Open-eyed, Sexton urges her daughter toward sexuality in terms that
include the tragic knowledge of woman's role:

> Keep on, keep on, keep on,
> carrying keepsakes to the boys,
> carrying powders to the boys,
> carrying, my Linda, blood to
> the bloodletter.[40]

The last line arrives at the intersection of the domestic sphere assigned to mothers and the wider world. To what purpose do we nurture these extensions of our identity? To what degree can we protect them? Carolyn Kizer in "Pro Femina" remarks on women's "well-known respect for life / Because it hurts so much to come out with it." That respect, beleaguered to the point of anguish and rage, informs the political poetry of Muriel Rukeyser, Denise Levertov, Robin Morgan, and many other poets whose work has been influenced by what Sara Ruddick calls "maternal thinking." "I'm alive to want more than life," exclaims Adrienne Rich, "want it for others hungry and unborn." Her anger is echoed in Susan Griffin's well-known "I Like to Think of Harriet Tubman," which juxtaposes a tribute to Tubman's defiance of slave law with Griffin's "hysteria"—literally "womb-suffering"—over "the problem of feeding children" and the president and other men who make and revere the law at the expense of starving children:

The legal answer
to the problem of feeding children
is ten free lunches every month,
being equal, in the child's real life,
to eating lunch every other day.
Monday but not
Tuesday.
And when I think of the President
and the law, and the problem of
feeding children, I like to
think of Harriet Tubman
and her revolver.

In *Of Woman Born* Adrienne Rich tells the anecdote of the Frenchwoman who ironically asked, when hearing that the poet had three sons, "*Vous travaillez pour l'armée,* madame?" (Are you working for the army?) Madeline Bass' "This Iliad" identifies the separation of boys from their mothers with their embrace of patriarchal violence: "They will all be killers." Sharon Olds, seeing the war between the sexes as an apocalyptic conflagration, wonders desperately how to save the children:

The only way out is through
fire, and I do not want a single
hair of a single head singed.[41]

For the poet who is a mother, this declaration has the force, if anything does, of a categorical imperative. Socially and politically, the mother-child attachment converges with the eroticizing of public life to become a maternal politics: an argument against hunger, poverty, violence, oppression, and war.

When we move to women's poems about their own mothers, from branches to roots, the experience of bonding seems almost magically strong. The daughters seek "clues / to our mother's unwritten life" in process of writing their own. Numerous poets record the experience of encountering the mother within the self, hearing the mother's voice in one's own, seeing the mother's face in the mirror. Mother and daughter are in some sense lovers. At the outset of sensuous life, says Adrienne Rich in "Sibling Mysteries," daughters are "brides of the mother," from whose goddesslike body they are exiled by the father. At the close of life, says Marie Ponsot's concisely titled "Nursing: Mother," the hospitalized mother is a goddess ("I flinch / before her sacredness"), and hers is the body which, in giving birth, effects both union and division. From between these mother's thighs that were splashed with Mercurochrome, Ponsot recognizes,

> I thrust into sight thirsting for air
> (So it must have been; so my children came;
> So we commit by embodying it, woman to woman,
> Our power to set life free.
> She set me free.)

When her mother has died ("Late") Ponsot understands the still stronger bond formed in infancy:

> We meant while we were together to create
> A larger permanence, as lovers do,
>
> Of perfecting selves: I would love you
> As you me, each to the other a gate.

Conversely, May Sarton's "Death and the Lovers" claims that lovers seek each other as infant seeks mother, "to make a strong one out of a frail two."[42] This sense that all desire threads back ultimately to the erotic mother is a primary component of women's poems to their mothers. Another is the ambivalence of maternal attachment, associated with ambivalent views of the mother as power figure.

Typically in women's poems the mother is perceived as both overwhelmingly powerful and devastatingly powerless. On the one hand she seems in many instances so awesome that she can be approached, actually and verbally, only when she lapses toward infirmity and death, and even then she commonly retains the attributes of a goddess. Among the metaphors Judith Hemschemeyer uses to describe her mother in one memorial sequence, the mother is a bear, a wolf, a giant redwood. Her hands were "'big as a foot,' she laughed." Her arms are like Joan of Arc's. Her glowing cigarette tip in the family car is a "tiny Vesuvius," and when she tries to wrench the car from the road she is Kali. In "Commandments," Hemschemeyer declares, "I went away, got straight A's, got children with a handsome husband, a stranger, a male":

> It didn't work.
> Delivered into her huge hands at birth,
> I lie there still.

On the other hand, daughter often perceives mother as someone who is powerless in the larger world of the fathers and has transmitted to the daughter a crippling expectation of weakness. As Adrienne Rich notes in her chapter on mothers and daughters in *Of Woman Born*,

> A mother's victimization does not merely humiliate her, it muti-lates the daughter who watches her for clues as to what it means to be a woman. Like the traditional foot-bound Chinese woman she passes on her own affliction. The mother's self-hatred and low ex-pectations are the binding rags for the psyche of the daughter.[43]

A mother locked into domesticity immobilizes her daughters in Rich's "A Woman Mourned by Daughters." What Plath sees in the mirror in "All the Dead Dears" is a mother, grandmother, and great-grandmother who "reach hag hands to haul me in." Her mother's desperate need to be useful paralyzes Plath in "The Disquieting Muses" and "Medusa." Karen Snow's extraordinary book-length *Wonders* is the fictionalized autobiography of a woman who has been literally cursed by a patholog-ically and aggressively humble mother. Susan Griffin's family poems give us a dynasty of failed and fragmented women and desperate fan-tasies of reunion and reintegration. Marilyn Hacker's mother-daughter poems fear that all women are "beasts that repeat themselves" in a cycle of self-despisal.

Resentful love, loving resentment, the need to affirm a bond per-ceived to be absolute, and the discovery that the mother or both parents are at once curse and blessing, animates some of our finest and most intense poems and poem sequences. In the title poem of *Satan Says*, Sharon Olds blasphemes her hated parents on Satan's instructions, only to discover that she loved them too, an insistence that at once captures and frees her forever. Mon Van Duyn's *Merciful Disguises* includes one good-mother and one bad-mother poem. Paradoxically, "The Creation"—the poem of elegiac tribute to her mother's strength, charm, beauty, and individuality—follows a conceit that the poet is erasing, feature by feature, the mother's image, while "Remedies, Maladies, Reasons"—an attack on a sickness-obsessed mother—concludes in a gesture of irrational love for this mother seen as giant savior. Marge Piercy's "Crescent Moon like a Canoe" struggles to articulate her connection with a conservative mother who refuses connection:

> You suffer
> and I cannot save you though I burn with dreams . . .
> You were taught to feel stupid; you
> were made to feel dirty; you were
> forced to feel helpless; you were trained
> to feel lost, uprooted, terrified.
> You could not love yourself or me.

Yet the same woman was a gardener who transmitted her lore about plants and birds to the daughter who now declares, "I am your poet, mother"; and at the end of the poem Piercy insists that the mother who slapped her down—"Don't do it, they'll kill you, you're bad"—secretly always wanted the "sword of hearts" her daughter has become.[44]

This pattern of angry division and visionary reunion is especially important, in fact almost universal, among black and third-world women poets. Where the factor of race augments the factor of gender, it imposes on mother and daughter a double powerlessness and a double degree of self-hatred but by the same token makes possible a stronger ultimate affirmation.[45] Audre Lorde's "Prologue" describes a typical pattern:

> When I was a child
> whatever my mother thought would mean survival
> made her try to beat me whiter every day
> and even now the color of her bleached ambition
> still forks throughout my words
> but I survived
> and didn't I survive confirmed.

The rejection of a black, Native American, Chicana, or Oriental heritage is a bitter memory in the work of many women's poems. In Lorde's "Black Mother Woman" the daughter becomes, like the mother, "split with deceitful longings." In "Generation II" the black girl submits to becoming the woman her mother desires because she is "afraid / of both their angers." Yet the split, for Lorde and others, must be healed, and reconciliation comes with recognition of the mother's strength, imaged as a darkness emerging from its shell in "The Woman Thing":

this woman thing my mother taught me
bakes off its covering of snow
like a rising blackening sun

Or in "From the House of Yemanja," the mother is divided, "one dark and rich and hidden / in the ivory hungers of the other," and the daughter invokes the deeper identity:

Mother I need
mother I need
mother I need your blackness now
as the august earth needs rain.

Less solemnly, Carolyn Rodgers records in *How I Got Ovah* a swing from defiance to reverence for a conservatively pious mother who thinks "Black" is "something ugly to kill it befo it grows":

she sd i mon pray fuh u tuh be saved. i sd thank yuh
    but befo she hung up my motha sd
    well girl, if yuh need me call me
i hope we don't have to straighten the truth out no mo
            . . . (then i sd)
        catch you later on jesus, i mean motha!

In the mother's stubborn endurance, her ability to work, love and sacrifice, Rodgers comes to recognize "a sturdy Black bridge that I / crossed over, on," and a means of strengthening her own identity.

The discovery of the mother-daughter bond as a necessary source of the daughter's art has also been described in the prose and poetry of numerous writers. Alice Walker's essay "In Search of Our Mothers' Gardens" celebrates the hidden creativity of the ancestresses whom black women today can begin to redeem. Cherríe Moraga in "La Guera" describes a moment of revelation significantly triggered by another woman poet:

I went to a concert where Ntozake Shange was reading. There, everything exploded for me. She was speaking language that I knew—in the deepest parts of me—existed, and that I had ignored in my own feminist studies and even in my own writing. What Ntozake caught in me is the realization that in my own development as a poet, I have, in many ways, denied the voice of my brown mother—the brown in me. I have acclimated to the sound of a white language which, as my father represents it, does not speak to the emotions in my poems—emotions which stem from the love of my mother . . . Sitting in that auditorium chair was the first time I had realized to the core of me that for years I had disowned the language I knew best—ignored the words and rhythms that were the closest to me. The sounds of my mother and aunts gossiping—half in English, half in Spanish—while drinking cerveza in the kitchen. And the hands—I had cut off the hands in my poems. But not in conversation; still the hands could not be kept down. Still they insisted on moving.

Moraga's "For the Color of My Mother" invokes a community of brown women, and her refrain describes the return to the mother and the mother tongue as that which empowers her writing:

> I am a white girl gone brown to the blood color of my mother speaking for her through the unnamed part of the mouth the wide-arched muzzle of brown women.

At the close of her long chantlike poem of mourning and tribute to her mother, "Getting Down to Get Over," June Jordan begs her "momma" to teach her a survival that is more than personal: "help me / turn the face of history / *to your face*." For women of color, it is clear that the return to the mother makes possible the freeing of the poet's voice and her ability to speak on behalf of a community which has given her substance as she gives it voice.[46]

4

> It hurts to pull off the old
> disguises and patches. They stick,
> the shields, veils, pasties,
> the band-aids of acquiescence,
> the diaphragm over the soul . . .
> until one of us lets fly
> and dazzles us all with her nakedness,
> her glorious black and blue.
>   —Lisel Mueller, "Levelling with Each Other"[47]

Chodorow's observation that the daughter's identification with the mother makes possible her identification with a larger world is a primary message of the poems we have just been examining. But this same sense of and need for connection with a community is present throughout women's writing, and the bond that shapes women's poems to lovers, children, and mothers extends through a wide web of other relationships. We have love poems to fathers, some of them frankly remembering the poignance of sexual attraction.[48] We have poems to women friends, often recording the difficult process of learning to remove the masks and become open.[49] And as Lynda Koolish has noted, "the woman poet's concept of the community as an extended family" reaches toward the past as well as the present, "creating new transtemporal bonds."[50]

In their quest for an identity that will be both personal and communal, women writers make poems for and from the lives of lost women, the insulted and injured of present and past history, the heroines, the writers and artists who are their spiritual sisters and ancestresses. And always the note is intimate. The implied faith is that without each other we are all incomplete and that the poet who recovers and articulates another's life not only redeems and honors it but supplies a necessary portion of her own being. "My lifetime listens to yours," says Muriel Rukeyser to the German artist Käthe Kollwitz. "Any woman's death diminishes me," says Adrienne Rich in a poem exploring the anonymous lives of American frontierwomen. "You are dead but not as dead as you / have been, we will avenge you," says Alta to the ostracized Anne Hutchinson, while a description of the Puritan foremother's "haughty and fierce carriage" makes the poet's shoulders straighten. Jayne Cortez' tribute to Fannie Lou Hamer ("Big Fine Woman from Ruleville") wears her heroine's "riverstone eyes splashed / with Mississippi blood / and your sharecropper shoes braided with your powerful stomp." Lucille Clifton identifies with and gathers fortitude from Harriet Tubman, Sojourner Truth, and her own grandmother ("harriet / if i be you"), and when she addressed the ruined "Miss Rosie" it is with both grief and resolution:

> When I watch you
> wrapped up like garbage
> sitting, surrounded by the smell
> of too old potato peels . . .
> you wet brown bag of a woman
> who used to be the best looking gal in Georgia
> used to be called the Georgia Rose
> I stand up
> through your destruction
> I stand up

The same conviction supports Judy Grahn's "common woman" sequence, ending with a vow sworn on her own common woman's head. Or, again, Marilyn Krysl's rowdy "Sestina for Our Revolution," an homage to the revolutionary heroines Emma Goldman and Anna Kil-

Ionta, celebrates their advocacy of opera, roses, and the "luxury" of free love, against the opposition of Emma's father and lover, Andrew Carnegie, Lenin, "Uncle Joe" Stalin, the poet's father ("What's your father's / profession? Mine was a butcher"), and others. Krysl's tour de force on sex and politics appropriately uses language as play and as rule breaking:

> "The luxury
> of love is completely un-Marxist." So Lenin the Great. "More
>
> bread, more wine, more lovers learning the language, more
> faces lit with radiance! Stop work, buy roses!" So Emma
> in Philadelphia.

Emma, explains the poet, is the "father of my revolution," much as George Washington is the father of Wakoski's country.

When women writers write of continuities from one writer, artist, or thinker to another, it is thus not, *pace* Harold Bloom, on the oedipal model of killing and superseding the precursor, but on the Demeter-Kore model of returning and reviving. As Joanne Feit-Diehl has observed, while the image of a male muse commonly provokes both fear and desire in the woman poet, a female muse functions as a giver of confidence and a representative of "an alternative line to the dominant male canon."[51]

Unlike the traditional male homage to a poetic ancestor, the female homage tends to be informal rather than formal, to focus on the precursor's personal qualities such as courage, passion, or hatred of injustice rather than on impersonal accomplishments, and to see the precursor as a practical support to her own creativity rather than an object of awe. Matthew Arnold's famous "Shakespeare" sonnet reverentially praises Shakespeare's inaccessible superiority: "Others abide our question. Thou art free . . . out-topping knowledge." Women poets seem not interested in praising, or becoming, superior beings in this sense. Even when another woman artist is seen as a negative model—Wakoski's long enraged poem on Sylvia Plath and Marge Piercy's grief-stricken one on the singer Janis Joplin's "rich stew of masochism" are examples—the grappling is never cool and judgmental but painfully personal. Self-destruction is a strong temptation to these poets, and they barely feel they are escaping it. Theirs is a far cry from, for example, W. H. Auden urbanely remarking in his elegy "In Memory of W. B. Yeats," "You were silly like us; your gift survived it all," or from Auden's conclusion that "poetry makes nothing happen."

Yet at the other end of the emotive spectrum, it is difficult to imagine

a male poet writing to and of a poetic master a poem anything like
Elizabeth Bishop's giddy "Invitation to Miss Marianne Moore," with its
"please come flying" refrain and its poignant picture of the poet as a
kind of scintillant good witch:

> Come with the pointed toe of each black shoe
> trailing a sapphire highlight,
> with a black capeful of butterfly wings and bon-mots,
> with heaven knows how many angels all riding
> on the broad black brim of your hat,
>   please come flying.
>
> Bearing a musical inaudible abacus,
> a slight censorious frown, and blue ribbons,
>   please come flying.
> Facts and skyscrapers glint in the tide, Manhattan
> is all awash with morals this fine morning
>   so please come flying . . .
>
> We can sit down and weep, we can go shopping,
> or play at a game of constantly being wrong
> with a priceless set of vocabularies,
> or we can bravely deplore, but please
>   please come flying.[52]

Bishop's sophisticated literary playfulness, resting as it does on an assumption of pre-existing feminine intimacy and understanding, differs
in surface but not in essence from the good humor of Carolyn Rodgers'
address to her black mother or Krysl's to Emma Goldman. If the deep
truth discoverable in men's poems is that all men are each other's rivals,
the equal and opposite truth discoverable in women's poems is that we
are allies and portions of one another.

5

> and he said: you pretty full of yourself ain't chu
> so she replied: show me someone not full of herself
>   and i'll show you a hungry person
>   —Nikki Giovanni, "Poem for a Lady Whose Voice I
>   Like"[53]

How can man escape
his animality?

Why
would he want to?
—Ann Darr, "Gaelic Legacy," [54]

Within the symposium of the self, women poets evidently wish to
reverse Yeats' dictum that from the quarrel with ourselves we make poetry. Instead they struggle to make poetry about healing the self through
reconciling internal antimonies. Coleridge, Rimbaud, and Woolf are
invoked for the idea of the androgynous being who combines intellect
and emotion, strength and gentleness. The integrated self of Piercy's
"The Woman in the Ordinary" is "a woman of butter and brass, / compounded of acid and sweet like a pineapple," set to explode like a hand
grenade and bloom like a sunflower. [55] Poems of self-integration through
visionary integration with both parents have been written by Rukeyser,
Celia Gilbert, Sharon Olds, Audre Lorde, and Jean Valentine. Often
the males in women's poems fill the role of courage-giving alter ego or
animus: Rich's "half-brother" Orion, Sexton's imaginary twin Christopher (based on Christopher Smart, the mad and mystic eighteenth-
century poet who inspires her psalm sequence "O Ye Tongues"), or
Maxine Kumin's spunky hermit neighbor in her "Henry Manly" poems.
    Adrienne Rich, brooding in poem after poem over "where the split
began," has created a sequence of healing images of integration which
have strongly influenced other poets. At the conclusion of "Snapshots,"
the new woman who approaches from the sky is "at least as beautiful as
any boy / or helicopter," while carrying a female "cargo." At the end of
"Necessities of Life," Rich imagines an androgynously figured self who
will be "trenchant in motion as an eel, solid / as a cabbage-head." The
figuratively male soul rejoins the figuratively female body at the close of
"In the Woods" when the alienated soul "burst into my body . . .
Found! ready or not." The first of Rich's "Two Songs" similarly reminds
us that body and mind need not be divided, for it is "pure happiness to
know / all our high-toned questions / breed in a lively animal." And
when she descends to the depths of personal and communal history in
"Diving into the Wreck," she is both naked mermaid and armored merman. "I am the androgyne," she says in "The Stranger"; and while Rich
has since repudiated the debated term "androgyny," [56] the idea of strength
combined with love remains attractive to her and to others.
    Denise Levertov, another poet haunted by polarities in need of heal-
ing, has for twenty years been proposing sensuous transformations of
dualistic texts. [57] Levertov's "Else a Great Prince in Prison Lies," from
The Jacob's Ladder (1961) implies, in contradistinction to John Donne's
famous formulation, that the "Prince" caught in human flesh is not a

transcendent soul but a beautiful animal. "The Fountain," Levertov's answer to *The Waste Land*, pleads "Don't say, don't say there is no water / to solace the dryness at our hearts." Where Eliot imagines a desert, Levertov imagines a spring that is at once outside and within the self. A few years later, the title poem of *O Taste and See* (1964) counters Wordsworth's declaration that the world is too much with us by claiming that "the world is / not with us enough" and urging that we should "savor, chew, swallow, transform" it all, living in the orchard and plucking the fruit. "Stepping Westward," taken from a Wordsworth poem structured around the duality of self and nature, announces that the poet as woman can be both "inconstant" as nature's tidal and seasonal changes and "true" as astronomy's North Star. The title poem of *The Freeing of the Dust* (1975), pressing further against the spirit-body hierarchy, urges that Ariel bless Caliban and that Caliban drink from the lotus of the spirit.

In the same volume a deceptively brief poem called "Knowing the Unknown" remarkably parallels Rich's "Diving into the Wreck" and is a sort of thumbnail prolegomenon to an intimate discourse on method. Reunion with a clouded planet is the quest, and its direction is—like Rich's—downward. Risking a descent from old holding patterns, riding on the "metallic bitter" wings of rationality, Levertov asks,

Can we dissolve
like coins of hail
touching down,
        down to the dense, preoccupied,
skeptical green world, that does not know us?

"Touching" is the fulcrum term, joining the technological and biological. Meanwhile the "unknown" object of thought itself has intellectual attributes, and the poet wonders whether the planet wants and will welcome its returning exiles. By implication, whatever is an unknown object to us is to itself a conscious subject to which we are the unknown—especially if we have mentally estranged ourselves, lost touch. One thinks of Keats' negative capability, but Levertov's point is sharper: it is not that we must lose our identities to gain contact with the identity of the other but that the process of a unifying discovery depends on our recognition that the not-us is like-us, that we share both ignorance and knowledge. We can know the unknown when we recognize that it is ourselves, hidden from ourselves, that we have denied.

For many women writers, the quest to reintegrate a split self is simultaneously a drive to topple the hierarchy of the sacred and the profane, redeeming and including what the culture has exiled and excluded. To deny the other is to deny the self. Conversely, it is dread of what seems loathsome within the self that produces a projection of it onto another. As all minorities come to know, this is the original significance of the scapegoat. In Lorde's "The Brown Menace, or, Poem to the Survival of Roaches," the speaker might be a self talking to itself, a cockroach talking to a human, a black speaking to a white, a body to a mind: anyone who has been marginalized to anyone who has been privileged.

> Call me
> your deepest urge
> toward survival
>   . . . call me
> roach and presumptuous
> nightmare on your white pillow
> your itch to destroy
> the indestructible
> part of yourself.

But respect for the indestructible parts of ourselves also means a readiness to challenge the concept of the "obscene," by using and detoxifying forbidden language and by recognizing (more fully than is recognized in the classic cases of Lawrence, Joyce, and Henry Miller) the link between outcast words and outcast persons. As with female bawdiness, the object is to dismantle an oppressive mystification. Muriel Rukeyser's "Despisals," one of the most important antidualistic poems of our period, equates the despised ghettos of our cities with the ghettos—taboo places and acts—of our bodies. Rukeyser vows, and the strong language confirms her vow,

> never to go despising the asshole
> nor the useful shit that is our clean clue
> to what we need. Never to despise
> the clitoris in her least speech.

> Never to despise in myself what I have been taught
> to despise. Nor to despise the other.
> Not to despise the *it*. To make this relation
> with the it: to know that I am it.

Like Rukeyser, Maxine Kumin urges respect for all bodily functions. Half-humorously meditating in the rhymed quatrains of "The Excrement Poem" while shoveling out the barn, she notes how sparrows pick seed from the manure pile, how coprinus mushrooms spring from it, and how "I honor shit for saying: We go on." Kumin's "Body and Soul:

A Meditation" materializes the soul in a run of typically demystifying speculations. The soul may be a "miners' canary flitting / around the open spaces," or a "little ball-bearing soul" that has tumbled its way down "the pinball machine / of the interior, clicking / against the sternum, / the rib cage, the pelvis," and has perhaps set up housekeeping in an erogenous zone. Such poems are not merely impudent. They represent a reimagining of the sacred.[58]

Then, as women relocate spirituality within the body and especially within the body's despised sexuality, we find certain radical redefinitions of art. When Sexton's uterus metaphorically sings, when clitoris and shit metaphorically speak, these figures signal the need we have already seen in connection with women's redefinitions of the body to represent the body as at one with the mind, an intelligently creative force. As Susan Friedman has observed, a number of contemporary women poets have begun to adapt the familiar masculine identification of pen with penis to their own purposes, identifying creativity with procreativity, so that the very function which once debarred a woman from writing now seems to privilege her.[59] The last major poems of H.D., "Hermetic Definition" and "Winter Love," written in the poet's late sixties, mystically identify writing and birth-giving. Denise Levertov's important essay "The Poet in the World" begins:

> The poet is in labor. She has been told that it will not hurt but it has hurt so much that pain and struggle seem, just now, the only reality. But at the very moment when she feels she will die, or that she is already in hell, she hears the doctor saying, "Those are the shoulders you are feeling now"—and she knows the head is out then, and the child is pushing and sliding out of her, insistent, a poem.

Lucille Clifton's "she understands me," the finale of a series of confrontations with the goddess Kali, describes a birth that is infant and poem:

> the thing
> drops out of its box squalling
> into the light. they are both squalling,
> animal and cage. her bars lie wet, open
> and empty and she has made herself again
> out of flesh out of dictionaries,
> she is always emptying and it is all
> the same wound the same blood the same breaking.

The title of Plath's *jeu d'esprit* called "Metaphors" can mean on the one hand that this poem is a series of riddling metaphors for pregnancy:

I'm a riddle in nine syllables,
An elephant, a ponderous house,
A melon strolling on two tendrils.

But on the other hand it can mean that Plath is refocusing, through the lens of pregnancy, on the root meaning of the term "metaphor" itself (to carry over or across) and its core function in literature (to assert the force of likeness-unlikeness in the world)—so that pregnancy becomes a metaphor for metaphors. As with Sexton's singing uterus, verbal fecundity appears to derive from physiological fecundity. Sharon Olds' "The Language of the Brag" celebrates childbirth as a "proud American boast" equivalent to Ginsberg's or Whitman's visions of literary valor, and incidentally redefines heroism as that which she shares with all mothers:

> I have done what you wanted to do, Walt Whitman,
> Allen Ginsberg, I have done this thing,
> I and the other women this exceptional
> act with the exceptional heroic body,
> this giving birth, this glistening verb,
> and I am putting my proud American boast
> right here with the others.

The path whereby these and other women have come to celebrate the female body as creative power is angrily and jubilantly described by Ntozake Shange in the autobiographical prose-poem "wow . . . yr just like a man," which details the odyssey of a poet from compliance with masculine standards:

> So anyway they were poets / & this guy well he liked this
> woman's work cuz it wazn't 'personal' / I mean a man can
> get personal in his work when he talks politics or bout his
> dad / but women start alla this foolishness bout their bodies
> & blood & kids & what's really goin on at home / well &
> that ain't poetry / that's goo-ey gaw / female stuff

until she announces her rebellion:

> I've decided to wear my ovaries on my sleeve / raise my
> poems on my milk / & count my days by the flow of my
> mensis / the men who were poets were aghast / they fled
> the scene in fear of becoming unclean.[60]

The appropriation of the creativity-procreativity metaphor by women is a conscious challenge to traditional poetics and beyond that to traditional metaphysics, for the gynocentric vision is not that the Logos condescends to incarnate itself, but that Flesh becomes Word.

With the dismantling of a logocentric conception of art, we find a variety of revisionist speculations on artistic form by women, all of which illustrate the impulse to eroticize, to dissolve boundaries, and to eliminate polarities. As the self reintegrates what has been excluded, so must the art object. Feminist essayists, for example, have argued that the division between art and craft which theoretically privileges the useless artifact above the useful one, and makes art an object of conspicuous consumption affordable only to the wealthy and idle, is also intrinsically misogynist, since it denies the name of art to precisely those domestic arts which women are most likely to practice. A number of women poets have therefore celebrated quilting as a paradigmatic female art which is life-supporting as well as beautiful, utilizes bits and scraps of the materials that are at hand, and is often communally created. Erica Jong, Sandra Gilbert, and Frances Mayes identify the making of poems with the making of food, and Jana Harris half-jokingly proposes laundry as an art form. Weaving is a centrally sacred female art in Robin Morgan's "Network of the Imaginary Mother" and in Judy Grahn's *Queen of Wands*.[61]

Again, several critics and poets have noted that women writers tend to defy genre categories by blurring distinctions between the private writing of the diary and the public writing of fiction and by creating nonlinear structures which appear to work as a diary works, on the basis of a continuing present rather than temporal progress.[62] Virginia Woolf's instruction to herself, defining the prose she hoped to write for her own pleasure in *A Writer's Diary*—"something loose knit and yet not slovenly, so elastic that it will embrace anything, solemn, slight or beautiful that comes into my mind"[63]—anticipates the open forms many women poets adapt from the work of Pound, Williams, Gertrude Stein, and Charles Olson while eschewing the "objectivist" poetics of their modernist precursors (such as Olson's desire to get rid of the "lyrical interference of the individual).[64] As Kathleen Fraser notes in her essay "On Being a West Coast Woman Writer," a woman employing open forms for self-exploration encounters conflict:

> For even though problems of established and agreed upon controls had their interest, it was the loss of these controls, the moving beyond them during the deepest writing engagement, that held the most rewards . . . [Yet] if you could ever hope, as a woman, to be taken seriously as a poet, you became aware of needing to pare down, of fitting, of bringing the clear light of the focused masculine intelligence into the central movement of the work.

In response, Fraser invents the term "the Gestate" to describe "a poem form for women" which is a mimesis of the biological process of gestation. As with women's erotic fantasies, the sensation of release rather than control is an aesthetic effect sought by women poets of many stripes and described in texts ranging from Denise Levertov's reasoned and lucid "Notes on Organic Form" to Diane Di Prima's repudiation of "what I used to like about poems: the words / standing still" in a poem on aesthetics which ends with a repudiation of closure:

> the earth is slippery w / rot, the words
> slide out of place;
> to be able to see it, to be able
> to say it,
> is nothing; but the process
> the bloody process[65]

Woolf's suggestively uterine metaphor of writing as elastic embrace is relevant to tone as well as structure. Among the most interesting mixes in women's poems is between solemnity, or that which is needed "to be taken seriously as a poet," and comedy. While tragedy has occupied a higher status than comedy in western culture since Aristotle, the imperative of intimacy often seems to shift the center of gravity in women's poems to a center of levity. In the first issue of the feminist literary journal *Sinister Wisdom*, editor Harriet Desmoines writes, "We rename the universe out of a subjectivity that is female and animal . . . New naming requires exaggeration, misstep, frequent plunges into absurdity." Similarly, Mary Daly describes gynocentric writing as "*ludic cerebration.*"[66] Women's attack on conventional privilege and authority means that many women's most characteristic poems are stubbornly undignified. They joke, they play, they are silly, they are ludicrous—which is to say they are *ludic*: anti-Apollonian, Dionysiac, Carnavalesque, in a way that has scarcely been seen in American poetry since E. E. Cummings, that Bad Boy of modernism who was also, not coincidentally, a shameless advocate of eros, and that exists in our own time only in the similarly shameless playfulness of Frank O'Hara and Allen Ginsberg. From time to time, and always when the craving for intimacy is being envisioned as satisfied rather than frustrated, there surfaces in women's poems a kind of giddy glee, a sense of absurdity which is antipodal to the familiar modernist "absurd" of despair and bitterness. It is as if instead of the universe revealing itself as irrationally cruel and meaningless, it revealed itself as irrationally (for we are supposed to know better) benign. Low-key versions of this tone might include the woman about to give birth in Sylvia Plath's "Three Voices," who thinks "I cannot help smiling at what it is I know." They might also include Elizabeth Bishop's poem to Marianne Moore, or the moment when Bishop's she-moose steps from the woods to refute our alienation from nature and allows the poet to ask on behalf of a busload of passengers:

> Why, why do we feel
> (we all feel) this sweet
> sensation of joy?

Other versions include Marie Ponsot's discovery in late middle age that the mythic "Grand / Mother" she has been seeking is herself, and "laughing she explains nothing." These examples are inoffensive. More likely to provoke either a complicit giggle or a censorious frown are the comedic confirmations of earthiness percolating throughout poets like Kumin, Sexton, Swenson, Mattison, and Krysl. Still more raucous are the hyperboles and extravagances in women's bawdy poems. See, for example, the lover's rising penis described by Ellen Bass as the head of a turtle, an accordion, and an expandable drinking glass, or Alta's magnanimous suggestion in a prose-poem essay ("Love") that a kiss while she is working "doesn't even interrupt the creative flow. in fact, it gets 2 creative flows going: top & bottom." Laughter is the most subversive agent in literature. If it will be difficult for the serious critic to determine exactly how seriously such playful poetry asks to be taken, there can be no question of the widespread tendency among women poets to promote a yeasty triumph of life over the exhaustion and annihilation that always threaten it. In her version of Williams' image of the "radiant gist" of a saving creativity in nature and humanity, Kathleen Fraser ("Coincidental") begins by confiding that "'Physics' becomes more cheerful every day and delights / in breaking the 'laws of nature,'" and ends by declaring:

> A great urge to be down-to-earth seems to show up in each
>   generation
> You can slice it as you would a flatworm . . .
> and still the tiny jiggles of light persist,
> as though some boogaloo of joy insisted on having its way—
> a full tank, a sunny day, a mailbox stuffed with envelopes

The notion that earthy manners are to conventional manners as quantum physics is to conventional physics—lawbreaking and playful—is reinforced by the rowdy metaphor of a "boogaloo of joy." We may compare Fraser's dance metaphor with Yeats' ecstatic solemnity in the dance trope at the close of "Among School Children" or Eliot's liturgical tone describing the dance in "East Coker". Fraser's final image of the stuffed mailbox is at once quasi-sexual, quasi-oral, and ingeniously represents communication as process: all potential, no disappointment.[67]

If such poetry ticklingly challenges our sense of poetic decorum, Judy Grahn's visionary "She Who" represents the position espoused by writers such as Mary Daly that the quest for an integrated female self is inseparable from linguistic revolution.[68] Grahn's title evokes a goddess figure yet might also be the secret tribal name of everywoman, and is less a name than a grammatical configuration pointing toward a potentially unlimited array of possible states and acts, which the sequence begins to exemplify. The chant of its opening poem moves from a question that is possibly curious, possibly insulting, to an affirmation which imitates the noise of a crowd or of the wind:

> She, she who? she WHO? she, WHO SHE? . . .
> She SHE who, She, she SHE
> she SHE, she SHE who
> SHEEE WHOOOOOO

Some of the poems in the "She Who" sequence are deadpan comedic fantasies, as when Grahn appropriates the third eye of Hindu mysticism. Note that because of the lack of punctuation the first two lines here can be read either as the commencement of a sentence or as a declarative statement followed by a question:

> She Who increases
> what can be done
>
> I shall grow another breast
> in the middle of my chest . . .
> slippery as a school of fish
> sounder than stone. Call it
> She—Who—educates—my—chest.

There are also animal fables, parables of female power and powerlessness, a poem of insults ("a cunt a bitch a slut a slit a hole a whore a hole"), a birth poem, a funeral song, a plainsong invoking the bonding of older and younger women ("are you not shamed to treat me meanly / when you discover you become me"), and a boasting rune which has become canonical in lesbian poetry:

> I am the wall at the lip of the water
> I am the rock that refused to be battered
> I am the dyke in the matter, the other
> I am the wall with the womanly swagger . . .
> and I have been many a wicked grandmother
> and I shall be many a wicked daughter.

With Grahn's "She Who" we arrive at the two final consequences of the imperative of intimacy in women's poetry: the self that is not merely a resolved pair of polarities but an uncircumscribed set of coexistent possibilities, and the poem that resists the closure of artifact to become a communal transaction. For as polarity yields to androgyny in women's poetic desires, so—the logical next step—androgyny yields to plurality. At the close of "Diving into the Wreck," Adrienne Rich learns not only "I am she: I am he" but "We are, I am, you are . . . the one who find our way / back to this scene." The speaker-protagonist of Levertov's "Knowing the Unknown" is "we . . . anyone, all of us." When Piercy's "The Queen of Pentacles" sees that other women enable her to touch "pruned selves, smothered wishes, small wet cries . . . and think how all together we make up one good strong woman," her "we" signifies both multiple interior selves and herself joined to other women.[69]

As the female self recognizes its multiplicity, it sometimes moves into extended chantlike forms which structurally exemplify the possibility of an unlimited plurality while tonally and rhythmically suggesting a sacred and communal primitivism. Some of our most striking contemporary poems, composed for oral performance, are incantatory. Audre Lorde, who constructs in *The Black Unicorn* an African-based mythology of a self who is female, black, powerful, passionately loving and hating, immortal and magic, frequently composes in chant from, as does Ntozake Shange. For both men and women black poets, the traditions of Afro-American music—field shout, gospel, blues, and jazz singing—and the highly rhythmed style of Afro-American preaching, have been vivifying formal influences. Among Hispanic poets, too, chant form is important. Examples are Sylvia Gonzales' bilingual "I Am Chicana," which moves from a memory of being Malinche's daughter, victim and bastard, to a rebirth as a holy mother, or Jessica Hagedorn's "Canto de Nada":

> she is nada   all music
> she is nothing   all music
> she is the punk   all music
> the dancing girl   all music
> she is the punk
> the dancing girl
> la cucaracha
> who can even get up
> from her own o.d.
> her name is nada
> mother to rashid
> roumiko
> carmen miranda

ruby delicious
the divine virgin
waiting for a trick . . .

Among white poets there is Anne Waldman's urban tribeswoman "Fast
Speaking Woman," a poem modeled on a shamaness-led peyote ceremony, with a written text on which the poet improvises in performance:

I'm the dulcimer woman
I'm the dainty woman
I'm the murderous woman
I'm the discerning woman
I'm the dissonant woman
I'm the anarchist woman
I'm the Bantu woman
I'm the Buddha woman
I'm the baritone woman
I'm the bedouin woman . . .

or the catalog of fifty-seven women at the climax of Grahn's quasi-tribal
"She Who":

the woman who eats cocaine
the woman who thinks about everything
the woman who has the tattoo of a bird
the woman who puts things together
the woman who squats on her haunches
the woman whose children are all different   colors

when She-Who-moves-the-earth will turn over
when She Who moves, the earth will turn over.[70]

The sensuous pleasure of such poetry, with its strong beat, its sound-
play, its joyous tapping of fantasy, is intimately bound up with its evocation of communality. Work of this kind pushes back from a conception
of poetry as secular, ornamental ("a superior entertainment," says Eliot,
which "makes nothing happen," says Auden), artifact, produced by and
directed to isolated individuals. It moves toward a much older situation
in which poetry is sacred, communal, popular, and inseparable from
the matrix of life.

6

It is difficult, even at this moment, to assert my
language in the powerful field of your reality.

Do you wonder why I've made so much of a barely
perceptible shift in our gaze? I wanted to catch it,
instead of pretending not to see. I want to begin to
talk to you. To bring into words the fragments I've
conspired with you to hide. It is part of my commitment
to myself and to you. It is my politics. My love.
—Kathleen Fraser, "Talking to Myself Talking to You"[71]

The chant poem assumes an audience either literally present or prepared to suspend disbelief and respond as if book-in-hand and lamp-on-
table were live ritual. But women's poetry is in fact filled with the idea
that the reader is and should be engaged in an active personal transaction with the writer. The imperative of intimacy may finally account for
the confessional or self-exploratory mode in women's poetry precisely
because of the intimacy this mode imposes on the audience. One cannot read, for example, Sexton or Wakoski without feeling that the objectivity of readership is under attack. In both cases the pull on the audience is directly related to an erotic ideology.

Sexton's *apologia pro poemata sua* appears at the outset of her career,
in response to a letter from her teacher and fellow poet John Holmes,
who disliked Sexton's flamboyance and advised her not to print the most
self-revealing poems in her first manuscript:

I distrust the very source and subject of a great many of your
poems . . . Something about asserting the hospital and psychi-
atric experience seems to me very selfish—all a forcing others to
listen to you, and nothing given the listeners, nothing that teaches
them or helps them . . . It bothers me that you use poetry this
way. It's all a release for you, but what is it for anyone else except a
spectacle of someone experiencing release?[72]

The poet's defense was double. She defiantly quoted as her epigraph to
To Bedlam and Part Way Back a letter from Schopenhauer to Goethe
celebrating the tragic courage of the philosopher willing to pursue the
most appalling truth: "But most of us carry in our hearts the Jocasta who
begs Oedipus for God's sake not to inquire further." The quotation implies a daring role reversal: Sexton takes the position of the tragic (male)
hero Oedipus, relegating her critic to the inferior (female) role of
Jocasta. The poem "For John, Who Begs Me Not to Inquire Further"
insists that personal truth is also transpersonal. In exploring "that narrow diary of my mind,"

At first it was private.
Then it was more than myself;

it was you, or your house
or your kitchen.
And if you turn away . . .

There is fear of rejection and contempt but also a pursuit of the point
that rejection of one another derives precisely from the dread of con-
templating our shared, frightening lives, and that denial will only intensify suffering:

This is something I would never find
in a lovelier place, my dear,
although your fear is anyone's fear,
like an invisible veil between us all . . .
and sometimes, in private,
my kitchen, your kitchen,
my face, your face.[73]

Sexton's biographer Diane Middlebrook, commenting on the Sexton-
Holmes relation, observes:

Sexton insists to Holmes that his rejection of her poetry is in part a
defense against the power of her art, which tells not a private but a
collective truth—which, to his horror, includes and reveals him.
Sexton may or may not have heard in literary circles gossip about
the gruesome suicide of Holmes' first wife, or about Holmes' successful recovery from alcoholism.[74]

Many of Sexton's poems are written to a "you" who may be mother,
father, daughter, husband, lover, psychoanalyst or God, but who is always also the reader. The fiction of a direct address expressing need,
hope, pain, joy, anger, despair, calling on our love and sympathy, is a
conscious—not an accidental and inadvertent—challenge to the poetics of distance advocated by Holmes and by conservative criticism.
    Diane Wakoski also repeatedly addresses a "you" who is sometimes
herself, sometimes a friend, lover, or lover-antagonist, sometimes the
reader, and sometimes—janglingly—all these in a single poem. To
read a Wakoski poem is to feel oneself jostled about by complicated
seductive-aggressive maneuvers, for she is as pleading, teasing, demanding, self-pitying, and hostile by turns toward readers as toward
lovers.
    Like Sexton, Wakoski understands that she is breaking the rules: "I
am screaming all this at the door / and you are privileged to say / it is in
'bad taste.'" Her mode, however, is ostentatiously theatrical rather than

therapeutic. In "Greed Part 6," a confession of the poet's obsessive jeal-
ousies, a lacerating self-examination alternates with histrionic addresses
to the audience. Having asked "Why am I telling you? Why do I think
you should be interested?" she gives a string of half-mocking answers:
she wants her readers "to know about it"; confession needs an audience
and she doesn't trust psychiatry or religion; "madness always interests
others a bit"; she wishes she had more dazzling images; she wants "you
to review yourselves and learn not about literature, but about life." At
this point she switches without missing a beat to telling a lover, Tony,
that she has nobly restrained herself from begging him to marry her.

Several of Wakoski's essays on art, most notably "The Emerald Essay" and "The blue swan, an essay on music and poetry," provocatively
mix prose with poetry, dicta on art and multiple versions of narratives
with personal confessions. She explains, not quite ingenuously, "I use
the letter format for these poem lectures because I want them to be as
personal as a letter, even though they are addressed to formal and abstract subjects." [75] What we understand is that her goal is to manipulate
the reader into personal response and paradoxically that Wakoski's grasp
of the personal depends on her ability to imagine a reader. Is she, in
this, so different from ourselves?

Sexton and Wakoski provide extreme but illuminating variations on
a core female position. Poet after poet testifies that the plural, self-
exploratory, open poem speaks of and to something larger than a sole
self. Here is a declaration in Marge Piercy's preface to *Circles in the
Water: Selected Poems*:

> I imagine that I speak for a constituency, living and dead, and that
> I give utterance to energy, experience, insight, words flowing from
> many lives.

Here is Ntozake Shange in a self-interview she calls "a conversation
with all my selves":

> quite simply a poem shd fill you up with something /
> cd make you swoon, stop in yr tracks, change yr
> mind, or make it up, a poem shd happen to you like
> cold water or a kiss.

And in a poem called "inquiry":

> poetry is unavoidable connection /
> some people get married / others join the Church
> i carry notebooks / so i can tell us what happened / . . .

whatever is here / is what you've given me /
if it's not enough for you /
give me some more.

June Jordan in the prefatory poem to *Things That I Do in the Dark* identifies language with the darkness of eros and exploration:

These poems
they are things that I do
in the dark
reaching for you
whoever you are
and
are you ready? . . .

whoever you are
whoever I may become.

Kathleen Fraser provocatively defends the poetics of intimacy to a reader-lover-critic:

Dear other, I address you in sentences. I need your nods and I hear your echoes. There is a forward movement still, as each word is a precedent for what new order . . . You are against confession because it is embarrassing. I want to embarrass you.

Here, outrageously, is Lenore Kandel in "Freak Show and Finale":

Expose yourself!
Show me your tattooed spine . . .
Admit your feral snarl . . .
Are you BOY 16 WEDS WOMAN 68 shaking with lust
Are you FATHER OF 3 SHOOTS SELF AND INFANT SON . . .
Are you UNKNOWN WOMAN LEAPS FROM BRIDGE

Here, polemically, Robin Morgan addresses her audience in "Phobophilia":

Do you smell smoke?
If you don't it's not
because a tenement isn't burning—
down the street, in Derry, Beirut or San Salvador.
Did you just hear a scream?
If you didn't, it's not

because a woman wasn't raped
since I asked if you smelled smoke.

Denise Levertov in the essay "Origins of a Poem" describes "the communion . . . between the maker and the needer within the poet; between the maker and the needers outside him." "The Poet in the World"
begins with the proposition that the poet is simultaneously a suffering
woman in labor, an anxious father in a man-made labor room, and an
infant being born; and it ends by advocating the poet's necessary involvement in political life. Levertov quotes E. M. Forster's "only connect."
"The words," she says, "reverberate through the poet's life, through my
life, and I hope through your lives."

A consensus exists among women poets that "the true nature of poetry" is, as Adrienne Rich claims, "the drive to connect. The dream of a
common language."[76] The divestment of masks means something for
reader as well as writer. As the poet refuses to distance herself from her
emotion, so she prevents us from distancing ourselves. To walk through
the mirror of the exoskeletal style which records fear of touch is to find a
set of devices which demand touch. We are obliged to witness, to experience the hot breath of the poem upon us. Or perhaps we want to
wrestle loose. The poem is impolite, crude, indecorous, it imposes too
much. In either case, we have been obliged to some degree to relin-
quish the role of reader and respond personally. That, evidently, has
been the aim of the poet.

If we are astute critics of women's poetry today we must recognize
that the distance between poet and reader is a literary convention like
any other and equally subject to manipulation. We need, and do not yet
have, a critical vocabulary able to describe the many types of interaction, transaction, and participation poets may demand of their readers.
If we are wise readers we may experience through our own dance of
identification and repulsion, in response to these demands, precisely
the tenuousness in the self-other relation which women poets seek to
reveal.

6 Thieves of Language: Women Poets and Revisionist Mythology

What would become of logocentrism, of the great philosophical systems, of world order in general if the rock upon which they founded their church were to crumble?

If it were to come out in a new day that the logocentric project had always been, undeniably, to *found* (fund) phallocentrism, to insure for masculine order a rationale equal to history itself?

Then all the stories would have to be told differently, the future would be incalculable, the historical forces would, will, change hands, bodies; another thinking as yet not thinkable will transform the functioning of all society.
    —Hélène Cixous, "Sorties"[1]

Nudgers and shovers
In spite of ourselves.
Our kind multiplies:

We shall by morning
Inherit the earth.
Our foot's in the door.
    —Sylvia Plath, "Mushrooms"[2]

A major theme in feminist theory on both sides of the Atlantic for the past decade has been the demand that women writers be, in Claudine

Herrmann's phrase, *voleuses de langue*, thieves of language, female Prometheuses.[3] Though the language we speak and write has been an encoding of male privilege, what Adrienne Rich calls an "oppressor's language" inadequate to describe or express women's experience, a "Law of the Father"[4] which transforms the daughter to "the invisible woman in the asylum corridor"[5] or "the silent woman" without access to authoritative expression,[6] we must also have it in our power to "seize speech" and make it say what we mean. More: there is a desire to make female speech prevail, to penetrate male discourse, to cause the ear of man to listen.[7]

Women writers have always tried to steal the language. Among poets more than novelists, the thefts have been filching from the servants' quarters. When Elaine Marks surveys the *Écriture féminine* movement in Paris, she observes that in its manifestos of desire "to destroy the male hegemony" over language, "the rage is all the more intense because the writers see themselves as prisoners of the discourse they despise. But is it possible," she asks, "to break out?"[8] Does there exist, as a subterranean current below the surface structure of male-oriented language, a specifically female language, a "mother tongue"? This is a debated issue. A variety of theorists argue in favor, others argue against, while a number of empirical studies in America seem to confirm that insofar as speech is "feminine," its strength is limited to evoking subjective sensation and interpersonal reponsiveness; it is not in other respects perceived as authoritative; it does not command men's respect.[9]

The question of whether a female language, separate but equal to male language, either actually exists or can (or should) be created, awaits further research into the past and further gynocentric writing in the present. My argument throughout this book has concerned the already very large body of poetry by American women, composed in the last twenty-five years, in which the project of defining a female self has been a major endeavor. What distinguishes these poets, I propose, is not the shared, exclusive *langage des femmes* desired by some but a vigorous and varied invasion of the sanctuaries of existing language, the treasuries where our meanings for "male" and "female" are themselves preserved. Where women write strongly as women, it is clear that their intention is to subvert and transform the life and literature they inherit. Among their important strategies we have already seen the revisionist use of gendered imagery. In this final chapter I turn to the large structures in which gendered images have always been embedded and suggest that revisionist mythmaking in women's poetry is a means of redefining both woman and culture.

At first thought, mythology seems an inhospitable terrain for a woman writer. There we find the conquering gods and heroes, the deities of pure thought and spirituality so superior to Mother Nature; there we find the sexually wicked Venus, Circe, Pandora, Helen, Medea, Eve, and the virtuously passive Iphigenia, Alcestis, Mary, and Cinderella. It is thanks to myth that we believe that woman must be either angel or monster.[10]

Yet the need for myth of some sort may be ineradicable. Poets, at least, appear to think so. When Muriel Rukeyser in "The Poem as Mask" exclaimed, "No more masks! No more mythologies," she was rejecting the traditional division of myth from a woman's subjectivity, rejecting her own earlier poem that portrays Orpheus and the bacchic women who slew him as separate from herself. "It was myself," she says, "split open, unable to speak, in exile from myself." To recognize this, however, is evidently to heal both the torn self and the torn god; the poem's final lines describe a resurrected Orpheus whose "fragments join in me with their own music." When Adrienne Rich in "Diving into the Wreck" carries with her a "book of myths / in which / our names do not appear" and declares that she seeks "the wreck and not the story of the wreck / the thing itself and not the myth," while enacting a watery descent that inverts the ascents and conquests of male heroism, she implies the necessity, for a woman, of distinguishing between myth and reality. Yet when Rich identifies with a "mermaid" and "merman" and says that "We are, I am, you are . . . the one who find our way / back to this scene," the androgynous being and the fluid pronouns imply that "the thing itself" is itself mythic.

When Circe in Margaret Atwood's "Circe/Mud poems" snarls at her lover, "It's the story that counts. No use telling me this isn't a story, or not the same story . . . Don't evade, don't pretend you won't leave after all: you leave in the story and the story is ruthless," she too describes the depersonalizing effects of myths on persons, the way they replay themselves over and over and "the events run themselves through / almost without us." But at the point of stating this, the poet declares that there are "two islands" that "do not exclude each other" and that the second "has never happened," "is not finished," is "not frozen yet." In all these cases the poet simultaneously deconstructs a prior "myth" or "story" and constructs a new one which includes, instead of excluding, herself.[11]

Let me at this point therefore define the term "revisionist mythmaking" and sketch the background behind the work I will discuss. Whenever a poet employs a figure or story previously accepted and defined by a culture, the poet is using myth, and the potential is always present that the use will be revisionist: that is, the figure or tale will be appropriated for altered ends, the old vessel filled with new wine, initially satisfying the thirst of the individual poet but ultimately making cultural change possible. Historic and quasi-historic figures like Napoleon and Sappho are in this sense mythic, as are folktales, legends, and Scripture. Like the gods and goddesses of classical mythology, all such material has a double power. It exists or appears to exist objectively, outside the self. Because it is in the public domain, it confers on the writer the sort of authority unavailable to someone who writes "merely" of the private self. Myth belongs to "high" culture and is handed "down" through the ages by religious, literary, and educational authority. At the same time, myth is quintessentially intimate material, the stuff of dream life, forbidden desire, inexplicable motivation—everything in the psyche that to rational consciousness is unreal, crazed, or abominable.

In the wave of poetic mythmaking that broke over England in the Romantic period, we hear two strains. One is public antirationalism, an insistence that there were more things in heaven and earth than were dreamt of by Newton and Locke. The other is an assurance that the poets had personally experienced forces within the self so overwhelming that they must be described as gods and goddesses, titans, demiurges, and demons. But Romantic revisionists do not simply take seriously what the Augustans took ornamentally. When Shelley invents for his defiant Prometheus an anima not present in any classical source, or when "knowledge enormous" of divine and human suffering makes a god and a poet of Keats' Apollo, who then dies into immortal life with a scream—that is mythic revisionism. (The same scream, by the way, tears through the young throat of Edna St. Vincent Millay, in a poem many women loved as girls and later learned to despise; "Renascence," too, is a poem about the genesis of a poet.)

Like the Romantics, the early moderns—Yeats, Pound, Eliot—turned to myth as a means of defying their culture's rationalism and materialism. Implicit in their writing is a conviction that civilization has declined from an earlier state more coherent than the fragmented present, in which the spiritual life represented by myth was culturally more central. From this conviction grew Yeats' syncretism of Irish lore and occultism, Pound's adaptations of classical myth, and Eliot's compound of fertility cult and medieval romance with Buddhist and Hindu sources, as well as his conversion to the Anglican Church. But while women poets in our time share a distrust for rationalism, they do not share the modernist nostalgia for a golden age of past culture, and their mythmaking grows at least as much from a subterranean tradition of female self-projection and self-exploration as from the system building of the Romantics and moderns.

As Emily Stipes Watts has demonstrated, American women poets have always used myth to handle material dangerous for a feminine "I."[12] The first poem by an American woman on a historical heroine was Anne Bradstreet's celebration of Queen Elizabeth, which after recounting a set of political triumphs greater, the poet claims, than any male monarch's, asks, "Now say, have women worth, or have they not?" The same Bradstreet describing herself as a poet is constrained to insist that her mind is feeble beyond repair and that "men can do best and women know it well." The slave-poet Phyllis Wheatley's longest poem is "Niobe in Distress for Her Children Slain by Apollo," and Niobe could rail despairingly against the gods in a way that Wheatley, who is elsewhere demurely Christian and patriotic, could not. These are both poems about women and power, as is Mercy Warren's "The Squabble of the Sea-Nymphs," a celebration of the Boston Tea Party enlivened by vigorously antityrannic females rather like herself.

In the nineteenth century, when American poetry was dominated by ideals of sexual purity and bourgeois gentility, women used heroines like Sappho and Eve as a cover for writing erotic verse and heroines like Medea and Ariadne for the forbidden theme of women's rage. Maria Brooks' highly esteemed *Zophiel, or the Bride of Seven*, evokes but does not consummate "the gushing torrent of attracted sense" for six cantos of steamy psuedo-mythology centered on a fallen angel and a virtuous Hebrew maid, followed by pages of footnotes rather like *The Waste Land*'s. Elizabeth Oakes Smith's "The Sinless Child," one of the most popular narrative romances of the mid-nineteenth century, has a heroine named Eva who is not only a new Eve but a female Christ who converts the wickedest of men by her beauty and purity. Dickinson did not use mythic heroines, but she did describe God as a burglar and banker, and she wrote a half dozen poems employing a figure which has subsequently become important for us: the witch.

Beginning in the late nineteenth century, while erotic and erotic-angry mythmaking continues, we also find mythic poems by women exploring the themes of woman as victim, as artist, and as force for social change. The best known of these is Emma Lazarus' "The New Colossus," which explicitly distinguishes between patriarchal glorification of "the brazen giant of Greek fame / With conquering limbs astride from land to land," and the "Mother of Exiles" who lifts her lamp and is "mighty" in a new way, through welcoming and sheltering refugees. Adelaide Crapsey's "Witch" traces the descent of an "I" who was Sphinx, Sappho, madonna, and finally a "wench" who knew too much and was hanged on the Salem green. Edna St. Vincent Millay's "An Ancient Gesture" ironically compares Odysseus' weeping at a feast over his lost shipmates—a bit of successful public relations—with the one from whom he learned the gesture, "Penelope, who really cried." Margaret

Walker's *For My People,* published in 1942, includes among its ballads
on black folk heroes such as Stagolee and John Henry the aggressive and
violent Kissie Lee and Mollie Means. May Sarton in "The Muse as
Medusa," says she has seen Medusa yet not been turned to stone, and
wonders "How to believe the legends I am told?" Sarton's poem records
a turning point in women's relationship to myth, as it moves from a
rejection of past authority to a personal illumination that recalls and
reproduces the psychic origin of all myth:

> I turn your face around! It is my face.
> That frozen rage is what I must explore—
> Oh secret, self-enclosed, and ravaged place!
> This is the gift I thank Medusa for.[13]

The recognition that the faces in mythology may be our own faces
which we "must explore" to gain knowledge of myth's inner meanings
and our own, has been crucial. As we approach our own time, women's
mythological poems demonstrate increasing self-consciousness, increasing irony, and increasing awareness that the poet may not only say
"Sappho" or "Ariadne" when the culture does not permit her to say "I"
but may also deviate from or explicitly challenge the meanings at-
tributed to mythic figures and tales. She may keep the name but change
the game, and here is where revisionist mythology comes in.

Since 1960 one can count over a dozen major works (poem sequences, long poems, or whole books) of revisionist myth published by
American women, and one cannot begin to count the individual poems
in which familiar figures from male tradition emerge altered.[14] These
poems generically assume the high literary status that myth confers and
that women writers have often been denied because they write "personally" or "confessionally." But in them the old stories are changed,
changed utterly, by female knowledge of female experience, so that they
can no longer stand as foundations of collective male fantasy or as the
pillars sustaining phallocentric "high" culture. Instead, they are correc-
tions; they are representations of what women find divine and demonic
in themselves; they are retrieved images of what women have collectively and historically suffered; in some cases they are instructions for
survival.

2

　　. . . she comes down from the remoteness of the ages, from
Thebes, from Crete, from Chichén-Itzá; and she is also the totem

set up deep in the African jungle; she is a helicopter and she is a
bird; and there is this, the greatest wonder of all: under her tinted
hair the forest murmur becomes a thought, and words issue from
her breasts.
    —Simone de Beauvoir, *The Second Sex*[15]

Women have had the power of *naming* stolen from us . . . To
exist humanly is to name the self, the world and God . . . Words
which, materially speaking, are identical with the old become
new in a semantic context that arises from qualitatively new
experience.
    —Mary Daly, *Beyond God the Father*[16]

Since the core of revisionist mythmaking for women poets lies in the
challenge to and correction of gender stereotypes embodied in myth,
revisionism in its most obvious form consists of hit-and-run attacks on
familiar images and the social and literary conventions supporting
them. The poems dismantle the literary conventions to reveal the social
ones, and reverse both, usually by the simple device of making Other
into Subject.[17] Thus in the stroke of a phrase, Sylvia Plath's Lady
Lazarus dismisses "Herr God, Herr Lucifer" as the two faces of a single
authoritarian and domineering being for whom a woman's body is "your
opus . . . your valuable" (p. 246). Anne Sexton in "Snow White," the
opening poem of *Transformations*, disposes of centuries of reverence for
the virgin "rolling her china-blue doll eyes . . . Open to say / Good
Day Mama, / and shut for the thrust / of the unicorn" (p. 224). Expen-
sive commodity, pretty toy, sacred victim: so much for her. Of one of her
avatars, the passive Euridice who exists only as the tragic object of
Orpheus' love, Alta writes a motto for any women poet:

> all the male poets write of orpheus
> as if they look back & expect
> to find me walking patiently
> behind them. they claim i fell into hell.
> Damn them, i say.
> i stand in my own pain
> & sing my own song. (p. 6)

The bacchante imagined by Sandra Gilbert has her own opinion of
Orpheus, "that show-off" who "gave the look that kills / to Eurydice on
the stony path":

> Her fur ruff twitches
> as she makes this case. It's clear

she never liked the bastard anyway,
the swaggering bastard with his silver flute,
precious proboscis, mean baton,

commanding silence, silence from everyone,
shutting the trees up, quieting the wind
and the quick birds, and the women.
Without his manly anthems,
everything, she says, would sing, would sing. (p. 43)

Another solution to the male creator–female muse convention is Erica
Jong's "Arse Poetica," a role-reversing prose-poem that contrives at once
to deflate centuries of male aesthetic pretentiousness and to assert the
identity of female sexuality and female creativity:

Once the penis has been introduced into the poem, the poet
lets herself down until she is sitting on the muse with her
legs outside him. He need not make any motions at all. (p. 27)

Rebelling against a family's imposition of feminine appearance and
docility, Jean Tepperman's "Witch" begins with the lines "They told
me / I smile prettier with my mouth closed" and ends:

I want my black dress.
I want my hair
curling wild around me.
I want my broomstick
from the closet where I hid it.
Tonight I meet my sisters . . .
Watch for us against the moon.
We are screaming,
we are flying,
laughing, and won't stop. (pp. 333–34)

With poems like these, one imagines the poets stepping out of the
ring dusting their hands off. But revisionist poems do not necessarily
confine themselves to defiance and reversal strategies. Mona Van Duyn's
"Leda" commences with Yeats' famous "Did she put on his knowledge
with his power / Before the indifferent beak could let her drop" as an
epigraph, followed immediately by the no-nonsense rejoinder, "Not
even for a moment." Van Duyn's Leda is an ordinary woman, not "abstract enough" for the immortality conferred upon her in men's tales.
After her encounter with the swan she "married a smaller man with a
beaky nose, / and melted away in the storm of everyday life" (p. 98).

The intention here is not directly to deny male power, divinity, or even "knowledge" as exemplified by the god in Yeats and his Greek sources, but to insist on the stubborn limitations of normal humanity as represented by woman, and perhaps to suggest that men would be wise to accept the truth that they are "smaller" than gods. In "Leda Reconsidered," Van Duyn reimagines her heroine as an experienced woman for whom the approach of the god becomes an occasion to meditate on her own sexuality, and who reaches "with practiced arms / past the bird, short of the god . . . to touch / the utter stranger" (pp. 78–80). Carolyn Kizer's "Semele Recycled" is a comic-romantic folktale of a goddess disassembled at her lover's departure and reassembled to make love on a compost heap at his return (pp. 13–15). In "The Copulating Gods" Kizer's Venus, in love with Vulcan, knows that men "deny our equal pleasure in each other" (p. 20). Such poems continue, though more assertively, a long tradition of female erotic mythmaking.

A more central set of preoccupations concerns female-female relationships and the relation of the female to suppressed dimensions of her own identity. Kate Ellis's "Matrilineal Descent" uses the Demeter-Kore story as an aid in discovering how we may reconstitute lost families, becoming spiritual mothers and daughters for each other in time of need. Mothers, daughters, sisters must be recovered as parts "of the original woman we are"; after dreaming that a rivalrous younger sister is a daughter, and killing her in the dream, the poet movingly realizes that like Demeter she can "go down and get her: / It is not too late" (pp. 31–34). In Helen Cooper's dramatic monologue "From the Mad Wife's Room in *Jane Eyre*," we discover that Bertha's sin was a self-pleasing autoeroticism learned from her mother and punished by her horrified husband. Sharon Barba's "A Cycle of Women" depicts women's history before and during patriarchy as "that dream world / . . . that dark watery place" presided over by a goddess, which each individual woman must try to remember, although the knowledge is locked from her. "Each one is queen, mother, huntress" and must reconstruct the past "until she knows who she is" and that she is not Botticelli's fantasy:

> Until she rises as though from the sea
> not on the half-shell this time
> nothing to laugh at
> and not as delicate as he imagined her:
> a woman big-hipped, beautiful, and fierce. (pp. 356–57)

Interlocked images of fertility and artistic creativity govern the poem sequence "Eurydice" by Rachel Blau DuPlessis. Here the heroine not only resents (like Alta's Euridice) the loss of herself to a husband whose powerful sex and art define her "like a great linked chain" but is herself the snake "whose deepest desire was to pierce herself." Withdrawing from her husband, far back into the moist, stony "fissure" and "cave" of herself, she becomes self-generating plant and finally, amid an efflorescence of organic images, her own mother, giving birth to the girlchild who is herself—or, since the sequence can be read as an allegory of female creativity, her poem. The idea of giving birth, unaided, to the self, is also the conclusion of Adrienne Rich's "The Mirror in Which Two Are Seen as One" and governs the "dry bulb" metaphor of "Necessities of Life."[18]

Toi Derricotte, in the extraordinary description of labor that is the central section of *Natural Birth*, goes from "the mountain of pain" to the experience of "some other woman, all muscle and nerve . . . tearing apart and opening under me." And as Derricotte is entered by and enters "her," like going into a tunnel, fast, with the headlights off,

i felt something pulling me inside, a soft call, but i could feel her power. something inside me i could go with . . . the more i gave to her, the more she answered me. i held this conversation in myself like a love that never stops. i pushed toward her, she came toward me, gently, softly, sucking like a wave. i pushed deeper and she swelled wider, darker when she saw i wasn't afraid. then i saw the darker glory of her under me. (p. 33)

The poet does not name this being—who recedes as her son is born. But as with H. D.'s *"Sage-Femme"* accompanying the birth agonies of "Winter Love" (*Hermetic Definition*, pp. 115–17), or Lucille Clifton's Kali in "she understands me," we feel that the text transcribes an authentic encounter with someone we might call God the Mother. We may also feel that the death and resurrection pattern of the labor experience described in *Natural Birth* is one possible source of that universal theme in pre-Christian and Christian religion.

All such poems are aspects of an attempt by women to retrieve, from our myth of a dominating abstract father god who creates the universe *ab nihilo*, the figure on which (according to feminist historians of early religion) that god was originally based—the female creatrix.[19] In women's versions the creatrix is not divided (as she is in C. G. Jung's and Erich Neumann's versions of her) into Sky Goddess (asexual) and Earth Mother (sexual but brainless).[20] Female writers commonly reunite attributes of flesh and spirit that traditional culture sets asunder. The Goddess for Denise Levertov is a furious woman who seizes the poet where she lies asleep in Lie Castle and hurls her against the walls. Prostrate

outside the castle "where her hand had thrown me," the poet tastes the
mud of a forest, bites the seed in her mouth, and senses the passing of
"her" without whom nothing "flowers, fruits, sleeps in season, / without whom nothing / speaks in its own tongue, but returns / lie for lie!"
("The Goddess," pp. 43–44). To identify an active, aggressive woman
with Truth is to defy a very long tradition that identifies strong females
with deception[21] and virtuous females, including muses, with gentle
inactivity.

Several of Levertov's poems depict her muse as a beautiful and teasing young male lover, but in "Song for Ishtar," one of Levertov's most
playful and compact poems, a Babylonian goddess of both Love and
War evokes images for what is divine and mundane, spiritual and animal, delicate and violent in female sexuality and female art:

> The moon is a sow
> and grunts in my throat
> Her great shining shines through me
> so the mud of my hollow gleams
> and breaks in silver bubbles
>
> She is a sow
> And I a pig and a poet
>
> When she opens her white
> lips to devour me I bite back
> and laughter rocks the moon
>
> In the black of desire
> we rock and grunt, grunt and
> shine (p. 3)

This resembles William Carlos Williams' early version of the muse as
crone, plunging him into "the filthy Passaic" in "The Wanderer."[22] Yet
it is different not only because of the far earthier and more sensual language but because of the gender difference. A muse imagined in one's
own likeness, with whom one can fornicate with violence and laughter,
implies the extraordinary possibility of a poetry of wholeness and joy, as
against the poetry of the age of anxiety in which Levertov was writing.
That a sacred joy can be found within the self; that it requires an embracing of one's sexuality; that access to it must be described as movement downward or inward, in gender-charged metaphors of water,
earth, cave, seed, moon: such is the burden of these and many other
poems by women. To Wallace Stevens' post-Nietzschean formula "God

and the imagination are one,"[23] these women poets would add a crucial third element: God and the imagination and *my body* are one.

At the opposite pole from the creatrix is the destroyer, a figure women's poetry has been inhibited from exploring in the past by the need to identify femininity with morality. When they traffic in the demonic, women poets have produced some of the most highly charged images in recent American poetry. One thinks immediately of Plath's "disquieting muses," the three ladies "with stitched bald head" who assemble around the poet, precipitated by the girl scout cheeriness of a mother who attempts to deny reality's darkness; or the clinging Medusa who is at once classic monster, jellyfish, and the poet's mother; or her image of herself as avenging Phoenix-fiend at the close of "Lady Lazarus"; or the depiction of demonic possession in "Elm." In Anne Sexton, demonic images associated with madness, guilt, and death proliferate with increasing intensity, from the witches in *To Bedlam and Part Way Back* to the set of "Angels" in *The Book of Folly* who the poet aquaints with "slime . . . bedbugs . . . paralysis" to the "Green Girls" who urge suicide in the "Dr. Y" poems and the staggering "death baby" who is the poet's alter ego in *The Death Notebooks*.[24]

Plath and Sexton are dramatic portraitists in contemporary poetry of what Joseph Conrad called "the horror . . . the horror." Like Conrad, they imply that the hypocrisies of civilized rationality are powerless to destroy what is destructive in the world and in ourselves—indeed, that "the horror" may well be the most devastating product of our demands for innocence and virtue. But what distinguishes their demonism from Conrad's, and from the standard personifications of "evil" throughout western poetry, is the common characteristic of passivity. Wherever in these two poets we find images of compelling dread, there we also find images of muteness, blindness, paralysis, the condition of being manipulated.

Inactivity is also a motif in several poems written by women about classic female monsters. Of Medusa, a perennial figure in male poetry and iconography, Ann Stanford's sequence "Women of Perseus" and Rachel Blau DuPlessis' "Medusa" both remind us of the key event in this female's life, though it goes unmentioned in either Bulfinch's or Edith Hamilton's *Mythology*: her rape by Poseidon before the snakes appeared on her head. In Stanford's poem the trauma "imprisons" Medusa in a self-dividing anger and a will to revenge that she can never escape, though she yearns to. Stanford makes clear that Medusa in this respect parallels all the women in the Perseus legend: Danae, whom her father nails into a box with her infant son and sets adrift; the three Graeae, stranded forever on a gray island; Andromeda, chained to a rock as a sacrifice to a sea monster, rescued by the Perseus who has just slain

Medusa. In DuPlessis' sequence the three Graeae—whose one eye Perseus steals—are conflated into one mother figure for Medusa; her rapist and killer are conflated into one male; and she herself becomes a static boundary "stone" and regresses to an infantile ur-language.

The Homeric earth-goddess and sorceress Circe, who turns Odysseus' fellow sailors to beasts and who throughout western literature represents the evil magic of female sexuality, is transformed in Margaret Atwood's "Circe/Mud Poems" into an angry but also quite powerless woman. Men turn themselves to animals; she has nothing to do with it. "Will you hurt me?" she asks Odysseus at his first armor-plated appearance. "If you do I will fear you, / If you don't I will despise you" (p. 208). Circe is "a desert island" or "a woman of mud" made for sexual exploitation, and her encounters with Odysseus are war games of rape, indifference, and betrayal, which she can analyze caustically, mounting a shrewd critique of the heroic ethos:

> Don't you get tired of killing
> those whose deaths have been predicted
> and are therefore dead already?
> Don't you get tired of wanting to live forever?
> Don't you get tired of saying Onward? (p. 206)

But this is passive, not active, resistance and cannot alter Odysseus' intentions. In Atwood's "Siren Song" the figure whose name still means "fatal seductress" sings a libretto of confinement turned vicious, "a boring song / but it works every time" (p. 196). What Atwood implies, as do other women who examine the blackness that has represented femaleness so often in our culture, is that the female power to do evil is a direct function of her powerlessness to do anything else.

3

> The short, passionate lyric has conventionally been thought appropriate for women poets if they insist on writing, while the longer, more philosophical epic belongs to the real (male) poet.
> —Susan Friedman, "Who Buried H.D.?" [25]

> I say there is only one image,
> one picture, though the swords flash;
> I say there is one treasure,
>
> one desire, as the wheels turn
> and the hooves of the stallions
> thunder across the plain,

and the plain is dust,
and the battle-field is a heap
of rusty staves and broken chariot-frames

and the rims of the dented shields
and desolation, destruction—for what?
a dream? a towered town?
        —H.D., "Helen in Egypt" [26]

If male poets write large, thoughtful poems while women poets write petite, emotional poems, the existence of book-length mythological poems by women on a literary landscape signifies trespass. To be great in our culture usually requires being big. Three such impressively big works are H.D.'s *Helen in Egypt*, Susan Griffin's extended prose-poem *Woman and Nature: The Roaring Inside Her*, and Anne Sexton's *Transformations*. They revise, respectively, ancient Greek and Egyptian mythology, the myth of objective discourse derived from the western concept of a God superior to Nature, and a set of fairy tales. All of them challenge not only our culture's concepts of gender but also its concepts of reality. [27]

In a 1928 poem entitled "Helen," written while she still had the reputation of the pure imagist poet, H.D. implies that the beautiful woman is always hated by the culture which pretends to adore her beauty and that the only good beauty, so far as patriarchal culture is concerned, is a dead one. H.D.'s Helen is passive, motionless, a bitter parody of her static appearance in poets from Homer through Poe and Yeats:

All Greece hates
the still eyes in the white face,
the luster of olives
where she stand
and the white hands . . .

Greece sees unmoved,
God's daughter, born of love,
the beauty of cool feet
and slenderest knees,
could love indeed the maid,
only if she were laid,
white ash amid funereal cypresses. [28]

Three decades later, in H.D.'s postwar masterpiece *Helen in Egypt*, Helen, "hated of all Greece" (p. 2) as the cause of the Trojan War, is again the subject. But the poet now announces that Helen of Troy, our culture's archetypal woman-as-erotic object, was actually a male-generated illusion, a "phantom," and that "the Greeks and the Trojans alike fought for an illusion."

H.D.'s sources are a fifty-line fragment by Stesichorus of Sicily (ca. 640–555 B.C.) and Euripides' drama *Helen*, which claim that Helen of Troy was a phantom and that "the real Helen" was transported by the Gods from Greece to Egypt where she spent the duration of the Trojan War waiting chastely for her husband Menelaus. These texts are themselves revisionist in that they propose a virtuous Helen instead of Homer's wanton adultress. But in H.D.'s version Menelaus is a trivial figure, and the poet makes clear that sexual chastity—or any conventional morality—is no more to be expected of an epic heroine than of an epic hero. The poet radically transforms these sources as well as the vast body of Greek and Egyptian mythology of which she was mistress, and which she believed composed "all myth, the one reality" in the same way that she believed all history was a "palimpsest," a reiterated layering of changeless patterns.

A more significant issue than the heroine's virtue is the redefinition of the relation between the feminine principle and what H.D. calls "the iron band of war," of which the war in Troy was the ancient exemplar and the two world wars the poet had lived through were the modern ones. Still more significant is the fact that the revised heroine is not woman-as-object at all, is not seen from the outside, but is instead a quintessential woman-as-subject, engaged in a quest for wholeness at once spiritual, psychological, and social.[29]

The narrative of *Helen in Egypt* resembles that of traditional epic in that it pursues a journey. The seeker Helen moves from Egypt to the Greek isle of Leuké and relives the pan-Hellenic travels of her past history, almost as if she were a female Odysseus. She is aided and protected by gods and heroes and survives perils. Unlike the epic hero, however, she does not know her own goal in advance and must discover it through fluid and nonlinear psychic processes which constitute her real adventure—meditation, memory, prayer, questioning, and associative weavings among "the million personal things, / things remembered, forgotten, / remembered again, assembled / and re-assembled in different order" (p. 289)—omitted from the accounts of Homer and all subsequent poets. Also unlike the epic hero, her role is not to support but to "unravel" and rewrite "the already-written drama or script" (p. 230) of religion and history.

Throughout *Helen in Egypt* H.D.'s "real Helen" is a "Psyche / with half-dried wings" (p. 166), a soul emerging from a chrysalis of ignorance and passivity. Spiritually her quest is to decipher symbols, begin-

ning with the hieroglyphs on the temple of the Egyptian god Thoth-
Amen, where we find her alone at the poem's opening. This Helen is an
"adept," an initiate seeking knowledge of the gods. Psychologically, she
is engaged in the recovery of her splintered selves, elements of her own
character and past which, we gradually discover, because they are
"hated of all Greece," have been "forgotten" by herself. This process
parallels the self-searching of classic psychoanalysis, and the episode in
which Helen is aided by the hero-father-lover figure Theseus is based
on H.D.'s sessions in the 1930s with Sigmund Freud.[30] These two tasks
are one task because "she herself is the writing" (p. 22). The goddess
who manifests herself as Isis-Aphrodite-Thetis is at first a mother-godess
to Helen but ultimately an aspect of her own identity. As in the closing
lines of Sexton's "Housewife" "a woman *is* her mother," so in H.D. a
woman *is* her mother-goddess. The centrality of the mother in women's
spirituality and eroticism is essential for understanding *Helen in Egypt*.

As an avatar of the love goddess Aphrodite, the heroine must recon-
cile herself with the Helen of Troy she has forgotten she ever was. That
is, the spiritual seeker must accept the erotic woman within herself.
These discoveries coalesce, again, with a third aspect of her quest: the
reconstitution of a primal family. Helen must determine the meaning to
herself of her Greek and Trojan lovers, the militant Achilles and the
seductive Paris. She must choose, rather than be chosen by, a "final
lover," and she must transcend the division between the virtuous role of
wife and mother that left her a stranger to herself, and the role of sinful
adultress, betrayer of her country, that left her "hated."

Achilles, the great protagonist of the *Iliad*, is H.D.'s paradigmatic
patriarchal male as Helen is the paradigmatic female. Heroic, male-
centered, immortality-seeking, Achilles ruthlessly leads a group of elect
warriors dedicated to discipline and control, called (punningly) "The
Command":

> The Command was bequest from the past,
> from father to son,
> the Command bound past to the present
>
> and the present to aeons to come,
> the Command was my father, my brother,
> my lover, my God. (p. 61)

H.D. draws clear parallels between this vocation, celebrated throughout
literary history, and fascism. To Achilles, woman is either sacrificial victim or sexual spoils. He has forgotten his boyhood love of the mother-

goddess Thetis. Precisely for this reason, Thetis—that is, the long-repressed and rejected feminine principle within him—can cause him to fall in love with the figure of Helen pacing the Trojan ramparts. In a moment of carelessness over an ankle-greave while he is gazing at her, Achilles receives the fatal and fated wound in his heel:

> This was the token, his mortality;
> immortality and victory
> were dissolved . . .
>
> some said a bowman from the Walls
> let fly the dart, some said it was Apollo,
> but I, Helena, know it was Love's arrow;
>
> the body honored
> by the Grecian host
> was but an iron casement,
>
> it was God's plan
> to melt the icy fortress of the soul,
> and free the man.

Helen's first perception of Achilles in Egypt is of a dim outline growing clearer,

> as the new Mortal,
> shedding his glory,
> limped slowly across the sand. (pp. 9–10)

H.D.'s attitude toward conquest, including the conquest of Time, anticipates Atwood's "Don't you get tired of killing. . . ? Don't you get tired of wanting to live forever?" Her image of masculine defense against feeling as a hard armor that should be dissolved and melted, for the man's own sake, parallels Rich's question in "The Knight": "Who will unhorse this rider / and free him from between / the walls of iron, the emblems / crushing his chest with their weight?" It also recalls the fates meted out to the male protagonists at the conclusions of *Jane Eyre* and *Aurora Leigh*, where the heroes must be wounded before the heroines can marry them. Brontë's and Browning's heroes are blinded in fires of sexual, and punitive, import. H.D.'s arrow penetrating a masculine chink is explicitly and evocatively sexual, and the image of this penetration of Achilles recurs like a refrain throughout the poem.

But the dissolving of male invulnerability in *Helen in Egypt* is part of a considerably larger pattern. Helen's Trojan lover, Paris, while a less violent, more sensuous, and more woman-centered figure than Achilles, is ultimately assigned the role of "son" rather than "father" in a mother-father-son romantic triangle. Moreover, late in the poem Helen hears within herself "an heroic voice, the voice of Helen of Sparta," one who glories in "the thunder of battle . . . and the arrows; O, the beauty of arrows" and must ask herself, "do I love War? / is this Helena?" (p. 177). The unveiling of a conflict-loving element in Helen balances the release of Achilles' eroticism. Replicating in mortal form the pattern of Isis-Osiris, Aphrodite-Ares (fecundity-knowledge, beauty-war), they link equal and opposite forces, generating a child ("Euphorion," pleasure or joy, equivalent of the Egyptian Horus and the Greek Eros) who will unite the attributes of both.

In its theology and its structuring of images, as well as in its quest plot, the driving intellectual impulse in *Helen in Egypt* is the synthesizing of opposites. Typhon and Osiris, killer and victim of Egyptian myth, were "not two but one . . . to the initiate" (p. 27). The daughter of Helen's sister Clytemnestra and her own daughter Hermione are identified as "one" sacrificial maiden (p. 69). The Greek Zeus and the Egyptian Amen are "One," though manifested as "a series of multiple gods" (p. 78). The same is true of some of the poem's key images or hieroglyphs: a beach of white "shells" and a beach of "skulls," the string of the lyre and the warrior's bowstring, the flaming brazier in the comforter's house and the flame of the burning Troy—these too are presented by the poem as cognate, related forms, mutually dependent polarities. Eventually Helen intuits that Love and Death, Eros and Eris (strife), unlike the Eros and Thanatos posited by the aged Freud as eternally dual principles, "will merge in the final illumination" (p. 271).

To analyze *Helen in Egypt* in a strand-by-strand fashion is to unweave, to pull threads from a fabric. Helen's quest invites a strenuous mental effort of meditation, intense reflection, associative leaping; but it resists the logocentric intellect. The poem does not explain its esoterica to the unenlightened reader, and it serenely neglects recognizable narrative. To a degree paralleled by very few poems in our literature, among them Blake's prophecies, it is pure psychodrama, nonmimetic of the world outside the psyche. Just as males in this poem play the relatively peripheral roles females have always played in male quests, so the external material world is represented in it largely by men in ships or at war, and the relation of such "realities" to Helen's identity is only one of the enigmas she is solving in the poem. Thus the fascinating, flickering alternation between prose and verse in *Helen in Egypt* is that of a single mind having an urgent dialogue with itself, probing, questioning—an extraordinarily large portion of the poem's text takes the form of ques-

tions—and persisting despite confusion ("What does he mean by that?
. . . Helena? who is she?") in the effort toward feminine self-definition:

I must fight for Helena (p. 37)

I am not, nor mean to be
The Daemon they made of me (p. 109)

I will encompass the infinite
in time, in the crystal,
in my thought here. (p. 201)

H.D. called the poem her "Cantos," and it is an implicit challenge to
Ezra Pound's culturally encyclopedic *Cantos*, not only because it assails
fascism and hero-worship but also for its uncompromising inwardness,
its rejection of all authority. For where Pound fills his poems with
chunks of authorized, authoritative literature and history, history and
literature are for *Helen in Egypt* never authoritative but always to-be-
deciphered, tangential to, incorporated within the feminine mind.

Helen in Egypt is first of all personal, one woman's quest epitomiz-
ing the struggle of Everywoman. Its interior life comes to include and
transcend the external historical world represented and inhabited by
males—but it does not reject that world. In Susan Griffin's *Woman and
Nature: The Roaring Inside Her*, male and female are also represented
as polar opposites, but from a different point of view and with a different
set of conclusions.

The dominating bulk of *Woman and Nature* consists of two long
books, "Matter" and "Separation," which constitute a definitive pastiche-
parody of the history of phallocentric intellect in the western world.
Griffin in these two books quotes and paraphrases hundreds of works,
ranging from the clean abstractions of theology, metaphysics, physics,
and mathematics, through the material facts of history, to such practical
subjects as forestry, agriculture, animal husbandry, mining, and office
management. The collective and anonymous paternal voice she creates
is emotionless, toneless, and authoritative. It does not say "I" or "we,"
but "it is said" or "it is stated":

It is decided that matter is passive and inert, and that all motion originates from outside matter.
That the soul is the cause of all movement in matter and that
the soul was created by God: that all other movement proceeds
from violent contact with other moving matter, which was first
moved by God. . . .

It is decided that the nature of woman is passive, that she is a vessel waiting to be filled. (p. 5).

The attitude of this voice toward Nature ("matter") and toward Woman is the same. It conceptualizes both as essentially, ideally, and properly inferior, passive, intended for man's use, yet at the same time potentially dangerous, threatening, wild, and evil, requiring to be tamed by force. Griffin here extends in two directions, theoretical and practical, the analogy formulated by the anthropologist Sherry Ortner that "Woman is to Nature as Man is to Culture." [31] On the one hand she makes clear the connection between the myth (in the sense of metaphor) of active male God and passive female Nature, and the myth (in the sense of falsity) of rational objectivity in the life of the intellect and of civilization. On the other she composes a huge collage of the multiple ways in which male superiority, buttressed by its myths, destroys life.

To justify their exploitation and destruction, woman and nature must be seen both as morally evil and as metaphysically nonexistent. Thus of the "'inordinate affections and passions'" of woman and the rich unpredictability of nature, "it is decided that that which cannot be measured and reduced to number is not real" (p. 11). From here to the rape of land and woman, land being consistently described as virgin or as mother, it is a short step. Scenes depicting depletion of nutrients in soil, courtship as a form of hunting, the extinction of species of beasts, the operation of clitoridectomy, the caging and drugging of a lioness, a woman muted by her husband's violence, the despoiling of forests, peasant women raped by invading soldiers are all the logical extrapolation of such axioms. Raskolnikov's desperate need in *Crime and Punishment* to dispose of the corpses of the two women he has murdered, and contemporary man's need to dispose of nuclear wastes, belong to the same pattern.

Toward the close of "Separation" Griffin documents some of the irrationalities, both creative and demeaning, in the lives of princes of rationality from Descartes to Darwin and Freud. There are also passages describing from a man's point of view man's dread of death and of the cosmic void, his dread of technology's killing consequences, and his ultimate dread, "so terrible he could scarcely hold onto it" that the difference between himself and the woman he lives with is not her "ignorance" but "the power he wields over her" and the intolerable fear that if "in an instant of feeling himself like her, he let this power go, then would he not become her" (p. 150).

Though satiric, Griffin's portrait of the myth of rational objectivity is also playfully inventive with numerous sorts of male discourse, from logic to legalese, from Dantean mysticism to Einsteinian thought-experiment. At times it is also beautiful, as in the section called "Territory"; at times ironic, as in the section called "The Show Horse." Throughout books I and II of *Woman and Nature* the female voice is muted. Occasionally we hear whispers of this suppressed female/natural voice—confused, suffering, angry.

In the third book, "Passage," and the fourth, "Her Vision," the female voice emerges from muteness and moves toward self-transformation. Through traditional female images of cave, water, earth, and seed, it gradually approaches images of light and flight. Altering from consciousness of "dreams" to knowledge of her body, her history, the body of the world, from passivity to rebellion, violence, dance, song, the "she" and "we" of this voice learn to accept "turbulence":

> When the wind calls, will we go? Will this wind come inside us? Take from us? Can we give to the wind what is asked of us? Will we let go? . . . Will the wind ask much of us, and will we be able to hear the wind singing and will we answer? Can we sing back, this we ask, can we sing back, and not only sing, but in clear voices? Will this be, we ask, and will we keep on answering, keep on with our whole bodies? And do we know why we sing? Yes. Will we know why? Yes. (p. 222)

Scenes from the first part of *Woman and Nature* reverse in the latter sections. Gynecologists become midwives. The lioness devours her captors. There is also a central assymmetry. Griffin portrays the relationships between mothers and daughters, midwives and birthing mothers; between women as friends, allies, and lovers; and between woman and earth as, in their ideal form, relationships of mirroring or interpenetration. Emotional closeness is derived from acknowledged likeness, not from the patriarchal relationship of dominance and submission, or from the dialectic between polarities envisioned by H.D. Consequently, in the last portion of *Woman and Nature*, the direct quotations are exclusively from women writers, and the male voice disappears from the book. At one point the "we" is a family of mourning elephants whose mother has been killed by a hunter and who vow to teach hatred and fear to their young:

> But though all traces of her vanish, we will not forget. In our life-times we will not be able to forget. Her wounds will fester in us. We will not be the same. The scent of her killer is known to us now. . . . We will pass this feeling to our young, to those who

follow in our footsteps, who walk under our bodies, who feel safe
in our presence, who did we not warn them, did we not teach
them this scent, might approach this enemy with curiosity . . .
They will learn fear. And when we attack in their defense, they
will watch and learn this too. From us, they will become fierce.
And so a death like this of our mother will not come easily to
them. This is what we will do with our grieving . . . And only
if the young of our young or the young of their young never know
this odor in their lifetime, only if no hunter approaches them as
long as they live, and no one with this scent attempts to capture
them, or use them to his purpose. . . . Only then . . . will we see
what we can be without this fear, without this enemy, what we
are. (pp. 217–18).

This pivotal passage offers a forceful metaphor for feminist separatism:
man is simply too dangerous, too much a killer, for woman to do anything but fear, fight, and avoid him.[32] The passage also, by virtue of
imagining a time "when no trace is left of this memory in us," releases
the author to conclude with a hymn of pleasure at once erotic and intellectual, a lesbian-feminist structural equivalent of the last movement of
Beethoven's Ninth Symphony, the close of Blake's *Jerusalem*, Molly
Bloom's soliloquy, or the Book of Revelation.

Lest these comparisons appear outrageous, it is worth noting with respect to the most (apparently) outrageous of them that the ratio of male
to female voices in the text of *Woman and Nature* is roughly equivalent
to that between Old and New Testaments, with the male coming first.
Like the Old Testament, the male books of *Woman and Nature* cover
a huge time span, are encyclopedic, multigenre, and polyvocal; they
concern conquest and law but also contain prophecy. Like the New
Testament, the female books cover a relatively brief time span, approach univocality, concern salvation and grace, and contain fulfillment of prophecy. I do not suggest that Griffin intended the parallels.
They are nevertheless visible and consonant with her overall purpose of
retrieving from patriarchal discourse a women's language.

Reading *Helen in Egypt* is like rafting on a swift river, confident notwithstanding meanders and eddies that one is traveling steadily down-
stream. Reading *Woman and Nature* is like watching the planet rotate,
watching the patches that mean farmland, mountain, desert go by,
watching ocean appear. But both books are about process and psychic
struggle. Despite the abstract nature of the masculine voice that dominates more than half of *Woman and Nature*, its structure is "intuitive."
In a recent essay Griffin has written that her initial attempts to organize
her material logically and chronologically "did not 'work.' It was like a

well-built bench that had no grace, and so one did not want to sit on it."
Thereafter she "simply followed the words intuitively, putting pieces
next to one another where the transition seemed wonderful, and that
was when the shape of the book began to seem beautiful to me." She
also explains that "all the time I wrote the book, the patriarchal voice
was in me, whispering to me . . . that I had no proof for any of my
writing, that I was wildly in error, that the vision I had of the whole
work was absurd."[33] Thus the gradual disclosure of the female voice in
the book reproduces the process of its creation.

Helen in Egypt and Woman and Nature are palpably difficult, intellectually complex works. Anne Sexton's Transformations, on the other
hand, looks superficially easy and entertaining, resting as it does on
what may be the one common narrative denominator left to modern
Americans from past traditions: the fairy tale. Its language is colloquial
and often comic; and it is full of ingratiating allusions to popular culture. Unlike both Helen in Egypt and Woman and Nature and unlike
most revisionist mythmaking by women, Transformations is not structured around the idea of male and female as polar opposites and is consequently not gynocentric in the fashion of these books. Rather, it is a
sharp synthesis of public "story" and psychological revelation, revisionist both in its systematically subversive readings of traditional plots,
characters, and morals and in its portrait of a lady who exists beyond the
plots, the female as creator.[34]

Transformations consists of a prologue and sixteen tales from the
Brothers Grimm, told in a wisecracking Americanese that simultaneously modernizes and desentimentalizes them, bringing them closer to
their often violent folk origins and reminding us that such stories were
once crackling with energy for their listeners. We have bits like "the
dwarfs, those little hot dogs" ("Snow White," p. 226); "a wolf dressed in
frills, / a kind of transvestite" ("Red Riding Hood," p. 270); or Sexton's
Gretel who, "seeing her moment in history . . . turned the oven on to
bake" (p. 289). Under the cover of entertainment, Sexton demolishes
many of the social conventions, especially those connected with femininity, that fairy tales ostensibly endorse. She mocks virginity and beauty
as values; the former makes one a fool ("Snow White, the dumb bunny"),
the latter cruel ("pretty enough / but with hearts like blackjacks"). Love,
in Sexton's versions, is a form of self-seeking. The happy ending of marriage is treated ironically as "a kind of coffin, / a kind of blue funk. / Is
it not?" (p. 232). Motherhood comes under scrutiny when Sexton describes a suffering mother as someone wearing "martyrdom / like a
string of pearls" (p. 260) and remarks, "a strange vocation to be a mother
at all" (p. 275).

An important source of Sexton's effectiveness is her striking ability to decode stories we thought we knew, revealing meanings we should have guessed. Her "Rapunzel" is a tale of love between an older and a younger woman, ultimately doomed by heterosexual normality. Her "Rumplestiltskin" is about the naivete and vulnerability of a dwarf manipulated by a calculating girl—or it is about the ability of the healthy ego to despise, suppress, and mutilate the libido. In "Hansel and Gretel," Sexton hints that the witch is a mother-goddess sacrificed by a female in alliance with the patriarchy.[35]

Though Sexton is obviously indebted to psychoanalytic method in the retrieval of latent content, she is not limited by its dogmas. For example, psychoanalytic commentary on the "sleeping virgin" pattern in fairy tales interprets the theme as that of feminine pubescence.[36] Sexton in "Briar Rose (Sleeping Beauty)" takes this insight almost contemptuously for granted and organizes her version like a series of clues to quite another mystery. There is no mother in Sexton's version, only a father. The psychoanalytically sophisticated reader may speculate that the thirteenth fairy, "her fingers as long and thin as straws, / her eyes burnt by cigarettes, / her uterus an empty teacup" (p. 291) is a displaced mother figure, as evil stepmothers commonly are. The protective father who not only got rid of spinning wheels but "forced every male in the court / to scour his tongue with Bab-o" (p. 292) is apparently a possessive parent hoping to keep his young daughter sexually pure. But after the denouement, the hundred years' sleep, and the arrival of the Prince, Sexton presents Briar Rose as a lifelong insomniac, terrified of sleeping. For when she sleeps she dreams of a dinner table with "a faltering crone at my place, / her eyes burnt by cigarettes / as she eats betrayal like a slice of meat" (p. 293). Why does the heroine identify with the crone? What betrayal does she allude to? Only the last lines tell us just why the mother is not "in" Sexton's story. Waking from sleep Briar Rose cries, like a little girl, "Daddy! Daddy!" as she did when the Prince woke her—and what she sees is "not the prince at all,"

> but my father
> drunkenly bent over my bed,
> circling the abyss like a shark,
> my father thick upon me
> like some sleeping jellyfish. (p. 294)

This is, of course, incest, a version of the Family Romance that neither orthodox psychoanalysis nor our legal system is ready to accept[37] but that countless women will recognize as painfully accurate.

In addition to the revivifying language and the revisionist interpretations of the stories, *Transformations* has another, framing element. The persona of the narrator-poet in the book's prologue is "a middle-aged witch, me" who talks like a den mother. Each of the ensuing tales has its own prologue, offering hints about the meaning of the story to come. The poet's personality alters with each prologue. In "Snow White" she is cynical, in "The White Snake" idealistic. Prior to "Rumplestiltskin" she announces that the dwarf is the suppressed "law of your members," out of St. Paul's epistles (p. 233), while in "One-Eye, Two-Eyes and Three-Eyes" she comments disapprovingly on the way parents with defective children "warm to their roles . . . with a positive fervor" where nature would sensibly let its malformed products die (p. 259). In the prologue to "The Frog Prince" she addresses a "Mama Brundig" psychoanalyst, gaily declaiming:

> My guilts are what
> we catalogue.
> I'll take a knife
> and chop up frog.

But the gaiety plummets abruptly to horror: "Frog is my father's genitals. / Frog is a malformed doorknob. / Frog is a soft bag of green" (p. 282).

Sexton as narrator is at times distant from the reader, at times intimate. Sometimes she identifies with life's sane ones, sometimes with the freaky and suicidal. She is unpredictably sensitive or brutal. It is important to notice here that while the tales themselves are fixed—and Sexton stresses their ruthless changelessness, never letting us think that her "characters" act with free will or do anything but fill their slots in predetermined plots—the teller is mobile. She emits an air of exhilarating mental and emotional liberty, precisely because she is distanced from the material she so penetratingly understands. Hers is an asexual role vis-à-vis her gendered characters. Thus the full force of *Transformations* lies not only in its psychosocial reinterpretations of Grimm's tales, however brilliant, nor in the fact that it expressly attacks literary and social conventions regarding women. Philosophically, the axis *Transformations* turns on is necessity (here seen as fixed and damaging social patterns) versus freedom; the "middle-aged witch, me" represents the latter.

4

And now we who are writing women and strange monsters
Still search our hearts to find the difficult answers,

Still hope that we may learn to lay our hands
More gently and more subtly on the burning sands.

To be through what we make more simply human,
To come to the deep place where poet becomes woman,

Where nothing has to be renounced or given over
In the pure light that shines out from the lover,

In the warm light that brings forth fruit and flower
And that great sanity, that sun, the feminine power.
        —May Sarton, "My Sisters, O My Sisters" [38]

The poems surveyed in this chapter have several characteristics in common. First, they treat existing texts as fenceposts surrounding the terrain of mythic truth but by no means identical to it. In other words, they are enactments of feminist antiauthoritarianism opposed to the patriarchal praxis of reifying texts. As Adrienne Rich declares in her definition of women's "writing as re-vision," "Re-vision—the act of looking back, of seeing with fresh eyes, of entering an old text from a new critical direction—is for women more than a chapter in cultural history: it is an act of survival." [39] Knowledge throughout women's mythmaking is achieved through personal, intuitive, and subjective means. It is never to be derived from prior authority and is always to be tested within the self. This is not to say that the poems, or the truths they represent, are merely private. As we have already seen, the private-public distinction is one that contemporary women poets tend to resist and attempt to dissolve in favor of a personal-communal continuum. As in women's love poems, the tacit assumption in women's myth poems is that the self in its innermost reaches is plural. The "I" is a "we," the myth contains and conveys common knowledge. The effectiveness of these poems rests on their power to release meanings that were latent but imprisoned all along in the stories we thought we knew.

Second, most of these poems involve reevaluations of social, political, and philosophical values, particularly those most enshrined in occidental literature, such as the glorification of conquest and the faith that the cosmos is—must be—hierarchically ordered with earth and body on the bottom and mind and spirit on the top. By the same token, none of these writers concerns herself with the achievement of immortality. On the contrary, the desire to live eternally tends to be mockingly deconstructed by women poets as a corollary of male aggressiveness and need for control.

Third, the work of women mythmakers is conspicuously different

from the modernist mythmaking of Yeats, Pound, Eliot, and Auden because it contains no trace of nostalgia, no faith that the past is a re-
pository of truth, goodness, or desirable social organization. Prufrock
may yearn to be Hamlet, but what woman would want to be Ophelia?
What woman's soul would seek monuments of its own magnificence in
Byzantium? While the myth of a Golden Age has exerted incalculable
pressure in the shaping of western literature and its attitude toward history, the revisionist woman poet does not care if the hills of Arcady are
dead. Or rather, she does not believe they are dead. Far from representing history as a decline or bemoaning disjunctions of past and present,
her poems insist that past and present are, for better or worse, essentially
the same. H.D.'s concept of the "palimpsest" seems to be the norm,
along with a treatment of time that effectively flattens it so that the past
is not then but now.

Fourth, degree of revisionism correlates with formal experiment.
This is important not only because new meanings must generate new
forms—when we have a new form in art we can assume we have a new
meaning—but because the strategies of defamiliarization draw attention to the discrepancies between traditional concepts and the conscious
mental and emotional activity of female re-vision. As it accentuates its
argument to make clear that there *is* an argument, that an act of theft is
occurring, feminist revisionism differs from Romantic revisionism,
although in other respects, such as its stress on personal feeling, it is
similar.

Some of the techniques that we have seen used throughout women's
poetry have a special relevance to the project of women's mythmaking.
The gaudy and abrasive colloquialism of Alta, Atwood, Plath, and
Sexton, for example, not only modernizes what is ancient, making
us see the contemporary relevance of the past. It also reduces the
verbal glow that we are trained to associate with mythic material. Even
H.D., who takes her divinities entirely seriously, avoids the elevated or
quasi-liturgical diction that, in the educated reader, triggers the self-
surrendering exaltation relied on by the creators of such poems as *Four
Quartets* or *The Cantos*. Levertov, too, consistently unites the liminal
with the experiential. With women poets we look at or into, but not up
at, sacred things; we unlearn submission.

A variant of colloquial language is childish or infantile language,
such as T. S. Eliot used in the nursery rhyme echoes of "The Hollow
Men" and at the close of *The Waste Land* to suggest a mix of regression and despair. We see similar effects, signaling primitive childhood
trauma, in Roethke's plaintive "Lost Son" poems, at the opening of

Berryman's "Dream Songs," and in the childhood poems of Lowell's *Life Studies*. In DuPlessis' "Medusa," passages of halting and sometimes punning baby talk become a way of revealing the power of sexual pain to infantilize, to thwart growth; the speaker's ultimate articulateness coincides with the sprouting of her avenging snakes. Regressive language also signals sexual trauma in Sexton. Another variant of the colloquial is the bawdy, a traditionally male linguistic preserve that women like Erica Jong and Carolyn Kizer have lately invaded.

The most significant large-scale technique in these poems is the use of multiple intertwined voices within highly composed extensive structures. The three long works discussed here employ the alternating prose and verse of *Helen in Egypt*, with occasional interludes when one of Helen's lovers speaks or she imagines him speaking; the male and female voices in *Women and Nature*, along with the multitudinous direct quotations; and prologue and story in *Transformations*.[40] These balancings are crucially important to the texture and sense of the poems, just as the multiple voices of *The Wast Land*, *The Cantos*, or *Paterson* are. Insofar as the subject of the poem is always the "I" of the poet, her divided voices evoke divided selves: the rational and the passionate, the animus and anima, analyst and analysand. Reading *Helen in Egypt* is uncannily like overhearing a communication between left brain and right brain.

Finally, these poems may challenge the validity of the "I," of any "I." Like the speaker of Adrienne Rich's "Diving into the Wreck," whose discovery of her submerged self is a discovery that she is a "we" for whom even the distinction between subject and object dissolves, and like the multiple self of women's chant-poems, the heroines we find in women's revisionist mythology are more often fluid than solid. But these are not books or heroines about which the authors are saying, as Pound tragically said of *The Cantos*, and his life, "I cannot make it cohere."[41] Although the divided self is probably the single issue women poets since 1960 most consistently struggle with, the most visionary of their works appear to be strengthened by acknowledging division and containing it, as H.D. says, "in my thought here." To return to Muriel Rukeyser's revision of her earlier "Orpheus" in "The Poem as Mask," the necessity is to drop the pretense that the fragmented gods are other than ourselves:

> when I wrote of the god,
> fragmented, exiled from himself, his life, the love gone down
>   with song,
> it was myself, split open, unable to speak, in exile from myself.

There is no mountain, there is no god, there is memory
of my torn life, myself split open in sleep, the rescued child
beside me among the doctors, and a word
of rescue from the great eyes.

No more masks! No more mythologies!

Now, for the first time, the god lifts his hand,
The fragments join in me with their own music. (p. 435)

Epilogue

Ezra Pound in *ABC of Reading* remarks that when poetry and music move too far from their origins in music and dance, they atrophy and need renewal. We should add that when poetry and the poet move too far from their origins in communal expression—too far from participatory performance and the expectation of shared human feeling, too far into a regulated and predictable literacy bound up in academic role playing, where the reader is either passive appreciator-student or judgmental critic-professor—they are again in need of reinvigoration. Today our schools for the most part train poets and critics into postures of detachment and impersonality, as if our encounters with the life of poetry ought to resemble our encounters with law and bureaucracy. We dread, it seems, the embarrassment and pain of personal and poetic self-disclosure. We have forgotten that "subjectivity" may be as severe and demanding a discipline as "objectivity." If poetry written by women today demands that we read as participants—identifying, gratified, terrified, irritated, disagreeing, even repelled—it may help us "discover self" and may also help us discover wider perspectives for art.

I have stressed throughout this book the adversary relation between the women's poetry movement and the "larger" culture, derived from women's cultural marginality. In our own time, a gynocentric poetics is necessarily adversarial. Yet in another sense it may be that women's poetry is simply a vehicle through which, at the present moment, the ongoing life of poetry is being preserved and extended. We must remember that all poetry is marginal in relation to the material preoccupations of society; that all poetry is potentially disruptive to rulers and institutions; and that all poetry depends for its survival not on literary fashions but on the interior needs of readers who for their own reasons respond with pleasure to it. When Whitman in *Song of Myself* wrote "Camerado, this is no book. Who touches this touches a man," and "What I assume you shall assume," he articulated an abiding impulse latent within all poetry. The women's poetry movement today is a carrier of that same impulse and makes it possible for us to "assume" more than we did before.

The subject of this book has been a collective endeavor to redefine "woman" and "woman poet." From this endeavor, because the nature of poetry always is to illuminate our darkness, we should discover not only more of what it means to be a woman but more of what it means to be human.

Notes

Introduction

1. Anne Bradstreet, *The Works of Anne Bradstreet*, ed. Jeannine Hensley, Forword by Adrienne Rich (Cambridge, Mass.: Harvard University Press, 1967), pp. 16–17.
2. Erica Jong, "Bitter Pills for the Dark Ladies," *Fruits & Vegetables* (New York: Holt, Rinehart and Winston, 1971), pp. 47–48.
3. Bradstreet, *Works*, p. 5.
4. T. S. Eliot, "Marianne Moore," in Charles Tomlinson, ed., *Marianne Moore: A Collection of Critical Essays* (Englewood Cliffs, N.J.: Prentice-Hall, 1969), p. 51.
5. Theodore Roethke, "The Poetry of Louise Bogan," *Selected Prose of Theodore Roethke*, ed. Ralph J. Mills, Jr. (Seattle: University of Washington Press, 1965), pp. 133–34.
6. Sandra M. Gilbert and Susan Gubar, eds., *Shakespeare's Sisters: Feminist Essays on Women Poets* (Bloomington: Indiana University Press, 1979), p. xviii.
7. Ralph Waldo Emerson, "The Poet," *Essays and Lectures*, ed. Joel Porte (New York: Library of America, Viking Press, 1983), p. 466; *Emerson in His Journals*, ed. Joel Porte (Cambridge, Mass.: Harvard University Press, 1982), p. 271.
8. Sandra M. Gilbert and Susan Gubar, *The Madwoman in the Attic: The Woman Writer and the Nineteenth-Century Imagination* (New Haven: Yale University Press, 1979), pp. 3–11.
9. Harold Bloom, *The Anxiety of Influence* (New York: Oxford University Press, 1973), p. 26.
10. Edwin Fussell, *Lucifer in Harness: American Meter, Metaphor and Diction* (Princeton: Princeton University Press, 1973), p. 12.
11. Caroline May, ed., *The American Female Poets* (Philadelphia: Lindsay and Blakiston, 1848), p. viii.
12. Roy Harvey Pearce, "Marianne Moore," in Tomlinson, *Marianne Moore*, p. 151.
13. Anne Stevenson, *Elizabeth Bishop* (New York: Twayne, 1966), p. 126.

14. Ruth Limmer, ed., *What the Woman Lived: Selected Letters of Louise Bogan: 1920–1970* (New York: Harcourt Brace Jovanovich, 1973), p. vii.

15. W. H. Auden, Preface to *A Change of World*, reprinted in *Adrienne Rich's Poetry*, ed. Barbara Charlesworth Gelpi and Albert Gelpi (New York: W. W. Norton, 1975), p. 127.

16. Robert Lowell, Introduction to *Ariel* by Sylvia Plath (New York: Harper and Row, 1965), p. vii.

17. John Cody, *After Great Pain: The Inner Life of Emily Dickinson* (Cambridge, Mass.: Harvard University Press, 1971), p. 495.

18. R. P. Blackmur, "Emily Dickinson: Notes on Prejudice and Fact," *The Southern Review* 3 (Autumn 1937): 346–47.

19. John Crowe Ransom, "Emily Dickinson: The Poet Restored," in Richard B. Sewall, ed., *Emily Dickinson: A Collection of Critical Essays* (Englewood Cliffs, N.J.: Prentice-Hall, 1963), pp. 89, 92.

20. David Porter, *Dickinson: The Modern Idiom* (Cambridge, Mass.: Harvard University Press, 1981).

21. Douglas Bush, *Mythology and the Romantic Tradition in English Poetry* (Cambridge, Mass.: Harvard University Press, 1937), p. 505.

22. Hugh Kenner, *The Pound Era* (Berkeley: University of California Press, 1971), p. 176.

23. See Susan Friedman, "Who Buried H.D.? A Poet, Her Critics and The Literary Tradition," *College English* 36, no. 7 (March 1975): 801–14.

24. Dennis Donaghue, review of Janice H. Robinson, *H.D.: The Life and Work of an American Poet*, *New York Times Book Review*, February 14, 1982, p. 23.

25. Yvor Winters, "Emily Dickinson and the Limits of Criticism," in Sewall, *Emily Dickinson*, p. 29.

26. For discussion of the continuing condescension toward Dickinson in contemporary criticism, see Suzanne Juhasz, ed., *Feminist Critics Read Emily Dickinson* (Bloomington: Indiana University Press, 1983), pp. 2–9. For discussion of the gendered (and racial) making of literary canons see Louise Bernikow, ed., *The World Split Open: Four Centuries of Women Poets in English and America, 1552–1950* (New York: Random House, 1974), Introduction, pp. 3–47; Suzanne Juhasz, *Naked and Fiery Forms: Modern American Poetry by Women, a New Tradition* (New York: Harper and Row, 1976), "The Double Bind of the Woman Poet," pp. 1–6; Gilbert and Gubar, *Shakespeare's Sisters*, Introduction, pp. xv–xxvi; Paul Lauter, "Race and Gender in the Shaping of the American Canon: A Case Study from the Twenties," *Feminist Studies* 9, no. 3 (Fall 1983): 435–63.

27. Carolyn Kizer, "Pro Femina," *Knock upon Silence* (Garden City, N.Y.: Doubleday, 1965), pp. 41–49.

28. Key texts sharing this position are Juhasz, *Naked and Fiery Forms*; Elaine Showalter, *A Literature of Their Own* (Princeton, N.J.: Princeton University Press, 1977); Ann Douglas, *The Feminization of American Culture* (New York: Knopf, 1977), which is, however, unsympathetic to the women writers discussed; Gilbert and Gubar, *Shakespeare's Sisters*; Gilbert and Gubar, *Mad-*

woman in the Attic; Cheryl Walker, *The Nightingale's Burden: Women Poets in America 1630–1900* (Bloomington: Indiana University Press, 1982). See also Florence Howe and Ellen Bass, eds., Introduction to *No More Masks: An Anthology of Poems by Women* (Garden City, N.Y.: Doubleday, 1973).

29. See Jan Clausen, *A Movement of Poets: Thoughts on Feminism and Poetry* (New York: Long Haul Press, 1982), for a personal account of the women's poetry movement, and Lynda Koolish, *A Whole New Poetry Beginning Here*, 2 vols. (Ann Arbor, Mich.: University Microfilms, 1981). Volume 1 analyzes the women's poetry movement, concentrating on its political dimensions; volume 2 is a collection of essays on poetics by thirty-five poets.

30. Judy Grahn, "Red and Black with Fish in the Middle," in Koolish, *Whole New Poetry*, vol. 1, p. 541; June Jordan, *Passion: New Poems 1977–1980* (Boston: Beacon Press, 1980), p. xix.

Chapter 1: I'm Nobody: Women's Poetry, 1650–1960

1. Virginia Woolf, *A Room of One's Own* (New York: Harcourt Brace, 1957), p. 79.

2. Alice Walker, *In Search of Our Mothers' Gardens* (New York: Harcourt Brace, 1983), p. 232.

3. Simone de Beauvoir, *The Second Sex*, trans. and ed. H. M. Parshley (New York: Knopf, 1953), chap. 9, "Dreams, Fears, Idols," chap. 10, "The Myth of Women in Five Authors."

4. Elaine Showalter, *A Literature of Their Own* (Princeton: Princeton University Press, 1977), traces the literary subculture of women's fiction in England. Joanne Feit-Diehl, "Come Slowly—Eden: An Exploration of Women Poets and Their Muse," *Signs* 3, no. 3 (Spring 1978): 572–87, discusses the woman writer's relation to Bloomian literary history and her use of female models as enabling muses. Sandra Gilbert and Susan Gubar, *The Madwoman in the Attic: The Woman Author and the Nineteenth-Century Imagination* (New Haven: Yale University Press, 1979), observe that the woman writer often can begin the struggle of self-definition "only by actively seeking a female precursor who, far from representing a threating force to be denied or killed, proves by example that a revolt against patriarchal literary authority is possible" (p. 49).

5. Anne Bradstreet, *The Works of Anne Bradstreet*, ed. Jeannine Hensley, Foreword by Adrienne Rich (Cambridge, Mass.: Harvard University Press, 1967), p. 15. The texts of Bradstreet's poems are quoted from this edition.

6. John Winthrop, *Winthrop's Journal: "History of New England," 1630–1649*, 2 vols., ed. James Kendall Hosmer (New York: Scribner's, 1908), vol. 2, p. 239.

7. Carl Holliday, *Women's Life in Colonial Days* (1922, reprint, New York: Frederick Ungar Publishing Co., 1960), p. 35.

8. Winthrop, *Journal*, vol. 2, p. 225.

9. Bradstreet, *Works*, p. 3. The text of Woodbridge's commendatory verse is from this edition.

10. The best account of Bradstreet's life is Elizabeth Wade White, *Anne Bradstreet: "The Tenth Muse"* (New York: Oxford University Press, 1971). The best critical book is Ann Stanford, *Anne Bradstreet: The Wordly Puritan* (New York: Burt Franklin & Co., 1974). Both stress Bradstreet's privileged girlhood as a formative influence on her writing. Her father, Thomas Dudley, a gentleman who claimed kinship with the family of Sir Philip Sidney, became steward to the fourth Earl of Lincoln when Anne was six or seven, and her youth was consequently spent in one of the "great houses" of England, among highly educated aristocrats and gentlefolk of nonconforming religion. After her marriage at the age of sixteen to Simon Bradstreet, her father's assistant, she lived in the household of the dowager countess of Warwick. In 1730 the Dudleys, Bradstreets, and other Puritan families emigrated to America, where Bradstreet lived successively in Salem, Newton (now Cambridge), Ipswich—a fast-growing community with a lively intellectual and political life—and Andover. Though she became the mother of eight children, who all survived to adulthood, her writing was evidently encouraged throughout her life by her father, her husband, and other relatives and friends, some of whom wrote verse themselves. It is important to remember that "Puritanism" did not necessarily mean opposition to belles lettres; many of Bradstreet's associates possessed large libraries of secular as well as religious works, and when her own house burned down in 1666, a library of more than eight hundred books was lost. See Stanford, *Anne Bradstreet*, for a list of Bradstreet's probable reading (pp. 135–44). Regarding the status of women writers in the late sixteenth and early seventeenth centuries, Stanford's anthology *The Women Poets in English* (New York: McGraw-Hill, 1972) makes clear that, notwithstanding opposition in some quarters to "female wits," ladies of noble or gentle birth could expect support and admiration for their efforts in verse. Nevertheless, as Wendy Martin demonstrates in *An American Triptych* (Chapel Hill: University of North Carolina Press, 1984), "the issue of power and powerlessness is the central concern" in Bradstreet's writing (p. 38).

11. Emily Stipes Watts, *The Poetry of American Women from 1632 to 1945* (Austin: University of Texas Press, 1977), points out that "the long tradition of poems concerning children by American women (more in number and much earlier than similar poems by English women) has generally been ignored" because real children did not interest male poets or critics before the twentieth century (p. 14). Watts discusses the theme of mother-child poetry and poetry for children on pages 14–17, 87–90, 93–96, 113–15, and elsewhere.

12. Josephine Piercy, *Anne Bradstreet* (New York: Twayne, 1965), p. 44.

13. Stanford, *Anne Bradstreet*, contains an appendix on Bradstreet's imagery, indicating that the poet's favorite images were of the human body; these outweigh by a good margin images of nature and biblical references (pp. 133–34). With the exception of Whitman, women poets from Bradstreet's time to our own consistently employ anatomical images more than their male cohorts do.

14. Watts, *Poetry of American Women*, enumerates the obstacles to female poetry in Puritan New England: lack of intellectual freedom in Massachusetts Bay; the Puritan marriage, which required female subjection; women's illiter-

acy in the New World; and the rugged physical conditions of Colonial life (pp. 21–22).

15. Watts, *Poetry of American Women*, p. 31. Watts' full discussion of Turrell and Wheatley is on pages 30–38.

16. Phillis Wheatley, "On Being Brought from Africa to America," in G. Herbert Renfro, *Life and Works of Phillis Wheatley* (Washington, D.C., 1916; reprint, Miami: Mnemosyne Publishing Co., 1969), p. 48. See, however, William H. Robinson, *Phillis Wheatley in the Black American Beginnings* (Detroit: Broadside Press, 1975). Robinson finds evidence of personal and racial pride in Wheatley's poetry and letters and discusses the value of Christianity to her as a doctrine whereby she and other blacks could claim equality to white Christians and superiority to unbelievers. Recently discovered, "Address to the Deist, 1767," in Wheatley's hand, begins "Must Ethiopians be employ'd for you?" (p. 79).

17. The Mercy Warren–John Adams correspondence is quoted in Jean Fritz, *Cast for a Revolution: Some American Friends and Enemies* (Boston: Houghton Mifflin, 1972), pp. 107–08.

18. Mercy Warren, *Poems, Dramatic and Miscellaneous* (Boston, 1790), p. 205.

19. Ann Eliza Bleecker, "To Mr. L.———," *Posthumous Works* (New York: T. and J. Swords, 1793), p. 201.

20. Elias Nason, *A Memoir of Mrs. Susanna Rowson* (Albany, N.Y.: Joel Munsell, 1870), p. 118.

21. Susanna Rowson, *Slaves in Algiers, or, a Struggle for Freedom* (Philadelphia: Wrigley & Berriman, 1804), p. 73.

22. Susanna Rowson, *Miscellaneous Poems* (Boston: Gilbert & Dean, 1804), pp. 99–115.

23. John Berryman, *Homage to Mistress Bradstreet* (New York: Farrar, Straus & Cudahy, 1956), n.p. Further quotes are from this edition.

24. See Bradstreet, *Works*, p. xxxi, for a summary of Bradstreet's success in the seventeenth century.

25. Moses Coit Tyler, *A History of American Literature During the Colonial Time*, 2 vols. (New York: Putnam, 1897), vol. 1, p. 283.

26. Charles Eliot Norton, Introduction to *The Poems of Mrs. Anne Bradstreet (1612–1672). Together with Her Prose Remains* (The Duodecimos, 1897), p. xx.

27. Adrienne Rich, Introduction to Bradstreet, *Works*, p. xvii. Rich has subsequently reprinted this essay in her collection *On Lies, Secrets and Silence: Selected Prose 1966–1978* (New York: W. W. Norton, 1979), pp. 21–32, apologizing for the condescension. Wendy Martin, *American Triptych*, still distinguishes between Bradstreet's public poems, which "reveal . . . grim determination to prove she could write in the lofty style of the established male poets" and later work "rooted in her actual experience as a wife, as a mother, and as a woman" (p. 15). Martin's subsequent reading of the public poems shows, however, that the line between intellectual and personal is not clear-cut.

28. Rufus Griswold, "Frances Sargent Osgood," in Mary Hewitt, ed., *The

Memorial: Written by Friends of the Late Mrs. Osgood (New York: George Putnam, 1851), pp. 13–14.

29. Frances Osgood, "Ah! Woman Still," *Poems* (Philadelphia: Carey and Hart, 1850), p. 46.

30. Quoted in Nancy F. Cott, ed., *Root of Bitterness: Documents of the Social History of American Women* (New York: Dutton, 1972), pp. 77–82.

31. Ann Douglas, *The Feminization of American Culture* (New York: Knopf, 1977), pp. 44–45.

32. *Ladies Magazine* 3 (1830), quoted by Douglas, *Feminization*, p. 46.

33. George Whicher, *This Was a Poet: A Critical Biography of Emily Dickinson* (New York: Scribner's, 1939), p. 136.

34. *Ladies Magazine* 2 (1829), quoted by Cheryl Walker, *The Nightingale's Burden: Women Poets and American Culture Before 1900* (Bloomington: Indiana University Press, 1982), p. 34.

35. Caroline May, ed., *The American Female Poets* (Philadelphia: Lindsay & Blakiston, 1848), pp. v–vi.

36. Rufus Griswold, *The Female Poets of America* (1848; Philadelphia: Moss, Brother & Co., 1860), pp. 7–8.

37. Griswold, "Osgood," p. 29.

38. Mary Clement, ed., *The Poetical Works of Alice and Phoebe Cary: With a Memorial of Their Lives* (New York: Hurd & Houghton, 1876), p. 82.

39. Hewitt, *Memorial*, p. 21.

40. Griswold, *Female Poets*, p. 232.

41. Griswold, *Female Poets*, p. 93.

42. May, *American Female Poets*, p. viii. The need of this period to ghettoize the female artist extends also to fictional representations of the supposed "type." Hawthorne's Hilda in *The Marble Faun* is a copyist of paintings and a shy soul, "a flower that finds a chink for herself and a little earth to grow in." The real-life Harriet Hosmer, whom Hawthorne knew in Rome, enjoyed an outdoor girlhood with her own horse, gun, and boat because her father wanted to ensure that she did not die young of tuberculosis like her mother. She climbed a mountain now known as Mt. Hosmer, was a friend of the Brownings in Rome, and executed large commissioned sculptures for notables and royalty. This interesting disparity is pointed out by Ernest Earnest in *The American Eve in Fact and Fiction* (Urbana: University of Illinois Press, 1974). Earnest also quotes diaries and letters of numerous well-read, bright, humorous, and unsentimental girls as evidence that they were nothing like the girls in Hawthorne's, Howells', or James' fiction. He is at particular pains to demonstrate that the typical American girl abroad was neither so vulgar as Daisy Miller nor so innocent as Isabel Archer.

43. Anna Maria Wells, "Hope," in May, *American Female Poets*, p. 114; Margaret Miller Davidson (untitled), in Griswold, *Female Poets*, p. 152.

44. Douglas, *Feminization*, pp. 5–6.

45. Douglas, *Feminization*, p. 203.

46. Louise Bogan, *Achievement in American Poetry* (Chicago: Gateway Editions, 1951), p. 19.

47. Watts, *Poetry of American Women*, pp. 5–6 and *passim*.

48. This is a shared premise of Elaine Showalter, *Literature of Their Own*; of Gilbert and Gubar, *Madwoman in the Attic*; of Suzanne Juhasz, *Naked and Fiery Forms: Modern American Poetry by Women* (New York: Harper and Row, 1976); of Margaret Homans, *Women Writers and Poetic Identity* (Princeton: Princeton University Press, 1980); and of Cheryl Walker, *The Nightingale's Burden: Women Poets and American Culture Before 1900* (Bloomington: Indiana University Press, 1982).

49. Homans, *Women Writers*, p. 166.

50. Griswold, *Female Poets*, p. 148.

51. Walker, *Nightingale's Burden*, p. 152. Walker's exposition of the dominant images of feminine ambivalence is on pages 21–58.

52. Maria Brooks, *Zophiël, or the Bride of Seven* (London: R. J. Kennet, 1833), pp. 35, 69. The book was later published in Boston. Extended excerpts are in Griswold, *Female Poets*, briefer ones in May, *American Female Poets*.

53. Griswold, *Female Poets*, p. 79.

54. May, *American Female Poets*, p. 57.

55. On Osgood, see Watts, *Poetry of American Women*, pp. 105–20, and Walker, *Nightingale's Burden*, pp. 28–29, 39–42.

56. Quoted by Watts, *Poetry of American Women*, p. 108.

57. Osgood, "A Song," *Poems*, p. 23.

58. Griswold, *Female Poets*, pp. 285, 284–85, 275.

59. Thomas Wentworth Higginson, quoted in Emily Dickinson, *Letters*, 3 vols., ed. T. H. Johnson (Cambridge, Mass.: Harvard University Press, 1971), vol. 2, p. 473. All quotations of Dickinson's letters are from this edition, designated *L* in the text.

60. Emily Dickinson, *Complete Poems*, 3 vols., ed. T. H. Johnson (Cambridge, Mass.: Harvard University Press, 1955), vol. 2, p. 365. All quotations of Dickinson's poems are from this edition, designated *P* in the text, and cited according to Johnson's numbering.

61. See Walker, *Nightingale's Burden*, chap. 4, pp. 87–116, for a full discussion of Dickinson's relation to other female poets, including Helen Hunt Jackson; Watts, *Poetry of American Women*, pp. 125–37; and Gilbert and Gubar, *Madwoman in the Attic*, chap. 16, pp. 581–650. The evidence refutes any ideas that Dickinson "took very little, in fact, from the available sources— from other poetry, for instance" (Dennis Donaghue, *Connoisseurs of Chaos* [New York: Macmillan, 1965], p. 112) or that "her stance is rarely belated, because of her exquisite good fortune in having precursors who were mainly male" (Harold Bloom, *A Map of Misreading* [New York: Oxford University Press, 1975], p. 184.) These assertions are variants of the "not another poetess" line, which depends on the assumption that good woman poets cannot be related to other women poets.

62. Adrienne Rich, "Vesuvius at Home: The Power of Emily Dickinson," *On Lies, Secrets and Silence*, pp. 158–83, esp. 172–74.

63. See Homans, *Women Writers*, pp. 176–212, especially the analysis of Dickinson's trick "of rendering equivalencies from polarities" and "the way in

which an apparently transparent poem invites two mutually exclusive readings" (p. 176). Homans' example here is "Success is counted sweetest," which she says can be read equally well literally or ironically. See also Albert Gelpi, *Emily Dickinson: The Mind of the Poet* (Cambridge, Mass.: Harvard University Press, 1965): "She is caught hesitating between the desire to be ravished and the fear of being violated, between the need for integration with something else and the assertion of self-contained individuality, between the need for union with or subservience to the not-me and the insistence upon the separate identity of the ego" (p. 3). This is a remarkably penetrating statement not only of Dickinson's personal dilemma but of her dilemma as a woman writer who is defined as submissive by male culture yet as assertive by her own ego and who feels both pulls equally keenly.

64. Donald Hall, "Goatfoot, Milktongue, Twinbird: The Psychic Origins of Poetic Form," *Claims for Poetry*, ed. Donald Hall (Ann Arbor: University of Michigan Press, 1983), p. 141.

65. See the discussion of "Goblin Market" in Gilbert and Gubar, *Madwoman in the Attic*, pp. 564–75. Gilbert and Gubar observe that Rosetti's is an "aesthetic of pain . . . a masochistic version of what Dickinson called 'the bouquet of abstemiousness'" (p. 573). Where the duplicities in Dickinson tend to revolve around issues of wicked power/virtuous powerlessness, in Rossetti they center on wicked pleasure/virtuous pain.

66. Richard Wilbur, "Sumptuous Destitution," in Richard B. Sewall, ed., *Emily Dickinson: A Collection of Critical Essays* (Englewood Cliffs, N.J.: Prentice-Hall, 1963), p. 128.

67. Louise Bogan, "I Saw Eternity," *The Blue Estuaries: Poems 1923–1968* (New York: Ecco Press, 1977), p. 50.

68. Marianne Moore, "The Paper Nautilus," *Complete Poems* (New York: Macmillan, 1967), pp. 121–22.

69. See Watts, *Poetry of American Women*, chap. 5, pp. 121–25, 137–47, and Walker, *Nightingale's Burden*, chap. 5, for discussions of late-nineteenth-century women's poetry and the transition to modernism.

70. Ella Wheeler Wilcox, *Poems of Passion* (Chicago: W. B. Conkey, 1883), p. 11.

71. A significant signpost of educated taste is Edmund Clarence Stedman's huge *An American Anthology: 1787–1900*, with selections from about six hundred poets. The proportion of women represented rises steadily through the volume's chronological divisions. For the final twenty-year period, 1880–1890, although the women poets are usually represented by fewer individual poems than the men, their total number comes to over one third of all the poets included.

72. Bogan, "The Alchemist," *Blue Estuaries*, p. 15.

73. The discussion in chapter 6 of Walker, *Nightingale's Burden*, of the continuities from sentimental to modernist to contemporary women poets suggests that women poets who ignore the lachrymose history of their grandmothers doom themselves to repeat it. One may also argue that the cultural oppression which produces female ambivalence regarding power, sexuality, and feminity

lifts only slightly in the twentieth century; the obvious analogue is the residue of
racism remaining after the legal abolition of slavery.

74. Adelaide Crapsey, *Verse* (New York: Knopf, 1922), pp. 81–83.

75. Sara Teasdale, *Collected Poems*, Introduction by Marya Zaturenska (New
York: Macmillan, 1966), p. 70.

76. Elinor Wylie, *Collected Poems* (New York: Knopf, 1966), p. 14.

77. Edna St. Vincent Millay, *Collected Poems* (New York: Harper and Brothers, 1956), p. 234.

78. Sara Teasdale planned to write a biography of Christina Rossetti and was
supposedly working on it when she killed herself with an overdose of sleeping
pills in 1933. Genevieve Taggard, *Life and Mind of Emily Dickinson* (New
York: Knopf, 1930), is the first commentator on the poet to see that "her life
was forcibly double and her mind divided" (p. xv) and to trace this division to
Dickinson's "primitive" relationship with her father. But in Louise Bogan, *Selected Criticism* (New York: Noonday Press, 1955), there are pieces, mainly from
the *New Yorker* column which Bogan wrote for thirty-eight years, on Hopkins,
Eliot, Sandburg, Jeffers, Rilke, Yeats, Auden, Spender, Frost, Pound, Lorca,
Winters, Graves, Betjeman; an enthusiastic review of Marianne Moore; a condescending one of Millay; and no other commentary on a living woman poet.
Asked in 1933 to edit a volume of women poets for *The New Republic*, Bogan
declined. "The thought of corresponding with a lot of female songbirds made
me acutely ill," she wrote John Hall Wheelock (*What the Woman Lived: Selected Letters of Louise Bogan, 1920–1970*, ed. Ruth Limmer [New York:
Harcourt Brace Jovanovich, 1973], p. 86).

79. John Crowe Ransom, "The Poet as Woman," *The World's Body* (New
York: Scribner's, 1938), pp. 76–78, 103–05.

80. Quoted by Carolyn Burke, "The New Poetry and the New Woman:
Mina Loy," in Diane Wood Middlebrook and Marilyn Yalom, eds., *Coming to
Light: American Women Poets in the Twentieth Century* (Ann Arbor: University
of Michigan Press, 1985), p. 37.

81. The best discussions of Stein's style are, on its indeterminacy, Marjorie
Perloff, in *The Poetics of Indeterminacy: Rimbaud to Cage* (Princeton: Princeton
University Press, 1981), pp. 67–108, and on its status as "antipatriarchal,"
Marianne De Koven, *A Different Language: Gertrude Stein's Experimental
Writing* (Madison: University of Wisconsin Press, 1983).

82. William Carlos Williams, *Autobiography* (New York: New Directions,
1957), p. 146.

83. Amy Lowell, *The Complete Poetical Works of Amy Lowell* (Boston:
Houghton Mifflin, 1955), pp. 409, 420.

84. Gertrude Stein, "Patriarchal Poetry," *Bee Time Vine and Other Pieces*
(1913–1927), ed. Virgil Thomson (New Haven: Yale University Press, 1953),
pp. 263–72; excerpts reprinted in Louise Bernikow, *The World Split Open: Four
Centuries of Women Poets, 1552–1950* (New York: Random House, 1974). The
poem was unpublished in Stein's lifetime. Virgil Thomson, who was a friend of
Stein, describes it as "genuinely hermetic," meaning that "direct communication of ideas is not its purpose" and that it cannot be understood in terms of

"common sense." In the same volume of posthumous writing is the long poem about love and happiness in daily life, "Lifting belly" (pp. 65–115), of which Thomson confesses, "I do not know the meaning of the title."

85. The poems are quoted and located in their cultural frame by Burke, "New Poetry," pp. 43–53. The standard edition of Loy's poems is *The Last Lunar Baedaker*, ed. Roger L. Conover (Highlands, N.C.: Jargon Society, 1982).

86. The definitive study of H.D.'s development of a woman-centered poetics is Susan Stanford Friedman, *Psyche Reborn: The Emergence of H.D.* (Bloomington: Indiana University Press, 1981). See also Susan Gubar, "The Echoing Spell of H.D.'s Trilogy," in Gilbert and Gubar, *Shakespeare's Sisters*, pp. 200–218; Rachel Blau DuPlessis, "Romantic Thralldom in H.D.," *Contemporary Literature* 20, no. 2 (Summer 1979): 178–203; Rachel Blau DuPlessis and Susan Stanford Friedman, "Woman Is Perfect: H.D.'s Debate with Freud," *Feminist Studies* 7, no. 3 (Fall 1981): 417–30; Alicia Ostriker, "The Poet as Heroine: Learning to Read H.D.," *Writing Like a Woman* (Ann Arbor: University of Michigan Press, 1983), pp. 7–41.

87. H.D., *Trilogy* (New York: New Directions, 1973), p. 103. Further quotations are from this edition.

88. Marianne Moore, *Complete Poems*, pp. 62–70. In the foreword to *A Marianne Moore Reader* (New York: Viking, 1961), Moore makes this disclaimer: "the thing (I would hardly call it a poem) is no philosophical precipitate; nor does it veil anything personal . . . It is a little anthology of statements that took my fancy" (p. xv).

89. William Carlos Williams, "A Memoir of Marianne Moore," in Charles Tomlinson, ed., *Marianne Moore: A Collection of Critical Essays* (Englewood Cliffs, N.J.: Prentice-Hall, 1969), p. 112.

90. Asked why H.D. and Bryher published her 1921 *Poems* without her knowledge, Moore replied, "To issue my slight product—conspicuously tentative—seemed to me premature." In 1925, "Desultory occasional magazine publication seemed to me sufficient and plenty conspicuous." Donald Hall, "An Interview with Marianne Moore," in Tomlinson, *Marianne Moore*, p. 27.

91. Donald Hall, *Marianne Moore: The Cage and the Animal* (New York: Pegasus, 1970), pp. 84–85. Hall's reading of "His Shield" (pp. 127–28) concludes that Moore's "contrived humility can only bespeak a soul not very humble." Similarly, Helen Vendler regards the young Moore's asperity as showing "the revengeful impatience of one not suffering fools gladly . . . Hers is the aggression of the silent, well-brought-up girl who thinks up mute rejoinders during every parlor conversation." (*Part of Nature, Part of Us: Modern American Poets* [Cambridge, Mass.: Harvard University Press, 1980], pp. 62–63).

92. Adrienne Rich, "When We Dead Awaken," *On Lies, Secrets and Silence*, p. 36.

93. William Gass, *Fictions and the Figures of Life* (New York: Knopf, 1971), pp. 79–86.

94. Carolyn Burke, "Supposed Persons: Modernist Poetry and the Female Subject," *Feminist Studies* 2, no. 1 (Spring 1985): 136.

95. Randall Jarrell, "Her Shield," in Tomlinson, *Marianne Moore*, p. 122.

96. See Susan Friedman, "Who Buried H.D.? A Poet, Her Critics, and 'The Literary Tradition,'" *College English* 36, no. 7 (March 1975): 801–14.

97. Elizabeth Bishop, *Complete Poems* (New York: Farrar Straus & Giroux, 1969), pp. 39–42.

98. Gertrude ("Ma") Rainey and Bessie Smith, in Bernikow, *The World Split Open*, pp. 272–77.

99. Hildegarde Flanner, "Let Us Believe," in Stanford, *Women Poets*, p. 224.

100. Margaret Walker, "Kissie Lee," *For My People* (New Haven: Yale University Press, 1942).

101. Muriel Rukeyser, "Poem Out of Childhood," *Collected Poems* (New York: McGraw-Hill, 1978), p. 3.

102. James E. B. Breslin, *From Modern to Contemporary: American Poetry, 1945–1965* (Chicago: University of Chicago Press, 1984), p. xiv.

103. Adrienne Rich, "Snapshots of a Daughter-in-Law," *The Fact of a Doorframe: Poems Selected and New, 1950–1984* (New York: W. W. Norton, 1984), p. 38.

104. Jane Cooper, "Nothing Has Been Used in the Manufacture of This Poetry That Could Have Been Used in the Manufacture of Bread," *Maps & Windows* (New York: Macmillan, 1974), pp. 31–55.

105. Adrienne Rich, "When We Dead Awaken: Writing as Re-Vision," *On Lies, Secrets and Silence: Selected Prose, 1966–1978* (New York: W. W. Norton, 1979), pp. 38–45.

Chapter 2: Divided Selves: The Quest for Identity

1. Rachel Blau DuPlessis, "Undertow," *Wells* (New York: Montemora Foundation, 1980), n.p.

2. Sylvia Plath, "Tulips," *Collected Poems*, ed. Ted Hughes (New York: Harper and Row, 1981), p. 161.

3. Audre Lorde: "An Interview with Karla Hammond," *American Poetry Review* (March–April 1980): 19.

4. Matthew Arnold, "Stanzas from the Grande Chartreuse," *The Poetical Works of Matthew Arnold*, ed. L. B. Tinker and M. F. Lowry (London: Oxford University Press, 1950), p. 302.

5. Adrienne Rich, "The Mirror in Which Two Are Seen as One," *The Fact of a Doorframe: Poems Selected and New, 1950–1984* (New York: W. W. Norton, 1984), pp. 159–61.

6. Karen Horney, "The Overvaluation of Love," *Feminine Psychology* (New York: W. W. Norton, 1967), p. 213. Simone de Beauvoir, *The Second Sex*, trans. and ed. H. M. Parshley (New York: Knopf, 1953), remains the most systematic and generative analysis of woman's entrapment in the passive vocation of love. See also Betty Friedan, *The Feminine Mystique* (New York: W. W. Norton, 1963); Germaine Greer, *The Female Eunuch* (New York: McGraw-Hill, 1971); Shulamith Firestone, *The Dialectic of Sex: The Case for Feminist Revolu-*

tion (New York: Bantam, 1970); and Dorothy Dinnerstein, *The Mermaid and the Minotaur: Sexual Arrangements and Human Malaise* (New York: Harper and Row, 1977).

7. Here and throughout this work I footnote in group form poems which share a key image, concept, or theme. Poems on the dilemma of romantic nonentity: Anne Sexton, "For My Lover, Returning to His Wife," *Complete Poems* (Boston: Houghton Mifflin, 1981), pp. 188–90. Ann Darr, "Dear James Wright," *Cleared for Landing* (Washington, D.C., and San Francisco: Dryad Press, 1978), p. 14. Judy Grahn, "Love came along," *The Work of a Common Woman: The Collected Poetry of Judy Grahn 1964–1977* (New York: St. Martin's Press, 1978), p. 136.

8. Jane Cooper, "Nothing Has Been Used in the Manufacture of This Poetry That Could Have Been Used in the Manufacture of Bread," *Maps & Windows* (New York: Macmillan, 1974), p. 55.

9. Poems of maternal nonentity: Jane Cooper, "Suicide Note," *Maps & Windows*, p. 23. Patricia Dienstfrey, "Circling the Pond," *Newspaper Stories* (Berkeley: Berkeley Poets' Workshop & Press, 1979), p. 17. Sylvia Plath, "Morning Song" and "Tulips," *Collected Poems*, pp. 157, 160.

10. Poems of sexual nonentity: Diane Wakoski, "Caves," *The Motorcycle Betrayal Poems* (New York: Simon and Schuster, 1971), pp. 116–18. Jane Cooper, "Waiting," *Maps & Windows*, p. 27. Sandra McPherson, "Sentience," *The Year of Our Birth*, (New York: Ecco Press, 1978), p. 31.

11. Susan Gubar, "The Blank Page and the Issue of Female Creativity," *Critical Inquiry* 8, no. 2 (Winter 1981): 243–63; issue on Writing and Sexual Difference. Among the women poets Gubar cites who use the metaphor of the passive female body as text are Sandra McPherson, Margaret Atwood, Christina Rossetti, Anne Sexton, Sylvia Plath, Adrienne Rich; among the novelists are Virginia Woolf, Isak Dinesen, George Eliot, Edith Wharton, Maxine Hong Kingston; among the artists and performance artists are Carolee Schneeman, Eleanor Antin, Judy Chicago.

12. Toi Derricotte, "The Mirror Poems," *The Empress of the Death House* (Detroit: Lotus Press, 1978), pp. 17–22.

13. Ntozake Shange, *For Colored Girls Who Have Considered Suicide When the Rainbow Is Enuf* (New York: Macmillan, 1977), p. 3.

14. Invisibility poems: Margaret Atwood, "This Is a Photograph of Me," *Selected Poems* (New York: Simon and Schuster, 1976), p. 8. Joyce Carol Oates, *Invisible Woman: New and Selected Poems 1970–1982* (Princeton: Ontario Review Press, 1982), p. 99. The postscript goes on to suggest that, like a woman who is judged by externals while knowing or hoping that her interior self is more complex than the outer eye can see, so "it might be argued that the poet, inhabiting a consciousness and a voice, is 'invisible' as well. It might be argued that all persons, defined to themselves rather more as what they think and dream, than what they do, are 'invisible.'" Oates' is among the few statements by a contemporary woman writer which hints that the marginal position of the woman may make her, in some respects, central. Suzanne Berger, "Vita," *These Rooms* (Lincoln, Mass.: Penmaen Press, 1979), p. 37. Marge Piercy, "In the men's

room(s)," *Circles on the Water: Selected Poems* (New York: Knopf, 1982), p. 80. Robin Morgan, "The Invisible Woman," *Monster* (New York: Random House, 1972), p. 46.

15. Phyllis Chesler, *Women and Madness* (Garden City, N.Y.: Doubleday, 1972) argues that classic psychotherapy "reflects a society which devalues women and socializes them to devalue themselves" (p. 4) and that the encouragement of mentally ill women to be passive and submissive exacerbates their illness.

16. Sandra Gilbert, "Soldier's Heart: Literary Men, Literary Women, and the Great War," *Signs: A Journal of Women in Culture and Society* 8, no. 3 (Spring 1983): 422–50, documents the advantages of World War I (and by implication of modernism) to women in the breakdown of the old order.

17. Muteness poems: Suzanne Berger, "The Mending," *These Rooms*, p. 11. Ann Darr, "August Hallucination," *Cleared for Landing*, p. 19. Louise Glück, "Portrait," "Grandmother," *Descending Figure* (New York: Ecco Press, 1980), pp. 21, 30. Adrienne Rich, "A Valediction Forbidding Mourning," *The Fact of a Doorframe*, pp. 136–37. Celia Gilbert, "Little Devil," "On Refusing Your Invitation to Come to Dinner," *Queen of Darkness* (New York: Viking, 1977), pp. 43–44, 57–58. Marge Piercy, "Unlearning to Not Speak," *Circles on the Water*, p. 97. (See also Piercy's related poems "Concerning the Mathematician," "Letter to Be Disguised as a Gas Bill," "The Secretary Chant," "The Nuisance," "A Shadow Play for Guilt," "High Frequency," "The Woman in the Ordinary," "Women's Laughter," "Councils," "Athena in the Front Lines," "Excursions, Incursions," *Circles on the Water*, pp. 17, 65–66, 77, 81, 84, 94–95, 96, 98–99, 116, 206–08, 237–41.) Adrienne Rich, "The Burning of Paper Instead of Children," "Diving into the Wreck," "Heroines," *The Fact of a Doorframe*, pp. 116–19, 162–64, 292–95. (See also, among key Rich poems concerned with the issue of language, "I Am in Danger—Sir," "Trying to Talk with a Man," "Cartographies of Silence," *The Fact of a Doorframe*, pp. 70–71, 149–50, 232–36; "Origins and History of Consciousness," *The Dream of a Common Language* (New York: W. W. Norton, 1978), pp. 7–9; and the discussion of Rich and the issue of language in Alicia Ostriker, "Her Cargo: Adrienne Rich and the Common Language," *Writing Like a Woman* (Ann Arbor: University of Michigan Press, 1983), pp. 112–14.) Susan Griffin, *Woman and Nature*, is discussed in chapter five.

18. See Elaine Marks, "Women and Literature in France," *Signs* 3 (Summer 1978): 832–42; Elaine Marks and Carolyn G. Burke, "Report from Paris: Women's Writing and the Women's Movement, *Signs* 3 (Summer 1978): 843–55; Carolyn G. Burke, "Irigaray Through the Looking Glass, *Feminist Studies* 7, no. 2 (Summer 1981): 288–306; Elaine Marks and Isabelle de Courtivron, eds., *New French Feminisms* (New York: Schocken, 1981); Mary Daly, *Beyond God the Father* (Boston: Beacon Press, 1973), and *Gyn/Ecology: The Metaethics of Radical Feminism* (Boston: Beacon Press, 1978).

19. Adrienne Rich, "When We Dead Awaken: Writing as Re-Vision," *On Lies, Secrets and Silence: Selected Prose 1966–1978* (New York: W. W. Norton, 1979), p. 35.

20. June Jordan, "Case in Point," *Passion* (Boston: Beacon Press, 1980), p. 13; Madelon Sprengnether Göhlke, "It's Cool Outside and Bright," *The Normal Heart* (St. Paul, Minn.: New Rivers Press, 1981), p. 13.

21. Margaret Atwood, "More and More," *Selected Poems*, p. 74.

22. Adrienne Rich, "Planetarium," *The Fact of a Doorframe*, p. 114–16.

23. Nancy Chodorow, *The Reproduction of Mothering: Psychoanalysis and the Sociology of Gender* (Berkeley: University of California Press, 1978), pp. 82–83, 110.

24. Dissolving-self poems: Elizabeth Bishop, "In the Waiting Room," *Geography III* (New York: Farrar Straus & Giroux, 1976), pp. 3–8. Anne Sexton, "Housewife," *Complete Poems*, p. 77. Sylvia Plath, "Medusa," *Collected Poems*, pp. 224–26. June Jordan, "Fragments from a Parable," *Things That I Do in the Dark: Selected Poems* (New York: Random House, 1977), p. 198. Louise Glück, "For My Mother," *The House on Marshland* (New York: Ecco Press, 1975), p. 6.

25. See Gilbert and Gubar, *The Madwoman in the Attic: The Woman Writer and the Nineteenth-Century Literary Imagination* (New Haven: Yale University Press, 1979), pp. 20–36 and passim.

26. Monster poems: Robin Morgan, *Monster.* Cynthia Macdonald, "Celebrating the Freak," "Francis Bacon (1561–1626; 1910———), The Inventor of Spectacles, Is the Ringmaster," "The Conception," "How to Order a Freak," "The World's Fattest Dancer," *W(h)oles* (New York: Knopf, 1980), pp. 14, 3–7, 41–42, 18–19, 89. Cynthia Macdonald, "Twice Too Long," *Amputations* (New York: Braziller, 1972), p. 72. See also Macdonald, "The Insatiable Baby," *Amputations*, p. 66. Margaret Atwood, "Speeches for Dr. Frankenstein," "Songs of the Transformed," "She Considers Evading Him," *Selected Poems*, pp. 64–69, 188–98, 143. Diane Di Prima, *Loba* (Berkeley, Calif.: Wingbow Press, 1978). Rochelle Owens, *The Joe 82 Creation Poems* (Los Angeles: Black Sparrow Press, 1974). Adrienne Rich, "Incipience," "Planetarium," "August," *The Fact of a Doorframe*, pp. 155–57, 114–16, 178.

27. H.D., "Fragment Thirty-Six," *Collected Poems 1912–1944,* ed. Louis L. Martz (New York: New Directions, 1983), pp. 165–68.

28. Margaret Atwood, *Surfacing* (New York: Simon and Schuster, 1972), p. 124.

29. Sandra M. Gilbert in the essay "My Name Is Darkness" (*Claims for Poetry,* ed. Donald Hall [Ann Arbor: University of Michigan Press, 1982], pp. 117–30) advances an argument parallel to mine, seeing self-definition as a central preoccupation in contemporary women's poetry and the double self as a central obstacle in the struggle. As support for the first point, Gilbert lists about fifty declarations pivoting on "I am" or, less often, "I am not," by Plath, Wakoski, Rich, Sexton, and Levertov—which, as she says, might all have been written "by one, anxiously experimental, modern Everywoman" (p. 122), and it would be easy to double or quintuple such a list. Gilbert's sense of the female double self, which stresses the frightening, amoral, supernatural quality of the double, takes a slightly different tack from mine. My own concern is with how the structure of the split self locks itself into a self-perpetuating division which reflects a cultural prescription opposed to female wholeness. Barbara Rigney,

Madness and Sexual Politics in the Feminist Novel (Madison: University of Wisconsin Press, 1978), sees a similar pattern in the doppelganger figures employed by Charlotte Brontë, Woolf, Lessing, and Atwood.

30. Denise Levertov, "In Mind," *O Taste and See* (New York: New Directions, 1964), p. 71. See also Denise Levertov, *The Double Image* (London: Cresset Press, 1946); "The Earthwoman and the Waterwoman," "Sunday Afternoon," *Collected Earlier Poems 1940–1960* (New York: New Directions, 1979), pp. 31, 78–79; "An Embroidery (I)," "A Cloak," *Relearning the Alphabet* (New York: New Directions, 1970), pp. 33–34, 44; "The Woman," *The Freeing of the Dust* (New York: New Directions, 1975), p. 53.

31. Diane Wakoski, "Beauty," *The Magellanic Clouds* (Santa Barbara: Black Sparrow Press, 1970), p. 127.

32. Wakoski identifies her poet-self explicitly as male in "Form Is an Extension of Content: Second Lecture": "A real poet is one who can make everything into poetry, including his life; he is a man who lives his life with imagery, metaphor and simile; he creates his own mythology, and lives that mythology." In "Little Magazines and Poetry Factions," she writes, "I hate being thought of as a Woman Poet. I am a poet and if that is not enough, then let my work fall in the garbage can." Again in "Poetry as the Dialogue We All Hope Someone Is Listening To," "a poet is a man who puts the richest part of himself on the page." These essays are all reprinted in *Toward a New Poetry* (Ann Arbor: University of Michigan Press, 1980), pp. 21, 56, 193. The earliest statement of the obsessive theme of the unbeautiful, hence unloved, woman is "Elizabeth and the Golden Oranges," *Trilogy* (Garden City, New York: Doubleday, 1974), pp. 12–13; the best known is "I Have Had to Learn to Live with My Face," *The Motorcycle Betrayal Poems*, pp. 11–15.

33. Wakoski, *Trilogy*, Preface, p. xv; "Creating a Personal Mythology: Third Lecture"; "Interview with Andrea Musher," *Toward a New Poetry*, pp. 112, 308; *Greed: Parts 5–7* (Santa Barbara: Black Sparrow, 1976), p. 13. The essay most exhaustively defining her personal self as a woman futilely "in love with love" and her artistic self as the inventor and fantasist able to make what is ordinary into something "exceptional" is "The Blue Swan, An Essay on Music in Poetry," *The Man Who Shook Hands* (Garden City, N.Y.: Doubleday, 1978), pp. 13–30. Double-self poems in Wakoski include "The Five Dreams of Jennifer Snow and Her Testament," *Trilogy*, pp. 76–81; "The Lament of the Lady Bank Dick," *The Motorcycle Betrayal Poems*, pp. 93–97.

34. Sylvia Plath, "In Plaster," *Collected Poems*, pp. 158–60. My reading of this poem is indebted to George Stade's introductory essay in Nancy Hunter Steiner, *A Closer Look at Ariel: A Memory of Sylvia Plath* (New York: Popular Library, 1973). Stade asserts that Plath's was a life "that experienced itself as double," quoting Plath's poet-husband Ted Hughes: "the opposition of a prickly, fastidious defense and an imminent volcano is, one way or another, an element in all her early poems" (p. 10). Prior to Plath's breakdown in 1953, she was working on an honors thesis on twins in James Joyce; she ultimately wrote the thesis on the double in Dostoevski. "In Plaster," for Stade, is a central Plath document. See also, as examples of split-self and multiple-self poems, "Two

Sisters of Persephone," "Face Lift," "Elm," "A Birthday Present," "Stings," "Fever 103°," *Collected Poems*, pp. 31–32, 155–56, 192–93, 206–08, 214–15, 231. Judith Kroll, *Chapters in a Mythology: The Poetry of Sylvia Plath* (New York: Harper and Row, 1976), reads Plath's mature poetry as exemplifying a "mythic system" revolving around an "original split into false and true selves" (p. 10). Mary Lynn Broe, *Protean Poetic: The Poetry of Sylvia Plath* (Columbia, Mo.: University of Missouri Press, 1980), sees Plath's career as embodying, throughout its development, an attempt to balance contrary impulses.

35. Sylvia Plath, *The Bell Jar* (New York: Bantam, 1972), pp. 180, 79.

36. The following are among the important split-self or multiple-self works by women poets in this century (listed alphabetically): Margaret Atwood, *Double Persephone* (Ontario: Hawkshead Press, 1961); "The Double Voice," *Selected Poems*, p. 104; *Two-Headed Poems* (Austin, Tex.: Touchstone Books, 1981). Elizabeth Bishop, "The Gentleman of Shallott," *Complete Poems* (New York: Farrar Straus & Giroux, 1977), p. 10. Louise Bogan, "Medusa," "The Crossed Apple," "The Sleeping Fury," *The Blue Estuaries: Poems 1923–1968* (New York: Ecco Press, 1977), pp. 4, 45–46, 78–79. Lucille Clifton, "in this garden," *Two-Headed Woman* (Amherst: University of Massachusetts Press, 1980), p. 23. Toi Derricotte, "the mirror poems," "doll poem," *Empress of the Death House*, pp. 17–27, 30. Rachel Blau DuPlessis, "Undertow," *Wells*, n.p. Kathleen Fraser, "One of the Chapters," *New Shoes* (New York: Harper and Row, 1978), pp. 5–6. Siv Cedering Fox, "Twins," *Mother Is* (New York: Stein and Day, 1975), p. 38. Tess Gallagher, *Instructions to the Double* (Port Townsend, Wash.: Graywolf, 1975). Joan Larkin, "Song," *Housework* (New York: Out & Out Books, 1975), pp. 23–24. Alicia Ostriker, "The Exchange," *A Woman Under the Surface* (Princeton: Princeton University Press, 1982), p. 7. Marge Piercy, "The Woman in the Ordinary," "The Strong Woman," *Circles in the Water*, pp. 96, 257. Naomi Replansky, "Two Women," *No More Masks! An Anthology of Poetry by Women*, ed. Florence Howe and Ellen Bass (Garden City, N.Y.: Doubleday, 1973), p. 119. Adrienne Rich, "Women," "The Mirror in Which Two Are Seen as One," *The Fact of a Doorframe*, pp. 94, 159; "Transit," *A Wild Patience Has Taken Me This Far* (New York: W. W. Norton, 1981), pp. 19–20. May Sarton, "The Muse as Medusa," *Selected Poems* (New York: W. W. Norton, 1978), p. 160. Anne Sexton, "The Double Image," "Old Dwarf Heart," "Again and Again and Again," "Rumplestiltskin," "The Ambition Bird," "The Other," "The Death Baby," *Complete Poems*, pp. 35–42, 54–55, 195–96, 233–37, 299, 317, 354–59. Jean Tepperman, "Witch," *No More Masks!*, pp. 333–34. Elinor Wylie, "Little Eclogue," *Collected Poems* (New York: Knopf, 1938), p. 288–90.

37. R. D. Laing, *The Politics of Experience* (New York: Random House, 1967), p. 79.

38. R. D. Laing, *The Divided Self* (New York: Pantheon Books, 1969), pp. 45–47, 48–49.

39. Judith Kroll, *Chapters in a Mythology*, employs the terms "true" and "false" selves differently. Plath's "true self is the child she was before things went wrong" and the creative self in whom she will be reborn. The "false self" is

"ineffectual, dominated, and powerless" (p. 10). The intolerable coexistence of the two selves—the true entrapped by the false—provides the dynamic of Plath's late poems (p. 11).

40. Laing, *Divided Self*, pp. 102, 122.

41. Poems on an armored, metal, or stone self: Judith Hemschemeyer, "I Used to Have Fur," *Very Close and Very Slow* (Middletown, Conn.: Wesleyan University Press, 1975), p. 67. Louise Glück, "Aphrodite," *Descending Figure* (New York: Ecco Press, 1980), p. 39. Margaret Atwood, "A Fortification," *Selected Poems*, p. 53. See also Wakoski's "In Gratitude to Beethoven," *Inside the Blood Factory* (Garden City, N.Y.: Doubleday, 1968), pp. 27–30:

I am like the guerrilla fighter
who must sleep with one eye open for attack, a knife
or poison, a bamboo dart could come at any time.

No one has loved me without trying to destroy me,
there is no part of me that is not armoured,
there is no moment when I am not expecting attack,

and her "disguise" poems, such as "Follow That Stagecoach," *Trilogy*, pp. 35–37, and "The Ice Eagle," *Inside the Blood Factory*, p. 93.

42. W. B. Yeats, "Sailing to Byzantium," *Collected Poems* (New York: Macmillan, 1956), pp. 191–92.

43. Hélène Cixous, "The Laugh of the Medusa," trans. Keith Cohen and Paula Cohen, in Elaine Marks and Isabelle de Courtivron, eds., *New French Feminisms* (New York: Schocken, 1981), pp. 245–46.

44. Gloria Anzaldúa, "La Prieta," *This Bridge Called My Back: Writings by Radical Women of Color*, eds. Cherríe Moraga and Gloria Anzaldúa (Watertown, Mass.: Persephone Press, 1981), p. 205.

45. Diane Wakoski, "No More Soft Talk," *Motorcycle Betrayal Poems*, pp. 66–68.

46. Margaret Atwood, "This Is a Photograph of Me," *Selected Poems*, p. 8.

47. As consciousness of cultural marginality comes to animate women's writing in general, so it comes more strongly to animate and empower the work of black, third-world, and/or lesbian women. See Gloria T. Hull, "Afro-American Women Poets: A Bio-Critical Survey," in Sandra M. Gilbert and Susan Gubar, eds., *Shakespeare's Sisters: Feminist Essays on Women Poets* (Bloomington: Indiana University Press, 1979), pp. 165–82; Paula Gunn Allen, "Answering the Deer: Genocide and Continuance in American Indian Women's Poetry," in Diane Wood Middlebrook and Marilyn Yalom, eds., *Coming to Light: American Women Poets in the Twentieth Century* (Ann Arbor: University of Michigan Press, 1985), pp. 223–32; Elly Bulkin, "'Kissing Against the Light': A Look at Lesbian Poetry," *Radical Teacher* 10 (December 1978): 8, an expanded version of which is available from the Lesbian-Feminist Study Clearinghouse, Women's Studies Program, University of Pittsburgh; Adrienne Rich, "It Is the Lesbian in Us . . ." and "Disloyal to Civilization: Feminism, Racism, Gynephobia," *On Lies, Secrets and Silence: Selected Prose 1966–1978* (New York: W. W. Norton,

1979), pp. 99–202, 275–310; Lynda Koolish, A Whole New Poetry Beginning Here: Contemporary American Women Poets, 2 vols. (Ann Arbor: University Microfilms, 1981). Important feminist journals carrying women's poetry and (often) reviews and essays concerning these and related issues include Calyx, Chrysalis, Conditions, Heresies, Thirteenth Moon, and Sinister Wisdom. For an extensive bibliography of writings by and about contemporary third-world and lesbian women writers, including anthologies, special editions of periodicals, and individual collections of poetry, see Moraga and Anzaldúa, This Bridge Called My Back.

48. Ordinary Women/Mujeres Comunes, ed. Sara Miles, Patricia Jones, Sandra Maria Esteves, Fay Chiang (New York: Ordinary Women Books, 1978).

49. Kathleen Fraser, "Flood," New Shoes, pp. 35–37.

50. Adrienne Rich, "Diving into the Wreck," The Fact of a Doorframe, p. 163.

Chapter 3: Body Language: The Release of Anatomy

1. Hortense Calisher, "No Important Woman Writer," quoted in Laura Chester and Sharon Barba, eds., Rising Tides: 20th Century Women Poets, Introduction by Anaïs Nin (New York: Washington Square Press, 1973), p. xxvi.

2. Marge Piercy, "The Friend," Circles on the Water: Selected Poems (New York: Knopf, 1982), p. 39.

3. Anne Sexton, "Little Girl, My String Bean, My Lovely Woman," Complete Poems (Boston: Houghton Mifflin, 1981), pp. 145–148.

4. A thousand lines from male poets in Stephen Berg and Robert Mezey's Naked Poetry: Recent American Poetry in Open Forms (Baltimore: Bobbs-Merrill, 1969), and Donald Hall's Contemporary Poetry (New York: Penguin, 1962), contain 127 references to human (or animal) bodies. A thousand lines from women poets in Barbara Segnitz and Carol Rainey's Psyche (New York: Dell, 1973) and Laura Chester and Sharon Barba's Rising Tides contain 236 body images, almost double the number in the men's poetry. Heads, faces, eyes, and hands commonly appear in the work of both sexes, and there is overlapping usage of many other terms. Terms used by male poets but not females were saliva, snouts, gills, loins, knees, all fours, lover's nuts, brains, skull, pubic beards, torsos, cock, balls, eyeball, fistbones, wishbones, funnybone, sacrum, luz-bone, ribcages, feather, tongue-bone, bruises, foot, left shoulder, right foot, palate, jaws, ends of fingers, nipples, forearms, eyebrows, corpse. Terms used by women poets but not men were lid, lids, nape, foetus, scalp, braincap, throat, scales, shoulders, ears, belly, finger, fingers, knucklebone, forehead, eyelashes, tit, fro (for afro, the hairdo), armfuls, abdomen, guts, muscle, muscles, skullplates, left ear, toes, fists, hairs, teeth, instep, orifice, wrinkles, lines, breast, breasts, wings of the nose, corners of the mouth, chin, earlobes, cunt, udders, duodenum, liver, membrane, scar, scars, scalp, legs, mustache, screwcurls, lap, cheeks, palm, legs, arm, arms, thumb, epiderm, valves, nerves, vein, pore, cells, ligaments, tissue, bladder, spit, sweat, fingernails, jelly (of an eye, during a lynching), pulse, little

toe, hips, (of the poet's father), *ovaries,* and *sperm sac* (of a queen bee). The women thus employed a greater range as well as a larger number of body images and included more "internal" parts; specificity of observation may be indicated by the fact that while poets of both sexes mentioned hair, for instance, the term was unmodified in the male poets but appeared variously in the women poets as "sticky gold hair," "eelgrass hair," "yellow hair," "acanthine hair," "fro," and "screwcurls." But the largest discrepancy between the sexes appears in the fact that the women poets referred both to their own bodies and to external figures, while the men's work included no more than a dozen references to the poets' own bodies.

The twenty male poets included in my count (fifty lines each, taken from the opening of the anthology selection for each one) were Roethke, Patchen, Stafford, Kees, Berryman, Lowell, Bly, Creeley, Ginsberg, Kinnell, Merwin, Wright, Levine, Snyder, and Berg (in *Naked Poetry*); Duncan, Nemerov, Dickey, Justice, and Ashbery (in *Contemporary American Poetry*). The twenty female poets were May Swenson, Levertov, Kizer, Sexton, Rich, Plath, Piercy, Owens, Wakoski, Atwood, Lifshin, Jong, and Giovanni (in *Psyche*); Van Duyn, Mueller, Kumin, Sanchez, Clifton, Pastan, and Jordan (in *Rising Tides*). A different selection might of course have produced slightly different figures, but if the selection were made from poems published only in the 1970s, the gap between masculine reticence and feminine expressiveness about the body would appear even more pronounced.

5. Ntozake Shange, *Nappy Edges* (New York: Bantam Books, 1980), pp. 14–17. A single citation of critical discomfort must suffice. Richard Howard fastidiously comments on Anne Sexton in *Alone with America: Essays on the Art of Poetry in the United States since 1950* (New York: Atheneum, 1980), p. 518:

> If you are wearing not only your heart on your sleeve, your liver on your lapel and the other organs affixed to various articles of your attire, but also a whole alphabet in scarlet on your breast, then your poetry must bear with losing the notion of *private parts* altogether and with gaining a certain publicity that has nothing to do with the personal.

Howard's final sentence is an example of the recurrent innuendo that a poetically assertive woman is a whore.

6. Simone de Beauvoir, *The Second Sex*, trans. H. M. Parshley (New York: Vintage, 1974. Original pub. 1953.) Quotations of de Beauvoir are from this edition.

7. Julia Kristeva, "La femme, ce n'est jamais ça" (Woman can never be defined), and "Oscillation du 'pouvoir' au 'refus'" (Oscillation between power and denial), trans. Marilyn A. August, in Elaine Marks and Isabelle de Courtivron, eds., *New French Feminisms* (New York: Schocken, 1981), pp. 137, 166.

8. Hélène Cixous, "The Laugh of the Medusa," trans. Keith Cohen and Paula Cohen in Marks and de Courtivron, *New French Feminisms*, pp. 256–59.

9. Luce Irigaray, "Ce sexe qui n'est pas un" (This sex which is not one),

trans. Claudia Reeder, in Marks and de Courtivron, *New French Feminisms*, p. 103.

10. Chantal Chawaf, "La chair linguistique" (Linguistic flesh), trans. Yvonne Rochette-Ozzello, in Marks and de Courtivron, *New French Feminisms*, pp. 177–78.

11. Adrienne Rich, *Of Woman Born: Motherhood as Experience and Institution* (New York: W. W. Norton, 1976), p. 62.

12. *Feminist Studies* 6, no. 2 (Summer 1980), contains four articles on de Beauvoir seen in the context of contemporary feminism, examining both achievements and limitations. Jo-Ann P. Fuchs, "Female Eroticism in *The Second Sex*," pp. 304–13, argues that de Beauvoir's vision of the female body and of female eroticism is limited to the "message of patriarchal culture: passivity, immanence, oppression lived in the erotic night, as well as in the day" (p. 309). Discussions and critiques of *l'Écriture féminine* and feminist "biocriticism" include Elaine Showalter, "Feminist Criticism in the Wilderness," in Elaine Showalter, ed., *The New Feminist Criticism: Essays on Women, Literature and Theory* (New York: Pantheon, 1985), pp. 250–56, and Ann Rosalind Jones, "Writing the Body: Toward an Understanding of *l'Écriture féminine*," in Showalter, *New Feminist Criticism*, pp. 361–77. The editors of *Questions féministes*, no. 1 (November 1977), contend that "it is also dangerous to place the body at the center of a search for female identity" because "the very theme of difference, whatever the differences are represented to be, is useful to the oppressing group." Against the notion that "woman's language is closer to the body, to sexual pleasure, to direct sensations, and so on," they argue that "there is no such thing as a direct relation to the body" without social mediation. See Marks and de Courtivron, *New French Feminisms*, pp. 218–19.

13. H.D., "Helen," *Collected Poems 1912–1944*, ed. Louis Martz (New York: New Directions, 1983), pp. 154–55.

14. Jane Kenyon, "Cages," *From Room to Room* (Cambridge, Mass.: Alice James Books, 1978), pp. 33–34.

15. Alice Walker, "Did This Happen to Your Mother," *Good Night, Willie Lee, I'll See You in the Morning* (New York: Dial Press, 1979), pp. 2–3.

16. Poems of psychic hurt described in somatic terms: Lynn Sukenick, "The Poster," in Laura Chester and Sharon Barba, eds., *Rising Tides*, p. 290. May Swenson, "Bleeding," *New and Selected Things Taking Place* (Boston: Little, Brown, 1978), p. 104. Lisel Mueller, "Life of a Queen," *The Private Life* (Baton Rouge: Louisiana University Press, 1976), pp. 15–16. Anne Sexton, "Snow White," *Complete Poems*, p. 224.

17. Passages by Sylvia Plath are quoted from *The Collected Poems*.

18. Annette Lavers, "The World as Icon: On Sylvia Plath's Themes," in Charles Newman, ed., *The Art of Sylvia Plath* (Bloomington, Ind.: University of Indiana Press, 1970), pp. 104–05.

19. See Ted Hughes, "Notes on the Chronological Order of Sylvia Plath's Poems," in Newman, *Art of Sylvia Plath*, pp. 187–95; Gary Lane, "Influence and Originality in Plath's Poems" in Gary Lane, ed., *Sylvia Plath: New Views on the Poetry* (Baltimore: Johns Hopkins University Press, 1979), pp. 116–37;

and Marjorie Perloff, "Sylvia Plath's 'Sivvy' Poems," in Lane, *Sylvia Plath*, pp. 163–69, for discussion of Plath's early imitativeness and influences.

20. A. A. Alvarez, *The Savage God: A Study of Suicide* (London: Weidenfield and Nicolson, 1972), p. 25.

21. Carolyn Kizer, "Pro Femina," *Knock upon Silence* (Garden City, N.Y.: Doubleday, 1965), p. 45.

22. William Butler Yeats, "Adam's Curse," *Collected Poems* (London: Macmillan & Co., 1950), p. 89.

23. Poems on the labors of beauty: Honor Moore, "My Mother's Moustache," in Lucille Iverson and Kathryn Ruby, eds., *We Become New* (New York: Bantam Books, 1975), pp. 39–41. Karen Swenson, "The Saga of the Small-Breasted Woman," *Thirteenth Moon* 2.2–3.1 (Winter 1975): 13. Kathleen Fraser, "Poem in Which My Legs Are Accepted," *What I Want* (New York: Harper and Row, 1974), pp. 25–27. Diane Wakoski, "I Have Had to Learn to Live with My Face," *The Motorcycle Betrayal Poems* (New York: Simon and Schuster, 1971), pp. 11–15. Nikki Giovanni, "Woman Poem," *Black Feeling, Black Talk/Black Judgement* (New York: Morrow, 1970), pp. 78–80. Marge Piercy, "A Work of Artifice," *Circles on the Water*, p. 75. Carolyn Kizer, "Pro Femina," *Knock upon Silence*, pp. 41–49. Erica Jong, "Aging," *Fruits & Vegetables* (New York: Holt, Rinehart & Winston, 1971), pp. 45–46.

24. Sharon Barba, "A Cycle of Women," in Chester and Barba, *Rising Tides*, pp. 356–57.

25. The female body as flower: Diane Wakoski, "In Gratitude to Beethoven," *Inside the Blood Factory* (Garden City, N.Y.: Doubleday, 1968), pp. 27–30. Marina La Palma, "Holding Fast," in Kelsey St. Press, eds., *Making the Park* (Berkeley: Kelsey St. Press, 1976), n.p.

26. The female body as water: Adrienne Rich, "Diving into the Wreck," *The Fact of a Doorframe: Poems Selected and New, 1950–1984* (New York: W. W. Norton, 1984), pp. 162–64. Sharon Barba, "Cycle of Women," in Chester and Barba, *Rising Tides*, pp. 356–57. Elizabeth Anne Socolow, "The Swimmer," in Rod Tulloss, David Keller, and Alicia Ostriker, eds., *US1: An Anthology: Contemporary Writing from New Jersey* (Union City, N.J.: William H. Wise, 1980), pp. 63–65. Marge Piercy, "Unclench Yourself," *Circles on the Water*, p. 174.

27. Simone de Beauvoir, *The Second Sex*, chap. 5, "Early Tillers of the Soil." Annette Kolodny, *The Lay of the Land: Metaphor as Experience and History in American Life and Letters* (Chapel Hill: University of North Carolina Press, 1975).

28. Earth as female identified with critical intelligence or creative imagination: Yosana Akiko, "Mountain Moving Day," in Elaine Gill, ed., *Mountain Moving Day: Poems by Women* (Trumansburg, N.Y.: Crossing Press, 1973), n.p. Meridel LeSueur, *Rites of Ancient Ripening* (Minneapolis: Vanilla Press, 1975), p. 52. Judith McCombs, "Loving a Mountain," *Against Nature: Wilderness Poems* (Paradise, Calif.: Dustbooks, 1979), p. 8. Anne Sexton, "In Celebration of My Uterus," *Complete Poems*, pp. 181–83.

29. Diana George notes that "the physical body is a nexus for meaning and

meaninglessness for nurture and deprivation, for wholeness and fragmentation" throughout Sexton's career. "The maker's voice seeks unity, speaks in metaphors and images of wholeness, and uses the body as a symbol for that wholeness." See Diana George, *Oedipus Anne: The Poetry of Anne Sexton* (Champaign, Ill.: University of Illinois Press, in press), chap. 3.

30. Robin Morgan, "The Network of the Imaginary Mother," *Lady of the Beasts* (New York: Random House, 1976), pp. 63–88.

31. A. R. Ammons, *Sphere: The Form of a Motion* (New York: W. W. Norton, 1974), n.p.

32. May Swenson, "Evolution," *New & Selected Things Taking Place* (Boston: Little, Brown, 1978), p. 271. Further quotations of May Swenson are from this volume.

33. Susan Griffin, *Woman and Nature: The Roaring Inside Her* (New York: Harper and Row, 1978), p. 226.

34. Estella Lauter, *Women as Mythmakers: Poetry and Visual Art by Twentieth-Century Women* (Bloomington: Indiana University Press, 1984), pp. 172–202.

35. Judith McCombs, "Atwood's Nature Concepts: An Overview," *Waves* 7, no. 1 (Fall 1978): 68–76. McCombs' conclusion locates Atwood among other writers of "women's nature myth."

36. Griffin, *Woman and Nature*, p. 219.

37. Maxine Kumin, *Our Ground Time Here Will Be Brief: New and Selected Poems* (New York: Penguin Books, 1982), p. 6. Further quotations of Kumin's poems are from this volume.

38. Maxine Kumin, *To Make a Prairie: Essays on Poets, Poetry, and Country Living* (Ann Arbor: University of Michigan Press, 1979), p. 107.

39. Robert Frost, "The Most of It," *Selected Poems* (New York: Holt, Rinehart and Winston, 1965), p. 224.

40. Elizabeth Bishop, "The Moose," *Geography III* (New York: Farrar Straus and Giroux, 1976), pp. 22–31. See the discussion of "The Moose" and "The Most of It" in Helen Vendler, *Part of Nature, Part of Us: Modern American Poets* (Cambridge, Mass.: Harvard University Press, 1980), pp. 107–110.

41. Margaret Atwood, "Circe/Mud Poems," *Selected Poems* (New York: Simon and Schuster, 1976), p. 206.

42. Adrienne Rich, "Two Songs," *The Fact of a Doorframe*, p. 65.

Chapter 4: Herr God, Herr Lucifer: Anger, Violence, and Polarization

1. William Shakespeare, *The Taming of the Shrew*, V.ii.161–165, *The Arden Shakespeare* (London and New York: Methuen, 1981), p. 296.

2. June Jordan, "Poem About My Rights," *Passion* (Boston: Beacon Press, 1980), pp. 86–89.

3. Phyllis Koestenbaum, "oh I can't she says" (Oakland, Calif.: Christopher's Books, 1980), n.p.

4. Nadezhda Mandelstam, *Hope Abandoned*, trans. Max Hayward (New York: Atheneum, 1981), p. 29.

5. The two proudest and angriest wronged women in Greek tragedy, Aeschylus' adulterous queen Clytemnestra and Euripides' sorceress Medea, significantly represent, respectively, a defeated prepatriarchal ethos of mother-right and an exotic primitivism. Both, in classic Greek culture, were seen as dangerous; neither was invested with the kind of dignity we find in, for example, the righteous but unaggressive Antigone, a model daughter of the patriarchy who tragically but willingly dies upholding the law of Zeus, just as the virtuous Cordelia dies upholding the daughter's duty to the father. Female anger is respectable generally in cultures to the degree in which the religion includes autonomous and powerful goddess figures; thus it has no rightful place within either Judaism or Christianity.

6. William Butler Yeats, "A Prayer for My Daughter," *Collected Poems* (New York: Macmillan, 1951), p. 187.

7. John Keats, "Ode on Melancholy," *The Poems of Keats* (London: Longman, 1970), p. 540.

8. "Poetic Aberrations," *Blackwood's* 87 (1860), quoted in Gardner B. Taplin, *The Life of Elizabeth Barrett Browning* (New Haven: Yale University Press, 1957), pp. 490–94. Mrs. Browning, says Taplin, was usually praised for "her understanding of the depth, tenderness and humility of the love which is given by women" (p. 417). The reviewer's agitation is all the more telling when one notes how carefully Browning has hedged the famous lines "A curse from the depths of womanhood / Is very salt, and bitter, and good" by the palliating context. First, an angel commands her to write, though she demurs, pleading that as a woman her vocation is heartbreak and weeping. As to the curse itself, dictated by Browning's "angel," it asserts merely that the hypocritical guilt of a nation dedicated to freedom yet permitting slavery shall be its own punishment—a rather mild anathema, after all.

9. Caroline Kizer, "Pro Femina," *Knock upon Silence* (New York: Doubleday, 1965), p. 41.

10. Jane Marcus, "Art and Anger," *Feminist Studies* 4, no. 1 (February 1978): 69–98.

11. Virginia Woolf, *A Room of One's Own* (New York and London: Harcourt Brace Jovanovich, 1957). See pp. 51, 58–59, 71, 63, 64, 108.

12. Woolf, *Room of One's Own*, p. 110.

13. Manifestos of the imperative of anger, in prose and poetry, include Adrienne Rich, "Vesuvius at Home," *On Lies, Secrets and Silence: Selected Prose 1966–1978* (New York: W. W. Norton 1979), p. 162. Robin Morgan, Introduction to *Sisterhood Is Powerful: An anthology of Writings from the Women's Liberation Movement* (New York: Vintage, 1970), p. xv. Audre Lorde, "Portrait," *The Black Unicorn* (New York: Norton, 1978), p. 51. Susan Griffin, "A Woman Defending Herself," *Like the Iris of an Eye* (New York: Harper and Row, 1976), p. 98.

14. Jane Marcus, "Art and Anger," *Feminist Studies* 4, no. 1 (February 1978): 69–98. The article concentrates on the feminist actress, novelist, and

264   STEALING THE LANGUAGE

playwright Elizabeth Robins and on Woolf's movement from A *Room of One's Own* to *Three Guineas*. Alex Zwerdling in "Anger and Conciliation in Woolf's Feminism," *Representations* 3 (Summer 1983): 68–89, examines the conflict between overt expression and tactical repression of anger as a conscious one in Woolf and relates it to opposed ideas of effective strategy within the feminist movement.

15. Geoffrey Chaucer, "The Wife of Bath's Prologue," 693–96, *Poetical Works*, ed. F. N. Robinson (Boston: Houghton Mifflin, 1933), p. 99.

16. Lyn Lifshin, "The No More Apologizing the No More Little Laughing Blues," *Upstate Madonna* (Trumansburg, N.Y.: Crossing Press, 1975), pp. 40–43.

17. Marge Piercy, "All Clear," *Living in the Open* (New York: Knopf, 1976), p. 42.

18. Domestic victimization poems: Cynthia Macdonald, "A Family of Dolls' House Dolls," *Amputations* (New York: Braziller, 1972), pp. 12–13. Marge Piercy, "Right Thinking Man," *Circles on the Water: Selected Poems* (New York: Knopf, 1982), pp. 90–91. Diane Di Prima, "The Quarrel," *Dinners and Nightmares* (New York: Corinth Books, 1974), pp. 75–76. Jana Harris, "Fix Me a Salami Sandwich, He Said," "When Mama Came Here as a Gold Panner," "The Last Voyage of the Eudora Dawn," *Manhattan as a Second Language* (New York: Harper and Row, 1982), pp. 59–60, 3–4, 5–7. Ntozake Shange, *For Colored Girls Who Have Considered Suicide When the Rainbow Is Enuf* (New York: Macmillan, 1977), pp. 40, 55, 58–63.

19. Rape became a central feminist issue with the publication of Susan Brownmiller's *Against Our Will: Men, Women and Rape* (New York: Simon and Schuster, 1975), the thesis of which is that rape is to be understood as a form of misogynist violence, officially condemned but actually sanctioned, in our and other societies, the victim being considered more blameworthy than the attacker. Among the important poems following Brownmiller are the following: Ntozake Shange, "With No Immediate Cause," *Nappy Edges* (New York: Bantam, 1980), pp. 111–13. Audre Lorde, "Need: A Choral of Black Women's Voices," *Chosen Poems Old and New* (New York: W. W. Norton, 1982), pp. 111–15. June Jordan, "The Rationale, or, She Drove Me Crazy," "Case in Point," "Rape Is Not a Poem," "Poem About My Rights," *Passion: New Poems 1977–1980* (Boston: Beacon Press, 1980), pp. 11, 13, 79, 86. Adrienne Rich, "Rape," *The Fact of a Doorframe: Poems Selected and New, 1950–1984* (New York: W. W. Norton, 1984), pp. 172–73. Marge Piercy, "Rape Poem," *Circles in the Water*, pp. 164–65. See also Shange, *For Colored Girls*, pp. 17–21. Ann Stanford, "The Intruder," *The Descent* (New York: Viking, 1970), pp. 21–22, "Medusa," *In Mediterranean Air* (New York: Viking, 1977), pp. 42–43. Rachel Blau DuPlessis, "Medusa," *Wells* (New York: Montemora Foundation, 1980), n.p. Madelon Sprengnether Gohlke, "It's Cool Outside and Bright," *The Normal Heart* (St. Paul, Minn.: New Rivers Press, 1981), p. 13. See also Alicia Ostriker, "Homecoming," *A Woman Under the Surface* (Princeton: Princeton University Press, 1982), pp. 49–50.

20. Fathers are less frequently attacked in women's poetry than are husbands

and lovers. Among important antifather poems, however, are the following: Sylvia Plath, "Daddy," *Collected Poems*, Ted Hughes, ed. (New York: Harper and Row, 1981), pp. 223–24. Adrienne Rich, "After Dark," *The Fact of a Doorframe*, pp. 68–70; "Sibling Mysteries," *The Dream of a Common Language: Poems 1974–1977* (New York: W. W. Norton, 1978), pp. 47–52. Sonia Sanchez, "A Poem for My Father," *We a BaddDDD People* (Detroit: Broadside Press, 1970), p. 14. Lynn Sukenick, "That Life, on Film," Laura Chester and Sharon Barba, eds., *Rising Tides: 20th Century American Women Poets* (New York: Washington Square Press, Simon and Schuster, 1973), p. 291. Judith Kroll, "Bed," *In the Temperate Zone* (New York: Scribner's, 1973), pp. 45–46. See also Anne Stanford, "Danae," *In Mediterranean Air*, pp. 33–39; Rachel Blau DuPlessis, "Voice," *Wells*, n.p.; and the father-forgiving poems in Lucille Clifton, *Two-Headed Woman* (Amherst: University of Massachusetts Press, 1980), and Ellen Bass, *I'm Not Your Laughing Daughter* (Amherst: University of Massachusetts Press, 1973), all of which see through a father's resented dominance to his weakness. Maxine Kumin's "Life's Work," *Our Ground Time Here Will Be Brief: New and Selected Poems* (New York: Penguin, 1982), pp. 102–03, retells the family anecdote of how her grandfather forbade her pianist mother to go on tour, thus cutting off her career, and how her own father forbade her, a swimmer, to join the Aquacade; she concludes, perhaps prematurely, "Well, the firm old fathers are dead."

21. Political victimization poems: Audre Lorde, "Power," *The Black Unicorn*, pp. 108–09. Susan Griffin, "Breviary," *Like the Iris of an Eye*, pp. 108–11. Robin Morgan, "The Network of the Imaginary Mother," *Lady of the Beasts* (New York: Random House, 1976), pp. 63–68; "Documentary," *Depth Perception* (Garden City, N.Y.: Doubleday, 1982), pp. 73–77. Carolyn Forché, "The Colonel," *The Country Between Us* (New York: Harper and Row, 1981), p. 16.

22. Doctor poems: Sylvia Plath, "Lady Lazarus," *Collected Poems*, pp. 244–46. Mona Van Duyn, "Death by Aesthetics," *Merciful Disguises: Published and Unpublished Poems* (New York: Atheneum, 1973), pp. 27–28. Judith Hemschemeyer, "The Carpenters," *Very Close and Very Slow* (Middletown, Conn.: Wesleyan University Press, 1975), pp. 54–56. Jana Harris, "What d'ya Get When You Cross a Gynecologist with a Xerox Machine," *Manhattan as a Second Language*, pp. 67–68.

23. The connection between masculine rationality and contempt for women, issuing in violence, appears in the following: Rochelle Owens, "The Power of Love: He Wants Shih (Everything)," *Salt & Core* (Los Angeles: Black Sparrow Press, 1968), pp. 38–40. May Swenson, "Bleeding," *New and Selected Things Taking Place* (Boston: Little, Brown, 1978), p. 104. Marge Piercy, "The Friend," *Circles on the Water*, p. 39. Kathleen Fraser, "The Baker's Daughter," *What I Want*, p. 6. Patricia Dienstfrey, "A Solid Plot," *Newspaper Stories & Other Poems* (Berkeley: Berkeley Poets' Workshop & Press, 1979), p. 4. Rachel Blau DuPlessis, "Breasts," *Wells*, n.p. Jill Hoffman, "The Emperor of Lies," *Mink Coat* (New York: Holt, Rinehart and Winston, 1973), p. 60. Celia Gilbert, "Life and Death of Hero Stick," *Queen of Darkness* (New York: Viking, 1977), pp. 48–51.

24. Rationalism, ideology, and dehumanization: Marge Piercy, "Song of the

266   STEALING THE LANGUAGE

Fucked Duck," *Circles on the Water* pp. 86–87; "The Box," *Living in the Open*, p. 44. Piercy's Tarot sequence "Laying Down the Tower" is an attempt to explore the political dimensions of the Tarot symbols; among its figures are the phallic "Tower of Baffle," emblem of the corrupt city and the Orwellian language used by its masters; the well-fed "Landlord" of the nine of cups; the "Emperor" who exploits women, blacks, and nature equally. Denise Levertov, "May Our Right Hands Lose Their Cunning," *The Freeing of the Dust* (New York: New Directions, 1975), pp. 33–34. Judith Leet, "Missile Launch Officer," *Pleasure Seeker's Guide* (Boston: Houghton Mifflin, 1976), p. 19. Anne Sexton, "I'm Dreaming the My Lai Soldier Again," *Complete Poems* (Boston: Houghton Mifflin, 1981), p. 575.

25. Masculine rationality imaged as cold, abstract, mechanical, armored, and capitalistic: Sylvia Plath, "The Rival," "Three Women," "The Colossus," "Daddy," "The Magi," "A Birthday Present," *Collected Poems*, pp. 166, 176–87, 129–30, 223–24, 148, 206–08. Erica Jong, "Touch," "His Silence," *Fruits & Vegetables* (New York: Holt, Rinehart & Winston, 1971), pp. 20, 22. Sandra Gilbert, "The Intruder," *In the Fourth World* (University, Ala.: University of Alabama Press, 1979), p. 8. Lynn Sukenick, "The Poster," in Chester and Barba, *Rising Tides*, p. 290. Adrienne Rich, "The Knight," *The Fact of a Doorframe*, pp. 32–33, 43–44. Margaret Atwood, "The City Planners," "my beautiful wooden leader," "there must be more for you to do," *Selected Poems* (New York: Simon and Schuster, 1976), pp. 10, 147, 206. Marge Piercy, "A Shadow Play for Guilt," "Song of the Fucked Duck," "The Emperor," *Circles on the Water*, pp. 84–86, 86–88, 99–101. Diane Wakoski, "Blue Monday," *Inside the Blood Factory* (Garden City, N.Y.: Doubleday, 1968), pp. 9–11. Kathleen Fraser, "Ships," *What I Want*, p. 8. Mona Van Duyn, "Advice to a God," *Merciful Disguises*, pp. 109–10.

26. Emily Stipes Watts, *The Poetry of American Women from 1632 to 1945* (Austin: University of Texas Press, 1977), pp. 6–7, 18–20, 127–28.

27. Anne Bradstreet, "To My Dear Children," *Works*, ed. Jeannine Hensley (Cambridge, Mass.: Harvard University Press, 1967), p. 243.

28. God as woman's adversary: Daniella Gioseffi, "Woman with Tongue in Cheek," in Chester and Barba, *Rising Tides*, pp. 304–06. Marge Piercy, "Right Thinking Man," *Circles in the Water*, pp. 90–91. Judith Kroll, "Who to Look Out For," *In the Temperate Zone*, pp. 9–10. Eloise Healy, "Dear Friend, My Priest," *A Packet Beating like a Heart* (Los Angeles: Books of a Feather Press, 1981), pp. 37–38. Sandra Gilbert, "The Dream of the Deathpill," *In the Fourth World*, p. 51. Marge Piercy, "Laying Down the Tower," *Circles on the Water*, pp. 118–38. Marie Ponsot, "de Religione Humanitas Vera," *Admit Impediment* (New York: Knopf, 1981), pp. 17–20.

29. Mary Daly, *Gyn/Ecology: The Metaethics of Radical Feminism* (Boston: Beacon Press, 1978).

30. Mona Van Duyn, "The Fear of Flying," *Merciful Disguises*, pp. 209–11.

31. Helen Chasin, "Fire," *Casting Stones* (Boston: Little, Brown, 1975), p. 4.

32. Anne Sexton, "The Death Baby," *Complete Poems*, pp. 354–59.

33. Revenge fantasies employing phallic weaponry: Sylvia Plath, "Daddy," "Purdah," *Collected Poems*, pp. 222, 242. Adrienne Rich, "The Phenomenology of Anger," "Hunger," *The Fact of a Doorframe*, pp. 165–69, 229–32. Marge Piercy, "A Just Anger," "The Window of the Woman Burning," *Circles in the Water*, pp. 88, 202–03. Audre Lorde, "The Women of Dan Dance," *The Black Unicorn*, pp. 14–15. Diane Wakoski, "Love Letter Postmarked Von Beethoven," *The Motorcycle Betrayal Poems* (New York: Simon and Schuster, 1971), pp. 16–18. Margaret Atwood, "They Eat Out," *Selected Poems*, pp. 145–46. Cynthia Macdonald, "Objets d'Art," "Reply to the Request from the Remaining Poet for Suicide Suggestions," *Amputations*, pp. 6, 39–42. See also Joan Larkin, "Revolutionary Practices," *Housework* (Brooklyn: Out & Out Books, 1975), pp. 68–69; Grace Schulman, "Burn Down the Icons," *Burn Down the Icons*, pp. 57–58, for fire images.

34. For explosion imagery, see, for example, Diane Di Prima, "my cunt a bomb exploding / yr christian conscience," in "To the Patriarchs," *Selected Poems 1956–1976* (Plainfield, Vt.: North Atlantic Books, 1977), p. 317; Ann Darr's volcano in "Relative Matter," *Cleared for Landing* (Washington, D.C.: Dryad Press, 1978), p. 27; Audre Lorde's images of language as snakes, as an explosion, and as "a diamond comes into a knot of flame," in "Coal," *Chosen Poems Old and New* (New York: W. W. Norton, 1982), pp. 10–11; and Wakoski's volcano and snakes in "No More Soft Talk," *Motorcycle Betrayal Poems*, pp. 66–68. Mary Jacobus discusses metaphors of earthquake and other moments of convulsion in women's writing as "transgression of literary boundaries," in Mary Jacobus, ed., *Women Writing and Writing about Women* (New York: Harper and Row, 1979), p. 16.

35. Erotic vengeance fantasies: Erica Jong, "His Silence," *Fruits & Vegetables*, p. 22. Marjorie Fletcher, "Fantasy, the dominant position," *US: Women* (Cambridge, Mass.: Alice James Books, 1973), p. 6. Helen Adam, "I Love My Love," in Florence Howe and Ellen Bass, eds., *No More Masks* (Garden City, N.Y.: Doubleday, 1973), pp. 86–89.

36. Vengeance as Logos: Muriel Rukeyser, "Myth," *Collected Poems* (New York: McGraw-Hill, 1978). Judith Leet, "Overlooking the Pile of Bodies at One's Feet," *Pleasure Seeker's Guide*, pp. 3–12. Erica Jong, "Back to Africa," in Chester and Barba, *Rising Tides*, pp. 341–42. Marilyn Krysl, "To the Banker: Sestina Against Money," "Sestina for Bright Cloud, Singing (But Not the Blues)," *More Palomino, Please, More Fuschia* (Cleveland: Cleveland State University Poetry Center, 1980), pp. 36, 40. See also Eloise Healy, "This Is Not Making Love," *A Packet Beating Like a Heart*, p. 46; Judith Kroll, "Dick & Jane," "Me Jane," *In the Temperate Zone*, pp. 4, 31; Susan Griffin, "I Like to Think of Harriet Tubman," "An Answer to a Man's Question, 'What Can I Do About Women's Liberation?'" *Like the Iris of an Eye*, pp. 10–12, 35–36; Toi Derricotte, "poem no. 1," *The Empress of the Death House* (Detroit: Lotus Press, 1978), pp. 37–38; and the role reversal in Judy Grahn's "I have come to claim," where the poet beats up a set of Marilyn Monroe cultists with Monroe's bones, which she has in a paper sack, *The Work of a Common Woman* (New York: St. Martin's Press, 1978), pp. 31–32.

37. Violence as waste product: Audre Lorde, "Power," *The Black Unicorn*, pp. 108–09. Denise Levertov, "A Poem at Christmas, 1972," *The Freeing of the Dust* (New York: New Directions, 1975), pp. 37–38.

38. Sigmund Freud, "Mourning and Melancholia," *Complete Psychological Works*, trans. and ed. James Strachey et al., 24 vols. (London: Hogarth Press, 1953–74), vol. 14, p. 252; "The Ego and the Id," vol. 19, p. 53. Freud's proposal of a "death instinct," developed in "Beyond the Pleasure Principle," should be distinguished from the concept of the death wish as contingent rather than instinctual and primal.

39. *The Diary of Alice James*, ed. Leon Edel (New York: Dodd, Mead, 1964), p. 149.

40. Among the poems delineating this interchangeability between the wish to kill and the wish to die are the following: Adrienne Rich, "The Phenomenology of Anger," *The Fact of a Doorframe*, pp. 165–69. Robin Morgan, "Monster," *Monster* (New York: Random House, 1972), pp. 81–86. Helen Chasin, "Fire," *Casting Stones*, p. 4. Ann Darr, "The Argument," "August Hallucination," *Cleared for Landing*, pp. 11, 19–20. Majory Fletcher, "Beginning Journals (Karen's Poem)," *US: Women*, p. 23. Sylvia Plath, "Daddy," "Lady Lazarus," *Collected Poems*, pp. 222, 244. Olga Broumas, "Maenad," *Beginning With O* (New Haven: Yale University Press, 1977), p. 17.

41. Phyllis Chesler, *Women and Madness* (Garden City, N.Y.: Doubleday, 1972).

42. Passive-erotic suicide and self-punishment imagery: Robin Morgan, "The Improvisers," *Monster*, p. 3. Marilyn Hacker, "Elegy," *Presentation Piece* (New York: Viking, 1974), pp. 93–96. Anne Sexton, "The Addict," "Wanting to Die," "Dr. Y," *Complete Poems*, pp. 165, 142, 561–62, are erotic death fantasies. "You, Dr. Martin," "Music Swims Back to Me," "Ringing The Bells," "Lullaby," "Cripples and Other Stories," "Making a Living," "The Death Baby," pp. 3, 6, 28, 29, 160–63, 350–51, 354–59, are fantasies of infantile regression, insofar as we can separate eroticism and regression in Sexton. Denise Levertov, "Hypocrite Women," *O Taste and See* (New York: New Directions, 1964), p. 70. Marge Piercy, "Women's Laughter," *Circles on the Water*, pp. 98–99. Sandra Gilbert, "Suicide (1)," "Suicide (2)," *In the Fourth World*, pp. 30, 33. Kathleen Fraser, "The Story of Emma Slide," *New Shoes* (New York: Harper and Row, 1978), p. 41. (Emma's search for romantic fulfillment/dissolution, "lit by clichéd expectations," as Fraser's Notes remark, cause her to see herself as infirm compared with others' firmness; as watery; as requiring "someone to love / as the tendrils of plants want a wall to climb"—thus a literal clinging vine, prehumanly prehensile but passive, incapable of independent life.) Sylvia Plath, "Suicide Off Egg Rock," "The Hanging Man," "Daddy," "A Birthday Present," "Getting There," "Ariel," "Lady Lazarus," *Collected Poems*, pp. 115, 141, 222, 206, 247, 239, 244.

43. A. A. Alvarez, *The Savage God: A Study of Suicide* (London: Weidenfeld and Nicolson, 1972), pp. 202, 203. Summarizing a 1910 symposium on suicide held by the Vienna Psychoanalytic Society, Alvarez cites the opinion of Adler that suicidal impulses are motivated by feelings of inferiority, revenge, and

antisocial aggression, and that of Stekel, "no one kills himself who has never wanted to kill another, or at least wished the death of another." Alvarez' personal account of suicide as simultaneously a seizing of freedom and a confession of failure, and his recurrent image of suicide as "a closed world with its own irresistible logic" (p. 105) feminizes the male suicide and coincides with women's self-representations and especially with their womb-and-embryo images. Explicit historical and political dimensions of the death wish, supplementing the psychosexual, are of paramount importance in Plath, Rich, Morgan, and less so in Sexton.

44. Olga Broumas, "Circe," *Beginning with O*, p. 15.

45. Margaret Atwood, *Power Politics* (New York: Harper and Row, 1971). Most, but not all, the poems in the sequence are included in Atwood's *Selected Poems*, which is the edition from which I quote. Omitted, however, are the initial "he reappears" and the concluding "he is last seen," here paraphrased though not quoted.

46. Linda Sandler, in her preface to the Atwood issue of the Canadian journal *Malahat Review* (January 1977), writes, "*Power Politics*, a book of poems which coolly dissects the foetid corpse of a love affair, made her one of the leading Cassandras of North American feminists, and the medusa of countless knights in shining armor" (p. 6). According to Jane Lilienfeld, "Silence and Scorn in a Lyric of Intimacy: The Progress of Margaret Atwood's Poetry," *Women's Studies* 7, i–ii, 185–94, "poem after poem skewers the mock-heroic lover, names him with witty ridicule . . . the speaker is safe from the desperation of need . . . Her wit gives her distance." Valerie Trueblood, "Conscience and spirit," *American Poetry Review* (March–April 1977), sees in *Power Politics* "a female sense of kinship with the natural world that waits to be plundered," but also notes that Atwood is "not a poet susceptible to happiness . . . Flushing out the harm-doers she keeps encountering herself" (p. 201).

47. See the jacket copy in the original edition of *Power Politics*; its frontispiece, which depicts a faceless armored figure roped, at its stiffly outstretched wrist, to the ankle of an upside-down bandaged woman in the pose of the Tarot hanged man; and Atwood's "Notes on Power Politics," *Acta Victoriana* 97, no. 2 (April 6–19, 1973). Eli Mandel in "Atwood Gothic," *Malahat Review* (January 1977), sees the Atwood persona as a self-styled "prisoner of mind police," but also suggests that the primal dread in *Power Politics* as in Mary Shelley's *Frankenstein* is a fear of birth and of life. Apropos of patterns and the mutual dependence of gender antagonists, Mandel usefully quotes Leslie Fiedler on the "maiden in flight" motif of the gothic novel (*Love and Death in the American Novel* [New York: Meridian Books, 1962], pp. 111–12):

Not the violation or death which sets such a flight in motion, but the flight itself figures forth the essential meaning of the anti-bourgeois gothic, for which the girl on the run and her pursuer become only alternative versions of the same flight. Neither can come to rest before the other, for each is the projection of his opposite . . . actors in a drama which depends on both for its significance.

If we substitute "fight" for "flight," we have *Power Politics* in a nutshell.
   48. Judith McCombs, "Power Politics," *Moving Out* 3, no. 2 (Spring 1973):
54–69; see p. 58. McCombs also suggests that Victor/Victim and Author/
Object may be polarized personae within a divided self.
   49. Robin Skelton, "Timeless Constructions: A Note on the Poetic Style of
Margaret Atwood," *Malahat Review* (January 1977): 107–20, is an excellent
examination of Atwood's high degree of parallel structure and its effects. Skelton
discovers that an Atwood poem can often be reversed or rearranged, stanza by
stanza or sentence by sentence, without altering its sense. He argues that this
"modular" structure accounts for our "unease" reading her:

> We perceive, subliminally, the poet's peculiar dealings with time. We be-
> come aware that while we are accumulating information, we are not in
> fact moving . . . beginnings could be conclusions and conclusions are
> not endings. We find ourselves in a universe where progress is impossible
> . . . The parallelisms are frightening because successive statements will
> often reflect and counter one another; they seldom move in logical stages
> towards resolution and conclusion. (p. 119)

See also McCombs' discussion of *Power Politics* as bringing "to static climax"
Gothic motifs in Atwood's earlier sequences *The Circle Game* and *Journals of
Susanna Moodie*: "Atwood's Haunted Sequences," in *The Art of Margaret Atwood: Essays in Criticism*, ed. Arnold E. Davidson and Cathy N. Davidson
(Toronto: Anansi Press, 1981), pp. 35–54.
   50. Diane Wakoski's *The George Washington Poems* originally appeared in
1967, and is reprinted in *Trilogy* (Garden City, N.Y.: Doubleday, 1974). Page
references in the text are to this edition.
   51. The double entendre of "The Father of My Country" is drawn to our
explicit attention not in the poem of that title but in an interview. See Diane
Wakoski, *Toward a New Poetry* (Ann Arbor: University of Michigan Press,
1980), p. 249.
   52. *Toward a New Poetry*, pp. 249–50.
   53. Estella Lauter summarizes Jungian definitions of this archetype by ob-
serving that "the phenomenon of the animus is often described by Jungians in
negative terms, as a voice within the woman that issues prohibitions, gives commands, and makes pronouncements, as if a woman could not express her mind
without animosity." Anima (the interior female self within a male) and animus
(the interior male self within a female) are asymmetrical concepts in classical
Jungian theory; the former is not primarily negative, the latter is. See "Visual
Images by Women: A Test Case for the Theory of Archetypes," in Estella Lauter
and Carol Schreier Rupprecht, eds., *Feminist Archetypal Theory* (Knoxville:
University of Tennessee Press, 1985), p. 62. An essay by Emma Jung, however,
suggests that the "animosity" of a woman's animus may be directed primarily
against herself:

> It comes to us as a voice commenting on every situation in which we find
> ourselves . . . we hear from it a critical, usually negative comment on

every movement, an exact examination of all motives and intentions, which naturally always causes feelings of inferiority, and tends to nip in the bud all initiative and every wish for self-expression. From time to time, this same voice may also dispense exaggerated praise, and the result of these extremes of judgment is that one oscillates to and fro between the consciousness of complete futility and a blown-up sense of one's own value and importance.

Quoted by Demaris S. Wehr, "Religious and Social Dimensions of Jung's Concept of the Archetype: A Feminist Perspective," in Lauter and Rupprecht, *Feminist Archetypal Theory*, p. 34. Adrienne Rich argues that Emily Dickinson's relation to powerful and dangerous male figures "are about the poet's relationship to her own power, which is exteriorized in masculine form" ("Vesuvius at Home," *On Lies, Secrets and Silence*, p. 165). Albert Gelpi, concurring, stresses that this figure both "holds the key to fulfillment" and is experienced as destructive of nature and femaleness: "impelled by the animus, she is empowered to kill experience and slay herself into art." See "Emily Dickinson and the Deerslayer: The Dilemma of the Woman/Poet in America," in Sandra M. Gilbert and Susan Gubar, eds., *Shakespeare's Sisters: Feminist Essays on Women Poets* (Bloomington: Indiana University Press, 1979), pp. 124, 131.

54. Anne Sexton's "The Jesus Papers" is included in its entirety in *Complete Poems*; page references in the text are to this edition. Estella Lauter, "Anne Sexton's Radical Discontent," *Women as Mythmakers: Poetry and Visual Art by Twentieth–Century Women* (Bloomington: Indiana University Press, 1984), examines Sexton's last five books "as a tragic part of the process of revisioning prescribed by Mary Daly for women who find it impossible to live with theologies designed to serve patriarchal ends" (p. 24).

55. A similar juxtaposition is in Daniella Gioseffi's "Woman with Tongue in Cheek," in Laura Chester and Sharon Barba, *Rising Tides*, which caustically remarks that "the knight / never comes riding . . . except to admonish me . . . or to drape a heavy blue robe around my shoulders / and rest his crucified head / in my big soft and tired lap" (p. 306).

56. Sexton as a flamboyant and provocative public performer is described in Maxine Kumin's introduction to the *Collected Poems* (pp. xxi–xxii). That her audience was often composed of cultists "pruriently interested in her suicidal impulses, her psychotic breakdowns, her hospitilizations" (p. xxxiv) both stimulated and aggrieved Sexton, as it does her "Jesus." See the essay "The Freak Show," in Anne Sexton, *No Evil Star: Selected Essays, Interviews, and Prose*, ed. Steven G. Colburn (Ann Arbor: University of Michigan Press, 1985), pp. 33–38, describing the poet's miseries as a performer.

57. Karen Horney's 1926 essay "The Flight from Womanhood," *Feminine Psychology* (New York: W. W. Norton, 1967) attributes the European man's (and by implication the psychoanalyst's) "dogma of the inferiority of women" to womb envy. In her 1932 essay "The Dread of Woman," she associates it with dread of the vagina and of absorption by "the sinister female genital," quoting abundantly from German poetry to prove the point.

58. Lauter's reading of this finale in "Anne Sexton's Radical Discontent,"

Women as Mythmakers, p. 32, is more optimistic than mine: "God emerges as nothing more or less than a ruthless demi-god, and for the moment, the poet emerges triumphant."

59. Adrienne Rich, "When We Dead Awaken," *On Lies, Secrets and Silence*, p. 49.

60. A comparable point is made by the poet and activist Alta in one of her prose meditations:

> women, we are learning, are as able to kill as men. this makes us equal. if the men do not celebrate birth, are we equal? as long as men beat off to pictures of women holding guns, do you really believe we are learning to be equal?

Nor, she declares, is the old polarization of females bonded by nurture, males bonded by war and hunting, acceptable: "this is not a new vision, i wish to see a new vision. this one tires my eyes." "Now About Life and Death," *The Shameless Hussy* (Trumansburg, N.Y.: Crossing Press, 1980), pp. 78–79.

Chapter 5: The Imperative of Intimacy: Female Erotics, Female Poetics

1. Sigmund Freud, *Complete Psychological Works*, trans. and ed. James Strachey et al., 24 vols. (London: Hogarth Press, 1953–74), *Civilization & Its Discontents*, vol. 21 (1929/1930), p. 145.

2. Alta, "Putting It All Down in Black and White," *The Shameless Hussy* (Trumansburg, N.Y.: Crossing Press, 1980), p. 196.

3. Siv Cedering Fox, "Both You Say," *Mother Is* (New York: Stein and Day, 1975), p. 39.

4. Maxine Kumin, "After Love," *Our Ground Time Here Will Be Brief: New and Selected Poems* (New York: Viking, 1982), p. 182.

5. The term "sexual thralldom" is originally Krafft-Ebbing's and is adapted by Freud. On the concept of "romantic thralldom" and its application to a woman writer's life and work, see Rachel Blau DuPlessis, "Romantic Thralldom and 'Subtle Genealogies' in H.D.," *Writing Beyond the Ending: Narrative Strategies of Twentieth-Century Women Writers* (Bloomington: University of Indiana Press, 1985). In fiction, the single most powerful and influential critique of "love" in women's lives and fictions is Doris Lessing, *The Golden Notebook* (New York: Ballantine, 1968). Ann Snitow discusses the widespread antiromanticism of contemporary American women's fiction in "The Front Line: Notes on Sex in Novels by Women, 1969–79," *Signs: Journal of Women in Culture and Society* 5, no. 4 (1980): 702–18, noting "the sharp split between high culture and low on this point," and making many of the same observations on the erotic element in women's fiction as I find in women's poetry.

6. Carol Gilligan, *In a Different Voice: Psychological Theory and Women's Development* (Cambridge, Mass.: Harvard University Press, 1982), p. 49.

7. Freud, *Civilization*, pp. 64–72.

8. The significance of "relationship" in female identity and self-definition has been a central topic in feminist theory. Among psychologists, the female tendency to define the self in terms of relationships is traditionally seen as a weakness; see, for example, Judith Barwick, *Psychology of Women* (New York: Harper and Row, 1971). Nancy Chodorow's widely accepted account of female identity formation, *The Reproduction of Motherhood* (Berkeley: University of California Press, 1978), views the mother-daughter bond and its consequences largely (though not entirely) in the context of male-dominated society and female powerlessness and therefore sees it as handicapping women's autonomy. Jean Miller, however, calls for a new psychological terminology to describe women's identity "organized around being able to make and then to maintain affiliations and relationships," in *Toward a New Psychology of Women* (Boston: Beacon Press, 1976), p. 83. Numerous writers indebted to Chodorow's analysis of women's personality formation take a positive view of its value and prospects. Carol Gilligan's treatise on gender and moral development proposes, for example, that while the impulse toward connection which images life as a web of personal affiliations and responsibilities "leaves women at risk in a society that rewards separation," it nevertheless represents valid moral principles and embodies the "truth" of "the ongoing process of attachment that creates and sustains the human community" (*In a Different Voice*, p. 156). Sara Ruddick's description of the flexible, other-centered mental strategies in what she calls "maternal thinking" advocates "the self-conscious inclusion of such thinking in the dominant culture." "Maternal Thinking," *Feminist Studies* 6, no. 2 (summer 1980): 343–67. Advocates of female empathy and capacity for nurturance as a social and political value may invite the charge that they are replicating retrograde nineteenth-century views of the virtuous (and powerless) female. Similarly, proponents of the body and of sexuality as sources of women's art are accused of "essentialism." See Elaine Showalter, "Feminist Criticism in the Wilderness," in Showalter, ed., *The New Feminist Criticism: Essays on Women, Literature and Theory* (New York: Pantheon, 1985), pp. 250–52, and Ann Rosalind Jones, "Writing the Body: Toward an Understanding of l'Écriture féminine," in Showalter, *New Feminist Criticism*, pp. 361–77, esp. p. 371:

> The psychic characteristics praised by advocates of *feminité* have in fact been determined by the familial and economic roles imposed on women by men. There is nothing liberatory . . . in women's claiming as virtues qualities that men have always found convenient. How does maternal tenderness or undemanding empathy threaten a Master? (p. 371)

For a powerful and wide-ranging presentation of the view that the polarization of male and female personalities and roles constitutes the "human malaise" which both men and women collaborate in maintaining, see Dorothy Dinnerstein, *The Mermaid and the Minotaur: Sexual Arrangements and Human Malaise* (New York: Harper and Row, 1976). My argument in this chapter is that the image of female desire which seems to dominate contemporary women's poetry does stress "empathy" and "tenderness" but is not at all "undemanding" and is strongly opposed to polarization.

9. See Judith Kegan Gardiner, "On Female Identity and Writing by Women," *Critical Inquiry* 8, no. 2 (Winter 1981): 347–61; Elizabeth Abel, "(E)Merging Identities: The Dynamics of Female Friendship in Contemporary Fiction by Women," *Signs* 6, no. 3 (Spring 1981): 413–35; Mary Jacobus, "The Difference of View," in Mary Jacobus, ed., *Women Writing and Writing about Women* (London: Croom Helm, 1979), p. 11; Rachel Blau DuPlessis, "For the Etruscans," in Showalter, *New Feminist Criticism*, pp. 275–76.

10. Kathleen Fraser, "The Recognition," *New Shoes* (New York: Harper and Row, 1978), p. 83.

11. Lucille Clifton, "If I stand in my window," *Good Times* (New York: Random House, 1969), p. 11.

12. Adrienne Rich, "Leaflets," *The Fact of a Doorframe: Poems Selected and New 1950–1984* (New York: W. W. Norton, 1984), pp. 116–20.

13. Mona Van Duyn, "Death By Aesthetics," *Merciful Disguises: Published and Unpublished Poems* (New York: Atheneum, 1971), pp. 27–28.

14. Poems on intimacy and the need for seeing and touch: June Jordan, "Who Look at Me," *Things That I Do in the Dark* (New York: Random House, 1977), pp. 2–21. Diane Di Prima, "The Party," *Selected Poems 1965–1975* (Plainfield, Vt.: North Atlantic Books, 1975), pp. 74–76. Kathleen Fraser, "What You Need," *New Shoes*, p. 9. Nikki Giovanni, "The Laws of Motion," *The Women and the Men* (New York: Morrow, 1975), n.p. "When I Die," *My House* (New York: Morrow, 1971), pp. 36–37. Anne Sexton, "Rowing," "The Touch," "The Kiss," "When Man Enters Woman," "The Fury of Cocks," *Complete Poems* (Boston: Houghton Mifflin, 1981), pp. 417, 173–74, 174–75, 369, 428. Marge Piercy, "Meditation in My Favorite Position," *Circles on the Water: Selected Poems* (New York: Knopf, 1982), p. 34. Diane Wakoski, "Love Song for O.K. Ready," *The Motorcycle Betrayal Poems* (New York: Simon and Schuster, 1971), p. 79. Jean Valentine, "Sanctuary," *The Messenger* (New York: Farrar Straus & Giroux, 1979), pp. 42–43.

15. Love poetry and the repudiation of the hero: Adrienne Rich, "Natural Resources," *The Fact of a Doorframe*, pp. 256–64. Carol Bergé, "Blues for a Cello Man," in Elaine Gill, ed., *Mountain Moving Day* (Trumansburg, N.Y.: Crossing Press, 1973), p. 30.

16. John Donne, "The Undertaking," *The Elegies and The Songs and Sonnets*, ed. Helen Gardner (Oxford: Clarendon Press, 1965), p. 57.

17. Love poetry and role reversal: Siv Cedering [Fox], "Like a Woman in the Kitchen," *Letters from the Floating World* (Pittsburgh: University of Pittsburgh Press, 1984), p. 57. Nikki Giovanni, "Seduction," *Black Feeling, Black Talk/ Black Judgement* (New York: Morrow, 1970), p. 38. Elizabeth Sargent, "A Sailor at Midnight," in Ellen Bass and Florence Howe, eds., *No More Masks* (Garden City, N.Y.: Doubleday, 1973), p. 228.

18. Sexual role reversal and female metaphor: Marge Piercy, "Unclench Yourself," "Doing It Differently," *Circles on the Water*, pp. 174, 108–13. De-

nise Levertov, "The Ache of Marriage," *O Taste and See* (New York: New Directions, 1964), p. 5.

19. Nongendered metaphors for sexuality: Nikki Giovanni, "The Way I Feel," *The Women and the Men*, n.p. Ntozake Shange, "When the Mississippi Meets the Amazon," *Nappy Edges* (New York: Bantam, 1979), pp. 31–32. Eloise Healy, "There Is Some Pain," "Separate Pieces," *Building Some Changes* (Los Angeles: Beyond Baroque Foundation, 1976), pp. 12, 20; "For Holly," "This Darknight Speed," *A Packet Beating Like a Heart* (Los Angeles: Books of a Feather Press, 1981), pp. 12, 19–20. Adrienne Rich, "Two Songs," *The Fact of a Doorframe*, pp. 65–66. Maxine Kumin, "This Day Will Self-Destruct," *Our Ground Time*, p. 101. Lenore Kandel, "Love in the Middle of the Air," *Word Alchemy* (New York: Grove Press, 1967), p. 8. Alice Mattison, "Husband," *Animals* (Cambridge, Mass.: Alice James Books, 1979), p. 11. Lisel Mueller, "Love Like Salt," *The Private Life* (Baton Rouge: Louisiana State University Press, 1976), p. 55. Lucille Clifton, "Salt," *An Ordinary Woman* (New York: Random House, 1974), p. 10.

20. Anne Snitow, "The Front Line," p. 711.

21. The identification of love with death in the Tristan and Isolde legend and throughout medieval and modern western culture is the theme of Denis De Rougemont's classic *Love in the Western World*, trans. Montgomery Belgion (New York: Pantheon, 1956). A recent and philosophical presentation of the theme is Georges Bataille, *Death and Sensuality* (New York: Walker, 1962); see also the identification of sexual excitement with hostility in psychologist Robert Stoller's *Sexual Excitement* (New York: Pantheon, 1979).

22. Karen Horney, "The Dread of Woman," *Feminine Psychology* (New York: W. W. Norton, 1967), pp. 137–38.

23. Love poetry and images of interpenetration and dissolved boundaries: Lenore Kandel, "Love-Lust Poem," *Word Alchemy*, p. 34. Metaphors of osmosis: Ann Darr, "Osmosis," *St. Ann's Gut* (New York: Morrow, 1971), p. 47. Susan Griffin, "Like Water in a Cell," *Like the Iris of an Eye* (New York: Harper and Row, 1976), pp. 119–22. Margaret Atwood, "Pre-Amphibian," "More and More," *Selected Poems* (New York: Simon and Schuster, 1976), pp. 35–36, 74. See also Lucille Day, "Neural Folds," *Self-Portrait with Hand Microscope* (Berkeley: Berkeley Poets' Workshop and Press, 1982), p. 7. Maxine Kumin, "We Are," *Our Ground Time*, p. 181; "Together," *The Nightmare Factory* (New York: Harper and Row, 1970). Alta, "Anybody could write this poem. All you have to say is yes," in Gill, *Mountain Moving Day*, p. 11. Susan Griffin, "The Woman Who Swims in Her Tears," *Like the Iris*, pp. 90–91. Adrienne Rich, "Origins and History of Consciousness," *The Dream of a Common Language* (New York: W. W. Norton, 1978), pp. 7–9. Audre Lorde, "Meet," "Recreation," *The Black Unicorn* (New York: W. W. Norton, 1978), pp. 33–34, 81. Daniella Gioseffi, "Paradise Is Not a Place," in Lucille Iverson and Kathryn Ruby, eds., *We Become New* (New York: Bantam, 1975), pp. 20–21.

24. Adrienne Rich, "Disloyal to Civilization: Feminism, Racism, Gynephobia," *On Lies, Secrets and Silence: Selected Prose 1966–1978* (New York: W. W. Norton, 1979), pp. 275–310.

276

STEALING THE LANGUAGE

25. On the identification of the personal and the political: Ann Snitow in "The Front Line," (p. 718) notes that "the making of visionary recombinations is one species of political work" and observes that women novelists

are insisting on the fusion of the realistic and the visionary . . . Doris Lessing, Toni Morrison, Margaret Atwood, Marge Piercy and a number of others begin with the traditional female concern with personal relationships and the details of daily life and then expand these concerns to include a wider and wider swath of human experience.

See Adrienne Rich, "The Blue Ghazals," "The Phenomenology of Anger," "Twenty-one Love Poems," *The Fact of a Doorframe*, pp. 120–23, 165–69, 236–46.

26. Judy Grahn, "A Woman Is Talking to Death," *The Work of a Common Woman* (New York: St. Martin's Press, 1978), pp. 113–31.

27. On women poets and the theme of responsibility for life, see, for example, the following: Barbara Greenberg, "The Game of Animals," *The Spoils of August* (Middletown, Conn.: Wesleyan University Press, 1974), p. 31. Judy Hemschemeyer, "That Summer," *Very Close and Very Slow* (Middletown, Conn.: Wesleyan University Press, 1975), p. 44. Marie Ponsot, "New York: Appendix of Predecessors," "From the Fountain at Vaucluse," *Admit Impediment* (New York: Knopf, 1981), pp. 7–15, 46–53, and note 34, below.

28. Celia Gilbert, "Voices," *Bonfire* (Cambridge, Mass.: Alice James Books, 1983), pp. 58–60.

29. Susan Griffin, "Mother and Child," *Like the Iris*, p. 99.

30. Anne Sexton, "Housewife," *Complete Poems*, p. 77; Sharon Olds, *The Dead and the Living* (New York: Knopf, 1984), p. 61.

31. Adrienne Rich, *Of Woman Born: Motherhood as Experience and Institution* (New York: W. W. Norton, 1976), p. 218.

32. Poets who write extensively of motherhood include Alta, Lucille Clifton, Patricia Dienstfrey, Susan Griffin, Marilyn Hacker, Shirley Kaufman, Marilyn Krysl, Maxine Kumin, Alice Mattison, Lisel Mueller, Sharon Olds, Robin Morgan, Alicia Ostriker, Marie Ponsot, Muriel Rukeyser, and Anne Sexton.

33. Abortion poems: Gwendolyn Brooks, "The Mother," *Selected Poems* (New York: Harper and Row, 1963), pp. 3–4. Lucille Clifton, "The Lost Baby Poem," *Good News About the Earth* (New York: Random House, 1972), p. 4. Summer Brenner, "Letter to an Unknown Daughter," Carol A. Simone, ed., *Networks: An Anthology of San Francisco Bay Area Women Poets* (San Francisco: Vortex, 1979), p. 24. Diane Di Prima, "Brass Furnace Going Out," in Simone, *Networks*, pp. 94–99.

34. Maternity and the defiance of stereotype: Diane Di Prima, "Jeanne Poems #5," *Selected Poems*, p. 30. Marilyn Krysl, "Sestina Extolling the Pleasures of Creation," *More Palomino, Please, More Fuschia* (Cleveland: Cleveland State University Poetry Center, 1980), p. 21. Alta, "you fell asleep," *Shameless Hussy*, p. 7. Lucille Clifton, "Admonitions," *Good Times*, p. 37. See also Alicia

Ostriker, "Letter to M," *The Mother/Child Papers* (Boston: Beacon, 1986), p. 33.

35. The conflict between mothering and creativity: Tillie Olsen, *Silences* (New York: Delacorte, 1978). Adrienne Rich, "When We Dead Awaken," *On Lies, Secrets and Silence,* and *Of Woman Born.* Judith Plaskow, "Woman as Body: Motherhood and Dualism," *Anima* 8, no. 1: 56–67. Both the conflict and the connections between motherhood and creativity are discussed in Alicia Ostriker, "A Wild Surmise: Motherhood and Poetry," *Writing Like a Woman* (Ann Arbor: University of Michigan Press, 1983), pp. 126–31. Sandra Donaldson, "Suddenly You've Become Somebody Else: A Study of Pregnancy and the Creative Woman,"*Women's Studies International Forum* 7, no. 4 (1984): 227–35. Susan Stanford Friedman, "Creativity and the Childbirth Metaphor: Gender Difference in Literary Discourse," *Feminist Studies,* forthcoming. See the discussion of maternal ambivalence and anger in women's poetry in Lynda Koolish, *A Whole New Poetry Beginning Here: Contemporary American Women Poets* (Ann Arbor, Mich.: University Microfilms, 1981), pp. 246–54.

36. Mother-child poems: Sylvia Plath, "The Munich Mannequins," "Morning Song," "Nick and the Candlestick," "Tulips," *Collected Poems,* Ted Hughes, ed. (New York: Harper and Row, 1981), pp. 262–63, 156–57, 240–42, 160. Madeline Bass, "To My Former Student on the Occasion of Birth," *Toward Spring Bank* (Wescosville, Pa.: Damascus Road, 1981), p. 12. Kathleen Fraser, "Poem Wondering if I'm Pregnant," *What I Want,* p. 51. Cynthia Macdonald, "The Insatiable Baby," *Amputations* (New York: Braziller, 1972). Joyce Carol Oates, "Baby," *Invisible Woman* (Princeton: Ontario Review Press, 1982), p. 11. Joan Larkin, "Story," *Housework* (New York: Out & Out Books, 1975), p. 29. Susan Griffin, "White Bear," *Like the Iris,* pp. 19–21. Miriam Goodman, "Notes," *Permanent Wave* (Cambridge, Mass.: Alice James Books, 1977), p. 60. Alice Mattison, "Husband," "The Crazy Baby," *Animals,* pp. 11–12, 57. Anne Sexton, "Hansel and Gretel," *Complete Poems,* pp. 286–90. Sharon Olds, "Young Mothers V," *Satan Says* (Pittsburgh: University of Pittsburgh Press, 1980), p. 43.

37. Poems of mother-child division and continuity: Ann Darr, "The Gift," *St. Ann's Gut* (New York: Morrow, 1971), p. 53. Lucille Clifton, "the thirty-eighth year," *Good Times,* pp. 92–94. Maxine Kumin, "The Envelope," *Our Ground Time,* pp. 65.

38. Maxine Kumin and the theme of the family: "Sperm," "Our Ground Time Here Will Be Brief," "The Retrieval System," "Splitting Wood at Six Above," *Our Ground Time,* pp. 96–98, 3, 45, 69–70.

39. Maxine Kumin and mother-child poems: "Changing the Children," "Family Reunion," "Leaving My Daughter's House," *Our Ground Time,* pp. 59, 18, 19–20.

40. Anne Sexton and the family; mother poems: "The Double Image," "Those Times . . . ," "The Division of Parts," and also "Christmas Eve," "Dreaming the Breasts," "Praying on a 707," *Complete Poems,* pp. 35–46, 118–21, 139–40, 314–15, 378–80. Daughter poems: "The Double Image,"

"A Little Uncomplicated Hymn," "The Fortress," "Pain for a Daughter," "Little Girl, My Stringbean, My Lovely Woman," "Mother and Daughter," *Complete Poems*, pp. 35–42, 148–52, 66–68, 163–64, 145–48, 305–07.

41. Poems of maternal politics: Caroline Kizer, "Pro Femina," *Knock upon Silence* (Garden City, N.Y.: Doubleday, 1965), pp. 41–49. Adrienne Rich, "Hunger," *The Fact of a Doorframe*, pp. 229–32. Susan Griffin, "I Like to Think of Harriet Tubman," *Like the Iris*, pp. 10–12. Madeline Bass, "This Iliad," *Toward Spring Bank*, pp. 49–56. Sharon Olds, "Late," *Satan Says*, p. 30. See also Alicia Ostriker, *The Mother/Child Papers* (Boston: Beacon Press, 1986).

42. The connection with the erotic mother: Sue Standing, "Watermark," *Deception Pass* (Cambridge, Mass.: Alice James, 1984), pp. 42–43. Adrienne Rich, "Sibling Mysteries," *The Dream of a Common Language*, pp. 47–52. Marie Ponsot, "Nursing: Mother," "Late," *Admit Impediment*, pp. 66–73. May Sarton, "Death and the Lovers," *Selected Poems*, p. 47.

43. Rich, *Of Woman Born*, p. 243.

44. Ambivalence in mother poems and the issue of the powerful-powerless mother: Judy Hemschemeyer, *The Ride Home*, unpublished volume of poems. Adrienne Rich, "A Woman Mourned by Daughters," *Fact of a Doorframe*, pp. 42–43. Sylvia Plath, "All the Dead Dears," "The Disquieting Muses," "Medusa," *Collected Poems*, pp. 70–71, 74–76, 224–26. Karen Snow, *Wonders* (New York: Penguin, 1980). Susan Griffin, "Grenadine," "Grandmother," "Archeology of a Lost Woman: Fragments," "Mother and Child," *Like the Iris*, pp. 39–42, 43–44, 49–55, 99–101. Marilyn Hacker, "Mother II," *Assumptions* (New York: Knopf, 1985), pp. 20–21. Sharon Olds, "Satan Says," *Satan Says*, pp. 3–4. Mona Van Duyn, "The Creation," "Remedies, Maladies, Reasons," *Merciful Disguises*, pp. 99–102, 134–42. Marge Piercy, "Crescent Moon like a Canoe," *Circles on the Water*, pp. 278–81.

45. Koolish discusses the pattern of division and return to the mother in black and third-world women writers in *A Whole New Poetry*, pp. 237–42.

46. Division and return to the mother in black and third-world writing: Audre Lorde, "Prologue," "Black Mother Woman," "Generation II," "The Woman Thing," *Chosen Poems Old and New* (New York: W. W. Norton, 1968), pp. 58–60, 52–53, 14–15; "From the House of Yemanja," *The Black Unicorn*, p. 6. Carolyn Rodgers, "Jesus Was Crucified, or It Must Be Deep," "It Is Deep," *How I Got Ovah* (Garden City, N.Y.: Doubleday, 1975), pp. 8–10, 11–12. Alice Walker, "In Search of Our Mothers' Gardens," *In Search of Our Mothers' Gardens: Womanist Prose* (New York: Harcourt Brace Jovanovich, 1983), pp. 231–43. Cherríe Moraga, "La Guera," "For the Color of My Mother," in Cherríe Moraga and Gloria Anzaldúa, eds., *This Bridge Called My Back: Writings by Radical Women of Color* (Watertown, Mass.: Persephone Press, 1981), pp. 27–34, 12–13. June Jordan, "Getting Down to Get Over," *Things That I Do in the Dark*, pp. 27–37.

47. Lisel Mueller, "Levelling With Each Other," *Private Life*, p. 36.

48. Love poems to fathers: Madeline Bass, "Tiger," *Toward Spring Bank*, pp. 14–15. Chana Bloch, "The Death of the Bronx," *The Secrets of the Tribe*, (New York: Sheep Meadows Press, 1980), pp. 3–11. Ann Darr, "Dear Oedi-

pus," *St. Ann's Gut*, (New York: Morrow, 1971), p. 41. Diane Di Prima, "To My Father," *Selected Poems*, p. 254, 29–30. Sandra Gilbert, "Five Meditations on One Who Is Dead," *In the Fourth World* (University, Ala.: University of Alabama Press, 1979), pp. 16–19. Maxine Kumin, "My Father's Neckties," "The Pawnbroker," *Our Ground Time*, pp. 49, 193–194. Carol Oles, *Quarry* (Salt Lake City: University of Utah Press, 1983). Sharon Olds, "The Victims," "The Ideal Father," "Fate," "My Father Snoring," *The Dead and the Living* (New York: Knopf, 1983), pp. 34, 38–39, 40, 41. Anne Sexton, "The Death of the Fathers," *Complete Poems*, pp. 322–32. Diane Wakoski, "The Father of My Country," *Trilogy* (Garden City, N.Y.: Doubleday, 1974), pp. 139–43.

49. Poems of female friendship: Lucille Clifton, "Sisters," *An Ordinary Woman* (New York: Random House, 1972), p. 5. Kathleen Fraser, "Notes to Lyn," *New Shoes*, pp. 26–29. Deena Metzger, "The Woman Who Swallows the Earthquake Gains Its Power," *The Streets Inside: Ten Los Angeles Poets* (Los Angeles: Momentum Press, 1978), pp. 98–103. Robin Morgan, "Portrait of the Artist as Two Young Women," *Lady of the Beasts* (New York: Random House, 1972), pp. 31–33. "Elegy," *Depth Perception* (Garden City, N.Y.: Doubleday, 1982), pp. 80–84. Marie Ponsot, "Sois Sage, O Ma Douleur," *Admit Impediment*, pp. 31–37. Holly Prado, "Crossings: For Deena's Birthday,"*Streets Inside*, pp. 57–59. Adrienne Rich, "For Julie in Nebraska," *A Wild Patience Has Taken Me This Far* (New York: W. W. Norton, 1981), pp. 16–18.

50. Koolish, *A Whole New Poetry*, pp. 227–28.

51. Joanne Feit-Diehl, "Come Slowly-Eden: An Exploration of Women Poets and Their Muse," *Signs* 3, no. 3 (Spring 1978): 572–87.

52. Poems of homage to heroines, spiritual ancestresses and sisters: Muriel Rukeyser, "Käthe Kollwitz," *Collected Poems* (New York: McGraw-Hill, 1978), pp. 479–84. Adrienne Rich, "From an Old House in America," *The Fact of a Doorframe*, pp. 212–22. (Rich's *The Dream of a Common Language* and *A Wild Patience* are preoccupied with the recovery of a female cultural heritage.) Alta, "The Vow," *Shameless Hussy*, p. 56. Jayne Cortez, "Big Fine Woman from Ruleville," *Firespitter* (New York: Bola Press, 1982), p. 14. Lucille Clifton, "harriet / if i be you," *Ordinary Woman*, p. 18; "Miss Rosie," *Good Times*, p. 5. Judy Grahn, "The Common Woman," *Work of a Common Woman*, pp. 59–73. Marilyn Krysl, "Sestina for Our Revolution," *More Palomino, Please*, pp. 38–39. Diane Wakoski, "Greed Part 9," *Greed/Parts 8, 9, 11* (Los Angeles: Black Sparrow, 1973), pp. 19–31. Marge Piercy, "Burying Blues for Janice," *Circles on the Water*, p. 100. Elizabeth Bishop, "Invitation to Miss Marianne Moore," *Complete Poems* (New York: Farrar Straus & Giroux, 1969), pp. 94–96. An important exception to the rule of intimacy between female subject and female poet is Pamela Hadas, *Beside Herself: Pocahontas to Patty Hearst* (New York: Knopf, 1983); these are traditional persona poems, deliberately distanced.

53. Nikki Giovanni, "Poem for a Lady Whose Voice I Like," *Women and the Men*, n.p.

54. Ann Darr, "Gaelic Legacy," *St. Ann's Gut*, p. 70–71.

55. Poems of self-integration and reconciliation: Marge Piercy, "The Woman in the Ordinary," *Circles on the Water*, p. 96. Poems of self-integration through

imaginary reintegration with both parents: Muriel Rukeyser, "Double Ode,"
Collected Poems, pp. 540–43. Celia Gilbert, "The Memory of Father and
Mother in the Bed," *Bonfire*, p. 34. Sharon Olds, "Satan Says," *Satan Says*,
p. 3. Audre Lorde, "Outside," *The Black Unicorn*, pp. 61–62. Jean Valentine,
"The Messenger," *The Messenger*, pp. 25–30. Adrienne Rich, "Orion," "Snap-
shots of a Daughter-in-Law," "Necessities of Life," "In the Woods," "Two
Songs," "Diving into the Wreck," *The Fact of a Doorframe*, pp. 79–80, 35–39,
55–56, 56–58, 65–66, 162–64; "The Stranger," *Poems Selected and New*
(New York: W. W. Norton, 1974), pp. 79–80. See also Anne Sexton, "O Ye
Tongues," *Complete Poems*, pp. 396–413; Maxine Kumin, the "Henry Manly"
poems, *Our Ground Time*, pp. 54–57, 166.

56. Advocates of "androgyny" argue that both women and men ideally
should develop attributes associated with both masculinity and femininity; see,
for example, Carolyn Heilbrun, *Toward a Recognition of Androgyny* (New York:
Knopf, 1973). Opponents argue that the term historically signifies the subsum-
ing of a feminine within a masculine psyche, representing male but not female
wholeness. See Barbara Charlesworth Gelpi, "An Androgynous Aesthetic," in
Karen Borden and Faneil Rinn, eds., *Feminist Literary Criticism: A Symposium*
(San Jose, Calif.: Diotima Press, 1974).

57. Denise Levertov's antidualistic poems include "Else a Great Prince in
Prison Lies," "The Fountain," *The Jacob's Ladder* (New York: New Directions,
1961), pp. 25, 30, 55; "O Taste and See," *O Taste and See* 53, "Stepping Westward," *The Sorrow Dance* (New York: New Directions, 1968); "The Freeing of
the Dust," "Knowing the Unknown," *The Freeing of the Dust* (New York: New
Directions, 1975), pp. 113, 6.

58. The breakdown of the sacred-profane boundary: Audre Lorde, "The
Brown Menace, or, Poem to the Survival of Roaches," *Chosen Poems*, pp. 92–
93. Muriel Rukeyser, "Despisals," *Collected Poems*, pp. 491–92. Maxine
Kumin, "The Excrement Poem," "Body and Soul: A Meditation," *Our Ground
Time*, pp. 72, 66–67.

59. Susan Friedman, "Creativity and the Childbirth Metaphor," forthcoming *Feminist Studies* (Summer 1986), discusses the history of this metaphor as it
has been used by male writers and as it is both employed and criticized by
women writers.

60. Works identifying creation and procreation: H.D., "Hermetic Defini-
tion," "Winter Love," *Hermetic Definition* (New York: New Directions, 1972),
pp. 49–55, 115–17. Denise Levertov, "The Poet in the World," *The Poet in the
World* (New York: New Directions, 1973), pp. 107–16. Lucille Clifton, "she
understands me," *An Ordinary Woman*, p. 50. Sylvia Plath, "Metaphors,"
Collected Poems, p. 116. Sharon Olds, "The Language of the Brag," *Satan
Says*, pp. 44–45. Ntozake Shange, "wow . . . yr just like a man," *Nappy
Edges*, pp. 14–18.

61. Poems identifying female "crafts" as art include Marge Piercy, "Looking
at Quilts," *Circles on the Water*, pp. 170–71. Erica Jong, "Fruits & Vegetables,"
"Where it Begins," *Fruits & Vegetables*, pp. 1–10, 85–86. Sandra Gilbert,
"Emily's Bread," "The Emily Dickinson Black Cake Walk," *Emily's Bread*,

pp. 35–36, 102–103. Frances Mayes, "Ars Poetica," *The Arts of Fire* (Woodside, Calif.: Heyeck Press, 1982), p. 39. Jana Harris, "Laundry," *Manhattan as a Second Language* (New York: Harper and Row, 1982), pp. 90–91. Robin Morgan, "Network of the Imaginary Mother," *Lady of the Beasts*, pp. 63–88. Robin Morgan, "Piecing," *Depth Perception*, pp. 3–5. Judy Grahn, *The Queen of Wands* (Trumansburg, N.Y.: Crossing Press, 1982).

62. See Judith Kegan Gardiner, "On Female Identity and Writing by Women," *Critical Inquiry* 8, no. 2 (Winter 1981): 355. Suzanne Juhasz, "Towards a Theory of Form in Feminist Autobiography," and Annette Kolodny, "The Lady's Not for Spurning: Kate Millett and the Critics," in Estelle C. Jellinek, ed., *Women's Autobiography: Essays in Criticism* (Bloomington: Indiana University Press, 1980). Women's writing and avant-garde form is the motif of the journal *HOW/ever*, ed. Kathleen Fraser and Frances Jaffer, and of *Feminist Poetics: A Consideration of the Female Construction of Language*, ed. Kathleen Fraser (San Francisco: San Francisco State University Creative Writing Department, private edition, 1984).

63. Virginia Woolf, *A Writer's Diary*, ed. Leonard Woolf (New York: Harcourt Brace Jovanovich, 1954), p. 13.

64. Charles Olson, "Projective Verse," *Selected Writings*, ed. Robert Creeley (New York: New Directions, 1966), p. 24.

65. Statements stressing the concept of a poetics which is both open in form and personal in content: Kathleen Fraser, "On Being a West Coast Woman Poet," *Women's Studies* 5 (1977). "The Gestate," discussed by Koolish, *A Whole New Poetry*, pp. 21–22. Denise Levertov, "Some Notes on Organic Form," *The Poet in the World*, pp. 7–13. Diane Di Prima, "The Colors of Brick," *Selected Poems*, p. 57.

66. Harriet Desmoines, "Notes for a Magazine II," *Sinister Wisdom* 1 (1976): 97; Mary Daly, *Gyn/Ecology: The Metaethics of Radical Feminism* (Boston: Beacon Press, 1978), p. 23.

67. The female erotic and the comic-ludicrous: Sylvia Plath, "Three Women," *Collected Poems*, pp. 176–87. Elizabeth Bishop, "Invitation to Miss Marianne Moore," *Complete Poems*, pp. 94–96. "The Moose," *Geography III* (New York: Farrar Straus & Giroux, 1976), pp. 22–31. Marie Ponsot, "Discovery," *Admit Impediment*, pp. 99–100. Ellen Bass, "In Celebration," *I'm Not Your Laughing Daughter* (Amherst: University of Massachusetts Press, 1973), p. 30. Alta, "On Love," *Shameless Hussy*, pp. 91–96. Kathleen Fraser, "Coincidental," *New Shoes*, pp. 14–15.

68. Judy Grahn, "She Who," *Work of a Common Woman*, pp. 77–109.

69. Poems of the plural self: Adriennne Rich, "Diving into the Wreck," *The Fact of a Doorframe*, pp. 162–64. Denise Levertov, "Knowing the Unknown," *Freeing of the Dust*, p. 6. Marge Piercy, "The Queen of Pentacles," *Circles on the Water*, pp. 120–21.

70. The plural self and chant form: Audre Lorde, *The Black Unicorn* (New York: W. W. Norton, 1978). Ntozake Shange, *For Colored Girls Who Have Considered Suicide When the Rainbow is Enuf* (New York: Macmillan, 1977). Sylvia Gonzales, "Chicana Evolution," *Networks*, pp. 112–17. Jessica Hagedorn,

"Canto de Nada," in Simone, *Networks*, pp. 55–56. Anne Waldman, "Fast Speaking Woman," *Fast Speaking Woman* (San Francisco: City Lights, 1974), pp. 1–36. Grahn, "She Who," pp. 75–109.

71. Kathleen Fraser, "Talking to Myself Talking to You," *Each Next: Narratives* (Berkeley: The Figures, 1980), p. 34.

72. John Holmes, quoted in Diane Wood Middlebrook, "I Tapped My Own Head: The Apprenticeship of Anne Sexton," in Diane Wood Middlebrook and Marilyn Yalom, eds., *Coming to Light: American Women Poets in the Twentieth Century* (Ann Arbor: University of Michigan Press, 1985), p. 203.

73. Ann Sexton, "For John, Who Begs Me Not to Inquire Further," *Complete Poems*, pp. 34–35.

74. Middlebrook, "I Tapped My Own Head," *Coming to Light*, p. 204.

75. Diane Wakoski, "How Do You Tell a Story," *The Man Who Shook Hands* (Garden City, N.Y.: Doubleday, 1978), pp. 60–65; "Greed Part 6," *Greed Parts 5–7* (Santa Barbara: Black Sparrow, 1976), pp. 23–34; "The Emerald Essay," "The Blue Swan, an Essay on Music and Poetry," *Virtuoso Literature for Two and Four Hands*, (Garden City, N.Y.: Doubleday, 1975), pp. 33–41; *The Man Who Shook Hands*, pp. 13–30.

76. The poetics of intimacy and the relation to the reader: Marge Piercy, Preface to *Circles on the Water*, p. xi. Ntozake Shange, "a conversation with all my selves," "inquiry," *Nappy Edges*, pp. 26, 57 (see also "ego," p. 134). June Jordan, "These Poems," *Things That I Do in the Dark*, n.p. Kathleen Fraser, *Each Next*, pp. 11–13. Lenore Kandel, "Freak Show and Finale," *Word Alchemy*, pp. 11–12. Robin Morgan, "Phobophilia," *Depth Perception*, pp. 26–29. Denise Levertov, "Origins of a Poem," "The Poet in the World," *The Poet in the World*, pp. 43–56, 107–16. Adrienne Rich, "Origins and History of Consciousness," *The Dream of a Common Language*, pp. 7–9.

Judith Kegan Gardiner mounts a similar argument regarding the novelist Jean Rhys in "Good Morning Midnight; Good Night, Modernism," *Boundary 2: A Journal of Postmodern Literature* 11, nos. 1 and 2, Fall–Winter 1982–83: 233–51. In Gardiner's view Rhys "challenges traditional dualisms between reader and character, men and women, good and bad, to show that they enshrine a peculiar historical privilege of exploiter over exploited" (p. 249). Yet "when a writer like Joyce or Eliot writes about an alienated man estranged from himself, he is read as a portrait of the diminished possibilities of human existence in modern society. When Rhys writes about an alienated woman estranged from herself, critics applaud her perceptive but narrow depiction of female experience and tend to narrow her vision even further by labeling it both pathological and autobiographical" (p. 247).

Chapter 6: Thieves of Language: Women Poets and Revisionist Mythology

1. Hélène Cixous, "Sorties," in *La jeune née*, trans. Ann Liddle (Paris: Union Generale d'Éditions, 1975), quoted by Elaine Marks in "Women and

Literature in France," *Signs: Journal of Women in Culture and Society* 3, no. 4 (Summer 1978): 832–42, esp. 841; appears also in Elaine Marks and Isabelle Courtivron, eds., *New French Feminisms: An Anthology* (New York: Schocken Books, 1981), pp. 92–93.

2. Sylvia Plath, "Mushrooms," *The Collected Poems*, Ted Hughes, ed. (New York: Harper and Row, 1981), pp. 139–40.

3. Claudine Herrmann, *Les Voleuses de langue* (Paris: Des Femmes, 1979).

4. Jacques Lacan's term for the symbolic order of language is widely used by psychoanalytically oriented French feminists; see Jane Gallop, "Psychoanalysis in France," *Women and Literature* 7, no. 1 (Winter 1979): 57–63.

5. Robin Morgan, "The Invisible Woman," *Monster* (New York: Random House, 1972), p. 46.

6. Marcia Landy, "The Silent Woman," in *The Authority of Experience: Essays in Feminist Criticism*, ed. Arlyn Diamond and Lee Edwards (Amherst: University of Massachusetts Press, 1977), pp. 16–27.

7. Elaine Showalter, Introduction to *The New Feminist Criticism: Essays on Women, Literature, and Theory* (New York: Pantheon, 1985), p. 10.

8. Marks, "Women and Literature," p. 836.

9. Robert Graves argues—without much evidence—in *The White Goddess* (New York: Creative Age Press, 1948) that a magical language honoring the Moon-goddess existed in prepatriarchal times, survived in the mystery cults, and was still taught "in the poetic colleges of Ireland and Wales, and in the witch covens of Western Europe" (p. x). Among French feminists, Herrmann claims that women use space and time, metaphor and metonymy differently from men, Cixous that women write with "mother's milk" or "the blood's language." Most interestingly, Luce Irigaray moves from *Speculum d'autre femme* (Paris: Editions de Minuit, 1974), which deconstructs Plato and Freud to demonstrate the history of systematic repression of woman as a concept in western culture, to *Ce Sexe qui n'est pas un* (Paris: Éditions de Minuit, 1977), which attempts to transpose the voices of Freud, Lacan, Derrida, and Lewis Carroll into a feminine language. Among Irigaray's techniques is the rejection of the "proper" name along with "property" and "propriety" to recover the self as "elle(s)," a plural being (see Carolyn Burke, "Irigaray Through the Looking Glass," *Feminist Studies* 7, no. 2 [Summer 1981]: 288–306). This work parallels in many ways Susan Griffin's *Woman and Nature: The Roaring Inside Her* (New York: Harper and Row, 1978), discussed below. Julia Kristeva, on the other hand, argues that woman has no linguistic existence but a negative, preoedipal one. For details of the debate, which in part centers on the question of whether feminists should use male abstractions, see Elaine Marks and Carolyn G. Burke, "Report from Paris: Women's Writing and the Women's Movement," *Signs* 4, no. 2 (Summer 1978): 84–55. The most important theoretical texts prophesying a woman's language are Mary Daly's *Beyond God the Father* (Boston: Beacon Press, 1973) and *Gyn/Ecology* (Boston: Beacon Press, 1978). *Per contra*, see Robin Lakoff, *Language and Women's Place* (New York: Harper & Row, 1975); Mary Hiatt, *The Way Women Write* (New York: Teacher's College Press, 1977); Barrie Thorne and Nancy Henley, eds., *Language and Sex: Differ-*

ence and Dominance (Rowley, Mass.: Newbury House, 1975); and the empirical studies referred to in Cheris Kramer, Barrie Thorne, and Nancy Henley, "Perspective on Language and Communication," Signs 3, no. 3 (Spring 1978): 638–51.

10. The case against myth is exhaustively stated by Simone de Beauvoir in chap. 9, "Dreams, Fears, Idols," of The Second Sex, trans. H. M. Parshley (New York: Vintage, 1974), pp. 157–223. A discussion of the usefulness of some myths for women writers is Susan Gubar's "Mother, Maiden and the marriage of Death: Women Writers and an Ancient Myth," Women's Studies 6, no. 3 (1979): 301–15. Gubar argues that the figure of the Sphinx and the Mother-Goddess represent "secret wisdom" which women identify with "their point of view," and that they use the myth of Persephone and Demeter "to re-define, to re-affirm and to celebrate female consciousness itself" (p. 302). See also Alicia Ostriker, "I Make My Psyche from My Need," Writing like a Woman (Ann Arbor: University of Michigan Press, 1983), pp. 132–45. Estelle Lauter, Women as Mythmakers: Poetry and Visual Art by Twentieth-Century Women (Bloomington: Indiana University Press, 1984). Rachel Blau DuPlessis, Writing beyond the Ending: Narrative Strategies of Twentieth-Century Women Writers (Bloomington: Indiana University Press, 1985), chaps. 7, "Perceiving the Other-Side of Everything: Tactics of Revisionary Mythopoesis," and 8, "The Critique of Consciousness and Myth in Levertov, Rich and Rukeyser."

11. Muriel Rukeyser, "The Poem as Mask," Collected Poems (New York: McGraw-Hill, 1978), p. 435. Adrienne Rich, "Diving into the Wreck," The Fact of a Doorframe: Poems Selected and New, 1950–1984 (New York: W. W. Norton, 1984), pp. 162–64. Margaret Atwood, "Circe/Mud Poems," Selected Poems (New York: Simon and Schuster, 1976), pp. 201–23, esp. pp. 221–23.

12. Emily Stipes Watts, The Poetry of American Women from 1632 to 1945 (Austin: University of Texas Press, 1977), esp. pp. 49–50, 74–82, 101–03, 153–57.

13. The following is a roughly chronological list of some myth-poems by poets prior to 1960, with the sources where they may most easily be found. All poems cited in the text are included in this list.

Anne Bradstreet, "In Honor of that High and Mighty Princess Queen Elizabeth," The Works of Anne Bradstreet, ed. Jeannine Hensley (Cambridge, Mass.: Harvard University Press, 1967).

Phyllis Wheatley, "Niobe in Distress for Her Children Slain by Apollo," in Herbert Renfro, Life and Works of Phyllis Wheatley (Washington, D.C., 1916; rpt., Mnemosyne Publishing Co., 1969).

Mercy Warren, Poems Dramatic and Miscellaneous (Boston: Thomas and Andrews, 1790).

Sarah Wentworth Morton, Ouabi: An Indian Tale (Boston: Thomas and Andrews, 1790).

Maria Gowen Brooks, Judith, Esther and Other Poems (Boston: Cummings and Hilliard, 1820); Zophiël; or, the Bride of Seven, ed. Zadel Barnes Gustafson (Boston: Lee and Shephard, 1879).

Harriet Fanning Read, "Medea," *Dramatic Poems* (Boston: Crosby and Nichols, 1848).

Mary E. Hewitt, "An Imitation of Sappho," "Sappho to the Sybil," "Clytia," "A Centaur and Bride of the Lapithae," *Poems: Sacred, Passionate and Legendary* (New York: Lamport, Blakeman, and Law, 1853).

Sara Clarke, "Ariadne," in *The American Female Poets*, ed. Caroline May (Philadelphia: Lindsay and Blakiston, 1848).

Elizabeth Oakes Smith, "The Sinless Child," *Poetical Writings* (New York: Redfield, 1845).

Lucy Larcom, "The Legend of Skadi," *Poetical Works* (Boston: Houghton Mifflin, 1884).

Emily Dickinson, #s 155, 593, 1046, 1158, 1583, 1708, *Poems*, ed. Thomas H. Johnson, 3 vols. (Cambridge, Mass.: Harvard University Press, 1955).

Helen Hunt Jackson, "Oenone," "Ariadne's Farewell," "Demeter," "Esther," "Vashti," *Poems* (Boston: Roberts Brothers, 1892).

Emma Lazarus, "Admetus," "Tannhauser," "The New Colossus," "Venus of the Louvre," *Poems*, 2 vols. (Cambridge, Mass.: Riverside Press, 1889).

Louise Guiney, "Astraea," "Happy Ending," *Collected Lyrics* (Boston: Houghton Mifflin, 1927).

Edith Wharton, "Artemis to Actaeon," *Artemis to Actaeon and Other Verse* (New York: Scribner's, 1909).

Amy Lowell, "The Captured Goddess," "Witch-Woman," *Complete Poetical Works* (Boston: Houghton Mifflin, 1955).

Adelaide Crapsey, "The Witch," "Susanna and the Elders," *Verse* (Rochester, N.Y.: Manas Press, 1915).

Sara Teasdale, "Helen of Troy," "Beatrice," "Guinevere," "Sappho," *Collected Poems* (London: Collier-Macmillan, 1966).

H.D., "Demeter," "Hymen," "Eurydice," "Callypso Speaks," "Helen," *Collected Poems 1912–1944*, ed. Louis L. Martz (New York: New Directions, 1983); *Trilogy* (New York: New Directions, 1973).

Edna St. Vincent Millay, "The Bean-Stalk," "Prayer to Persephone," "The Singing-Woman at the Wood's Edge," "Invocation to the Muses," "An Ancient Gesture," *Collected Poems* (New York: Harper and Row, 1967).

Babette Deutsch, "The Mother," "Nike at the Metropolitan," "Epistle to Prometheus," *Collected Poems* (New York: Doubleday, 1969).

Louise Bogan, "Medusa," "Cassandra," "The Sleeping Fury," *The Blue Estuaries* (New York: Farrar, Straus and Giroux, 1968).

May Sarton, "She Shall Be Called Woman," "The Furies," *Collected Poems 1930–1973* (New York: W. W. Norton, 1974).

Margaret Walker, "Mollie Means," "Kissie Lee," *For My People* (New Haven: Yale University Press, 1942; rept., New York: Arno Press, 1968).

Muriel Rukeyser, "The Minotaur," "Orpheus," *Selected Poems* (New York: New Directions, 1951); "The Birth of Venus," *Body of Waking* (New York: Harper and Brothers, 1958).

14. The following are representative post-1960 myth-poems, listed alphabetically by author. References to all works discussed in the present chapter are to these editions. Extended poems and poem sequences are indicated by an asterisk (*).

Alta, "euridice," *I Am Not a Practising Angel* (Trumansburg, N.Y.: Crossing Press, 1980), p. 6.

Margaret Atwood, "Eventual Proteus," "Speeches for Dr. Frankenstein," "Siren Song," "Circe/Mud Poems,"* *Selected Poems*, pp. 12–13, 64–69, 195–96, 201–23.

Sharon Barba, "A Cycle of Women," in Laura Chester and Sharon Barba, eds., *Rising Tides: 20th Century Women Poets* (New York: Washington Square Press, 1973), pp. 356–57.

Olga Broumas, "Twelve Aspects of God,"* *Beginning with O* (New Haven: Yale University Press, 1977), pp. 3–24.

Grace Butcher, "Assignment," in Chester and Barba, *Rising Tides*, p. 231.

Lucille Clifton, Kali Poems,* *An Ordinary Woman* (New York: Random House, 1974), pp. 37, 47–57.

Helen Cooper, "From the Mad Wife's Room in Jane Eyre," in *Advance Token to Boardwalk: 28 New Jersey Poets* (Scotch Plains, N.J.: Poets & Writers of New Jersey, 1977), pp. 44–47.

Toi Derricotte, *Natural Birth* (Trumansburg, N.Y.: Crossing Press, 1983).

Patricia Dienstfrey, "Blood and the Iliad: The Paintings of Frida Kahlo," *Newspaper Stories & Other Poems* (Berkeley: Berkeley Poets' Workshop & Press, 1979), pp. 28–29.

Diane Di Prima, *Loba** (Berkeley: Wingbow Press, 1978).

Rachel Blau DuPlessis, "Medusa,"* "Eurydice,"* *Wells* (New York: Montemora Foundation, 1980), n.p.

Kate Ellis, "Matrilineal Descent," in Rod Tulloss, David Keller, and Alicia Ostriker, eds., *US1: Contemporary Writing from New Jersey* (Roosevelt, N.J.: US1 Poets' Cooperative, 1980), pp. 31–34.

Elizabeth Fenton, "Under the Ladder to Heaven," in Florence Howe and Ellen Bass, eds., *No More Masks: An Anthology of Poems by Women* (Garden City, N.Y.: Doubleday, 1973), pp. 298–99.

Celia Gilbert, "Lot's Wife,"* *Bonfire* (Cambridge, Mass.: Alice James Books, 1983), pp. 65–71.

Sandra Gilbert, "Bas Relief: Bacchante," "Daphne," "Scheherazade," "Psyche," *Emily's Bread* (New York: W. W. Norton, 1984), pp. 43–44, 82–88.

Nikki Giovanni, "Ego Tripping," *The Women and the Men* (New York: Morrow, 1975), n.p.

Louise Glück, "Gretel in Darkness," "Jeanne d'Arc," *The House on Marshland* (New York: Ecco Press, 1975), pp. 5, 20.

Judy Grahn, "She Who,"* *The Work of a Common Woman* (New York: St. Martin's Press, 1978), pp. 75–109; *The Queen of Wands** (Trumansburg, N.Y.: Crossing Press, 1982).

Susan Griffin, *Woman and Nature: The Roaring Inside Her** (New York: Harper and Row, 1978).

Marilyn Hacker, "For Elektra," "The Muses," "Nimue to Merlin," *Presentation Piece* (New York: Viking Press, 1974).

Pamela Hadas, *The Passion of Lilith* * (St. Louis: Cauldron Press, 1976); *Designing Women* * (New York: Knopf, 1979) *Beside Herself: Pocahontas to Patty Hearst* * (New York: Knopf, 1983).

H.D., *Helen in Egypt* * (New York: New Directions, 1961); *Hermetic Definition* * (New York: New Directions, 1972).

Erica Jong, "Arse Poetica," *Fruits & Vegetables* (New York: Holt, Rinehart & Winston, 1970); "Back to Africa," "Alcestis on the Poetry Circuit," *Halflives* (New York: Holt, Rinehart & Winston, 1973).

Carolyn Kizer, "Semele Recycled," "The Copulating Gods," "The Dying Goddess," *Yin* (Brockport, N.Y.: Boa Editions, 1984), pp. 13–15, 20, 45.

Denise Levertov, "The Goddess," *With Eyes at the Back of Our Heads* (New York: New Directions, 1959); "The Jacob's Ladder," "The Well," *The Jacob's Ladder* (New York: New Directions, 1961), pp. 37–38; "Song for Ishtar," *O Taste and See* (New York: New Directions, 1964), p. 3; "An Embroidery, (I)," "A Tree Telling of Orpheus," *Relearning the Alphabet* (New York: New Directions, 1970), pp. 33–34, 81–85.

Robin Morgan, "The Network of the Imaginary Mother," * "Voices from Six Tapestries," * *Lady of the Beasts* (New York: Random House, 1976), pp. 63–88, 105–31.

Lisel Mueller, "The Queen of Sheba Says Farewell," "Eros," "'O Brave New World . . .'" *Dependencies* (Chapel Hill: University of North Carolina Press, 1965), pp. 19–20, 23, 44; "Letter from the End of the World," *The Private Life* (Baton Rouge: Louisiana State University Press, 1976), p. 63.

Alicia Ostriker, "Homecoming," "The Impulse of Singing," "Message from the Sleeper at Hell's Mouth," * *A Woman Under the Surface* (Princeton: Princeton University Press, 1982), pp. 41–50.

Rochelle Owens, *The Joe 82 Creation Poems* * (Los Angeles: Black Sparrow Press, 1974).

Marge Piercy, "Icon," "Laying Down the Tower," * *Circles on the Water* (New York: Knopf, 1982), pp. 102, 118–38.

Sylvia Plath, "The Disquieting Muses," "The Colossus," "Witch Burning," "Magi," "Elm," "Medusa," "Lady Lazarus," "Mary's Song," *Collected Poems*, pp. 74–76, 129–30, 135–36, 148, 192, 224–26, 244–47, 257.

Adrienne Rich, "The Knight," "Orion," "Planetarium," "I Dream I'm the Death of Orpheus," *The Fact of a Doorframe*, pp. 32, 79–80, 114–16, 119–20.

Muriel Rukeyser, "The Poem as Mask," "Private Life of the Sphinx," "Orpheus," "The Birth of Venus," "Myth," "Waiting for Icarus," "In the Underworld," *Collected Poems* (New York: McGraw-Hill, 1978), pp. 278–80, 291–300, 417, 495, 519, 523.

May Sarton, "The Invocation to Kali," "The Muse as Medusa," "At Lindos," "At Delphi," *Selected Poems* (New York: W. W. Norton, 1978), pp. 155–66.

Anne Sexton, *Transformations,* * "Angels of the Love Affair," "The Jesus Papers," * "Gods," "Rats Live on No Evil Star," "The Furies," "Mary's Song,"

"Jesus Walking," *Complete Poems* (Boston: Houghton Mifflin, 1981), pp. 221–95, 332–36, 337–46, 349, 359–60, 363–78, 381–84.

Ann Stanford, "Women of Perseus," * In *Mediterranean Air* (New York: Viking, 1977), pp. 33–48.

Jean Tepperman, "Witch," in Howe and Bass, *No More Masks*, pp. 333–34.

Mona Van Duyn, "Outlandish Agon," "Advice to a God," "Leda," "Leda Reconsidered," *To See, to Take* (New York: Antheneum, 1970), pp. 3–4, 12, 23–24, 77–80.

Diane Wakoski, "The George Washington Poems," * *Trilogy* (Garden City, N.Y.: Doubleday, 1974), pp. 113–66.

Eleanor Wilner, "Epitaph," "Maya, Journey from the East," "Twice-gold," "Iphigenia, Setting the Record Straight," *Maya* (Amherst: University of Massachusetts Press, 1979), pp. 5, 13, 17, 20–21; *Shekinah,* * (Pittsburgh: University of Pittsburgh Press, 1984).

15. de Beauvoir, *Second Sex*, p. 811.

16. Daly, *Beyond God the Father*, p. 8.

17. Rachel Blau DuPlessis, *Writing Beyond the Ending*, pp. 108–112, calls this device "displacement," as against the larger strategies of "delegitimation," when a poet revises the plot of a known narrative.

18. Adrienne Rich, "The Mirror in Which Two Are Seen as One," "Necessities of Life," *Fact of a Doorframe*, pp. 159–60, 55–56.

19. The feminist attempt to construct a redefined "Goddess" or "Great Goddess" is, of course, not confined to poetry or even to literature. See, in *Chrysalis: A Magazine of Women's Culture*, no. 6 (1978), Gloria Z. Greenfield, Judith Antares, and Charlene Spretnak, "The Politics of Women's Spirituality," pp. 9–15; and Linda Palumbo, Maurine Revnille, Charlene Spretnak, and Terry Wolverton, "Women's Survival Catalog: Spirituality," an annotated listing of classic and recent texts, journals, and (a few) environmental artworks relating to "The Goddess," pp. 77–99. The Spring 1978 *Heresies* was devoted to "The Great Goddess." Journals of the women's spirituality movement, *Lady Unique* and *WomanSpirit*, regularly publish essays on Goddesses. See also Z. Budapest, *The Feminist Book of Lights and Shadows* (Los Angeles: Luna Press, 1976). *The Holy Book of Women's Mysteries* (Los Angeles: Luna Press, 1979). Carol Christ, *Diving Deep and Surfacing: Woman Writers on Spiritual Quest* (Boston: Beacon Press, 1980). Carol Christ and Judith Plaskow, eds., *Womanspirit Rising: A Feminist Reader in Religion* (San Francisco: Harper and Row, 1979). Mary Daly, *Gyn/Ecology: The Metaethics of Radical Feminism* (Boston: Beacon Press, 1978). Helen Diner, *Mothers and Amazons: The First Feminine History of Culture* (Garden City, N.Y.: Doubleday, 1973). Nor Hall, *The Moon and the Virgin: Reflections on the Archetypal Feminine* (New York: Harper and Row, 1980). Jane Ellen Harrison, *Mythology* (1924; rpt., New York: Harcourt Brace and World, 1963); *Prolegomena to the Study of Greek Religion* (New York: Meridian, 1957). Estella Lauter, *Women as Mythmakers: Poetry and Visual Art by Twentieth-Century Women* (Bloomington: Indiana University Press, 1984). Judith Ochshorn, *The Female Experience and the Nature of the Divine* (Bloomington: Indiana University Press, 1980). Sylvia Brinton Perera, *The Descent of Inanna*

(Toronto: Jung Society, 1981). Starhawk, *The Spiral Dance* (New York: Harper and Row, 1979). Merlin Stone, *When God Was a Woman* (New York: Harcourt Brace Jovanovich, 1978). Diane Wolkstein and Samuel Noah Kramer, *Inanna: Queen of Heaven and Earth* (New York: Harper and Row, 1983).

20. See Erich Neumann, *The Great Mother: An Analysis of the Archetype*, trans. Ralph Manheim (Princeton: Princeton University Press, 1963).

21. Levertov treats the association of women with falsity in "Hypocrite Women," which redefines feminine deception (and self-deception) as compliance with male demands for mothering and with the male pronouncement that "our cunts are ugly," *O Taste and See*, p. 70.

22. William Carlos Williams, "The Wanderer," *Collected Early Poems* (New York: New Directions, 1951), pp. 3–12.

23. Wallace Stevens, "Final Soliloquy of the Interior Paramour," *Collected Poems of Wallace Stevens* (New York: Knopf, 1954), p. 524.

24. Anne Sexton, "Her Kind," "Angels of the Love Affair," "The Death Baby," "Letters to Dr. Y," *Complete Poems*, pp. 15–16, 332–35, 354–59, 571–72, 575–77. The best discussion of these motifs in Sexton is Diana George, *Oedipus Anne: The Poetry of Anne Sexton* (Champaign: University of Illinois Press, 1986), chs. 8 and 9.

25. Susan Stanford Friedman, "Who Buried H.D.? A Poet, Her Critics, and Her Place in 'The Literary Tradition,'" *College English* 37 (March 1975): 807.

26. H.D., *Helen in Egypt* (New York: New Directions, 1961), p. 243. Further quotations are from this edition.

27. I have selected these three works for both their excellence and their diversity—including their diverse perspectives on female sexuality, from which much else, ideologically and formally, follows. H.D.'s orientation is (in this book) heterosexual, Griffin's lesbian, Sexton's (in this book) asexual. I believe that these works illuminate both the common ground and the differences among these three orientations toward women's sexuality, and I believe it is vital for feminist critics not to "prefer" one to the others.

28. H.D., "Helen," *Collected Poems 1912–1944*, ed. Louis C. Martz (New York: New Directions, 1983), pp. 154–55.

29. Susan Stanford Friedman, *Psyche Reborn: The Emergence of H.D.* (Bloomington: Indiana University Press, 1981) documents H.D.'s revisionist use of occult and mystical tradition in her quest for what she called "spirituality," and her revisionist use of psychoanalytic doctrines and methods in her quest for self-affirmation, both in her life and in *Helen in Egypt*. Rachel Blau DuPlessis, "Romantic Thralldom and 'Subtle Genealogies' in H.D.," *Writing Beyond the Ending*, chap. 5, examines H.D.-Helen's need to construct a "sufficient family" centered in the mother-child dyad rather than in heterosexual romance. Helen's successful quest for (1) knowledge of the gods, (2) integration of self, (3) a family consisting of parent figures, siblings, lover, and progeny might be related to a revisionist scheme of superego, ego, libido, in terms of what is sought and necessary for human wholeness.

30. Friedman, *Psyche Reborn*, p. 66.

31. Sherry Ortner, "Is Female to Male as Nature Is to Cultue?" in Michelle Zimbalist Rosaldo and Louise Lamphere, eds., *Women, Culture and Society* (Stanford, Calif.: Stanford University Press, 1974). Annette Kolodny, *The Lay of the Land* (Chapel Hill: University of North Carolina Press, 1975), pursues the metaphor of land as "virgin" or "mother" in American history and literature, with findings parallel to Griffin's. Daly, *Gyn/Ecology*, might provide a gloss on much of Griffin; Griffin and Daly review each other's books in *Chrysalis*, no. 7 (1979): 109–12.

32. Lauter, however, reads *Woman and Nature* as a work contributing to a developing myth of humanity within nature which is ultimately nonseparatist, in *Women as Mythmakers*, p. 223.

33. Susan Griffin, "Thoughts on Writing: A Diary," in Janet Sternburg, ed., *The Writer on Her Work* (New York: W. W. Norton, 1980), pp. 112–113.

34. See Suzanne Juhasz, *Naked and Fiery Forms: Modern American Poetry by Women, A New Tradition* (New York: Harper and Row, 1976), pp. 126–27.

35. Louise Glück's "Gretel in Darkness" similarly hints that Gretel has inadvertently killed the mother-goddess and been trapped in the house of patriarchy.

36. See, for example, Bruno Bettelheim, *The Uses of Enchantment: The Meaning and Importance of Fairy Tales* (New York: Knopf, 1976), pp. 225ff. See Juhasz, *Naked and Fiery Forms*, pp. 118–32, for a discussion of "the psychoanalytical model" and Sexton's outgrowing of it.

37. See Florence Rush, *The Best-Kept Secret* (Englewood Cliffs, N.J.: Prentice-Hall, 1980), esp. chap. 7, "The Freudian Cover-Up," which discusses Frued's conviction that incest is a female fantasy and the consequences of Freudian orthodoxy for incest victims today. See also Judith Lewis Herman (with Lisa Hirshman), *Father-Daughter Incest* (Cambridge, Mass.: Harvard University Press, 1981), esp. appendix, "The Incest Statutes," by Leigh Bienen.

38. May Sarton, "My Sisters, O My Sisters," *Selected Poems*, pp. 192–93.

39. Adrienne Rich, "When We Dead Awaken: Writing as Re-vision," *On Lies, Secrets and Silence* (New York: W. W. Norton, 1979), p. 35.

40. Similar techniques appear in Diane Wakoski's "George Washington Poems," Robin Morgan's "Network of the Imaginary Mother," and other works. I cannot think of any major modern poem by a man in which the self is presented as split or plural while the total poetic structure remains cohesive rather than fragmented. In the closest approximation, John Berryman's *Dream Songs* (New York: Farrar Straus & Gerioux, 1969), the "blackface" voice plays a distinctly minor role. *The Waste Land, The Cantos,* and *Paterson* are of course, all classics of personal, social, *and* aesthetic fragmentation. James Merrill's ouija trilogy *The Changing Light at Sandover* (New York: Atheneum, 1982) has a great deal in common with women's major works of revisionist mythology, including a double protagonist, a nonauthoritarian stance, and an emphasis on personal relationships. It differs in two fundamental ways: The posture toward history and culture is benign rather than adversarial, reflecting the privileged social position of the protagonists. By the same token, while much of Merrill's

supernatural and metaphysical "reality" is shifting, hazy, elusive, and insecure, the identities of the human protagonists JM and DJ are firm, nonmarginal, and not at issue. JM is a chosen/choosing vessel of cosmic enlightenment—however quizzical—much like Dante and Milton.

  41. Ezra Pound, *The Cantos of Ezra Pound* (New York: New Directions, 1970), p. 796.

Selected Bibliography

I Volumes by Individual Women Poets

Ai. *Cruelty.* New York: Houghton Mifflin, 1973.

———. *Killing Floor.* New York: Houghton Mifflin, 1979.

Alta. *I Am Not a Practicing Angel.* Trumansburg, N.Y.: Crossing Press, 1980.

———. *The Shameless Hussy.* Trumansburg, N.Y.: Crossing Press, 1980.

Atwood, Margaret. *Selected Poems.* New York: Simon & Schuster, 1976.

Bass, Ellen. *I'm Not Your Laughing Daughter.* Amherst: University of Massachusetts Press, 1973.

Bass, Madeline Tiger. *Toward Spring Bank.* Wescosville, Pa.: Damascus Rd., 1981.

Berger, Suzanne. *These Rooms.* Lincoln, Mass.: Penmaen Press, 1980.

Bishop, Elizabeth. *Complete Poems.* New York: Farrar, Straus & Giroux, 1969.

———. *Geography III.* New York: Farrar, Straus & Giroux, 1976.

Bleecker, Ann Eliza. *Posthumous Works.* New York: T. and J. Swords, 1793.

Bloch, Chana. *The Secrets of the Tribe.* New York: Sheep Meadow Press, 1980.

Bogan, Louise. *The Blue Estuaries: Poems, 1923–1968.* New York: Ecco Press, 1977.

Bradstreet, Anne. *The Works of Anne Bradstreet.* Edited by Jeannine Hensley. Cambridge, Mass.: Harvard University Press, 1967.

Brooks, Gwendolyn. *Selected Poems.* New York: Harper & Row, 1963.

Brooks, Maria. *Zophiël, or The Bride of Seven.* London: R. J. Kennet, 1833.

Broumas, Olga. *Beginning With O.* New Haven, Conn.: Yale University Press, 1977.

Cedering [Fox], Siv. *Letters from the Floating World Selected and New Poems.* Pittsburgh: University of Pittsburgh Press, 1984.

Chasin, Helen. *Casting Stones.* New York: Little, Brown, 1975.

Clifton, Lucille. *Good Times.* New York: Random House, 1969.

———. *Good News About the Earth.* New York: Random House, 1972.

———. *An Ordinary Woman.* New York: Random House, 1974.

———. *Two-Headed Woman.* Amherst: University of Massachusetts Press, 1980.

Cooper, Jane. *Maps & Windows*. New York: MacMillan, 1974.

Cortez, Jayne. *Firespitter*. New York: Bola Press, 1982.

Crapsey, Adelaide. *Verse*. New York: Knopf, 1922.

Darr, Ann. *St. Ann's Gut*. New York: Morrow, 1971.

———. *Cleared for Landing*. Takoma Park, Md.: Dryad Press, 1978.

Day, Lucille. *Self-Portrait with Hand Microscope*. Berkeley, Calif.: Berkeley Poets & Workshop, 1982.

Derricotte, Toi. *Empress of the Death House*. Detroit: Lotus Press, 1978.

———. *Natural Birth*. Trumansburg, N.Y.: Crossing Press, 1983.

Di Prima, Diane. *Dinners & Nightmares*. New York: Corinth Books, 1974.

———. *Selected Poems, 1965–75*. Plainfield, Vt.: North Atlantic Books, 1975.

———. *Loba*. Berkeley, Calif.: Wingbow Press, 1978.

Dickinson, Emily. *Complete Poems*. Edited by T. H. Johnson. 3 vols. Cambridge, Mass.: Harvard University Press, 1955.

Dienstfrey, Patricia. *Newspaper Stories*. Berkeley, Calif.: Berkeley Poets & Workshop, 1979.

H. D. [Hilda Doolittle]. *Trilogy*. New York: New Directions, 1973; orig. pub. 1944–46.

———. *Helen in Egypt*. New York: New Directions, 1961.

———. *Collected Earlier Poems 1940–1960*. Edited by Louis Martz. New York: New Directions, 1983.

DuPlessis, Rachel Blau. *Wells*. New York: Montemora Foundation, 1980.

Fletcher, Marjorie. *Us: Women*. Cambridge, Mass.: Alice James, 1973.

Forché, Carolyn. *The Country Between Us*. New York: Harper & Row, 1981.

Fox, Siv Cedering. *Mother Is*. New York: Stein & Day, 1975. Also see Cedering [Fox], Siv.

Fraser, Kathleen. *What I Want*. New York: Harper & Row, 1974.

———. *New Shoes*. New York: Harper & Row, 1978.

———. *Each Next*. Berkeley, Calif.: Berkeley Poets & Workshop, 1980.

Gallagher, Tess. *Instructions to the Double*. Port Townsend, Wash.: Graywolf, 1975.

Gilbert, Celia. *Queen of Darkness*. New York: Viking, 1972.

———. *Bonfire*. Cambridge, Mass.: Alice James, 1980.

Gilbert, Sandra. *In the Fourth World*. University, Alabama: University of Alabama Press, 1979.

———. *Emily's Bread*. New York: Norton, 1984.

Gilliland, Mary. *Gathering Fire*. Ithaca, N.Y.: Ithaca House, 1982.

Gioseffi, Daniela. *Eggs in the Lake*. Brockport, New York: Boa, 1979.

Giovanni, Nicki. *Black Feeling Black Talk/Black Judgment*. New York: Morrow, 1970.

———. *The Women and the Men*. New York: Morrow, 1975.

Glück, Louise. *The House on Marshland*. New York: Ecco Press, 1975.

———. *Descending Figure*. New York: Ecco Press, 1980.

Gohlke, Madelon Sprengnether. *The Normal Heart*. St. Paul: New Rivers Press, 1981.

Goodman, Miriam. *Permanent Wave* (with Kathleen Aguero, *Thirsty Day*). Cambridge, Mass.: Alice James, 1977.

Grahn, Judy. *The Work of a Common Woman*. Introduction by Adrienne Rich. New York: St. Martin's, 1979.

———. *The Queen of Wands*. Trumansburg, N.Y.: Crossing Press, 1982.

Greenberg, Barbara. *The Spoils of August*. Middletown, Conn.: Wesleyan University Press, 1974.

Griffin, Susan. *Like the Iris of an Eye*. New York: Harper & Row, 1976.

———. *Woman and Nature: The Roaring Inside Her*. New York: Harper & Row, 1978.

Hacker, Marilyn. *Presentation Piece*. New York: Viking, 1974.

———. *Assumptions*. New York: Knopf, 1985.

Hadas, Pamela. *The Passion of Lilith*. St. Louis: Cauldron Press, 1976.

———. *Designing Women*. New York: Knopf, 1979.

———. *Beside Herself: Pocahontas to Patty Hearst*. New York: Knopf, 1983.

Harris, Jana. *Manhattan as a Second Language*. New York: Harper & Row, 1981.

Healy, Eloise Klein. *Building Some Changes*. Los Angeles: Beyond Baroque Foundation, 1976.

———. *A Packet Beating Like a Heart*. Los Angeles: Books of a Feather Press, 1981.

Hemschemeyer, Judith. *I Remember the Room was Filled with Light*. Middletown, Conn.: Wesleyan University Press, 1973.

———. *Very Close and Very Slow*. Middletown, Conn.: Wesleyan University Press, 1975.

Jong, Erica. *Fruits and Vegetables*. New York: Holt, Rinehart, 1971.

Jordan, June. *Things That I Do in the Dark*. New York: Random House, 1977.

———. *Passion*. Preface by the poet. Boston: Beacon Press, 1980.

Kandel, Leonore. *Word Alchemy*. New York: Grove Press, 1970.

Kaufman, Shirley. *From One Life to Another*. Pittsburgh: University of Pittsburgh Press, 1979.

Kenyon, Jane. *From Room to Room*. Cambridge, Mass.: Alice James, 1978.

Kizer, Carolyn. *Knock Upon Silence*. Garden City, N.Y.: Doubleday, 1975.

———. *Yin*. Brockport, N.Y.: Boa, 1984.

Koestenbaum, Phyllis. *Oh I Can't She Says*. Oakland, Calif.: Christopher Books, 1980.

Kroll, Judith. *In the Temperate Zone*. New York: Scribner, 1973.

Krysl, Marilyn. *More Palamino Please, More Fuschia*. Cleveland: Cleveland State University Poetry Center, 1980.

Kumin, Maxine. *The Nightmare Factory*. New York: Harper & Row, 1970.

———. *Our Ground Time Here Will Be Brief: New and Selected Poems*. New York: Viking, 1982.

LaPalma, Marina, et al. *Making the Park*. Berkeley, Calif.: Kelsey St. Press, 1976.

Larkin, Joan. *Housework*. New York: Out & Out Books, 1975.

Leet, Judith. *Pleasure Seeker's Guide*. Boston: Houghton Mifflin, 1976.

LeSueur, Meridel. *Rites of Ancient Ripening*. Minneapolis: Vanilla Press, 1975.

Levertov, Denise. *With Eyes at the Back of Our Heads.* New York: New Directions, 1959.
―――. *The Jacob's Ladder.* New York: New Directions, 1961.
―――. *O Taste and See.* New York: New Directions, 1964.
―――. *The Sorrow Dance.* New York: New Directions, 1968.
―――. *Relearning the Alphabet.* New York: New Directions, 1970.
―――. *The Freeing of the Dust.* New York: New Directions, 1975.
―――. *Life in the Forest.* New York: New Directions, 1978.
―――. *Collected Earlier Poems 1940–1960.* New York: New Directions, 1979.
―――. *Candles in Babylon.* New York: New Directions, 1982.
Lifshin, Lyn. *Upstate Madonna.* Trumansburg, N.Y.: Crossing Press, 1975.
Lorde, Audre. *The Black Unicorn.* New York: Norton, 1978.
―――. *Chosen Poems, Old and New.* New York: Norton, 1982.
Lowell, Amy. *The Complete Poetical Works.* Boston: Houghton Mifflin, 1955.
Loy, Mina. *The Last Lunar Baedeker.* Edited by Roger Conover. Highlands, N.C.: Jargon Society, 1982.
Macdonald, Cynthia. *Amputations.* New York: Braziller, 1972.
―――. *W(h)oles.* New York: Knopf, 1980.
Mattison, Alice. *Animals.* Cambridge, Mass.: Alice James, 1979.
Mayes, Frances. *The Arts of Fire.* Woodside, Calif.: The Heyeck Press, 1982.
McCombs, Judith. *Against Nature: Wilderness Poems.* Paradise, Calif.: Dustbooks, 1979.
McPherson, Sandra. *The Year of Our Birth.* New York: Ecco Press, 1978.
Millay, Edna St. Vincent. *Collected Poems.* New York: Harper and Brothers, 1956.
Moore, Marianne. *A Marianne Moore Reader.* New York: Viking, 1961.
―――. *Complete Poems.* New York: Macmillan, 1967.
Morgan, Robin. *Monster.* New York: Random House, 1972.
―――. *Lady of the Beasts.* New York: Random House, 1974.
―――. *Depth Perception.* Garden City, N.Y.: Doubleday, 1982.
Mueller, Lisel. *Dependencies.* Chapel Hill: University of North Carolina Press, 1965.
―――. *The Private Life.* Baton Rouge: Louisiana State University Press, 1976.
―――. *The Need to Hold Still.* Baton Rouge: Louisiana State University Press, 1980.
Oates, Joyce Carol. *Invisible Woman: New and Selected Poems 1970–1982.* Princeton, N.J.: Ontario Review Press, 1982.
Olds, Sharon. *Satan Says.* Pittsburgh: University of Pittsburgh Press, 1980.
―――. *The Dead and the Living.* New York: Knopf, 1983.
Oles, Carol. *Quarry.* Salt Lake City: University of Utah Press, 1983.
Osgood, Frances. *Poems.* Philadelphia: Carey and Hart, 1850.
Ostriker, Alicia. *Songs.* New York: Holt Rinehart: 1969.
―――. *Once More out of Darkness.* Berkeley, Calif.: Berkeley Poets & Workshop, 1976.
―――. *A Dream of Springtime: Poems 1970–1978.* New York: Smith/Horizon, 1979.

————. *The Mother/Child Papers.* Boston: Beacon Press, 1986; orig. pub. Momentum, 1980.

————. *A Woman Under the Surface.* Princeton, N.J.: Princeton University Press, 1983.

Owens, Rochelle. *Salt and Core.* Santa Barbara: Black Sparrow, 1968.

————. *The Joe 82 Creation Poems.* Santa Barbara: Black Sparrow, 1974.

Piercy, Marge. *Circles on the Water: Selected Poems.* Introduction by the author. New York: Knopf, 1982.

Plath, Sylvia. *Collected Poems.* Edited by Ted Hughes. New York: Harper & Row, 1981.

Ponsot, Marie. *Admit Impediment.* New York: Knopf, 1981.

Rich, Adrienne. *Adrienne Rich's Poetry.* Edited by Barbara Charlesworth Gelpi and Albert Gelpi. New York: Norton, Critical Edition, 1975.

————. *The Dream of a Common Language.* New York: Norton, 1978.

————. *A Wild Patience Has Taken Me This Far.* New York: Norton, 1981.

————. *The Fact of a Doorframe: Poems, Selected and New 1950–84.* New York: Norton, 1984.

Rodgers, Carolyn. *How I Got Ovah.* Garden City, N.Y.: Doubleday, 1975.

Rowson, Susanna. *Slaves in Algiers, or, A Struggle for Freedom.* Philadelphia: Wrigley & Berriman, 1804.

————. *Miscellaneous Poems.* Boston: Gilbert & Dean, 1804.

Rukeyser, Muriel. *Collected Poems.* New York: McGraw-Hill, 1978.

Sanchez, Sonia. *We a BaddDDD People.* Detroit: Broadside Press, 1970.

Sarton, May. *Selected Poems.* New York: Norton, 1978.

Schulman, Grace. *Burn Down the Icons.* Princeton, N.J.: Princeton University Press, 1975.

Sexton, Anne. *Complete Poems.* Boston: Houghton Mifflin, 1981. With a Foreword by Maxine Kumin.

Shange, Ntozake. *For Colored Girls Who Have Considered Suicide When the Rainbow is Enuf.* New York: Macmillan, 1977.

————. *Nappy Edges.* New York: St. Martin's, 1978.

Snow, Karen. *Wonders.* New York: Penguin, 1978.

Stanford, Ann. *In Mediterranean Air.* New York: Viking, 1977.

Stein, Gertrude. *Bee Time Vine and Other Pieces.* New Haven, Conn.: Yale University Press, 1953.

Swenson, May. *New & Selected Things Taking Place.* New York: Little, Brown, 1978.

Teasdale, Sara. *Collected Poems.* Introduction by Marya Zaturenska. New York: Macmillan, 1966.

Valentine, Jean. *The Messenger.* New York: Farrar, Straus & Giroux, 1979.

Van Duyn, Mona. *To See, To Take.* New York: Atheneum, 1970.

————. *Merciful Disguises: Published and Unpublished Poems.* New York: Atheneum, 1971.

Wakoski, Diane. *Inside the Blood Factory.* Garden City, N.Y.: Doubleday, 1968.

————. *Greed Parts 5–7.* (Santa Barbara: Black Sparrow, 1971).

————. *The Motorcycle Betrayal Poems*. New York: Simon & Schuster, 1971.

————. *Greed/Parts 8, 9, 11*. Santa Barbara: Black Sparrow, 1973.

————. *Trilogy*. Garden City, N.Y.: Doubleday, 1974.

————. *Virtuoso Literature for Two and Four Hands*. Garden City, N.Y.: Doubleday, 1975.

————. *The Man Who Shook Hands*. Garden City, N.Y.: Doubleday, 1978.

————. *The Magellenic Clouds*. Santa Barbara: Black Sparrow, 1978.

Waldman, Anne. *Fast Speaking Woman*. San Francisco, Calif.: City Lights, 1974.

Walker, Alice. *Good Night, Willie Lee, I'll See You in the Morning*. New York: Dial, 1979.

Walker, Margaret. *For My People*. New Haven, Conn.: Yale University Press, 1942.

Warren, Mercy. *Poems, Dramatic and Miscellaneous*. Boston, 1790.

Wheatley, Phyllis. *Life and Works of Phyllis Wheatley*. Edited by G. Herbert Renfro. Washington, D.C., 1916; reprinted Miami: Muemosyne Publishing Co., 1969.

Wilcox, Ella Wheeler. *Poems of Passion*. Chicago: W. B. Conkey, 1883.

Wilner, Eleanor. *Maya*. Amherst: University of Massachusetts Press, 1979.

————. *Shekinah*. Pittsburgh: University of Pittsburgh Press, 1984.

Wylie, Elinor. *Collected Poems*. New York: Knopf, 1966.

II Anthologies of Poetry

Bernikow, Louise, ed. *The World Split Open: Four Centuries of Women Poets in England and America, 1552–1950*. Introduction by Louise Bernikow, Preface by Muriel Rukeyser. New York: Random House, 1974.

Barba, Sharon, and Laura Chester, eds. *Rising Tides: 20th Century American Women Poets*. Introduction by Anaïs Nin. New York: Washington Square Press, 1973.

Brodine, Karen, Marina La Palma, Patricia Dienstfrey, et al., eds. Introduction by Susan Griffin. *Making the Park*. Berkeley, Calif.: Kelsey St. Press, 1976.

Gill, Elaine, ed. *Mountain Moving Day: Poems by Women*. Trumansburg, N.Y.: Crossing Press, 1973.

Griswold, Rufus. *The Female Poets of America*. Philadelphia: Moss, Brother, 1860.

Howe, Florence, and Ellen Bass, eds. *No More Masks!: An Anthology of Poems by Women*. Introduction by Florence Howe. Garden City, N.Y.: Doubleday, 1973.

Iverson, Lucille, and Kathryn Ruby, eds. *We Become New: Poems by Contemporary American Women*. New York: Bantam, 1975.

May, Caroline, ed. *The American Female Poets*. Philadelphia: Lindsay and Blakiston, 1848.

Miles, Sara, et al., eds. *Ordinary Women/Mujeres Comunes: An Anthology of*

Poetry by New York Women. Introduction by Adrienne Rich. New York: Ordinary Women Books, 1978.

Mohr, William, ed. *The Streets Inside: Ten Los Angeles Poets.* Los Angeles: Momentum, 1978.

Moraga, Cherríe, and Gloria Anzaldúa, eds. *This Bridge Called My Back: Writings of Radical Women of Color.* Foreword by Toni Cade Bambara. Watertown, Mass.: Persephone Press, 1981.

Poets and Writers of New Jersey. *Advance Token to Boardwalk: 28 New Jersey Poets.* Scotch Plains, N.J.: Poets & Writers of New Jersey, 1977.

Segnitz, Barbara, and Carol Rainey, eds. *Psyche.* New York: Dell, 1973.

Simone, Carol A., ed. *Networks: An Anthology of San Francisco Bay Area Women Poets.* San Francisco: Vortex, 1979.

Stanford, Ann, ed. *The Women Poets in English.* Introduction by Ann Stanford. New York: McGraw-Hill, 1972.

Tulloss, Rod, David Keller, and Alicia Ostriker, eds. *US 1: An Anthology: The Contemporary Writing From New Jersey.* Union City, N.J.: Wm. H. Wise, 1980.

III   Critical Studies and Feminist Theory

Abel, Elizabeth, ed. *Critical Inquiry.* Vol. 8, No. 2, Winter 1981. Issue on Writing and Sexual Difference.

Alvarez, A. A. *The Savage God: A Study of Suicide.* New York: Radom House, 1972.

Bettelheim, Bruno. *The Uses of Enchantment: The Meaning and Importance of Fairy Tales.* New York: Knopf, 1976.

Bloom, Harold. *A Map of Misreading.* New York: Oxford University Press, 1975.

————. *The Anxiety of Influence.* New York: Oxford University Press, 1979.

Bogan, Louise. *Achievement in American Poetry.* Chicago: Gateway Editions, 1951.

————. *Selected Criticism.* New York: Noonday Press, 1955.

————. *What the Woman Lived: Selected Letters, 1920–1970.* Edited by Ruth Limmer. New York: Harcourt Brace Jovanovich, 1973.

Borden, Karen, and Faneil Rinn, eds. *Feminist Literary Criticism: A Symposium.* San Jose, Calif.: Diotima Press, 1974.

Breslin, James E. B. *From Modern to Contemporary: American Poetry, 1945–1965.* Chicago: University of Chicago Press, 1984.

Broe, Mary Lynn. *Protean Poetic: The Poetry of Sylvia Plath.* Columbia, Mo.: University of Missouri Press, 1980.

Brownmiller, Susan. *Against Our Will: Men, Women and Rape.* New York: Simon & Schuster, 1975.

Bush, Douglas. *Mythology and the Romantic Tradition in English Poetry.* Cambridge, Mass.: Harvard University Press, 1937.

Chesler, Phyllis. *Women and Madness.* Garden City, N.Y.: Doubleday, 1972.
Chodorow, Nancy. *The Reproduction of Mothering: Psychoanalysis and the Sociology of Gender.* Berkeley: University of California Press, 1978.
Clausen, Jan. *A Movement of Poets: Thoughts on Feminism and Poetry.* New York: Long Haul Press, 1982.
Cody, John. *After Great Pain: The Inner Life of Emily Dickinson.* Cambridge, Mass.: Harvard University Press, 1971.
Cott, Nancy F., ed. *Root of Bitterness: Documents of the Social History of American Women.* New York: Dutton, 1972.
Daly, Mary. *Beyond God The Father.* Boston: Beacon Press, 1973.
————. *Gyn/Ecology: The Metaethics of Radical Feminism.* Boston: Beacon Press, 1978.
de Beauvoir, Simone. *The Second Sex.* Translated and edited by H. M. Parshley. New York: Knopf, 1953.
De Koven, Marianne. *A Different Language: Gertrude Stein's Experimental Writing.* Madison: University of Wisconsin Press, 1983.
Diamond, Arlyn, and Lee Edwards, eds. *The Authority of Experience: Essays in Feminist Criticism.* Amherst: University of Massachusetts Press, 1977.
Dickinson, Emily. *Letters.* Edited by T. H. Johnson. Cambridge, Mass.: Harvard University Press, 1971.
Dinnerstein, Dorothy. *The Mermaid and the Minotaur: Sexual Arrangements and Human Malaise.* New York: Harper & Row, 1977.
Donaghue, Dennis. *Connoisseurs of Chaos.* New York: Macmillan, 1965.
Douglas, Ann. *The Feminization of American Culture.* New York: Knopf, 1977.
DuPlessis, Rachel B. *Writing Beyond the Ending: Narrative Strategies of Twentieth-Century Women Writers.* Bloomington: Indiana University Press, 1985.
Emerson, Ralph Waldo. *Emerson in His Journals,* edited by Joel Porte. Cambridge, Mass.: Harvard University Press, 1982.
————. *Essays and Lectures,* edited by Joel Porte. New York: Library of America, Viking Press, 1983.
Firestone, Shulamith. *The Dialectic of Sex: The Case for Feminist Revolution.* New York: Bantam, 1970.
Freud, Sigmund. *Complete Psychological Works.* Translated and edited by James Strachey et al. 24 vols. London: Hogarth Press, 1953–74.
Friedan, Betty. *The Feminine Mystique.* New York: Norton, 1963.
Friedman, Susan Stanford. *Psyche Reborn: The Emergence of H.D.* Bloomington: Indiana University Press, 1981.
Fussell, Edwin. *Lucifer in Harness: American Meter, Metaphor and Diction.* Princeton, N.J.: Princeton University Press, 1973.
Gass, William. *Fictions and the Figures of Life.* New York: Knopf, 1971.
Gelpi, Albert. *Emily Dickinson: The Mind of the Poet.* Cambridge, Mass.: Harvard University Press, 1965.
George, Diana. *Oedipus Anne: The Poetry of Anne Sexton.* Champaign: University of Illinois Press, 1986.
Gilbert, Sandra M., and Susan Gubar, eds. *Shakespeare's Sisters: Feminist Essays on Women Poets.* Bloomington: Indiana University Press, 1979.

————. *The Madwoman in the Attic: The Woman Writer and the Nineteenth-Century Literary Imagination.* New Haven: Yale University Pres, 1979.

Graves, Robert. *The White Goddess.* New York: Creative Age Press, 1948.

Greer, Germaine. *The Female Eunuch.* New York: McGraw-Hill, 1971.

Hall, Donald. *Marianne Moore: The Cage and the Animal.* New York: Pegasus, 1970.

————, ed. *Claims for Poetry.* Ann Arbor: University of Michigan Press, 1983.

Harrison, Jane E., *Mythology.* New York: Harcourt Brace and World, 1963; orig. pub. 1924.

————. *Prolegomena to the Study of Greek Religion.* New York: Meridian, 1957.

Heilbrun, Carolyn. *Toward a Recognition of Androgyny.* New York: Knopf, 1973.

Herman, Judith L. (with Lisa Hirschman). *Father-Daughter Incest.* Cambridge, Mass.: Harvard University Press, 1981.

Homans, Margaret. *Women Writers and Poetic Identity.* Princeton, N.J.: Princeton University Press, 1980.

Horney, Karen. *Feminine Psychology.* New York: Norton, 1967.

Howard, Richard. *Alone with America: Essays on the Art of Poetry in the United States since 1950.* New York: Atheneum, 1980.

Irigaray, Luce. *Speculum d'autre femme.* Paris: Editions de Minuit, 1974.

————. *Ce Sexe qui n'est pas un.* Paris: Editions de Minuit, 1977.

Jacobus, Mary, ed. *Women Writing and Writing About Women.* New York: Harper & Row, 1979.

James, Alice. *The Diary of Alice James.* Edited by Leon Edel. New York: Dodd, Mead, 1964.

Jellinek, Estelle C., ed. *Women's Autobiography: Essays in Criticism.* Bloomington: Indiana University Press, 1980.

Juhasz, Suzanne. *Naked and Fiery Forms: Modern American Poetry by Women.* New York: Harper & Row, 1976.

————, ed. *Feminist Critics Read Emily Dickinson.* Bloomington: Indiana University Press, 1983.

Kolodny, Annette. *The Lay of the Land: Metaphor as Experience and History in American Life and Letters.* Chapel Hill: University of North Carolina Press, 1975.

Koolish, Lynda. *A Whole New Poetry Beginning Here: Contemporary American Women Poets.* 2 vols. Ann Arbor, Mich.: University Microfilms, 1981.

Kroll, Judith. *Chapters in a Mythology: The Poetry of Sylvia Plath.* New York: Harper & Row, 1976.

Kumin, Maxine. *To Make a Prairie: Essays on Poets, Poetry, and Country Living.* Ann Arbor: University of Michigan Press, 1979.

Laing, R. D. *The Politics of Experience.* New York: Random House, 1967.

————. *The Divided Self.* New York: Pantheon, 1969.

Lakoff, Robin. *Language and Women's Place.* New York: Harper & Row, 1975.

Lane, Gary, ed. *Sylvia Plath: New Views on the Poetry.* Baltimore: Johns Hopkins University Press, 1979.

Lauter, Estella. *Women as Mythmakers: Poetry and Visual Art by Twentieth-Century Women*. Bloomington: Indiana University Press, 1984.
————, and Carol S. Rupprecht, eds. *Feminist Archetypal Theory*. Knoxville: University of Tennessee Press, 1985.
Levertov, Denise. *The Poet in the World*. New York: New Directions, 1973.
Marks, Elaine, and Isabelle de Courtivron, eds. *New French Feminisms*. New York: Schocken, 1981.
Middlebrook, Diane W., and Marilyn Yalom, eds. *Coming to Light: American Women Poets in the Twentieth Century*. Ann Arbor: University of Michigan Press, 1985.
Miller, Jean. *Toward a New Psychology of Women*. Boston: Beacon Press, 1976.
Morgan, Robin, ed. *Sisterhood is Powerful: An Anthology of Writings from the Women's Liberation Movement*. New York: Vintage, 1970.
Neumann, Erich. *The Great Mother: An Analysis of the Archetype*. Translated by Ralph Mannheim. Princeton, N.J.: Princeton University Press, 1963.
Newman, Charles, ed. *The Art of Sylvia Plath*. Bloomington: University of Indiana Press, 1970.
Ostriker, Alicia. *Writing Like A Woman*. Ann Arbor: University of Michigan Press, 1983.
Perloff, Marjorie. *The Poetics of Indeterminacy: Rimbaud to Cage*. Princeton, N.J.: Princeton University Press, 1981.
Piercy, Josephine. *Anne Bradstreet*. New York: Twayne, 1965.
Porter, David. *Dickinson: the Modern Idiom*. Cambridge, Mass.: Harvard University Press, 1981.
Ransom, John Crowe. *The World's Body*. New York: Scribner, 1938.
Rich, Adrienne. *Of Woman Born: Motherhood as Experience and Institution*. New York: Norton, 1976.
————. *On Lies, Secrets and Silence: Selected Prose 1966–1978*. New York: Norton, 1979.
Rigney, Barbara. *Madness and Sexual Politics in the Feminist Novel*. Madison: University of Wisconsin Press, 1978.
Robinson, William H. *Phyllis Wheatley in the Black American Beginnings*. Detroit: Broadside Press, 1975.
Roethke, Theodore. *Selected Prose of Theodore Roethke*. Seattle: University of Washington Press, 1965.
Rosaldo, Michelle, and Louise Lamphere, eds. *Women, Culture and Society*. Stanford, Calif.: Stanford University Press, 1974.
Sewall, Richard B., ed. *Emily Dickinson: A Collection of Critical Essays*. Englewood Cliffs, N.J.: Prentice-Hall, 1963
Sexton, Anne. *No Evil Star: Selected Essays, Interviews, and Prose*. Edited by Steven E. Colburn. Ann Arbor: University of Michigan Press, 1985.
Showalter, Elaine. *A Literature of Their Own*. Princeton, N.J.: Princeton University Press, 1977.
————, ed. *The New Feminist Criticism: Essays on Women, Literature and Theory*. New York: Pantheon, 1985.

Stanford, Ann. *Anne Bradstreet: The Worldly Puritan.* New York: Burt Franklin, 1974.

Steiner, Nancy Hunter. *A Closer Look at Ariel: A Memory of Sylvia Plath.* Introduction by George Stade. New York: Popular Library, 1973.

Sternburg, Janet, ed. *The Writer on Her Work.* New York: Norton, 1980.

Stevenson, Anne. *Elizabeth Bishop.* New York: Twayne, 1966.

Stone, Merlin. *When God Was a Woman.* New York: Harcourt Brace Jovanovich, 1978.

Taggard, Genevieve. *Life and Mind of Emily Dickinson.* New York: Knopf, 1930.

Tomlinson, Charles, ed. *Marianne Moore: A Collection of Critical Essays.* Englewood Cliffs, N.J.: Prentice-Hall, 1969.

Vendler, Helen. *Part of Nature, Part of Us: Modern American Poets.* Cambridge, Mass.: Harvard University Press, 1980.

Wakoski, Diane. *Toward a New Poetry.* Ann Arbor: University of Michigan Press, 1980.

Walker, Alice. *In Search of Our Mothers' Gardens.* New York: Harcourt Brace Jovanovich, 1983.

Walker, Cheryl. *The Nightingale's Burden: Women Poets and American Culture before 1900.* Bloomington: Indiana University Press, 1982.

Watts, Emily S. *The Poetry of American Women from 1632 to 1945.* Austin: University of Texas Press, 1977.

Whicher, George. *This Was a Poet: A Critical Biography of Emily Dickinson.* New York: Scribner, 1939.

White, Elizabeth. *Anne Bradstreet: "The Tenth Muse."* New York: Oxford University Press, 1971.

Williams, William Carlos. *Autobiography.* New York: New Directions, 1957.

Woolf, Virginia. *A Writer's Diary.* Edited by Leonard Woolf. New York: Harcourt Brace Jovanovich, 1954.

———. *A Room of One's Own.* New York: Harcourt Brace, 1957.

Index